Praise for *The Holocaust*

"[An] incisive analysis of the genocidal endgame that unfolded from Nazi antisemitism."
—*Wall Street Journal*

"This vital history shatters many myths about the Nazis' genocide. . . . Drawing on the latest scholarship in English and German, Stone's brisk, energetic book fizzes with ideas. Indeed, even if you think you know the subject, you'll probably find something here to make you think. . . . An excellent book."
—*Sunday Times*

"Rescu[es] the Holocaust from distortion and cliché. . . . Historian Dan Stone seeks to amend—and expand—our understanding of the genocide. . . . A concise and accessible history that extends beyond the death camps."
—*New York Times Book Review*

"A stunning, original, concise analysis, culling the latest research and the most observant eyewitness accounts of the time. The parallels to fascism today are extremely unsettling. Few scholars could write this masterful synthesis and even fewer would take on a closer examination of its darkest features and unsettling questions about the broader significance of Holocaust education today."
—Wendy Lower, author of *Hitler's Furies*,
a National Book Award finalist

"A Holocaust history for our times, passionate as well as scholarly, and written with a sharp eye to the growing threat of the radical right in the present. Stone is not afraid to question the verities that have become attached to this most catastrophic epoch of modern history, and he challenges readers to confront its scope and enormity anew."

—Jane Caplan, professor emerita of European history,
University of Oxford

"Stone's remarkable book offers both a narrative overview and an analysis of the events, challenging many common assumptions and often returning to how this terrible history remains 'unfinished.'" —*The Guardian*

"A significant new history of the Holocaust from the director of the Holocaust Research Institute at Royal Holloway. . . . Stone delivers a gripping account. . . . A painfully revealing, vital history." —*Kirkus Reviews* (starred review)

"A book that turns on their head some of the widely held notions about that terrible era of genocide eighty years ago."

—*Daily Mail*

"An important and challenging work." —*Jewish Chronicle*

"A brilliant study, lucid, powerful, moving, and full of original insights. Few general studies of the Holocaust have so successfully integrated the international, indeed global, dimensions of the Nazi genocide and its aftermath."

—Mark Roseman, Pat M. Glazer Chair in Jewish Studies and
professor of history at Indiana University

"A timely account of the Holocaust and its many consequences. Troubling and thought-provoking for a world in which post-war certainties are now dissolving. It deserves the widest possible readership."

—Richard Overy, professor of history at the University of Exeter and *New York Times*–bestselling author of *Blood and Ruins: The Last Imperial War, 1931–1945*

"One of the best new publications presenting more complicated narratives of the Holocaust. . . . Dan Stone's *The Holocaust: An Unfinished History* is an outstanding survey that updates the history of the European genocide of the Jews in a thought-provoking and informative way. . . . Powerful."

—*The Times Literary Supplement*

"Drawing on his own extensive research and a vast range of work by historians from across the last eight decades, Stone sets about showing how our mental picture of the Holocaust is dangerously wrong. . . . A vital and provocative book."

—*Irish Times*

"An outstanding book: well written, deeply felt, always perceptive, and exhibiting considerable knowledge of decades of Holocaust scholarship. It will become the standard work in English on the subject for some time to come."

—*History Today*

"Outstanding. . . . Deeply haunting. . . . An engaging and accessible read that never hurries or shields the reader from its dark subject matter."   —*The Telegraph*

"Stone [is] one of the foremost Holocaust historians in the world. . . . Instead of presenting Holocaust history as a tidy affair wrapped in a bow with neat moral messages, Stone

proposes that we examine its unfinishedness, its unknowability, and its very incompleteness. . . . By confronting these uncomfortable truths, Stone hopes to jolt us out of complacency. We have not, he suggests, sufficiently learned the lessons of the Holocaust."
—*The New Republic*

"[A] sobering and meticulous exploration of aspects of the Shoah that have remained, until now, underanalyzed. And these aspects of the Holocaust are especially salient today. . . . Stone also examines, with great sensitivity, the deep trauma that survivors carried with them their entire lives. . . . Stone's disturbing findings, tragically, resonate all too clearly."
—*Commentary*

"Stone is one of the foremost historians of the Holocaust. . . . Breaks new ground and ties the Holocaust to modern times in ways that are valuable and important."
—Dan Carlin, *Hardcore History* podcast

"For those who believe there is an oversaturation of books on the Holocaust and little to add to the history of the Jewish genocide, this volume is a corrective. Stone has written an indispensable account of the Holocaust."
—*Choice*

The Holocaust

DAN STONE

The Holocaust
An Unfinished History

MARINER BOOKS
New York   Boston

HarperCollins books may be purchased for educational, business, or sales promotional use. For information, please email the Special Markets Department at SPsales@harpercollins.com.

The Mariner flag design is a registered trademark of Harper-Collins Publishers LLC.

Originally published in the United Kingdom in 2023 by Penguin Random House UK.

A hardcover edition of this book was published in 2024 by Mariner Books.

FIRST MARINER BOOKS PAPERBACK EDITION PUBLISHED 2025.

Library of Congress Cataloging-in-Publication Data has been applied for.

ISBN 978-0-06-334892-9

24 25 26 27 28 LBC 5 4 3 2 1

Contents

List of Figures and Maps

Figures

Maps

Image Sources

What Is the Holocaust?

'There are no clean or unclean people, at least, not in principle. There are no chosen nations. However, there are those who know of a dividing line between what is and what is not permitted, and others who not only do not know it, but who do not want to know it either.'
— Abel Jacob Herzberg[1]

'The program of action against the Jews included disenfranchisement, stigmatization, denial of civil rights, subjecting their persons and property to violence, deportation, enslavement, enforced labour, starvation, murder, and mass extermination. The extent to which the conspirators succeeded in their purpose can only be estimated, but the annihilation was substantially complete in many localities of Europe. Of the 9,600,000 Jews who lived in the parts of Europe under Nazi domination, it is conservatively estimated that 5,700,000 have disappeared, most of them deliberately put to death by the Nazi conspirators. Only remnants of the Jewish population of Europe remain.'
— From the indictment, International Military Tribunal, Nuremberg, 7 June 1946[2]

In the diary that she kept in Bergen-Belsen, the young Jewish Yugoslav Hanna Lévy-Hass writes at one point of a boy whose body has been infested by fleas and who is rejected by his family:

> [He] couldn't kill the vermin that had settled on his body because he couldn't see them; they've burrowed deep into his skin and swarmed through his eyebrows. His chest is completely blackened by these fleas and their nests. We have never seen such a thing; we never imagined such a thing could occur . . . Everyone avoids him. His brothers and sister dread his presence, his fleas, his howling . . . The other night, he dragged his useless body from one bed to the other . . . begging people to make room for him. Everyone pushed him away in disgust . . . Painful story. His case is not unique.[3]

This merging of animal and human, this deeply traumatic destruction of the self and the revulsion it causes amongst others who fear the same thing happening to them, is an extraordinary description. In it we glimpse the nightmarish consequences of Nazi persecution.

In one of his stories written in the Łódź ghetto, Isaiah Spiegel describes a rabbi who, at the morning prayers, appears to go mad after being mocked by German soldiers in the street:

> For a moment, Reb Bunem was paralysed, overcome by shame and nausea. The blood rushed from his heart into his hands, which began to tremble. His eyes flashed an uncanny green flame. With a surge of preternatural strength, he suddenly turned to the praying Jews and

started ripping the prayer books from their hands. The frightened Jews moved off to the side while Reb Bunem continued tearing the Psalm books from their grasp and casting imprecations on their heads. He shouted with the voice of one possessed, while in the darkness of the synagogue his beet-red face glowed with divine wrath:

'Jews!!! Stop reciting Psalms!!! God is on the side of our enemy! . . . God is with the Germans! . . . I beseech you, recite no more Psalms! . . . Our world is shrouded in darkness!'[4]

A rabbi desecrates the holy books and pleads with his congregants to abandon their prayers.

There are still major parts of the history of the Holocaust that have not been understood in the prevailing narrative. In the region of Romanian-occupied Ukraine which the Romanians called Transnistria, Jews were herded into pigsties, where they froze to death and suffered inescapable epidemics. They were not paid for the work they did, although payment was promised. They were robbed and often tricked into handing over valuables or clothing in exchange for food that was never provided. In Acmecetca, 'Driven by hunger, most of the Jews were naked in a matter of weeks, covering their hips with rags or paper.' The prefect, Modest Isopescu, 'who preferred this camp over all other camps in the Golta județ [county], inspected it a few times, each time amusing himself with the fate of the prisoners; he took pictures of the deportees "grazing" in the grass on their hands and knees.' In Peciora, 'Extreme hunger quickly reduced the prisoners to eating plant roots, twigs, leaves, human excrement, and even dead bodies. Romanian and Ukrainian guards raped Jewish young women, who in turn killed themselves. Such conditions fostered mental illness and suicide.'[5]

These vignettes take us a long way from the notion of 'industrial murder' that still prevails in the public consciousness. Even in the Nazi death camps, the perception of 'factory-like' genocide is misleading: as we will see, even at Auschwitz the murder process was brutal and far from efficient.

The Holocaust turned the victims' world upside down, not just destroying their homes and families, leaving most of the small minority of survivors unable to return to the lands of their birth, but in terms of values. Both during and after the war years, the Nazi assault on the Jews left them, in many cases, unable to lead lives guided by morality or established norms, as the above examples show. Those trapped in Nazi ghettos and camps found themselves not on 'another planet' but certainly in the *anus mundi*, in which literal and metaphorical filth governed existence.[6] These were places made by human beings in which human beings were destroyed. As Hannah Arendt said, perhaps the Holocaust was an attempt to eradicate the very concept of the human being.[7]

Arendt's radical claim reminds us that we have in some ways either forgotten, or ignored altogether, what the Holocaust was and how devastating its effects were. The depth of the trauma caused by the Holocaust means we must move beyond a mechanistic interpretation of 'industrial genocide'. The ubiquity of collaboration across Europe, driven by a coincidence of wants between the Nazis' ideologically driven aspiration to rid the world of Jews and the desires of many nation-states' leaders to create ethnically homogeneous populations, means we need to stop thinking of the Holocaust as solely a German project. It was, however, driven and largely perpetrated by Germans (including Austrians), thus we must focus on ideology, understood as a kind of phantasmagorical conspiracy theory, as the kernel of Nazi thinking and action. And finally we need to understand the ways in which the after-effects of the Holocaust shaped the postwar years and continue to be felt today.

The trauma of the Holocaust has been largely written out of the historiography and decidedly excluded from commemorative ceremonies and the discussion of the Holocaust in the public sphere. It is not the case that people are not moved or informed or that they do not find the events terrible; but the real depths of suffering the Holocaust caused beyond the level of the individual or family and its deep implications for the nature of the modern state and the modern world in general are just too unpleasant and uncomfortable for people to deal with – or so it seems. This problem is partly caused by vocabulary; as the scholar of Holocaust literature Lawrence Langer noted thirty years ago in his landmark study of Holocaust testimonies:

Words like *survival* and *liberation*, with their root meanings of life and freedom, entice us into a kind of verbal enchantment that too easily dispels the miasma of the death camp ordeal and its residual malodours . . . Available vocabulary educes a unified view of the self, which invites us to adapt the Holocaust experience to ideas of heroism *during* the event and a process of *recovery* afterward that are inconsistent with the realities of the disaster.[8]

But there is also a generalized *looking away* in evidence – strange though that might sound given the extent to which representations of the Holocaust pervade popular culture. This argument applies not just to saccharine treatments of the Holocaust such as those found in popular books and films, but to the underpinnings of much Holocaust education and to pious ceremonies which characterize Holocaust commemoration. Tears may flow, but the truly destructive nature of the Holocaust for its victims – and for the societies they came from – and the radical implications of the Holocaust for our modern world are passed over in silence.

We must also remember that the Holocaust was not just a German affair.[9] One of the roots of the revival of fascism in Europe today can be found in the fact that the genocide of the Jews could not have been so thorough and so brutal without almost ubiquitous collaboration across Europe and beyond. Historians have long known this, but the true extent of this collaboration has remained covered up by successive governments across the continent. The drip-feed of revelations and apologies means we still have not taken the measure of what truly happened in what can only be partly described as 'Hitler's Europe', but can truly be called 'antisemitic Europe' in the period of the Second World War. The third volume of the United States Holocaust Memorial Museum's *Encyclopedia of Camps and Ghettos* covers sites created by regimes allied to Nazi Germany; it is over 900 pages long and contains information on almost 700 places, from the far north of Norway to the Atlas Mountains, from Brittany to Ukraine, not a single one of them a camp administered by the Germans. Not all were 'Holocaust sites' in the sense that Jews were sent there to die. But the majority were 'Holocaust camps' in the sense that Jews were held in them and died performing forced labour, through serious neglect and lack of food and medicine, and through being deported from them to their deaths. In some cases, especially in Transnistria, Jews were massacred in the tens of thousands or left to the elements to die a 'natural death'. Not only do these places and events show that the postwar narrative of a German Holocaust was only partially correct, they also show that the concept of industrial genocide – though certainly appropriate in part – fails to capture the experiences of a large proportion of the Holocaust's victims. Almost half of the victims of the Holocaust died of starvation in ghettos or were shot in face-to-face killing actions, and even the gas chambers, as we will see, were brutal and hardly the epitome of technological efficiency – the victims died in agony, having been terrorized and deported in unspeakably filthy means of transport, many driven insane before they ever saw the entrance to a gas chamber.

The Holocaust was a truly transnational affair. By this, I mean that policies implemented by the Nazis were replicated by their allies but also vice-versa; often collaborating states forced the hand of the Nazis by taking the initiative where persecution of Jews was concerned. The Vichy government, for example, pre-empted the Nazis by introducing its first Statut des Juifs without the Nazis' encouragement. Persecution in one place emboldened others elsewhere, and the sharing of fascist ideology across Europe made this interconnectedness possible, facilitating a continent-wide crime that the Germans on their own would have found much harder to implement.

The same is true from the victims' perspective. Historians

are only just investigating in detail the experiences of Jews not directly caught in the Nazi net. The deportation and murder of the Jews of France, the Netherlands, Belgium, Slovakia, Poland, Hungary, Greece and elsewhere has been described many times. Nevertheless, revelations continue to come, especially concerning the roles played by local, non-German actors and the extent to which the Holocaust was experienced as a constant movement. Many Eastern European Jews were killed where they lived in the summer and autumn of 1941; many others were rounded up and deported to their deaths; but the process of arrest, assembly, detention, deportation, travelling and arrival is often neglected. And for many Holocaust victims, the story was far more complicated, as they were dragged from one incarceration site to another. As we will see, some victims endured five, six or more concentration camps, especially in the later stages of the war, when Jews were used as slave labourers in small camps linked to specific firms which hired the 'work Jews' (*Arbeitsjuden*) from the SS.

Additionally, historians are only now describing the fact that the Holocaust exceeded the boundaries of Europe. North Africa has been almost entirely omitted from most histories of the Holocaust, yet in the Vichy-controlled Maghreb and in areas occupied by the Germans and Italians, the persecution of the Jews forms part of the wider Holocaust story. Jews in North Africa were subjected to French and Italian racial laws, had their property stolen, and were interned and made to perform forced labour. Some were deported to death camps in Europe as were some North African Jews living in France.[10] The growing research on the experiences of Jews in North Africa challenges our perception of where the Holocaust took place, making the designation of the genocide as a 'continent-wide crime' seem no longer entirely adequate, even given that the countries we now think of as forming 'North Africa' were at the time European colonies and thus in some ways part of 'Europe'.[11] There were also several hundred thousand Jews who fled or were deported from eastern Poland in the autumn of 1941, to spend the war years as refugees in the Soviet Union. Although they did not feel the full weight of Nazi occupation, their stories are ones of massive loss of life. At the end of the war, they returned to a country where they swiftly found that they could not stay because of ongoing antisemitism. Yet little is known about these Jews, many of whom fought in the Polish army and returned to Europe via Iran, and of many others who tell extraordinary stories of survival in Central Asia or Siberia, grateful to the Soviets for saving their lives but having to fight against Kafkaesque Soviet bureaucracy and restrictions on their rights.[12] Maria Tumarkin's aunt Lina, for example, was deported as a baby with her family from Kiev to Uzbekistan, where they all contracted malaria and tried to keep alive doing hard labour. Only a chance meeting in Samarkand between Lina's aunt Tamara with her former professor from the Kharkiv Medical Institute saved them, as they were sent to Station Malyutinskaya to set up a medical station.[13] Such chance occurrences were how many of the Polish-Jewish refugees survived the harsh reality of the Soviet Union. Jews were dispersed around the world, from Mauritius to Japanese-occupied Manchuria, from Bolivia to the Philippines. Although Nazi-occupied Europe was the heart of the genocide, its effects were felt worldwide.[14]

Thus, although the persecution of the Jews that led to the Holocaust was a German project – a point which cannot be overemphasized – it chimed with the programmes of many European fascist and authoritarian regimes. Without the Germans' umbrella project, the Holocaust in Europe would not have happened. Nor were its allies as obsessed with the 'world-historical threat' posed by the Jews as the Germans were, although some came close, especially certain figures in the Croatian, Romanian and French leadership strata. But without the willing participation of so many collaborators across Europe, the Germans would have found it much harder to kill so many Jews. In Norway, France and Hungary, local police rounded up, guarded and deported Jews; in Slovakia the impetus to deport Jews came from the indigenous 'clerical-fascist' regime rather than from the Germans. The same is true in the country of the Enlightenment, where French officials drafted the legislation and provided the manpower to arrest and deport Jews from France, the 'only country in Western Europe where Jews were deported from a zone not under direct German occupation'.[15] In the Romanian case, the regime of the *conducător* (leader), Ion Antonescu, grasped the opportunity provided by the German plans to carry out a Holocaust of its own, deporting Jews from recently annexed areas of Romania and killing them alongside local Jews and Roma in Transnistria. The scope of the killing implicates the whole of Europe, not just the Nazi regime and a few quislings. The legacy of collaborationist Europe remains visible in the resistance to research that appears from a nationalist perspective to 'defame' the good name of the nation as in the Polish government's attempts to prosecute historians who have uncovered information about Poles who handed Jews over to the Nazi occupiers; in the erection of memorials and promotion of museums which selectively interpret the past so as to make one's nation appear an innocent victim or rescuer of Jews, as in controversial monuments recently erected in Hungary; and, most worryingly, in the ease with which increasingly large sections of the European populace reach for the store of ideas, imagery and vocabulary associated with fascism, as for example the association of migrants with criminality or disease.

Many have interpreted the 'Final Solution' as a mechanistic process – a plan for industrial genocide – but this distracts us from what happened to most victims. The Jews killed in the Holocaust died in brutal, face-to-face shootings, were starved to death in ghettos or were murdered in death camps. But not only is the prevailing notion of 'industrial genocide' a stock phrase which prevents us from thinking, it is not even accurate to describe a process that was violent, vicious and deeply traumatic, whether one looks at the death pits of the western Soviet Union or the extermination camps, where the killing process could, at its height, be remarkably swift.

A third aspect that I want to emphasize is that we need a 'return to ideology' following the movement away from it in several recent major synthetic histories which stress instead the reactive nature of German decision-making, driven primarily by military circumstance.[16] By a return to ideology, I do not mean a simple 'intentionalist' rendering in which the Nazis murdered the Jews because they had always intended to do so, but a cultural imaginary in which the Nazis dreamed of a world without Jews long before they had a genocidal programme to implement. Throughout, this book will draw on Nazi documents, of course, but also on diaries written during the Holocaust, postwar testimonies and records, and fiction, all of which, when attended to carefully, allow us to appreciate the terrible destruction caused by the Holocaust. Only a few scholars have combined scholarship with the emotions; all too often, scholarship erects a barrier against feeling, forgetting the reasons that the Holocaust demanded our attention in the first place.[17]

Although there was no plan to murder the Jews of Europe before the Second World War, what became the Holocaust started as a genocidal fantasy long before the killing began. The Nazis had been dreaming of a 'world without Jews' since the Nazi Party's inception.[18] But so too had many European nation-states. The successors to the Austro-Hungarian Empire, slightly earlier creations such as unified Italy or Belgium, as well as longer-established states such as France all witnessed the emergence of large-scale nativist movements in the age of nationalism whose dreams of creating ethnically pure nations chimed with Nazi goals of eradicating Jews and other minority groups. The actual process of arriving at a genocidal programme was in many ways ad hoc and, as recent scholarship suggests, heavily dependent on the military situation: the Nazis could not deport Jews from countries they had not occupied or from Axis countries whose leaders did not want to deport them, such as Italy before 1943 or Finland. Yet that does not mean that the murder of the Jews was an accident.[19] Hatred and, more important, *fear* of Jews was deeply ingrained into Nazi thinking. The Holocaust was not predetermined by an actual, physical blueprint but nor is it to read history backwards to say that the genocide of the Jews was foreshadowed in the writings, speeches and actions of the Nazis from the 1920s onwards. We need a renewed emphasis on Nazi ideology, in particular on race thinking in the broad sense: not just racial science but the mysticism of race, in which Nazi thinkers set out a metaphysics and an anthropology of German superiority and proposed that the movement of history was driven by a clash between good and evil, represented by the Germans on the one side and the threatening race-destroyers, the Jews, on the other.[20] Such writings were echoed in race thinking across Europe; irrespective of which country one examines, what these writings have in common was their demonization of the Jews.[21]

Ideology in this broad sense – not simply as a consciously held political position but as a 'whole way of life' – also ties in with Nazi fantasies about obtaining *Lebensraum* (living space) in Eastern Europe and creating a 'racial community' (*Volksgemeinschaft*) in the Reich. These dreams actually went hand in hand. The notion of a unified and harmonious society of Aryans necessitated the 'removal' of those deemed to block its coming into existence.[22] In particular this meant the Jews, for they were not merely aesthetically unpleasing marks of the community's imperfection, such as the disabled, but were, so the Nazis believed, actively seeking to destroy the Germans. Although one can take each of these categories – antisemitism, empire and the racial community – in turn and analyse the ways in which they contributed to the unfolding of the Holocaust, for the Nazis they were inseparable.[23] A Nazi empire in the east – replicating in Hitler's mind the British Empire in India or, more emphatically, the spread of 'white' civilization across the expanding United States – was of necessity antisemitic, since the Nazis regarded Soviet communism as synonymous with Jews ('Judaeo-Bolshevism'); and the racial community at home was founded on the radical exclusion of Jews. Hence ideology here means the very belief in, and attempt to create, an immanent community whose self-construction could only come about through genocidal destruction.

This argument creates, to some extent, tension with the previous point about ubiquity: the focus on ideology reveals the difference between the Nazi regime and its collaborators. There is no doubting the antisemitic obsessions of leaders such as Tiso, Antonescu or Horthy, but they regarded Jews primarily as cunning competitors who prevented the titular nation from achieving its potential, not, as the leading Nazis did, as the incarnation of evil or as a kind of world-threatening, metaphysical malignity. Collaboration in the Holocaust occurred for many reasons: nation-building, greed and venality being the most obvious, but also, at a more grassroots level, fear, desperation and avarice. As historian Peter Hayes writes, commenting on German corporate involvement in the Holocaust, 'if hatred was the fuel that propelled Nazi Germany on the road to the Holocaust, that road was paved not just by indifference, as Ian Kershaw has remarked, but by self-interest'.[24] Since the Holocaust was a German project first and foremost, which found willing collaborators everywhere, it is crucial to note how ideology, especially antisemitism, constituted an unspoken shared framework, a consensus or offer that could be taken up by others.[25] Besides, in all of the countries occupied by Nazi Germany, as well as its allies, it is not hard to find viciously antisemitic texts and examples of collaborators whose ideological stance was closely aligned with Nazism. Collaboration was not merely opportunistic.

Finally, it is important to remember that the Holocaust did not just end in May 1945 with the liberation of the camps. Rather, the remnants of European Jewry, shocked and angry, found themselves (with the exception of the small numbers of Western European Jews who could return home relatively easily) homeless, without families, communities and home-lands. Jewish Poles who returned to Poland – many after spending the war years as refugees in the Soviet Union – were subjected to pogroms; Hungarian Jews who returned were met with incredulity and disdain by those who had stolen their apartments; Dutch Jews encountered resistance to their sto-ries, since the Dutch were consumed with their own suffering during the 'hunger winter' of 1944–5. The creation of DP (dis-placed persons) camps in, of all places, Germany and Austria (and, to a smaller extent, in Italy), and the incarceration of Jewish 'illegal' migrants (*Aliyah bet*) in Cyprus by the British left many Jewish survivors with a feeling that there was no future for them any more in Europe. Having expected help from the Allies to resettle where they wanted, their bitter dis-appointment at being detained further manifested itself in a knee-jerk Zionism. Although some half of all survivors eventu-ally found their way to the US, Palestine became the destina-tion of choice for most, at least in the first instance, and the creation of the state of Israel – in the context of a war in which a large proportion of soldiers were Holocaust survivors – followed, in a sequence of events that might otherwise never have come to pass.

In the decades that followed, the memory of the Holocaust continued to be felt in world affairs: civil rights and anti-Apartheid struggles, anti-colonialism and wars in Algeria and other colonies. Memories of collaboration, fascist interpretations of history and anti-fascism were all mobilized in ways that made for a complex and in some cases toxic brew.[26] In Israel, the resistance fighters of the Warsaw ghetto were regarded as forerunners of the IDF (Israeli Defence Force) and the militarized stance of the new state. The 1953 creation of Yad Vashem, Israel's memorial and research centre on the Holocaust, unsurprisingly placed the Holocaust at the heart of the new state's self-perception – this was the instinctive Zionism of the DPs, rejected by Europe and the US, in action. It would take several decades for the events which accompanied the creation of the state of Israel, especially the Nakba, or Palestinian catastrophe, when Palestinians were expelled from their towns and villages to make way for Jewish settlers, to make its mark on Israeli intellectuals and the public.[27] In the student revolts of 1968 across Europe and the Americas, the memory of the Holocaust was instrumentalized as a way of criticizing the older generations, often in ways which suggested that the students themselves, for all their anti-fascist credentials, had failed to understand the real horror of the Holocaust.[28] This is most infamously illustrated in the hijacking of an Air France plane en route from Israel to France in 1976. Landing at Entebbe in Uganda, the West German and Palestinian hijackers 'selected' Jewish and Israeli passengers as hostages while the rest were set free. In this action, the failure to work through their parents' fascism was clear. It constituted 'a compulsive repetition of

Nazi crimes by those who had tried to distance themselves from them', as student leader Joschka Fischer later put it.[29]

Yet the effects of the Holocaust were also felt globally, from the ratlines that allowed Nazis to escape to South America to the creation of an international legal framework on the rights of refugees. The Holocaust played a role in West Germany's attempts to reassert itself as a sovereign nation, for example in negotiating reparations treaties, in international debates about the Armenian genocide and the problem of Armenian terrorism in the 1980s, and in the Cold War relations between East and West.[30] Since the end of the Cold War, a breaking down of many postwar myths has gone hand in hand with a proliferation of revisionist narratives. We now know more about local collaboration across Europe, for example, but we can also witness newly confident fascist interpretations of the past which would have been unpublishable, whether for legal or marketing reasons, a few decades ago. Holocaust imagery, especially references to the *Kindertransport*, have become common in debates over how best to respond to the 'refugee crisis' in Europe since 2015 and in arguments over the position of Islam in multicultural societies.[31] There is something strange going on when European radical right parties and movements are allied with Benjamin Netanyahu, the prime minister of Israel; no wonder that some scholars see the need to stress the ways in which Muslims and Jews to some extent shared similar fates under Nazism, for example in the murder of Muslim Roma, as a way of detoxifying contemporary intergroup relations.[32]

There was thus a Holocaust effect seen in international politics, intergenerational struggles and geopolitical crises even before 'Holocaust consciousness' became prominent through commemoration, education and popular representation. For example, negotiations over reparations payments from West Germany to Israel in 1950, the trial of Adolf Eichmann in Jerusalem in 1961 and the 1963–4 Frankfurt trial of Auschwitz guards all brought the genocide of the Jews into the public sphere, beginning the use of the term 'Holocaust' to describe it. From the 1980s onwards, and especially in the 1990s, the explosion of films, books, documentaries and other forms of representation of the Holocaust was quite remarkable. From the airing of the 1978 TV series *Holocaust* to the multi-Oscar-award-winning movie *Schindler's List* in 1993, awareness of the Holocaust grew rapidly, primarily across the US, West Germany (in all sorts of complex ways) and Western Europe. This process had many way-stations. When Ronald Reagan visited Bitburg cemetery in May 1985, Holocaust survivors led by Elie Wiesel expressed their outrage, especially when it was discovered that SS men were buried there alongside ordinary Wehrmacht soldiers (as if it were fine to pay homage to the Wehrmacht). In the *Historikerstreit*, or Historians' Debate, in West Germany, argument raged in the quality press over whether the Holocaust could be compared to Stalin's gulag. And concerns over renewed German power following unification at the end of the Cold War were amplified in the furore over the Crimes of the Wehrmacht exhibition of 1995, which revealed the remarkable extent of ordinary soldiers' involvement in war crimes.[33] Since then, there has been an unstoppable barrage of Holocaust representations, with some critics arguing that just about all of them, from beer bottles labelled with fascist leaders to 'cats that look like Hitler' websites, from computer games to scholarly debates about comparative genocide, are trivializations of the subject.[34] In fact, this very proliferation shows just how successful Holocaust consciousness has been. The images of the camps, and other Holocaust iconography, have become instantly recognizable. Besides, some caution needs to be exercised before simply condemning all ways of dealing with the Holocaust, apart from those considered appropriate by self-designated gatekeepers of morality. In other words, the fact that these discussions exist indicates how the history of the years since the Holocaust is also part of the history of the Holocaust. Rather than simply take a position in those debates, this book will analyse the debates themselves in terms of what they tell us about the changing perception of the Holocaust over time.

Trauma, collaboration, genocidal fantasy and postwar consequences are the four main frameworks used to shape this book. They will be woven into a narrative that moves between Nazi policy and its effects on individuals, the immense scale of murder across Europe and microhistories from across Europe and beyond. Each helps to explain the vast trauma caused by the Holocaust and its terrible ubiquity. Finally, there is also the curious fact that both 'Holocaust consciousness' and the rise of xenophobic nationalism characterize our age. Despite the best intentions of those who promote Holocaust education, the rise of the populist right suggests that teaching about the Holocaust is largely irrelevant in the face of wider socio-economic challenges.

The commemoration of the Holocaust was institutionalized by the United Nations in 2005, and many countries in the world now recognize 27 January, the day of the liberation of Auschwitz by the Red Army, as Holocaust Memorial Day. The Holocaust has become part of school curriculums across Europe and the English-speaking world. Organizations such as the Holocaust Educational Trust have the ear of politicians, who then promote Holocaust education and commemoration. There are Holocaust museums not just in the US, UK, Israel and Australia, but also in Norway, Macedonia, Brazil, Uruguay and even the West Bank. Holocaust films, graphic novels, plays, documentaries, websites and Holocaust imagery are ubiquitous. Surely, one might think, Holocaust consciousness has done its job?

And yet. We live in an age of increasing nationalism, right-wing populism and xenophobia, all of which are pressing hard against the mainstream acceptance of international cooperation and multiculturalism that have characterized, however partially and imperfectly, the postwar Western world. How else do we explain the elections of Donald Trump and Jair Bolsonaro, the vote for Brexit, the election of a radical-right component to the Austrian and Italian governments, the success of self-styled illiberal democracy in Hungary and Poland, or the rise of radical-right movements? We are seeing these movements not just in countries such as Greece, which have only recently 'discovered' their role in the Holocaust, but also in Germany, with the Alternative für Deutschland, Spain, with Vox, and France, with the National Rally (formerly the National Front), and in countries with longstanding and deep commitments to Holocaust education and commemoration such as the US, the UK and Germany. In countries such as Austria, Hungary and Poland, recently created Holocaust memorials and museums have generated national discussions on the topic of the Holocaust.

Part of the answer is that research and popular representations have brought to the fore a realization that not only Germans were responsible for the Holocaust. Resentment against 'cosmopolitan memory', which is meant to promote democratic values, tolerance, multiculturalism and internationalism, has grown in the countries concerned.[35] Revelations that Jews were killed by states and organizations with longstanding nationalist aspirations to create ethnically homogeneous nation-states, especially in Hungary, Romania, Croatia and France, have led many – perhaps primarily descendants of those whose families fought on the Axis side or who regard nationalism as an anti-communist duty – to feel embittered and angry at what they see as an attempt to air the nation's dirty laundry in public. Even in Poland, which had no official collaborationist organization, Jews were murdered by their Polish neighbours as well as by the German occupiers; saying so in today's Poland now carries the risk that one will be prosecuted for defaming the Polish nation. In the Baltic states, the discourse of 'double genocide' claims to place the Holocaust side by side with the victims of Stalinism but, all too often, seeks to obscure the former by emphasizing the latter, often by appealing to the myth of Judaeo-communism, a conspiracy theory that promotes the idea that the Jews brought communism to Eastern Europe.[36] In Hungary, government-sponsored memorials and museums present the embattled nation as the victim of larger, sinister outside forces, in a move that is not only mendacious about the past but, with its obsession with financier George Soros, who has supposedly single-handedly threatened Hungary's national integrity, fans a new version of a well-worn antisemitic fantasy.[37] In France there is a direct line from the anti-Dreyfusards to the Vichy collaborators, to the torturers during the Algerian War (1954–62), to the National Front under Jean-Marie Le Pen and his successors.

However, it would be quite erroneous to claim that Holocaust research and Holocaust commemoration were directly to blame for the current upsurge in right-wing movements and nationalist sentiments across the world. Indeed, to believe so would be bordering on antisemitism, since it is one of the oldest tropes of antisemitism to believe that the Jews' influence in world affairs is decisive. What is more likely is that those who work on this subject have overestimated the extent to which Holocaust consciousness might change the world for the better. Rather, as in the 1930s, it is the wider socio-economic situation that counts. Knowledge of the past might act as a warning and a brake but cannot provide lessons that will change the course of events. The driving forces today are austerity, economic recession and the feeling among the 'just managing' that immigration brings Islamist fundamentalism. The Covid-19 pandemic presents opportunities to blame others for spreading the virus and a reason to erect border controls against those of whom one is frightened. Memories of the Second World War held by those who fought on the losing side, including those in collaborating or occupied countries, are part of the mix and provide a vocabulary and aesthetic to which many turn easily and unthinkingly.[38] The fact is that Holocaust education goes out of the window if people feel that their life chances are narrowing.

We often get it the wrong way around: the answer to increasing levels of hatred is not more Holocaust education, for that is asking education to do more than it can provide. Rather, if we want Holocaust education to prove effective, we have first to build a society that desires equality and tolerance, and in which the values promoted by Holocaust education chime with the values of society at large.

This is how it begins. Economic recession, protectionism, nativist movements promising to protect 'the nation'. When the policies deriving from this position end by making people poorer, more afraid of others, and more turned in on themselves, then their positions harden and become more strident, since those promoting them can only explain their failure by claiming they have been thwarted by an unseen hand. We are not yet at that stage; fascism is not yet in power. But it is knocking on the door and the circumstances which allow it to do so – primarily the impoverishment of large swathes of the population through forty years of neo-liberal economics and the consequences of austerity since 2008 – remain unaddressed. One might argue that prolonging this situation will only lead to more ground being given to those with simplistic protectionist solutions. If we refuse to deal with this challenge, then the postwar order built on internationalism and individual freedom, which has already been attenuated in the last thirty years, will be decisively done away with and we will have sleepwalked into authoritarianism, if not full-blown fascism.[39] The Holocaust is not a lesson about the dangers of bullying, nor even a tale of the dangers of hatred. It is a warning that states, when elites become desperate to hold on to power, can do terrible, traumatic things, and that the deep psychology of modernity produces monsters the likes of which even the sleep of reason would struggle to generate. I will return to these problems, which are more pressing now than at any time since historians began to write about the Holocaust at the end of the Second World War, later in the book.

What Is the Holocaust?

Before proceeding, it might be worth offering a condensed summary of what is to follow, since this very complex history can be told in many different ways.

Nazism emerged from the crisis of post–Great War Europe and the Great Depression. The Nazis thought of themselves as carrying out an 'anti-colonial' struggle: that is to say, reversing the 'Diktat' of Versailles and revealing it to have been the work of the 'hidden hand' of international Jewry meant, from the Nazis' point of view, freeing Germany from foreign control. The context of postwar violence, and not just in Germany's eastern borderlands, and the ways in which the Freikorps foreshadowed extra-legal military forces, are crucial here, as is, in general, the impact of the First World War on European societies.[40] For the first time, concepts such as 'statelessness', refugee camps and 'states of exception' became unmissable fixtures on the European landscape and the Bolshevik revolution fuelled the rise of fascism in Italy and elsewhere. The crisis of Weimar is usually written with the emphasis on the rejection of the republic and the polarization of politics. But it was economic depression after 1929 that proved crucial, since only after that date did Nazism in Germany rise to prominence, as the middle classes felt the ground shifting beneath their feet. Most important, Nazism was part of broader European trends and did not come from nowhere: mass politics; unemployment; post-1918 violence; Italian Fascism; anti-communism; appeasement and the underrating of Hitler and his ideas, especially the importance of 'race'; traditional Christian Jew-hatred and its mutation into modern antisemitism; the notion of fascism as 'colonialism returned home' – all of these contributed to the appeal of Nazism, which was not an explosion of 'collective madness' with no links to anything that had gone before in European history. Rather, Nazism was the most extreme manifestation of sentiments that were quite common, and for which Hitler acted as a kind of rainmaker or shaman. It would be nice if it were true that Nazism was simply a return of the barbarians, for then we could agree with Peter Viereck, who in 1941 argued that Nazism was an outgrowth of German romanticism, and concluded pithily: 'The result is apes in evening dress, Neanderthalers in bomb-laden airplanes, very efficient and intelligent barbarians speeding debonairly in civilization's latest-model motor-cars: applying to uncivilized ends the highest technical achievements of civilization.'[41] However, Nazism, as Arendt said, may have come from the gutter, but the gutter is also part of European civilization.[42]

The first years of Nazi rule were characterized by antisemitic legislation and attacks, an attempt to 'coordinate' German society, and the attack on political enemies. Crucial to this process were the early concentration camps. These first concentration camps were not set up for the incarceration of Jews but for 'political enemies' and, in the years 1936–8, for 'asocials', in other words, 'Aryan' Germans who did not conform to the Nazis' ideals of social and political behaviour.

There were, of course, Jews in the camps, and, being Jews, they received in general worse treatment than other inmates.[43] But Jews and concentration camps were not linked then in ways that were imagined after the war and that still cause confusion today – the SS's concentration camp system and the Holocaust intersected only late in the war, even if the existence of concentration camps drove the Nazis' violent imagination and supported dreams of a purified society.

That said, Jews were immediately and violently targeted as soon as the Nazis took power, and Jews faced daily struggles in trying to deal with this onslaught on their ways of life and inclusion in the wider community. The November pogrom (*Kristallnacht*) was the turning point in the persecution of the Jews in Germany, for it marked the first time that Jews had been incarcerated in large numbers, even if most of them were able (that is to say, forced) to emigrate after leaving the camps. On the domestic front, Jews were now isolated in the Third Reich, which now included Austria. On the international front, the low point of the Hitler-Stalin Pact (August 1939) and Britain's isolation meant that the Jews were abandoned to their fate, trapped in an increasingly Nazified Europe.

The start of the war marked a shift in Nazi *Judenpolitik*, as a dynamic of violence unfolded and as the changing fortunes of the war exposed more Jewish communities to danger. Even before the establishment of ghettos in Nazi-occupied Poland – before a plan to murder the Jews held in them existed – the war in Poland saw the use of *Einsatzgruppen* (action squads) for rounding up and killing members of Poland's establishment (priests, politicians, academics, etc.).

This radical attack on Poland as such exacerbated gulfs in Polish society that existed before the war and indicated how a country already on the brink of introducing its own anti-semitic legislation before September 1939 would respond to the Nazi persecution of the Jews. It also set the scene for worse violence to come.

The military situation is clearly crucial here: attempts to crush Britain and keep the US out of the war, such as in Hitler's threat of world war in his 'prophecy' of 30 January 1939, clearly linked Nazi Jewish policies with the war, as the Nazis imagined that 'the Jew' was the puppet-master behind Roosevelt and Churchill, as well, of course, as the 'Judaeo-Bolshevik' Stalin. The inability to control the Indian Ocean, for example, precipitated the failure of the German Foreign Office's plans to deport the Jews to Madagascar, in the so-called 'territorial solution'. Yet the links between practical possibilities for targeting Jews and the military situation do not explain everything. Instead, from the choice of the Jews as victims to arguments between different agencies over what to do with the Jews in the ghettos in occupied Poland, we see that the unfolding of the Holocaust was shaped, but not de-termined, by the war.

With the invasion of the USSR on 22 June 1941, the war against the Jews merged with the military war, since in the eyes of the Nazis 'Judaeo-Bolshevism' was synonymous with the Soviet system, representing the antithesis to everything the Nazis stood for and wanted to achieve. In terms of the persecution of the Jews, a new and far more bloody stage than anything that had gone before now took place: the so-called 'Holocaust by bullets', which saw some 1.5 million Jews shot by the SS's *Einsatzgruppen*, in two 'sweeps': autumn 1941 and spring 1942. This was still not a Europe-wide project of genocide but was fast becoming one: the Operation Reinhard death camps (Bełżec, Sobibór and Treblinka) were already being planned to eliminate the Jews of Poland before the Wannsee Conference took place on 20 January 1942; gas vans in Chełmno and, in early 1942, Serbia were carrying out mass murder without involving face-to-face shooting; the eradication of the Jews of Latvia was fast completed, and preparations for deportations in France were also under way before the SS wrested full control over Jewish policy away from Goering, Frank, Rosenberg and other competing parties. What we now know as the 'Final Solution' was arrived at through a series of steps, not a single decision, culminating in spring 1942, when the programme was recognizably in place.

At this point, Jews were still not very relevant to the SS's camp system, since they were being killed in face-to-face shootings in Eastern Europe or in death camps in Nazi-occupied Poland. The key year was 1942: in March, some 75–80 per cent of the Holocaust's victims were still alive, whereas by mid-February 1943, some 80 per cent of the Holocaust's victims were dead.[44] The victims at this stage were primarily religious Eastern European Jews, and their struggles to comprehend what was happening to them are vitally important for showing how just as there was not one form of persecution, so different people amongst the victim groups in different places responded in different ways to the attacks on them.

The Holocaust, however, was a European phenomenon with many perpetrators, not just Germans. Collaboration is most obviously evident in countries such as France, Norway,

Croatia, Slovakia, Hungary and Romania, where killing Jews fitted with long-held nationalist aspirations to create ethnically homogeneous nation-states. It also refers to organizations, from the OUN in Ukraine, which allied itself with Nazi Germany in the hope of obtaining a Ukrainian state, to Nazi movements such as Norway's Nasjonal Samling or the Dutch NSB. These ideologically aligned groups believed in the Nazi vision of a racially cleansed Europe and thought that their national interests were best served under German hegemony. It also included millions of individuals, such as those who signed up to join the Waffen-SS, from Denmark to Bosnia, as well as Ukrainian and Baltic camp guards and, at a local level, so-called *szmalcowniki* in Poland (those who bribed Jews or who betrayed them to the SS).[45] The shocking extent of collaboration, which took many forms for different reasons – from ideological to a simple life-or-death decision for Soviet POWs – has become clearer since the end of the Cold War; the *ressentiment* its discovery has bred is all too clear in revived radical right movements today.

Among the clearest examples of collaboration are the Holocaust in Romania and the deportation of the Jews of Hungary in spring 1944. With these cases, we see an independent state choosing to participate in the Holocaust and a collaborating state under Nazi occupation assisting in deporting hundreds of thousands of Jews to their deaths in a very short space of time. We also gain a sense of the determination of the Nazi regime to 'finish the job', even in the face of impending military defeat. We gain a sense of how collaborating states enjoyed considerable freedom of manoeuvre (in Croatia, for example, the common description of NDH as a 'puppet state' does not reflect Ante Pavelić's Ustaša regime's independent input) and understand how it was possible for the Nazis to deport Jews across Europe as a whole, from Norway to Crete, Alderney to the Caucasus, the Baltic states to North Africa. The Holocaust did not only happen where the state was destroyed, as in Poland;[46] Romania shows exactly the opposite, that is, that where a functioning state wants to carry out criminal policies on a huge scale, it will find reasons and resources to do so.

This massive Europe-wide crime met something of a mirror-image in the response of the 'free world'. The War Refugee Board, the Atlantic Charter and the creation of the United Nations show how, despite the best intentions of their creators, they hardly matched the scale of the crime which precipitated their establishment. This inability quite to take the measure of Nazism was an echo of interwar appeasement and a failure, even by 1943, to believe that the Nazis meant what they said in their apocalyptic declarations. Recognizing this mismatch helps to explain why the Allies, despite the existence of a large literature on Nazi camps since the 1930s and an insightful intelligence network, were unprepared for what they found in the final stages of the Holocaust.

In the last stages of the war, the increasingly desperate needs of the war economy drove the Nazi leadership to reconsider its killing programme – a remarkable fact given that the drive to murder Jews was central to Nazism. From 1943 onwards, Jews and others were as likely to end up in slave labour sub-camps attached to the SS's main camps as they were to be murdered outright. The rapid growth in the sub-camp system is something that popular histories of the Holocaust often fail to explain, but it does not downplay Nazi genocidal plans to show that they were attenuated to a small extent in the final year and a half of the war. Rather, when one considers the ways in which slave labourers were treated, the exact opposite is the case. If one cannot always talk of 'annihilation through labour' (this is a term which does not occur very often in the sources), nevertheless the Nazis' attitude, even when labour needs were acute, was that Jews were expendable and that no effort should be made to ensure that productivity levels could become anything like those for normal labourers.

These sub-camps were often very small, and those who went through them often endured more than one. Indeed, the trajectories of many survivors include a number of small sub-camps whose names rarely mean anything today (who has heard of Neu-Dachs, Eintrachthütte, Christian-stadt, Überlingen or Dondangen?). As the need for labour increased and as the approach of the Allies forced camps to be relocated, the Holocaust became increasingly 'mobile'. We think of the Holocaust as having taken place in fixed in-stallations, but this only captures a small part of the Holo-caust experience. From deportation by various means of transport, to being shunted around the camp system, to the 'death marches' at the end of the war, the Holocaust took place on the move across Europe. Indeed, the Holocaust oc-curred over vastly different terrains and experiences (ghet-tos, camps, trains, ships), climates, languages, occupation or collaborating regimes – but all headed in the direction of a homogeneous conclusion: the murder of the Jews. Excep-tions to this rule such as Bulgaria and Denmark need care-ful consideration, not simplistic statements about 'good

Italians' and the like, which elide the differences between the actions of individuals and state policies. For the victims, this movement was overwhelmingly bewildering, and sub-camp inmates often did not even know where they were. The fact is, however, that the use of Jews as slave labourers saved the lives of many who would otherwise have simply been killed. Even if their deaths were being deferred, their lives were prolonged as a result of the unexpected flexibility of the Nazis' racial laws from late 1943 onwards. It was because they were in slightly better physical condition than they would have been had they not been in the sub-camps, that some Jews were able to survive until the liberation.

The images of the Holocaust which still dominate the collective memory are those from the liberation of the camps, especially of Belsen, Buchenwald and Dachau. But Jews were only in those camps in Germany in large numbers because of the 'death marches'. As the Red Army approached from the east, Himmler's order that camp inmates should not fall alive into enemy hands resulted in the bizarre phenomenon of the camp evacuations, or 'death marches'.[47] Here the concentration camp and Germany became synonymous as the inmates passed through just about every small locality in Central Europe, especially across Silesia, Thuringia, Bohemia and Bavaria. The complicity of the population at large was assured, and claims, commonly heard after the war, that 'no one knew' became impossible to defend. More importantly, the marchers were killed in huge numbers, such that perhaps a third of the more than 714,000 concentration camp inmates as of January 1945 were dead by the end of the war. They died of exhaustion or were shot on the route and buried, often in unmarked graves, by the roadside where they fell or in local cemeteries.

Thus, although camps such as Belsen and Dachau had not been created to house Jews and, up until late 1944, had hardly been associated with the Holocaust at all (apart from in the training of camp guards, in the case of Dachau), by 1945 these camps were effectively functioning as death camps. This is especially so in the case of Belsen, where the British, on the surrender of the camp on 15 April, found some 60,000 dying inmates. The horror of Belsen remains a scar on the world's conscience, and the sources from that moment remain painful to read, see and hear.

'Liberation', then, needs to be understood in inverted commas: many survivors died soon afterwards, too ill to be helped, and many more, amazed to have outlived the Nazi regime, were shocked to discover that they remained captive, unable to go where they wanted, deeply disappointed that the 'free world' did not grant them the right to start a life of their choosing, now that everything that characterized their old one was destroyed. The loneliness of the survivors was profound, as is indicated in the desperate way in which they set off to search for relatives at the slightest rumour. Yet over time, the DP camps became functioning societies, with political, religious, social and sporting clubs and organizations, a press, theatre and schooling, and vocational training to prepare new immigrants for life outside the camps. Amongst these people Zionism was inescapable, for they felt rejected by Europe, which they rejected in turn. Even so, the so-called 'hard core' of DPs – those who could not or would not leave Germany – remained for many years, until the last DP camp, at Föhrenwald near Munich, closed in 1957, by which point it had become an embarrassment to a West Germany trying to assert its sovereignty in the comity of nations. The Holocaust, in other words, did not simply 'end' in May 1945.

Indeed, the 'afterlife' (or, as Lawrence Langer aptly calls it, the 'afterdeath') of the Holocaust is now inescapably part of its history, especially when we consider that 1945 was not the end of the story. This is to be expected given that we are talking about an event of world-historical significance. The stages of 'collective memory' through which 'Holocaust consciousness' has passed, moreover, are important markers of postwar European society and culture in general. The rise of 'Holocaust consciousness' can be charted through numerous media: film, law, education and culture in the widest sense. The Holocaust has moved, as Jeffrey Alexander puts it, from 'war crime to trauma drama', and perhaps one of the most unedifying spectacles – indicating the law of unintended consequences – is the way in which an increased awareness of the Holocaust has led to it being banalized and exploited.[48] Unsurprisingly, it remains a key topic of contestation for the radical right across the world and a barometer of political culture, whether in Israel or Poland. But perhaps most problematic is what we might call the 'beautifying' of the Holocaust in the Western world: the lauding of survivors and their moving stories and a desire to 'learn' from the Holocaust. The Holocaust teaches nothing except that deep passions that owe nothing to rational politics can move human beings to do terrible things. Which is to say, the Holocaust teaches us nothing, since nothing in the end can stop people from supporting these dark forces in times of crisis.

That grim thought raises the question: what does the Holocaust tell us about modernity?[49] The Holocaust was not the logical conclusion of means–ends rationality but rather the consequence of a modern world that creates and canalizes deep passions that have no obvious outlet. In principle, there is nothing wrong with Holocaust education or Holocaust commemoration. But we should be willing to face the radical conclusions to which these activities should lead us: that the Holocaust was a deeply traumatic event for its victims; that the consequences of the Holocaust have not only led to good (the creation, for the time being, of a democratic Germany, the absence of war in most of Europe since 1945) but have left a dark legacy, a 'deep psychology' of 'fascination with fascism' that people turn to instinctively in moments of crisis; and that the Holocaust not only reveals the fragile identity but awesome power of the modern nation-state and the 'pillars' which support it (rule of law, the military, religion, ruling elites) but also calls their very organization and functioning into question. The Holocaust cannot be explained as the vicious actions of a mad regime; it has political, religious, cultural and social implications for modern societies, and that is why its impact is so keenly felt even if public commemorative ceremonies rarely articulate its significance in these terms. In this book, I show what these implications are and why the Holocaust is not just a 'lesson' about intolerance or hatred but tells us how societies in crisis can slide into horror, with the majority, including established elites, colluding in the worst sort of crimes if they sense that their positions might otherwise be threatened.

Thinking about the Holocaust

Anyone who studies the Holocaust quickly discovers – often to their dismay, at least initially – that the scholarship on the subject is vast. Across all disciplines, there is a stupendous literature that no one person can master. Even restricting oneself to historical writing on the Holocaust, the size and scope of the scholarly literature is truly remarkable. This should not be taken as a sign of overproduction or, even more cynically, of an unbridled 'Holocaust industry'. Rather, it signals that the Holocaust is a phenomenon which troubles all thinking people, as it should, and that many scholars – as with people in general – feel compelled to grapple with it. In fact, the scope of the historiography is an opportunity: to learn a great deal from different perspectives, to appreciate the work done by scholars, whether writing minute studies of a single person or family, or grand synthetic overviews, to understand a phenomenon which seems to elude understanding, and to see how the afterlife of the Holocaust has been shaped in the years since 1945 to the present. In doing so, we chart our own changing times.

For several decades now, the historiography of the Holocaust has been unmanageably large. Even if one is aware of the main trends and can manage an overview of what is appearing in every European language, reading it all is impossible. Since then, the scholarship has branched out in terms of topics and approaches and new insights are being generated all the time. Some of the most innovative approaches include gendered studies, showing how gender affected the experiences of men and women during the Holocaust; the use of archaeology and forensic science, for example to learn more about camp sites; the geographical concept of space to enrich our understanding of the topographies of the Holocaust; the turn to microhistory, with its concept of the 'normal exceptional', that is, how seemingly minute occurrences can illuminate the bigger picture; and ideas borrowed from refugee studies, anthropology, psychoanalysis, environmental studies and other cognate disciplines.

Historians have recently turned to studies of the Holocaust in places and regions which have previously seemed marginal to or escaped the notice of scholars, from Subcarpathian Ruthenia to North Africa, as well as a focus on multiethnic relations in particular locales, especially in Eastern Europe. There are also detailed studies of little-known institutions, especially the huge number of sub-camps across Nazi-occupied and Axis Europe; a more nuanced examination of the role played by so-called bystanders; a greater focus on Aryanization, i.e. the appropriation and theft of Jewish property, in Germany and elsewhere; the fate of Jewish refugees in the Soviet Union, the Iberian peninsula, and elsewhere; the so-called death marches, as camps were forcibly evacuated in the face of the Allied advance in late 1944 and early 1945; and a host of aftermath issues, from studies of DP camps in Italy to the creation of camp survivors' organizations, from the Yiddish-language newspapers printed in the DP camps to the remigration of Jewish refugees in far-flung places such as Mauritius, Shanghai and the Dominican Republic, from trials of *kapos* in Israel to the writing of *yizker-bikher* (memorial books), to the lost communities of Eastern Europe, from the early postwar search for Jewish missing persons to the remarkable operation of the International Tracing Service.[50] In the vast, interdisciplinary literature on Holocaust memory, increasingly sophisticated studies of testimony have appeared, showing how individuals' testimonies vary depending on when and where they are given, and assessing the impact of collecting practices and methodologies on the construction of archives of testimonies.[51] Studies of memorial sites, museums, historical commissions, restitution, the return of looted property, Holocaust-related trials in settings as varied as communist Poland to post–Cold War France, and historiography itself, all of which describe the institutionalization of Holocaust consciousness, have become prominent and represent a substantial share of the scholarly literature on the subject.[52] The rediscovery of numerous early postwar texts by survivors is enriching our understanding of the victims' responses. If we add in debates in genocide studies concerning the extent to which the Holocaust bears comparison with other cases of genocide, the literature becomes even bigger.[53]

Yet there are still many topics which remain understudied. Nazi thought has not yet been the subject of a sustained engagement, probably because historians fear being seen to grant Nazism too much intellectual credence or coherence. There are exceptions, of course, as the growing literature on the sciences in Nazi Germany indicates, but for most historians the notion of a history of ideas of Nazism is oxymoronic, since the concept of Nazi thinkers or philosophers, as opposed to ideologues, seems outrageous. Current scholarly research projects suggest that we can expect far more scholarship on child survivors of the Holocaust, on DP camps and refugees, especially using digital mapping techniques to show survivors' trajectories and networks, on microhistories of places across Europe, and far more attempts to integrate the responses of the victims into a historiography which has until recently been dominated by perpetrator-centric research. The work of the early postwar historians, many of whom wrote in Yiddish or who were not university-based, such as Philip Friedman, Rachel Auerbach and Eva Reichmann, has been rediscovered and, especially with a view to emphasizing a victim-centred approach, bears further scrutiny.[54]

These are all empirical topics, research on which is based on the historian's *sine qua non* of access to archives. But ideas about what to do with the material are also subject to change. As well as the methodological innovations like gender history, digital humanities and so on, key interpretive frameworks have changed considerably over the years. From the keywords such as fascism or totalitarianism in the postwar period, to antisemitism and modernity in the years just before and after the end of the Cold War, to genocide and ideology in recent years, historians have offered competing interpretations of the Holocaust which can themselves be historicized. Interpretive frames are shaped by the questions historians ask, who are themselves shaped by the socio-cultural circumstances in which they are living and writing. Today, as a historian writing under the shadow of the end of the postwar order, when the architecture of international co-operation is being dismantled, with nationalism, xenophobia and racism growing in the shadow of the threat to the planet caused by climate change, the Holocaust seems to take on a different hue than it did to historians writing only a few years ago.[55] It is certainly true, as Alon Confino writes, that 'The historian's best narrative renders the process of dehumanization and brutality without condemnation or tears but in terms that illuminate the reality of the events that took place.'[56] There should be no need to moralize when writing about a topic so obviously disgusting. Nevertheless, the reasons for holding such a position – which are fundamental to the writing of what is normally considered good history – are shakier now than at any time since 1945.[57]

In this book, my focus on ideology is not meant to suggest a simplistic belief in an 'ideas-into-action' model. It is not the case that because Hitler wrote diatribes against the Jews in *Mein Kampf* that the Jews of Europe were murdered. At the same time, there *is* a connection between Hitler's statements and the genocide of the Jews.[58] I suggest that in the context of the interwar crisis in Europe, which allowed Hitler's ideas to gain support, Jews functioned as symptoms of modernity that fascism was designed to overcome: rootlessness, cosmopolitanism, universality, loss of community, rapid change, standardization, soullessness. This was the ideological framework in which the Holocaust took place, which is not the same thing as saying that a plan to murder the Jews existed in 1933 or even in 1940. Nazi antisemitism attacked an abstract concept – the Jew – that was, the Nazis believed, the embodiment of everything that was wrong with modernity. In turn, this led to the murder of some six million individuals because they were, according to Nazi definitions, Jewish. This is why the focus here is on the Jews. Roma, the disabled, Soviet POWs, homosexuals and other groups were victims of the Nazis, and it is entirely legitimate to study

WHAT IS THE HOLOCAUST?

their fate alongside one another.[59] But using the term 'Holocaust' to encompass all of these groups with the aim of being inclusive and not prioritizing one group's suffering, actually does a disservice to groups other than Jews. For the Nazis persecuted these groups for different reasons, reasons we fail to appreciate if we collapse them all together.

Thus, although the Nazis placed great store on what I term 'race mysticism', this was no atavistic regression but a response to a modern crisis. But by attacking the Jews as a symbol of that modernity, the Nazis left in place much that caused the crisis in the first place, especially the rampant nature of unregulated interwar capitalism which led to the Great Depression, instead focusing discontent on a 'personification of its social form'.[60] It was not an accident that the Nazis focused their hatred on the Jews; Jews were the traditional Other of the Christian West, both constituent of Western civilization and a reminder of that which was supposed to be overcome. Christian European history had periodically re-enacted the crucifixion through ritual murders and pogroms of Jews. As one strident critic puts it, the Holocaust 'exposes the pulsation of an unconscious behavioural cliché transferred to the secular religion of Nazism – which reenacted it systematically'.[61] In its modern variant, antisemitism was a projection onto an Other whose outsider–insider status needed no explanation, of fears brought about by conditions that were thoroughly modern in origin.

In the words of the great Holocaust historian Saul Friedländer: 'the very notion of "outsider" applied by modern antisemitism to the Jew owed its tenacity not only to Jewish difference as such but also to the depth of its religious roots'.[62]

It was a 'reactivated millenarian phantasm' built on the deep psychology of European fantasies as applied to a modern crisis.[63] For example, in the explanation put forward by philosopher Ernst Cassirer, the Nazi myth consisted of attacking the people whose religion represented the rejection of myth *par excellence* – in the forbidding of graven images, for example, which implies a rejection of the sort of race worship to which the Nazis were devoted. This led Cassirer to the conclusion that Nazi antisemitism was far more than a mere technique of domination or a means of distracting the masses but demanded 'a life and death struggle which could only find its end in the complete extermination of the Jews'.[64] Hence what we see in the Holocaust is, as Friedländer succinctly puts it, 'the use of bureaucratic measures to enforce magical beliefs'.[65] If much the same is true today – the radical right attacks immigrants, Muslims, Others of all varieties, thereby mistaking a symbol for the concrete – then saying so is not about using present-day problems to explain the past. Instead, it is the reverse: it is showing how the appeal of Nazism could lead to the commission of a crime that exceeds the cognition of the rational mind, even as we are ourselves sleepwalking into a twenty-first-century catastrophe.

Historians sometimes shy away from offering explanations, preferring to detail the mechanics of how something occurred. This is especially so when the explanations tend towards the psychoanalytical, or towards other factors which cannot easily be backed up empirically.[66] But the need to try is not outweighed by the obvious truth that any explanation will only ever be partial, suggestive and a spur to further thinking. It is easy to feel bamboozled and overwhelmed in the face of the horror of the Holocaust, and no book can be the last word on the subject – as is of course true for all subjects. But in the case of the Holocaust, it is perhaps especially apt that history should be unfinished; the idea of endless questioning and an openness to new ideas operates as a logical counterweight to the desire for final solutions, last words and completion.

The Holocaust

CHAPTER 1

Before the Holocaust

'The idea of the community as a body is *always* a "mythic" idea, and it *always* (not only in case of the Christian community) establishes a *corpus mysticum*.'
— Eric Voegelin[1]

Introduction

Ideology does not come from nowhere. The history of ideas is crucial, though it is insufficient for explaining the historical origins of Nazism. Ideas that seemed marginal at one moment became decisive at another, following the German defeat in the First World War and, especially, after the terrible effects of the Great Depression. In order to grasp the power of the forces that fuelled the Holocaust, we have to understand the toxic mix of ideas and events which propelled an apocalyptic movement to the fore. Nazism was not merely a political programme but sought to be, as Goebbels put it, 'the very air which we breathe'. It was not just an ideology but a *Weltanschauung*, or worldview.[2]

Worldviews have to come from somewhere, however. Historians have long traced the origins of the Nazi worldview in the mystical, *völkisch* antisemitism, racial supremacism and cultural pessimism of nineteenth-century writers such as Arthur de Gobineau, Houston Stewart Chamberlain and Georges Vacher de Lapouge on the one hand, and in the scientific racism of social Darwinism, eugenics, racial psychology (*Völkerpsychologie*) and criminology on the other, bodies of thought that were considered avant-garde at the start of the twentieth century. The largely unreadable tracts produced by these racial evangelists were simplified after the Great War by Nazi thinkers such as early theorist of Nazism Dietrich Eckart, Hitler's close associate and 'Party philosopher' Alfred Rosenberg, the 'blood and soil' theorist and early Nazi Party member Richard Walther Darré and race theorist Hans F. K. Günther, who in their different ways converted turgid philosophical racism into propagandistic platitudes. At the same time, many interwar intellectual fashions – such as *Lebensphilosophie*, futurism or vitalism – tended towards fascism, emphasizing breaking with bourgeois dependability and seeking the essence of life in the organic 'body' of a narrowly defined community. While eugenics and the idea of the *Volksgemeinschaft* (racial community) were by no means exclusively right-wing ideas in the interwar period, they became so in Germany after 1930 – a periodization which is telling, since it was only in the context of the Great Depression that the fault-lines which had riven the Weimar Republic since its inception truly began to take effect.[3]

Yet to some extent debates about which trend – *völkisch* thought or racial science – more properly explains the origins of Nazism miss the point, which is one that Dutch novelist Harry Mulisch understood: 'The truth is that Hitler did not need the writing from Gobineau to Rosenberg. He appreciated it as some sort of canonical tradition, which continued next to or behind what he himself possessed, something much more awful: a mystical revelation. He did not need to write or think. *He knew*.'[4] In other words, the leading Nazis did not need to study these texts, many of which they would barely have understood. Rather they absorbed simplified versions of them in slogans such as the 'survival of the fittest' and 'knew' that they made sense because they *wanted* to believe in the idea of race. They wanted to believe because they were at the helm of a movement which promised national regeneration, the end to national humiliation at the hands of foreign powers and the elimination of the enemy within. That does not mean that, since Nazism was a mish-mash of prior ideas, lacking originality or intellectual rigour, it was not lethally effective or that it should not be taken seriously as a worldview. In fact, quite the opposite is the case: those who failed to take Nazism seriously 'felt its deadly power on their own flesh' and, even when we are 'only' discussing Nazi rhetoric, we are still dealing with judgements over life and death.[5]

Antisemitism was especially important in the Nazi worldview. Nazism's self-perception as an anti-colonial struggle – that is to say, reversing the Diktat of Versailles and revealing it to have been the work of the hidden hand of international Jewry – meant, from the Nazis' point of view, freeing Germany from foreign control. And for the leading Nazis 'foreign control' meant more than the punitive debt repayments and the war guilt clause; it meant exposing 'the Jew' as the puppet-master controlling these events, finagling world leaders into doing the secret cabal's bidding. Such ideas built on the legacy of European Jew-hatred which had existed since the high medieval period but also went far beyond it, radicalizing stereotypes about Jews, making the abstract Jew do service as the embodiment of modernity's ills and turning antisemitism into a metaphysical *vade mecum*.[6]

In his novel about a Yugoslav *kapo* who survives Auschwitz and is later tormented by his behaviour in the camp, the Serbian novelist Aleksandar Tišma ventriloquizes the catchall reasons for antisemitism, placing these thoughts in the minds of Lamian, his eponymous *kapo*. Lamian is himself of Jewish origin, though baptized by his parents in the vain hope of avoiding prejudice and persecution, and articulates a classic variety of antisemitism which sees Jews as the opposite of every healthy trait:

> Their rootlessness, their lack of allegiance to country or language, or an allegiance they changed according to need, contemptuous of all affiliations and borders, disdaining the shackles of history, geography, national colours and symbols. Marxists, Freudians, Esperantists, feminists, nudists, supporters of every revolution, receptive to every novelty, they scampered here and there like mice, until speared by the claws of the cat, who preferred to lie in the sun.[7]

None of this owed much to race philosophy or to social Darwinism, though both form part of the background to this classic statement of Nazi antisemitism, which brought together ancient and modern tropes in a hate-filled narrative of regeneration through elimination. Nazism was a paranoid conspiracy theory which believed in history as a redemption story. The struggle between good and evil – Aryan versus non-Aryan – lay at the heart of history and the need for living space for the German *Volk* necessitated the elimination of social and political enemies of all sorts, but above all the life-and-death fight to annihilate the puppet-master who sought to destroy Aryan civilization: the Jew.[8] Dietrich Eckart argued that 'the secret of Jewishness' was that it 'wants the *despiritualization* of the world and nothing else; but this would be the same as its *annihilation*'. Alfred Rosenberg claimed in a 1923 analysis of the famous tract that purported to be an account of a secret cabal at the heart of the Jewish world conspiracy, *The Protocols of the Elders of Zion*, that 'the incorporation of the German colony into the pan-Jewish private syndicate is taking place'. No wonder that the Nazi Party's programme, from its earlier incarnation in 1921, demanded the abrogation of the Versailles Treaty, the acquisition of land 'for the nourishment of our people and for the settlement of our excess population', and then insisted: 'Only he who is a folk comrade can be a citizen. Only he who is of German blood, regardless of his church, can be a folk comrade. No Jew, therefore, can be a folk comrade.'[9] And no wonder that contemporary observers saw in Nazi antisemitism something more than a mere aspiration, political position or technique of domination. As the lawyer and Anglo-Jewish notable Neville Laski wrote in 1939: 'Anti-Semitism is not a side-issue of Nazism. It is the very root of the Nazi creed and, particularly in the mind of the Leader, the very essence of his doctrine.'[10] The Nazis' victims understood this especially clearly. As Ella Lingens-Reiner, survivor of Auschwitz and noted anti-fascist activist, wrote in her book published shortly after the war: 'Anti-Semitism was not only one of the fundamental tenets of the Nazi creed, it was probably the only point of the doctrine, apart from the sacred person of the Fuehrer, which even the more rationally minded Nazis would refuse to discuss. Either you were of the faith or you were not.'[11]

After the Great War

Can these intellectual trends alone account for the emergence of Nazism? Naturally, the answer must be no, for in order to be operationalized, or put into practice, ideas require the impetus of changing social and political circumstances. Economic change, demographic shifts, social change in the wake of industrialization – all are part of the necessary background to Nazism. But that is equally true of all twentieth-century movements. We can account for the large-scale context, the background from which Nazism emerged, but not the specific verve and voraciousness which characterized the Nazi world-view, even in comparison with other fascist groups or authoritarian regimes, and it is important to remember that Nazism was a radical variant of fascism.[12] As the historian Thomas Mergel observes, no other post-1918 European dictatorship 'came even close to radically reshaping their societies as the Nazis did'.[13] Even set alongside Stalin's Soviet Union – with which Nazi Germany is most commonly compared – the characteristically apocalyptic dimension of Nazism, and the huge popular support for it, are distinctive.[14] There is thus a circular argument at work: ideas drive actions, especially when we look for ideology fuelling violent, criminal regimes; and ideas are born from changing circumstances. We need some specifics in order to offer more precise explanations for the appearance of such an extraordinary phenomenon as National Socialism. Many ideas such as those espoused by the new antisemites, the *völkisch* thinkers and the eugenicists were in the air in the early twentieth century, but what happened to allow them to become fundamental drivers of state policy in Germany?

The Great War was the most important catalyst for change. Its significance has hardly been missed, either by contemporary commentators, including the Nazis themselves as well as their enemies, or by generations of historians. As the historian Benjamin Ziemann notes, the Great War 'had a massive impact on the political imaginary of all political groups in Germany, and fundamentally shaped notions of national belonging, class, and citizenship'.[15] From the outset, parties of left and right threatened to compromise the Weimar Republic's integrity or even to destroy it altogether. On all sides, German politicians remained in thrall to the memory of the Wilhelmine Empire under the Kaiser and the putative harmony of Germany under the wartime military dictatorship, which supposedly transcended party squabbling, leading to a contradiction between the conflict inherent to party democracy and the yearning for stability. The Versailles Peace Treaty brought these internal contradictions to the fore at the very birth of the republic. Only a slim majority in the Reichstag supported it, and even most of those supporters from across the political spectrum had to hold their noses in distaste at the war-guilt clause, which the Allies insisted on including. 'In this sense', as Mergel notes, 'the first German democracy was characterized from the very beginning by the desire to revise precisely those conditions which had enabled its existence in the first place.'[16]

Generations of schoolchildren since then have grown up

being taught that the Versailles Treaty was the main cause of the rise of Hitler. But in fact almost all politicians, of all ideological stripes, in the Weimar Republic opposed the treaty. Nazism came to power in 1933 and not in 1923, when debates about the treaty were still fresh. As the philosopher and historian R. G. Collingwood said of Versailles, 'the spark in a fuse is not the sole cause of an explosion'.[17] The sense of humiliation and a desire to restore German honour were certainly key issues throughout the interwar period, but they were not specific to the Nazis. By the time of the Great Depression, however, and after seemingly endless changes in government, the Nazis seemed to many voters to be the last untried option, and one untainted by involvement with the *Herrenklub*, that is to say, the elite club of politicians, who seemed, so ordinary voters believed, to have come through the Depression unscathed while the majority suffered. The trend towards presidential rule after 1925, and decisively so after 1930, permitted by the famous Article 48 of the Weimar constitution, made rule by emergency decree seem normal and, in that sense, the turn to the Nazis seemed less decisive than might otherwise have been the case. Besides, bringing the Nazis into power not only was a decision made by traditional conservative elites, in the vain hope of clinging on to power, but was made possible by the Nazis' electoral success: 37.3 per cent of the votes in July 1932 and 33 per cent in November 1932, making the NSDAP by far the largest party in Weimar Germany.

Even more important, the Great War brought about new meanings of citizenship and belonging that threatened ordinary people's sense of how the world worked, generating a sense that only a dictatorship could restore stability.

'Everything in the fatherland had begun to stagger' in the autumn of 1918, said one National Socialist.[18] The legend that Germany had been stabbed in the back by Jews and Bolsheviks – or Jewish Bolsheviks – runs like a red thread through the anti-republican rhetoric of the right during the Weimar period and, after the Nazis came to power, was appealed to again and again as justification for the Nazis taking the measures they did. The state of exception that Weimar's Article 48 embodied was not new: both Germany and France were run as military dictatorships during the war, with President Poincaré imposing a state of siege on France which lasted until 12 October 1919.

One of the most characteristic phenomena of the state of exception was the camp. Camps – with the relatively recent invention of the wooden barrack now ubiquitous[19] – held POWs in unprecedented numbers: between eight and nine million soldiers, or one in every nine men in uniform. Such huge numbers tell us something about the capabilities of modern states to transport and hold people, and thus also something about modern technology being put at the service of warfare and how that changed people's understanding of their place in the world. Large numbers of POWs died – over 9 per cent of Habsburg POWs in Russian captivity, or nearly 20 per cent of Italian soldiers in Austrian captivity, for example – but that was because of states' decisions not to provide sufficient food rather than because of an inability to sustain life.[20]

The Great War also saw huge numbers of civilians interned for the first time on European soil. Such practices had occurred regularly in the European powers' overseas colonies, from the age of slavery onwards, as whole population groups were dispossessed and forcibly removed, as in the expanding United States, German South West Africa or Australia under British governance. Now, in a move that would support the post–Second World War claims of anti-colonial writers such as Frantz Fanon or Aimé Césaire that fascism represented a kind of 'colonialism come home', such camps were seen in Europe itself. At the end of the First World War, some 111,879 'enemy civilians' were interned in Germany, as were 24,255 Germans, Austrians and Hungarians in Britain. Italians in the Austro-Hungarian Empire were deported for being 'out of place' or held in what were called concentration camps. Whatever the reason given for rounding up and interning civilians in this way – fear of fifth columnists, as reprisal, or to obtain forced labourers being the most common – the actions bespeak a new nervousness and paranoia around states' conceptions of themselves, as the transition from empires to nation-states was taking shape at the end of the Great War. The concept of statelessness stems from this period, as does the first large wave of refugees on European soil, with refugee camps being established to house Russian émigrés in the wake of the Revolution and civilians subjected to euphemistically named 'population transfers' at the end of the war. Europe after the war was more obsessed with narrowly defined national belonging, accompanied by fears and fantasies of threatening outsiders – especially outsiders within – than it had been before.

These tremendous population movements and shifts in the meaning of citizenship intersected with pre-existing fears and fantasies about certain groups of people. For example, when it came to the fear of communism, one of the drivers of fascism across Europe, the presence of Russian POWs heightened

Germans' fears – which were unfounded – that a successful communist revolution was imminent. With more than 1.4 million Russian POWs being held in camps across Germany, it was all too easy to imagine that, once released, 'they would form a revolutionary army dedicated to the aim of spreading world revolution all the way to the Rhine'.[21] President Ebert's decision to call in the Freikorps – the radical right paramilitary groups who refused to be demobilized in 1918 – to put down the Spartacist uprising marked the continuity between the war, the emergence of fascism, and the democrats' dilemma in Weimar. Ebert, the social democrat president, had to rely on armed members of the radical right to put down this communist uprising. And as Hitler claimed in *Mein Kampf*, in a reading of the postwar chaos that would gain in popularity as the Nazis' influence increased, the war had drained an 'irreplaceable' amount of 'German heroes' blood', and the '*real* organizer of the revolution and its actual wirepuller' was 'the international Jew'.[22]

Such fears easily took shape and became widespread in the chaos that followed the end of the war. The collapse of the old empires and the violent birth of new nation-states such as Poland with formally democratic constitutions but with ethnically nationalist aspirations, completely reshaped the demographic, political, religious and linguistic landscape of Central and Eastern Europe. The chaos and dislocation that accompanied this reshaping contributed greatly to what the historian Cathie Carmichael calls 'eliminationist groups' across Europe, that is to say, extremists who aimed at achieving ethnic homogeneity through violence.[23] In the case of Germany, where the new republic was born amidst hostility, where the loss of the war was ascribed to treason and where national humiliation and the will to overcome it provided one of the few sources of social cohesion, the stage was set for something radical. A combination of *völkisch* thinking and the impact of the First World War explains the emergence of Nazism's vision and the violence to which it gave rise. The contingent circumstances of the Great Depression provided the push for the popular surge of enthusiasm for Nazism as well as the elite's gamble in following the electorate and inviting Hitler into power. But to understand the drive for *Lebensraum*, the creation of a German empire in Europe in which the racial community could thrive, one has to grasp the overriding significance of race for the Nazis.

Race: Thinking with the Blood

It would be a mistake to look for a clear intellectual lineage for Nazism, just as it would be a mistake to believe that Nazis held a coherent view of race, applied consistently over time and place. But that lack of consistency or intellectual rigour does not mean that the Nazis' racial obsessions were not passionately held, or lethal.

In Hitler, the Nazis found a leader who embodied many of the fears and fantasies that were common on the German right after the Great War, but also a strange character who switched from shyness to on-stage charisma, from sullenness to ranting. His 'Landsberg bible', *Mein Kampf* (My Struggle), written following the failed coup of 1923, was mocked by the educated and fought over by translators but turned out not only to make Hitler rich, but also to be a reasonably accurate guide to what he would do once in power.[24] Most importantly, it revealed the extent of Hitler's grandiose sense of his own world-historical mission. Any page offers suitably pompous and unselfconscious verbiage:

> And so the Jew today is the great agitator for the complete destruction of Germany. Wherever in the world we read of attacks against Germany, Jews are their fabricators, just as in peacetime and during the War the press of the Jewish stock exchange and Marxists systematically stirred up hatred against Germany until state after state abandoned neutrality and, renouncing the true interests of the peoples, entered the service of the World War coalition.[25]

Few commentators at the time took this seriously. They saw Hitler as ripe only for satire, a satire which was important but which also facilitated a fatal misstep: not realizing that Hitler meant what he said. Many people, wrote Labour Party intellectual Harold Laski, 'could not bring themselves to believe that any child of the twentieth century could seriously contemplate a world in which the vast majority were the helpless slaves of a cruel and corrupt oligarchy, ruling by the right of force alone, and concerned deliberately to emphasize their conviction that force alone is a full title to rule.'[26] One exception was Sebastian Haffner, the émigré lawyer who fled Germany in 1938. Haffner understood that:

> to tabulate Hitler, as it were, in the History of Ideas and degrade him to an historical episode is a hopeless undertaking, and can only lead to perilous miscalculations. Much more progress towards an accurate estimate of the man can be made if one takes exactly the opposite course and considers German and European history as a part of Hitler's private life.[27]

Mein Kampf might have been a rambling, incoherent product of a second-rate mind but, in its violence, self-certainty, limitless hatred and gargantuan fantasy, it provided the basis for a worldview which, when presented to the public through speeches and legislation, proved to have powers of attraction that had nothing to do with rational decision-making, or the cost–benefit analyses of the sort that commentators tend to assume motivates voters.

A small number of contemporaries, mostly Germans acquainted with Nazism through first-hand experience, were well aware of the Nazis' racial obsessions.[28] In a book published in 1933, and still one of the most insightful studies of Nazi race-thinking, philosopher Eric Voegelin noted how 'astonishing' it was that the Jews had become the 'counteridea' of the Germans when they constituted so small a percentage of the population. This was thanks, he argued, to 'a feeling of inferiority on the part of the Germans, to their fear – repeatedly expressed in antisemitic literature – of being dominated by the Jews, to the Germans' belief in a worldwide organization of all Jews directed with diabolical cleverness towards the ultimate, total economic enslavement of the Aryans and, most particularly, of the Germans'. According to Voegelin, this idea revealed 'nothing about Jews but a great deal about the community regarded as positive, in contrast to which Jews are simply nothing'.[29] Well aware of the Nazis' attempts to find scientific evidence to underpin their racial fantasies, Voegelin argued that antisemitism served primarily a political purpose, that of creating a cohesive and radically exclusive community. Working with a 'system of dogmas' that 'is neither transcendentally shaken by philosophical anthropology nor deeply affected inherently by the course of biology and scientific anthropology', race theory was in fact 'a system of scientific superstition'.[30]

Voegelin himself came under suspicion of harbouring quasi-mystical views about race, accused of being a 'fascist savant of rare acumen and coolness' by the phenomenologist (and convert from Judaism to Catholicism) Aurel Kolnai.[31] Kolnai overstated the extent of Voegelin's sympathy for fascism, but in 1938, when he published *The War Against the West*, still one of the finest studies of Nazi thought, the claim was perhaps understandable. In this large book, the 120-page chapter titled 'Nation and Race', consciously echoing *Mein Kampf*'s most notorious chapter, is a masterpiece of critical analysis. Without making the mistake of dismissing Nazi thought as an oxymoron, Kolnai delved into the Nazi race philosophers' thoughts, resulting in a trenchant critique. With reference to writers like Ewald Banse, Ludwig Schemann, Ludwig Ferdinand Clauss, Ernst Krieck, Alfred Baeumler, Hans F. K. Günther, Alfred Rosenberg and many others (mostly academics, and all men), Kolnai shows how Nazism equates the state with the *Volk*, how it is devoted to warfare and how it seeks above all to preserve Aryan blood. Stressing the mystical rather than strictly scientific aspects of race thinking, Kolnai, like Voegelin, argued that with Nazism 'we are in no way concerned with the anthropological subject of human races or racial fitness as such, only with the neo-German emphasis attached to race for political, social and philosophical reasons'. Or, with a greater sense of distaste, and with particular reference to Ernst Krieck, Kolnai noted that 'the philosophic creed of race has a claim to a sort of primeval, religious dignity, by no means dependent on cor-roboration by scientific research with its chancy and chang-ing results'.[32] Such insights were perhaps easier to stomach in the 1930s; even in 1942, Kolnai's argument was being rec-ommended to British fellow travellers of Nazism: 'Persons like Lord Londonderry, and Sir Nevile Henderson, and the whole Anglo-German Fellowship, should be compelled to read M. Kolnai's book' since 'it contains as damning a revela-tion of mental perversion and wickedness as any the world has seen'.[33] By contrast, after the war, when Europe lay dev-astated and millions were dead, this sort of philosophical analysis that took Nazism seriously as a system of thought was regarded as distasteful; it was easier to dismiss Nazism simply as a kind of 'madness'. Indeed, after 1945 analytical frameworks which understood Nazism as a deviation from a Western liberal norm were to prevail. All had their merits but all evaded the need to subject Nazi ideology to rigorous analysis and failed to appreciate the seriousness with which Nazism devoted itself to the mystical idea of racial union.

Before the war, few commentators outside of Germany had the insight or understanding to appreciate the serious-ness of the Nazis' devotion to race. This is somewhat surpris-ing, given the fact that thinking in racial terms was common across all social groups, whether educated or not, in the first half of the twentieth century. Notions of superior and inferior races had accompanied – if not driven – European imperial expansion in the nineteenth century and the worst colonial brutalities do not make sense in military or cost–benefit terms alone, but can be accounted for only through racialized lenses – the Belgian Congo, for example, or British 'small wars' in Sierra Leone, Perak or Sudan.[34] Eugenics, with its aim of 'improving the race', was an avant-garde position held by leftist intellectuals almost as commonly as those on the right, at least until the 1920s, although those on the left rarely articulated their visions with quite the same violent eagerness as those, like Anthony M. Ludovici, who were strangely aroused by the idea of doing away with 'the weak'.[35] White supremacists, especially but by no means only in the US, built on the notion of polygenism – the idea that human races had separate evolutionary origins – to question whether blacks and whites belonged to the same species and to justify Jim Crow post-emancipation segregation.[36] Nevertheless, the emphasis on nature to the exclusion of nurture came to characterize German eugenics – or, as it was called in Germany, racial hygiene (*Rassenhygiene*) – more than anywhere else in the interwar period.[37] In the UK, the provision of public infrastructure such as sewers offered an obvious rejoinder to arguments that the lower classes were inherently diseased or degenerate; in the US, the country of immigrants, German-born anthropologist Franz Boas demonstrated that with better social and economic conditions, the children of immigrants were healthier and more robust than their parents, thereby disproving the hard-line eugenicists' claim that the degenerate classes were inherently unchangeable.[38] In Catholic countries, whilst there was some collaboration between Catholic intellectuals and eugenics, there was also considerable opposition to the idea of interfering with God's plan.[39]

The difference between Germany, where race-thinking became so dominant, and other countries was not therefore a question of scientific proof. Rather, Nazism offered a quasi-mystical sense of belonging. Postwar historians such as George L. Mosse and Uriel Tal stressed the faith-like qualities of Nazism, understanding it as a form of apocalypticism which drove Europe down a fatal path to destruction, in the name of waging a war against what the leading Nazis regarded as the source of all evil: the 'international Jew'.[40] But the construction and suppression of difference in the Third Reich was, on a day-to-day basis, supposedly the preserve of racial science and the bodies set up to administer it, the racial courts and genealogical assessors. Their remit ranged from assigning people to racial categories that allowed them to obtain an *Ariernachweis* (Aryan proof), a passport to welfare and a recognition of one's right to belong to the community, to setting out the eugenic principles which underlay sterilization legislation and later the euthanasia programme, to campaigning against asocials, the workshy and other undesirables, including Roma, homosexuals and prostitutes. Difference and exclusion from the *Volksgemeinschaft* was supposedly a question of the application of scientific principles.[41]

For the Nazis, race was understood as underlying all social phenomena, and thus race provided a kind of unifying framework for the Third Reich. At the same time, race was neither a homogeneous nor a stable concept. Historians have shown that ideology is not a single, unchanging phenomenon – indeed, Nazi ideology was constructed and radicalized as the Third Reich developed – and, likewise, race did not carry a single charge or meaning. It could refer to the nation or a supranational notion of kinship among related peoples; it could refer to physical and psychological traits; it was subjected to scientific analysis and popularizing propaganda. Although they could not be neatly separated in practice, the construction and suppression of difference in the Third Reich rested on a scientific strand and a mystical strand. Scientific and mystical race-thinking ultimately led in the same direction – to the glorification of the Aryan race, a concept which we understand today to be wholly chimerical. At the time, however, much race theory was accepted across the world as being rooted in science. It therefore makes sense on the one hand to examine what the Nazis thought of as scientifically justified arguments about the threats posed by lesser races or 'degenerates' within the Aryan race. But we should also distinguish these 'scientific' arguments from claims about the political aspirations of the Jews: their conspiracy to destroy the Aryan race and take over the world on the other. This charge owed nothing to science except insofar as it rested on a notion that this Jewish plot emerged from a fixed, innate racial quality that the Jews could not help but possess.

The task of making racial propaganda simple and consistent fell to Walter Gross. Gross, head of the NSDAP's Office of Racial Policy (*Rassenpolitisches Amt*), devoted himself, through radio broadcasts, speeches and the pages of his popular journal *Neues Volk*, to spreading the Nazi message of the protection of the Aryan race from the weak and ill. In doing so, he made the *Volkskörper* (racial body), rather than the individual, the measurement of social value and worth. He appealed to science for legitimization, while emphatically proclaiming that his message was not primarily a scientific one, as can be seen in this passage from a radio broadcast written for children: 'for us the teaching of blood and race does not mean primarily an important and interesting bit of biological science, but above all a political and philosophical principle which basically determines our attitude on many questions of life.' This position was based on the principles of heredity, which revealed that an individual's abilities were a result of his belonging to a particular racial stock and were not reflections of the individual's worth alone; 'a recognition of the deep, even spiritual meaning of the racial differences within mankind' which argued against the 'sickly ambition' of trying to bring about an 'equalization' of the world's races.[42] Gross' worldview was a fairly crude one, dressed up in philosophical-sounding terminology, arguing along familiar Nazi lines that the 'international Jew', who had swapped an effete ethics of democracy and care for the weak with authentic German values, was the cause of racial degeneration. Gross' enthusiastic propounding of racial welfare was based on his belief in 'the voice of the blood streaming through history' and his dismissal of 'false humanism' and 'exaggerated pity'.[43] Blood was what counted above all.

These were views derived far less from science than from ethics or politics. 'Nazi theorists,' one scholar writes, 'blamed Jews not only for the racial contamination of the Germans but also for having introduced ethics into history, and specifically the moral institution of conscience into Western ethical discourse.' The consequence was that the strong could no longer rule over the weak with the clarity and assuredness that they once supposedly could.[44] The victory of racial antisemitism, noted the physicist and Nobel Prize winner Johannes Stark in the SS journal *Das Schwarze Korps*, would only be a 'partial victory'. 'We also have to eradicate the Jewish spirit, whose blood can flow just as undisturbed today as before, if its carriers hold beautiful Aryan passes.'[45] These arguments about the Jews were racial insofar as they supposedly conformed to the laws of nature and identified the Jews' allegedly immutable traits. But they owed little if anything to science, in the sense of physical anthropological measurements, or to laboratory experiments on disease, serology or genetics. The difference between a popular race theorist such as Günther and Gross lay in their respective abilities to exercise real power. Günther, though lauded by Hitler and profoundly influential in the field of *Judenforschung* (the academic study of the Jews), was not a decision-maker; Gross was, and constantly exhorted Nazi policy-makers to take sterner action against the Jews – something which he soft-pedalled when addressing the public at large. Not being a member of the SS, Gross never achieved the levels of power of men such as Adolf Eichmann or Reinhard Heydrich; nevertheless, his blend of scientific vocabulary and asking the 'spiritual question' of being for or against Germany, as US ambassador William Dodd put it, made him a representative figure of the Nazi race ideologue.[46]

Powerful race thinkers such as Gross spread their message of the superiority of the Aryan race, the need to eradicate the weak and the threat posed by the Jews through claiming it was backed up by science. Under this scientific patina, however, Gross was essentially making political assertions about the danger to the Germans of not attending to a racial or eliminationist agenda. As historian Claudia Koonz notes, 'Hitler and his comrades were self-taught bigots who mingled romantic Nordic racism with crude antisemitism. Arcane jargon about genotypes, phenotypes, skull measurements, and Mendelian inheritance laws meant nothing to them.' Gross, with his medical background, impressed them by appearing to give their views scientific backing.[47] But it was really a mystical political-ethical agenda that he and the Nazi leaders were espousing. The eugenicist Fritz Lenz, who had praised Hitler as early as 1931,[48] was closer to the truth when he spoke in 1933 of race as a 'principle of value'. Likewise, Ernst Krieck, the political scientist and rector of Heidelberg University, wrote with startling honesty that 'we have learned from Chamberlain's and especially from the Führer's teachings that the verification of the existence of race, and perhaps of existence in general, does not require artificial scientific tools . . . the fact of the existence of race is not doubtful, because man carries it in his heart, his spirit, his soul, or because man wants race to become a fact.'[49] More important, someone with genuine power, Joseph Goebbels, could in 1943 describe the 'disappearance of all Jews from Europe' as a matter of state security, since the Jew, who cannot help acting in accordance with his inner essence, 'destroys states and peoples' and therefore had to be destroyed himself.[50] This was a perfect example of Nazi race ideology, but the argument is neither amenable to nor dependent on science – except insofar as scientists used their authority also to defend such statements.

The point here is that the regime was not interested in a complex genealogy of *völkisch* ideas or in academic debates about racial origins and development. Rather, it wanted clear and straightforward messages about the greatness of the German *Volk* to set against its fears and hatred of the Jews and to act as justifications for aggression. This is not a simple materialist view in which ideas are sought to justify naked aggression; indeed, the naked aggression was partly an outcome of the power of such ideas. But for the Nazi leadership, their persuasiveness lay in their simplicity and the desire to believe in racial destiny, in contrast to a conclusion reached after long study. A political scientist such as Ernst Krieck, for example, could espouse a '*völkisch* political anthropology' in the scholarly journal *Volk im Werden*, but doing so led to conflict with 'official' Nazi theorist Alfred Rosenberg; the scholarly approach was too complex.[51]

Race science and racial mysticism are not easily separated; nor, for the Nazi thinkers, was the distinction meaningful. Yet whilst race science flourished everywhere in Nazi-dominated Europe – largely thanks to the power, funding and appeal of German eugenics and racial anthropology – the attack on the Jews which has come to be known as the Holocaust was not (or not only) a logical outgrowth of Nazi eugenics. The very idea of the Jews as a separate race with particular, dangerous traits was, of course, an expression of racial ideology; but it grew from a mystical notion of 'thinking with the blood' and the need for a Nazi ethics based on the coherence of the racial community and a distancing from the dangerous Jewish ethic and world conspiracy far more than it did out of eugenic or anthropological research into Jews' physical or psychological characteristics.[52] As one expert on Nazi medicine and racial science notes, 'Science was a factor in the vast system of population clearance and destruction, but had to be blended with devotion to Nazi values that are difficult to derive from evolutionary biology.'[53] Hitler certainly spoke a vulgar scientific jargon, arguing in the manner of many eugenicists around the world that nature limits the possibility of racial crossings and causes them to die out, and claiming that a 'natural, slow process of regeneration' could occur 'as long as a basic stock of racially pure elements is still present and a further bastardization does not take place'.[54] Likewise, the SS and SD (Sicherheitsdienst – the SS's intelligence service) intellectuals were enamoured of race science, of course, but primarily because it was grist to their pre-existing racial mill, in which Jews were *a priori* considered racially dangerous.[55] If the biological and political (or biopolitical) race theories were to some extent inseparable, nevertheless the biological race theories were so successful only because they provided backing for the political race theories which existed independently of the world of science. Accordingly, both the *Volksgemeinschaft*, to the extent it actually existed, and the Holocaust resulted less from the statistics generated by scientists' measurements than from a political diagnosis of the threat posed to the Aryan race by a Jewish conspiracy.

So much for race. It is crucial not to mystify the concept, to make it into something sacred in the way that some Nazis sought to do; at the same time, by insisting, as we do now, that race is meaningless as a biological or anthropological concept, even though it retains its power as a social and conceptual marker and source of prejudice, we fail to see probably the single most important driver for the Nazi leadership. Irrespective of the unstable and multivalent nature of the concept for Nazi thinkers and in Nazi practice, it is clear that the Third Reich 'racially groomed' itself, in one striking phrase.[56] In Nazism's apocalyptic worldview of a battle between good and evil, synonymous with Aryan versus Jew, the Jews represented a metaphysical evil which had to be destroyed in order that Aryan civilization might triumph. Hitler was seen

as a kind of shaman who had revealed this dialectical movement of history that led towards Aryan redemption. As social
theorist Norbert Elias wrote, 'Hitler had a function and characteristics in Germany similar to those of a rainmaker, a medicine man or a shaman in simpler tribal groups. He reassured
a distraught and suffering people that he would give them
everything they most wanted, just as a rainmaker promises a
people threatened with hunger and thirst by a long period of
drought that he will make it rain.'[57] Or, as the great anthropologist Bronislaw Malinowski argued when, in old age, he
embarked on a lecture tour of the US to alert the public to
the dangers of Nazism, fieldwork in Melanesia which revealed
the importance of magic in everyday life, could apply equally
well to current-day totalitarianism: 'The whole doctrine
of Aryan superiority in race,' wrote Malinowski, 'and of the
right to world domination by the master race, is essentially
mystical.'[58] For Malinowski, magic is not simply 'a system of
daydreaming, not a spontaneous outburst of hate or despair';
rather, it is pragmatic, 'a form of action' whose 'binding function' is its most notable characteristic.[59] For the Nazis, race
was the magic that bound the Aryan community together.

Indeed, this 'binding function' is crucial, for the reasons
why so many Germans bought in to this racial scheme are
not simple. Certainly, many chose to believe it, and the presence of antisemitism as a cultural code in Germany from the
Wilhelmine period, coupled with traditional Christian Jew-
hatred in a country where 95 per cent of the population were
paid-up members of a church, provides an important background.[60] But it is improbable that the vast majority of the
German population truly believed that 'the Jew' presented

a threat to the Aryan race to such an extent that what the historian Saul Friedländer calls 'redemptive antisemitism' needed to be placed at the heart of state policy.[61] More proximate causes, such as the sense of national humiliation felt by Germans after Versailles and the loss of certainty brought about by inflation and then depression, made many Germans ripe for simple answers to their problems, especially when these promised a rebirth of German greatness to people who, as historian Lucie Varga put it in the 1930s, had 'the feeling of losing the ground beneath their feet'.[62] One man whose father had to remortgage the family farm explained his turn to the Nazis as the result of a realization that:

> The Jew threatened to drive him from the soil his ancestors had tilled for over 300 years . . . The Jew at the bottom of it all had to tame the farmer in order to achieve his plans . . . After 1930 I turned my back on the Deutschnationale Volkspartei [DNVP, the right-wing German National People's Party] and after attending National Socialist party meetings regularly, I was won over to National Socialism.[63]

After Hitler's accession to power, only a small minority of true believers ever devoted themselves to Nazism's sacred narrative of redemption through annihilation, but the large majority of Germans rapidly acquired Aryan identification cards (*Ahnenpässe*), thronged to exhibitions and cinemas displaying racial propaganda, attended labour camps which sought to mould the *Volksgemeinschaft* and lauded the idea that Germany would once again become a great nation on the world stage. The crowds gathering in the streets waiting for Hitler to pass by, wrote English educationalist Amy Buller in her

Darkness over Germany, published in 1943, were 'like drowning men and women who saw in Hitler a chance of salvation'.[64] Despite the 'irrational foundations of racial scientific claims', one historian writes, giving a contemporary twist to Krieck's racial philosophy, which distinguished between race belief and science: 'a great many Germans *wanted* to believe that racist ideas had been scientifically proven'.[65] Or, as Karl Weber, from the Ministry of Culture, told Amy Buller on one of her study tours to Germany in the mid-1930s:

> It is plain to all who are willing to see, that this philosophy
> involves a call to the younger generations to heroic living,
> for this reality of race is something which claims them,
> gives them a standard and orientates their whole life. This
> great inspiration does not only come from intellectual
> conceptions, it comes because there has been called
> forth in this country what we term a deep feeling for life
> (*Lebensgefühl*) which is inevitably bound up with the fact
> of blood and race. The Führer expresses what all of us in
> some measure have experienced, that we have passed from
> mere existence into inexhaustible life.[66]

Nazism succeeded as a movement not only because of its radicalism but because it appeared to be untainted by association with the Weimar establishment. It offered access to the political process for the masses who felt disenfranchised, and because it became a focal point for a populist uprising which promised 'a renovated nation, the Third Reich'.[67] Indeed, in due course – that is to say, quite quickly – 'most Germans came to believe that National Socialism had healed German history'.[68] The idea of history being something organic that could be injured and therefore in need of healing is telling: Nazism saw the fight between Aryan and Jew as the dynamic motor of history and believed that it was Hitler's destiny to bring that fight to a victorious conclusion. The creation of the *Volksgemeinschaft* would be realized by defeating the Jew; this idea was fundamental to Nazism from the start.[69] And since so many Germans voluntarily coordinated themselves with the new regime, it should be no surprise that 'National Socialism added up to an extraordinary endeavour to establish a new racial morality, one that pulled Germans at all levels further and further into active, self-willed complicity with Nazi projects.'[70]

This total absence of compromise, an inability to regard anything or anyone other than himself as correct, was why Hitler was so impervious to criticism, so assured of his own destiny – and why so many Germans were attracted to him. It was why British and American commentators did not really understand him, regarded him as buffoonish and failed to take him seriously, why appeasement was such a disastrous failure – other than in gaining time for the Western powers to rearm – and thus why it was left to émigrés like Haffner to state the obvious: that the impossibility of 'meeting Germany half-way' was 'sufficient reason to destroy the man as a mad dog'. The democratic spirit of compromise having proved useless, Haffner noted in 1940, it was now clear that Hitler could be dealt with only on terms he understood: 'The spell of Hitler will be broken the moment he is no longer treated as a statesman and ruler, but as the swindler that he is – whose removal is the preliminary basis of any negotiations for peace.'[71] It was partly the dwindling democracies' fault that Hitler was not unmasked but continued to be negotiated with instead. As Laski noted in 1940 of the appeasers, 'It did not occur to them until it was too late that their view was wholly mistaken.'[72] But a combination of exhaustion with the established elites, the desire for national renewal, the lack of popular and elite faith in the Weimar Republic, the bitterness and desperation caused by the Great Depression and the radicalism and all-embracing promises of Nazi ideas all contributed to the fatal attraction of the Nazi movement which did far more than Anglo-American diplomacy to keep Hitler in power.[73] Besides, although Hitler 'had his ideological *idées fixes*, he could nonetheless demonstrate an extraordinary degree of flexibility, which confounded both opponents and colleagues and made him unpredictable even to those who knew him best'.[74]

A generation of Germans 'sought to "redeem" Germany from its recent defeat and humiliation' and 'its members yearned for discipline and order, to be realized in the creation of a *Volksgemeinschaft*, a homogeneous and harmonious "community of the people".'[75] Alfred Rosenberg had already promised in 1924 that 'the leaders of National Socialism have unequivocally let it be understood that they would either help the new idea of state to victory, in spite of all opposition and necessary disappointments, or, if necessary, perish with the entire German people'.[76] And the feeding-through of the memory of 1918 into Nazi ideology is a textbook example of the power of traumatic memory, of what has been called 'the perpetrator's "never again" syndrome'. 'They should not have staged 9 November 1918 with impunity', fumed Hitler to the Czechoslovak foreign minister in 1939. 'That day shall be avenged . . . The Jews shall be annihilated in our land.'[77] Hitler was simply reaffirming what he had said in *Mein Kampf*, that 'the Jew' is '"a ferment of decomposition" among peoples and races' whose 'Bolshevisation of Germany', that is, the oppression of the German working class under Jewish world finance, 'is conceived only as a preliminary to the further extension of this Jewish tendency of world conquest'.[78] These statements describe well not just the trajectory of Nazism from victory to destruction but the power of Nazism's attraction and the remarkable commitment to it displayed by its adherents, not to mention the classic genocidaire's tactic of attributing to one's putative enemy one's own fantastical schemes – in this case, extermination and world conquest. Once Nazism came to power, it bolstered this attraction with a powerful dose of political violence, intimidation and shock tactics such as concentration camps for the regime's self-declared enemies, and utilizing the threat of them as a means of keeping others in line. Nazism, as we have seen in this chapter, did not come from nowhere: mass politics; unemployment; post-1918 violence; the rise of Italian Fascism; anti-communism; nationalism in the post-imperial 'successor states'; appeasement and the underrating of Hitler and his ideas, especially the importance of 'race'; the notion of fascism as 'colonialism returned home' – all contributed to the appeal of Nazism.

Nazism was thus built on and radicalized existing belief structures. The historian Uriel Tal, who more than many sought to uncover Nazism's underlying driving forces, put it beautifully: Nazism was 'not simply a negation of religion. Instead, Nazism appropriated the messianic structure of monotheism, especially of Christian monotheism, deprived it of its authentic content, reversed the meaning of the redemptive rhythm of Christianity, and went on to exploit that new pseudo-religion for its own political ends, in a most effective way.'[79] Only the most perceptive commentators recognized the extent to which Nazism was driven by this apocalyptic dynamic and what that would mean for its victims. In 1938, Max Mayer, a sixty-five-year-old Jewish man living in Freiburg, wrote a letter to his grandson Peter Paepcke, a *Mischling* (or 'mixed breed') in Nazi racial terms, to explain that the Nazis believed that Germany needed 'to be cleansed and liberated from Jewish members and elements'. Although the letter was never sent, its clarity of thought is striking:

> In fulfilment of this theory [*Weltanschauung*], which
> is dressed up as an 'ideology', an orgy of racial hatred
> has been instituted, together with a process whereby
> Jewish persons are subjected to total and systematic
> disqualification. The entire Party machine, the press,
> vocational training, broadcasting, official propaganda, the
> political education of the young, the whole of national
> life – all have been harnessed to the task of stripping Jews
> of their good name and social acceptability, regardless of
> personal standing. They are being ousted from their homes
> and livelihoods and compelled to emigrate destitute of
> means, and the belief in their human inferiority is being
> duly incorporated in the Aryan world of ideas.[80]

In 1940, close to the end of his life, the Oxford philosopher and historian R. G. Collingwood – one of the most unusual and remarkable British thinkers of the first half of the twentieth century – published an article entitled 'Fascism and Nazism'. In it he argued that fascism was successful because its supporters were inspired by a passion which defenders of liberalism and parliamentary democracy could not summon. 'Fascist and Nazi activity,' Collingwood wrote, 'exhibits a driving power, a psychological dynamism, which seems to be lacking from the activity of those who try to resist it.' This presented a serious problem for anti-fascists:

> The anti-Fascists and anti-Nazis feel as if they were opposed, not to men, but to demons; and those of them who have analysed this feeling say with one accord that Fascism and Nazism have succeeded in evoking for their own service stores of emotional energy in their devotees which in their opponents are either latent or non-existent. Fascism and Nazism may be silly, but those who believe in them believe in them intensely, care enormously that they should win their fight, and win it because they so greatly care to win it.

Fascism and Nazism, then, 'owe their success to the emotional forces which they have at their command'.[81] Or, in the words of the unorthodox Marxist philosopher Ernst Bloch, who was unusual in that he regarded Nazi ideology as worthy of analysis in its own right and not merely as a diversionary tactic unleashed by big business to stop the masses from recognizing their true interests: 'It is not the "theory" of the National Socialists but rather their energy which is serious, the fanatical-religious strain which does not merely stem from despair and stupidity, the strangely roused strength of faith.'[82] This drive was directed inwards, at the creation of the Aryan community, and outwards, unleashing in a few short years waves of unstoppable violence against the Jews in what came to be known as the Holocaust. That this would happen was not inevitable solely because of the writings of ideologues like Eckart or Rosenberg. But, as we will see in the following chapters, the nature of the Nazi dictatorship and the circumstances which it engineered into existence, and above all the war and its disastrous consequences, facilitated a process whereby Hitler, Himmler and the leading Nazis opted for ever-more extreme measures.

CHAPTER 2

Attack on the Jews, 1933–8

'Racial ideology precludes deviations, allows for
no exceptions, and is ruthlessly deterministic.'
— Michał Głowiński[1]

Antisemitism was the kernel of Nazi ideology. For the leaders of the Third Reich, the attack on the Jews was regarded as a means of saving the Aryan race from destruction at the hands of the international Jew. Historians sometimes note the gradual development of Nazi racial policy, yet six or seven years is a short time in which to isolate and destroy a group that has been part of one's social environment for generations. As early as August 1933, the Hamburg-based Jewish lawyer Kurt Rosenberg wrote in his diary that: 'Day by day the assault on human rights and the human dignity of Jews continues, fragmented into a thousand individual affronts, while much noise is made for passage of an animal protection law that will outlaw vivisection and promotes kindness to animals. It is impossible to count all the small incidents that daily plague us.'[2] In the six years before the war, the Nazis reduced the German (and, after 1938, Austrian and Czech) Jews from prosperous communities, simply parts of the state in which they lived, to abject destitution and, moreover, removed them from the majority population's sense of obligation, morality and civility. How did this come to pass?

Given the Nazi leaders' obsession with the Jewish world conspiracy, it is no wonder that they addressed the topic in mystical, metaphysical terms. 'At stake,' wrote Alfred Baeumler, one of the leading Nazi philosophers, in 1940, 'is nothing less than to create anew in the light of consciousness a form of existence that hitherto resided in the unconscious . . . to nurture the irrational with rational means . . . proceeding from the purest impulses of the race.'[3] A few years earlier, Walter Gross, the man responsible for translating 'scholarly' race theory for a popular audience, noted that: 'Racial antisemitism is the consummation and at the same time our most sacred symbol of the far-reaching revolution brought about by National Socialism against rigid rationalism . . . It leads us to the rebirth of our racial life-force, which has been drained of its strength by the abstract Jewish modes of thinking.'

No wonder that passages such as these are interpreted as showing that 'in the eyes of many of the Nazi leaders it was precisely the irrationalism of racial antisemitism that bore witness to the greatness of the Nazi revolution'.[4] By the time Baeumler had written his celebration of the irrational, the Jews of Germany were finished as a community: half had emigrated, and the rest were trapped, and it would not be long before they were deported to their deaths.

We should first of all note, as many commentators did at the time, that antisemitism was not merely one aspect of National Socialism, even if the Nazis themselves played it down in some quarters in the early 1930s, or even if some critics believed that it was nothing but an opportunist way of uniting Germans around a convenient scapegoat. Rather, as the author of a book on the Jews in Nazi Germany published in 1939 noted, 'it is not true that the Jews would have been left alone if the Nazi regime had not met with any internal or external difficulties'. Instead, he went on, 'As almost every one of the prominent Nazi leaders has stated, the racial question, and that is in the main the Jewish question, is one of the fundamental principles, nay, the fundamental principle, of the Nazi creed.'[5] As soon as Hitler came to power – even before the stranglehold on the country which was quickly established as the Nazis' coalition partners and rivals were outmanoeuvred and whilst President Hindenburg was still alive – attacks on Jews began. These attacks 'expressed the antisemitic hatred, fury and violence that lay at the heart of Nazism at every level', as Richard Evans puts it, and unleashed a dynamic whereby the leading Nazis wanted to be able to control the violence but 'in practice continually fuelled it with their rhetoric, and with the constant antisemitic diatribes in the Nazi press'.[6]

The Nazis' main ambition, as is now well understood, was to eradicate any opposition, through a combination of carrot and stick. The latter was the threat of incarceration in one of the newly created concentration camps, established, as the Nuremberg judgement put it, 'to imprison without trial all those persons who were opposed to the Government, or who were in any way obnoxious to German authority'.[7] The SA and Gestapo first set up impromptu 'wild' camps in basements of their headquarters. When these were replaced by Dachau, the first purpose-built camp to be opened, its operations were keenly advertised by the regime.

The former, for the majority of the population, was the promise of order, jobs and a sense of belonging.

The Nazis' first victims were political opponents, communists and social democrats. Representatives and supporters of other parties more or less willingly 'coordinated' themselves, as the phrase went, so as to fit in with the new reality; few politicians from the right of centre were willing to challenge what the Nazis were doing, partly because they shared some of the same views, even if they disapproved of the tactics, and partly out of justifiable fear for their own safety. Politicians from the left of centre were not given the choice: they were targeted irrespective of their bravery or otherwise in speaking out. But while communists were the Nazis' first target, the link between communism and Jews in the Nazis' minds should not be overlooked. As the historian Saul Friedländer notes,

> during the early years of Hitler's career as an agitator –
> and this includes the writing of the text of *Mein Kampf* –
> political Bolshevism, although always recognised as one
> of the instruments used by the Jews to achieve world
> domination, is *not* one of Hitler's central obsessions: It is a
> major theme only insofar as the Jews from whom it derives
> are *the* major theme.[8]

As the immediate threat, however, the Nazis targeted their political opponents first. Amongst them were many Jews, who were also victims of the so-called Law for the Restoration of the Professional Civil Service of 7 April 1933, whose 'Aryan paragraph' began to follow through on the Nazis' promise to remove Jews from public life as a step towards revoking their German citizenship and excluding them from the community. Actions and laws directed specifically against Jews were crucial to this process, such as the 'boycott' – in fact, better understood as a blockade – of Jewish shops on 1 April 1933,[9] the banning of Jews from swimming pools and the prosecution of both Jews and non-Jews for race defilement (*Rassenschande*). An overtly sexualized fear of Jewish contamination and the attempt to save German blood could be clearly seen as the motivating forces of many of these actions, as it could in the education of the young in Jew-hatred. For example, the text of the children's book *Der Giftpilz* (The Poisonous Mushroom) is truly poisonous, to the point of inculcating murderous hatred. At the end of the book, three young friends plan to attend a talk by Nazi ideologue Julius Streicher, which they see advertised on one of the wall posters used to such powerful effect by the *Völkischer Beobachter*, the Nazi party's paper (figure 1).

The eldest, a Hitler Youth, recalls the last time he heard Streicher speak, two years earlier. First Streicher spoke about the years of struggle before the Nazis came to power. Then he turned to the Jewish question:

> What he set out was so clear and simple that even we boys
> could understand him. Again and again he brought forward
> examples from life. At one moment he spoke cheerfully and
> cracked jokes, so that we all had to laugh. But then he again
> spoke with profound seriousness, and it was so still in the
> hall that you could hear a pin drop. He spoke of the Jews
> and their horrific crimes. He spoke of the grave danger that

Figure 1
Image from *Der Giftpilz*, showing a wall poster advertising a talk by Julius Streicher.

Jewry means for the world: 'Without solving the Jewish question, there can be no salvation for humanity!' Thus he urged us. We all understood him.[10]

All of this was observed by outsiders who sought to explain what was happening in Germany. In 1936 the British publisher Victor Gollancz brought out a book called *The Yellow Spot: The Extermination of the Jews in Germany*. Its prescient title is immediately striking, but its real worth lies in its meticulous documentation of the persecution of the Jews that had taken place in the first three years of Nazi rule. The book began: 'Ever since National Socialism assumed power, it has never ceased its endeavours to uproot the Jewish population of Germany.' It warned against the sort of complacency which regarded Nazi antisemitism as a passing phase, perhaps a short-term characteristic of a radical reshaping of the social order but one which would soon end:

> Until quite recently, many well-meaning people both in Germany and outside it believed that the persecution of Jews in the Third Reich was only a sort of cataclysm that might temporarily cause great hardship to individual Jews, but which was bound to pass in time. In all countries there were optimists who hoped for and expected a gradual tolerance, the attainment of some, if an inferior, form of equilibrium. There were even Jews in Germany who took this view. They refused to believe that they were all to be harried from the country in which their ancestors had lived for centuries and to whose art, science and economic progress they had contributed so substantially.[11]

What changed these optimists' minds? The crucial event was the promulgation of the so-called Nuremberg Laws in September 1935, 'laws and decrees whose sole purpose was to deprive the German Jews of the ordinary rights of citizens', as one contemporary observer rightly noted.[12] The first of these, the Reich Citizenship Law, established the fact that there were now two categories of persons in Germany: citizens and subjects. By placing Jews in the latter category, the Nazis effectively fulfilled one of the main aims of their party programme as it had existed since the early 1920s: 'A citizen of the Reich is that subject only who is of German or kindred blood and who, through his conduct, shows that he is both desirous and fit to serve the German people and Reich faithfully.'[13] The second of the Nuremberg Laws was the so-called Law for the Protection of German Blood and German Honour. It included an article preventing Jews from flying the 'Reich or national flag' – a seemingly minor law but one which served the purpose of effectively making the exclusion of Jews from the community more conspicuous, as 'there are a great many occasions in Germany when a whole town or village is adorned with flags'.[14] Moreover, the law outlawed marriage between 'Jews and citizens of German or kindred blood', forbade 'sexual relations between Jews and nationals of German or kindred blood' and stopped Jews from employing 'female citizens of German or kindred blood under 45 years of age as domestic servants'.[15] In fact, as was often the case with Nazi legislation, this law was a reaction to change as much as a driver of it in Germany: when August Landmesser and Irma Eckler (she Jewish, he not) declared their intention to marry in

August 1935, a month before the Nuremberg Laws, the Hamburg register office rejected their banns.[16]

The sexual aspect of Nazi antisemitism did not go unnoticed – even if some coyly conceded only that a psychiatrist would be needed to make sense of the phenomenon[17] – and as well as revealing the extent of the Nazis' fears about racial purity, the law gave rise to the bizarrely complicated question of *Mischlinge*, or 'half-breeds', and what to do with them. This question in fact acts as a kind of barometer for the increasing radicalization of Nazi antisemitism as well as indicating the limits of its racial pretensions. Bernhard Lösener, the Interior Ministry's expert on Jewish affairs, admitted the scientific impossibility of establishing the Jewishness of a *Mischling* in a revealing statement:

> An effective means of determining for a given person, according to his behaviour or his blood or the like, whether he has Jewish infiltration, does not exist, or at least for the time being has not been found . . . Our expert for racial study [Achim Gercke] is in fact an expert on family research; that is, when he is given the task to determine for a certain person whether he has Jewish blood, he will trace the family tree and in this manner, that is by genealogical research, find out whether Jewish ancestry is present.[18]

Since no scientific definition of the Jewish race could be found (for the simple reason that no such thing exists), the Nazis resorted to genealogical research and defined Jewishness as descent from grandparents who were Jewish by religious belonging, that is, synagogue membership. The survival of *Mischlinge* with just one or two Jewish grandparents became increasingly doubtful with the passage of time.

Even so, it is sometimes asserted that the German Jews accepted the Nuremberg Laws with resigned equanimity, seeing them as a return to a pre-emancipation condition that was in existence just a few generations before. The Nuremberg Laws, especially the ban on mixed marriages, essentially confirmed the status quo, in a process whereby law was passed only to set the stamp on already-established practices in the Third Reich.[19] Bodies like the *Reichsvertretung der deutschen Juden* (RV, the Reich Representation of German Jews), the core Jewish organization in Nazi Germany, could hope after the Nuremberg Laws that 'by being no longer defamed and boycotted, the Jews and Jewish communities in Germany will be able to sustain themselves spiritually and economically'. But they were not dupes; at the same time, the RV also advocated emigration, knowing that such emigration would bring about the end of Jewish life in Germany.[20]

In fact, outside observers were much more likely to be fooled by the Nazis' intents than German Jews, however patriotic or assimilated they felt. By no means were all outsiders as revolted as Gollancz and other outspoken critics of the Nazi regime. In her book *Modern Germanies as Seen by an Englishwoman*, the suffragette, actress and former resident of Germany Cicely Hamilton excused the Nazi assault on the Jews as a valid response to the latter's venality:

> Envy, no doubt, supplies most of the motive-power of the *Judenhetze*; perhaps the ugliest of human passions, yet one for which, in the circumstances, a certain amount of excuse

can be made. A people that has suffered and is bitterly poor sees a race that climbs and flourishes upon the ruin of its own fortunes; small wonder if envy does stir in its heart and it snarls accusations of profiteering against all who belong to the race. Is it not because he has fattened on the miseries of others that Israel to-day dwells lordly in the Kurfürstendamn [*sic*]? which once was the aristocratic quarter, the Mayfair of Imperial Berlin![21]

What Hamilton called the *Judenhetze* (agitation against the Jews) took many forms, from outright violence to varieties of social exclusion and petty legislation. Gollancz describes the 'Battle of Kurfürstendamm', for example, which represents 'the main residential area of the Jewish bourgeoisie' of Berlin in a rather different light from Hamilton.[22] Under the absurd pretext of having booed in the dark of a cinema when a Swedish antisemitic film was being shown, the Jews were targeted, following incitements in the *Völkischer Beobachter* and Goebbels' *Der Angriff*. In Gollancz's description:

> The first row of tables was upset, the cutlery and china broken, the glass of the door smashed to smithereens. There were shouts and some blows struck. Some of the customers were pushed out into the street and forced to beat a retreat through rows of striking fists. Others, beaten and bleeding, lay on the ground. After a few minutes the café was turned into a shambles . . . Customers fled bleeding into the back rooms. Cries of pain were heard over the whole street. But even louder were the old pogrom battle-cries and slogans: 'Perish Judah!' 'death to Jewry!'

Pogroms, Gollancz noted, 'had moved from the inconspicu-
ous backwater of village life straight on to the doorstep, so
to speak, of the foreign correspondents', who could hardly
ignore this outburst of violence, though some still considered it aberrant in July 1933.[23]

Yet pogroms such as this were relatively rare, although
in the wake of the Kurfürstendamm riot anti-Jewish measures across Germany were stepped up, from the displaying
of antisemitic slogans to beatings;[24] far more common was
verbal abuse, being shamed and humiliated on the street,
in a tram or at school. In the first few years of the Third
Reich, Jews were subjected to a barrage of legislation, curtail-
ing their freedom of movement and action. As well as being
forbidden access to swimming pools, Jews were sometimes
excluded from some resort towns altogether. Jews were forbidden from voting, from arranging meetings, from attending festivals such as the Oktoberfest, from speaking on the
radio, from serving in the military, from attending the same
schools as Aryans, from acting as doctors to Aryan patients,
from exhibiting paintings, and on and on. Gollancz accurately
called this 'the pogrom of "Verbot"'.[25] He also accurately
argued that even more decisive than outbursts of violence or
the displaying of offensive banners was the Nazis' systematic
depriving of the Jews of the means of earning a living:

> The most serious problem confronting German Jews is
> their gradual squeezing out from economic life. Other
> aspects of the persecution may excite more horror, such
> as acts of violence or incitement, other aspects may incite
> more pity, for example the position of the children, but

in the end the factor that must prove most crushing is
the closure to them of every profession, of every avenue
of trade and employment, of every path to livelihood or
skill in labour for the new coming generation. This side of
the campaign is carried through without physical force,
without massacre, without bullets, but it means, none the
less, decisive destruction.[26]

The process of 'Aryanization' was set in motion, a euphemism for forced dispossession, whereby Jewish business
owners were obliged to sell their businesses at vastly reduced
rates. This included the majority of Jewish businessmen who
were shopkeepers, traders, artisans and the like, who had already been subjected to boycotts from the beginning of the
Nazi regime. Indeed, small Jewish shopkeepers and traders
in small towns across Germany were swiftly ruined after the
Nazis came to power.[27] Jews were forbidden from taking part
in the Mannheim Autumn Fair and a large cattle auction in
Münster in 1935, reported the local press.[28] They were, in
other words, deprived of their means of existence. A formal
legal 'Aryanization' procedure was not adopted until after the
November pogrom in 1938, however, showing once again how
official policy in Nazi Germany was often playing catch-up
with realities on the ground. Yet even before the pogrom, the
Jews were economically eliminated – it made little difference
to the Jews concerned whether their financial means were
plundered as they were forced into emigration or whether, as 'Aryanization' provided for, their property was legally
transferred into non-Jewish ownership. Thus, long before the
mass-murder of Jews across Europe, when the Nazis and their

accomplices carried out one of the largest thefts in history, the Third Reich had already shown itself to be a kleptocracy from the start. As it 'recovered' wealth 'stolen' from the *Volk* (the German term *Volksgut* encompasses this notion very precisely), many Nazis grew rich, and the means of extortion became ever more brutal.[29] At the same time, this was a process in which millions of Germans were involved, 'as competitors, purchasers, financiers, profiteers of all sorts, brokers, trustees, experts, and finally, as representatives of specialist groups, economic associations, and chambers of industry and commerce'. Aryanization is one of the clearest examples of how the Third Reich created a deep-seated complicity among the German people, showing that the Nazi regime was 'more than a dictatorship operating from the top down. It was a coherent social practice that involved German society in manifold ways.'[30]

Perhaps the most harmful measure enacted between the Nuremberg Laws and the November pogrom, and far more destructive than it might at first appear, was the August 1938 law requiring Jews to take the name Israel (for men) and Sarah (for women).[31] The passage of this law was based on several assumptions: that Jews needed to be outed since, as the Nazis believed, they were trying to hide their Jewishness by assuming German names; and that despite outward differences of dress, class, religious observance and so on, Jews were basically homogeneous. 'There is no difference between one Jew and another,' as Goebbels wrote several years later. 'Every Jew is a sworn enemy of the German people. If he does not make his hostility plain, it is only from cowardice and shyness, not because he loves us.'[32] Seemingly absurd, the law actually cut to the heart of individuals' identities. It did not matter to which branch of Judaism they belonged, or whether they were irreligious and belonged to none; it did not matter what their political views were, whether they were German nationalists or anarchists; it did not matter which football team they supported, what food they liked, what clubs they belonged to, how rich or poor they were. They were only Jews.

These official acts against the Jews are well known, but one must consider the responses by those who were affected by them really to appreciate what they meant. The sense of exclusion from one's community, the gradual and, at the same time, rapid break with all that one held to be normal, as all that was solid melted into air. The threat and the reality of violence, the threatening atmosphere: all added up to the destruction of the German Jews' world. As Kurt Rosenberg wrote in his diary on 26 April 1936:

The sphere of activity open to Jews grows ever more constrained. One regulation follows another. Now the Jewish pharmacists and the veterinarians are affected. And tomorrow? And the day after tomorrow? And things that don't fall under law and regulations fall into the category of boycott. For weeks the Jews have been whispering into each other's ears that it will become even worse after the Olympics in August. A road without end. Long ago we lost the ability to take pleasure in small things and celebrations – because over everything hangs the eternal question, Is it still worth it? Followed by the other question, Where are we headed?[33]

Long before 'the Holocaust', understood as the extermination of all the Jews of Europe, the Jews in Nazi Germany had been destroyed as a community, abandoned and left as fair game. All of which suggests that through the violence that was perpetrated against them in Germany before the war, 'Jews were not rivals who had to be defeated, they were "pests" who should be eliminated.'[34]

November Pogrom

For all that Jews were randomly attacked, subjected to intimidation, excluded from their jobs and forced to sell their businesses, they had not been the victims of physical violence on a large scale in Germany up to that point. That was to change with the November pogrom, of 9–10 November 1938, commonly known as *Kristallnacht*, or the night of broken glass. Two days earlier, Ernst vom Rath, a diplomat in the German embassy in Paris, had been shot and subsequently died on 7 November. His killer, a seventeen-year-old Polish boy named Herschel Grynszpan, was seeking revenge for the dumping of some 18,000 Polish Jews, including his parents, brother and sister, on the German–Polish border. Local outbursts of anger against Jews had already begun in the days following the shooting, including in Kassel and other towns nearby.[35] But permission to launch a wider assault came from the Nazi leadership, and vom Rath's murder was but an excuse to expedite the flight of Jews from Germany.[36] In response to the shooting of vom Rath, the *Völkischer Beobachter* ran eight stories, one calling it a 'crime against the peace of Europe'. *Der Angriff*, Goebbels' newspaper, insisted that the Jews should pay 'the sharpest consequences', and a local Berlin paper demanded that Germans should see a 'full and genuinely just punishment of the Jews' for the murder.[37] The international dimension was key here; in the wake of appeasement, Hitler was enjoying seemingly unstoppable foreign policy successes, having annexed Austria and the Sudetenland. The Nazi regime's popularity following the Olympics, the elimination of open opposition and an economic revival which only a few keen observers such as Haffner understood was predicated on the need for warfare, since it was placing Germany on a war footing, was at its height. These foreign policy successes left Hitler believing in his own invincibility and 'fed Hitler's determination to proceed with an escalation of the campaign against the Jews at home'.[38]

In the wake of the announcement that vom Rath had died, Goebbels delivered a thunderous speech in Munich – where NSDAP 'old fighters' (longstanding members of the party) were gathered to commemorate the 1923 Beer Hall Putsch, the failed coup d'etat that led to Hitler's imprisonment – in which he insinuated that the people should feel able to show their anger towards the Jews. As a confidential Nazi Party report later explained, Goebbels' speech suggested to those present that 'outwardly . . . the party was not to give the appearance of having provoked the demonstrations, while in reality it was to organize and carry them out'.[39] This they did, telephoning their local constituencies, with well-known consequences: 177 synagogues across Germany were burned down, and many more were severely damaged; some 8,000 Jewish business premises were destroyed along with numerous homes. In Vienna, 42 synagogues were burned down, and 2,000 families were forced out of their homes. About 100 Jews were murdered, many more injured, and 30,000 Jewish men were dragged off to Dachau, Buchenwald and Sachsenhausen, with more than a thousand dying as a result.

But more was going on that night. In the audience in Munich when Goebbels spoke was Reinhard Heydrich, Heinrich Himmler's young deputy in the increasingly powerful SS. Surprised by Goebbels' actions, and annoyed at being surprised, Heydrich telephoned Heinrich Müller, the head of the SS, in the middle of the night and issued instructions that would ensure the SS took control of the situation.[40] Acknowledging that the demonstrations should go ahead, Heydrich ordered that 'Only such measures are to be taken as do not endanger German lives or property (i.e. synagogues are to be burned down only where there is no danger of fire to neighbouring buildings).' He also ordered, in a move that signalled a curious adherence to petit bourgeois morality also displayed by Himmler, that 'Places of business and apartments belonging to Jews may be destroyed but not looted' and was firm in noting that 'Foreign citizens – even if they are Jews – are not to be molested.'[41] Heydrich was clearly annoyed not only at Goebbels' initiative taking but at what he regarded as the inconvenience of street violence; he favoured a more systematic and supposedly rational approach to the Jewish problem. Nevertheless, Goebbels' actions were ultimately favourable for the SS, for Heydrich took the opportunity to assert the SS's dominance in Jewish policy – a process that would only accelerate in the coming years – and was pleased to see that one consequence of the pogrom was to increase German Jews' desire to leave the country.[42]

Heydrich and the SS were at the forefront of the persecution of the Jews, which, following the annexation of Austria, took a new turn with the creation of a Central Office for Jewish Emigration, headed by Adolf Eichmann. The office hastened Jewish emigration from Austria and extracted as much money from them as possible in the process. Shortly after the *Anschluss*, Himmler and Oswald Pohl, chief of the SS administrative office, inspected the quarries of Mauthausen, near Linz, and decided to create the first major concentration camp in Austria (now known as the Ostmark).[43] Heydrich also expressed his opinions in print; in *Das Schwarze Korps*, the SS's in-house journal, he wrote in 1935 that 'Since the beginning of time, the Jew has been the mortal enemy of all nations and peoples joined by Nordic leadership and racial bonds. His aim has been and remains world domination at the hands of a more or less visible Jewish elite.' He added ominously that 'the Aryan laws are by no means sufficient to eliminate the danger that Judaism presents to Germany'.[44] There is no evidence that in 1935 such words referred to a plan to kill all the Jews – this was true even of statements such as 'One does not fight rats with guns but with poison and gas', which was an attack on 'mob antisemitism' rather than a statement of intent – but the fantasy of getting rid of the Jews one way or another was always present in the minds of the leading Nazis.[45] This fantasy thinking is especially obvious after the November pogrom, when '"marks of a genocidal mentality" were in clear evidence in the Nazi leadership'.[46]

Given that underlying genocidal logic, the consequences for the victims were terrifying. Rudolf Bing, a Great War veteran, and his wife, Gertrud, were woken in the middle of the night by a mob outside their building in Nuremberg. When he phoned the police, he was asked, 'Are you Aryan?'

53

When he replied in the negative, the operator hung up. Hearing a neighbour being attacked, the Bings tied sheets to the window frame, threw a mattress out of the window and, as the mob was breaking down the door to their apartment, jumped out. 'My wife decided that the window frame and linen sheets would not hold her weight,' Bing wrote in 1940. 'Suddenly she was hanging by her fingertips from the window ledge, let go, and fortunately fell into my arms, for I had been standing right under her on the mattress that I had thrown down.' They hid that night in a shed housing Christmas trees. Thus they escaped physically unharmed but were robbed of most of their money when they managed to leave Germany for Palestine.[47] In Treuchtlingen (Middle Franconia), many local women were involved in inciting and carrying out attacks on Jews and their property. In Rimbach (Hesse), a group of NSDAP members physically abused a Jewish family and then burned down their house. The pogrom represented, in historian Wolfgang Benz's words, a 'release of energy' which allowed participants 'to indulge in sadistic, infantile, sexist, aggressive behaviour', an opportunity that many took up.[48]

When on 12 November 1938 leading Nazis met at Goering's Air Ministry, the outcome was the remarkably named *Decree for the Restoration of the Street Scene in Relation to Jewish Business Premises*. This stated that proprietors of Jewish businesses would be responsible for paying for repairs, and, even more extraordinary, it imposed a fine on the Jewish community of one billion Reichsmarks in return for the 'hostile attitude of the Jews towards the German people and Reich which does not shrink even from cowardly murders'.[49] In this Nazi topsy-turvy world, the Jews were the guilty ones, and it was they who should pay. The idea that Germany was fighting back against Jewish subjugation could hardly have been clearer, and it was one which would have terrible consequences later. No wonder Goering commented towards the end of the discussion: 'I wouldn't like to be a Jew in Germany.' It was an aside, an afterthought, but profoundly insightful in its simplicity.[50]

The production of antisemitic texts, from the vulgar propaganda rag *Der Stürmer* to the popular propaganda of Walter Gross to the refined philosophical antisemitism of Klages, Baeumler and the like, continued apace throughout the twelve years of the Nazi regime. In fact, this outpouring was truly extraordinary; from legislation to legal commentaries, from scholarly antisemitism (*Judenforschung*) to journalism, from criminology to anthropology, from training manuals for the Wehrmacht to schoolbooks, antisemitic ideas pervaded German society and really did become the very air the Germans breathed in a way that is now hard to imagine. It is still the case that historians have not taken the measure of this radical shift in German cultural life.[51] Around the time of the November pogrom, for example, a book on the 'Jewish swindler' argued that the existence of a criminal underground 'that is largely the product of Jews' was evidence of the 'contrast between the Jews and the other peoples of the earth' and of 'a perspicuous sense of *inferiority*'.[52] Anthropologist and SS officer Fritz Arlt argued, in an article entitled 'The Final Struggle against Jewry', that antisemitism had always existed but had lost its political teeth since the rise of Christianity, and especially Protestantism. Hitler's new blood revolution not only revived antisemitism but went further than the churches ever did, since it did not offer Jews a bridge to acceptance in non-Jewish circles through baptism. Instead, 'anti-Judaism that is based on blood firmly establishes one thing: the Jew can arbitrarily extol his beliefs and declare his national allegiance according to his inclination . . . There is no bridge he can cross to join the community of non-Jews. *Hence, anti-Judaism on a racial basis represents the final struggle in the history of all struggles against the Jew.*'[53] As the poet and historian Peter Viereck wrote in his 1941 study of 'the roots of the Nazi mind': 'Nazism is the revolt against conditioning by environment', by which he meant that Nazism 'denies that environment can give German morals or culture to, say, a Jew or a Slav. Such qualities are determined unalterably before birth.'[54]

Yet just as not all Germans were persuaded by this racialization of the social sphere, this universalization of the 'race soul', neither was everyone in Germany impressed with the idea of violence against a minority group taking place in broad daylight. Much of the population was shocked, as many secret Nazi reports noted. In Lahr, for example, the Office for [Ideological] Training observed that 'The *Jew's Operation*, which was also carried out in our district, did not find approval in the eyes of many people. That is proof of the extent to which broad circles of our population, indeed even extending to party members and political leaders in the NSDAP, still are helpless when confronting the Jewish Question.'[55] Indeed, this distaste registered with Himmler and Heydrich, confirming them in their support for systematic measures which would not give rise to public displays of violence, at least not inside the borders of the Reich.

Although there was widespread dislike of the violence, however, those Germans who objected, for the most part, did so to the fact that they had to see it and not to the idea that it was wrong to persecute Jews. It simply had to be done 'correctly'.[56] Thus, although Heydrich and Himmler concluded that any future attacks on the Jews needed to be more orderly, they also felt emboldened to proceed with more radical measures. As historian Peter Fritzsche notes, the pogrom confirmed that:

> Jews in Germany were not simply a persecuted minority but a racial enemy whom the Nazis were willing to murder as 'free game' if Jews did not or could not emigrate on their own. What the pogrom demonstrated as well was that the Nazis could carry out the most extreme policies with the help of police, town officials, and other citizens.[57]

Despite some misgivings and expressions of distaste, overall there was 'an alarming degree of consensus and cooperation among local inhabitants'.[58] The November pogrom was thus a crucial moment in the radicalization of Nazi policy towards the Jews, precipitating not only growing confidence among the Nazi elite that they could move against the Jews with impunity but, in light of the decreasing possibilities for emigration, options that edged ever closer towards genocide.[59]

The victims of these atrocities were now facing not just personal catastrophe but the end of their communities and, beyond that – especially for the majority of assimilated, middle-class Jews – the collapse of the familiar world. A 1941 study carried out at Harvard on the basis of more than 200 essays submitted for an essay competition on the theme 'My life in Germany before and after January 30, 1933' noted that people 'shopped around for islands of security, sampling in turn political Zionism, rumors of underground movements, religious activities – anything, in short, that would provide distraction and hope'.[60] Jews were worn down by the endless legislation, any one piece of which would have been an inconvenience but taken together constituted an assault on their lives. They faced the threat of violence and what has aptly been called social death. And those who made up their minds to leave the country faced not only a bureaucratic nightmare but stood to be fleeced in the process. One testimony, written from safety in New York City at the end of December 1938, offers a vivid insight into the Kafkaesque world of the Jewish émigré trying to leave Nazi Germany. From applying for visas to different countries, including Uruguay and Brazil, to be on the safe side if the US ones did not come through, to sorting out containers, 'because we were fortunate in that our furniture had not been smashed to pieces', to dealing with the *Devisenstelle* (foreign currency office), this was a merry-go-round of often fruitless activity. The report goes on:

> As you know, I had an *Unbedenklichkeitsschein* [clearance certificate] for both of us from the *Finanzamt* [tax office] in . . . and the city of . . . We now heard that no more of these *Unbedenklichkeitsscheine* were being distributed, and that before one could be drawn up people would have to make the 20% *Kontribution* [the reparation decree of 12 November]. Yet as I have already explained to you, no one was allowed to sell securities, so how was I supposed to pay this 20% and on top of that the *Reichsfluchtsteuer* [Reich departure tax] for *Mama*, which I had not yet paid? . . . And then there was usually the *Zollfahndung* [customs investigation], which checked every last detail with a fine toothcomb.[61]

Another, this time a letter written by the doctor Gerhard Kann, reveals his fears at being left behind and also the need not to appear too desperate for fear of alienating friends and relatives who might be able to help. To his friend Heinz Kellermann in New York, Kann wrote from Berlin:

> Each day we see the walls around us grow higher, and each week brings new obstacles to leaving the country. Hopes and plans are buried, and the number of fellow sufferers in Central Europe grows ever greater.

Speaking of his 'serious, dogged search for a way to emigrate', Kann seemed to see only obstacles:

> Our plans and hopes have all more or less come to naught. Despite registering at the consulate here, America seems like a very remote possibility, something you have said. There now appears to be some chance of going to Peru. In any event, entering the country would cost 4,000 French francs per person, which would need to be raised for us abroad. Then we would need to get visas. I still have no idea how I could pull this off.[62]

In fact, Kann did manage to leave for Palestine before the war, and then moved on to Bolivia, where he worked as a doctor. Stories like Kann's remind us that Jews were desperate to leave, and that the urgency put them in a position where they were willing to leave behind everything they knew for an uncertain future in places such as Bolivia or Peru, which, for the vast majority of Germans in the 1930s, were little more than names on a map.

A few years later, Jews and non-Jewish political enemies of

Germany experienced a similarly frustrating bureaucratic entrapment in Lisbon, the last port of exit from Europe for the US in 1940–1. Given that very few countries were willing to take in Jewish refugees from Nazi Germany, the combination of hurdles in the way of emigration from the German side and obstacles in the way of obtaining entry to a new country meant that large numbers of German and Austrian Jews were unable to leave. Nor was there a contradiction with the policy of encouraging Jews to leave in making it difficult to do so – this was about exporting antisemitism by dumping impoverished Jews in new host countries.

Among those who were unable to leave was the Frühauf family. Although Hilde Frühauf was born in New York City and had US citizenship – her parents had emigrated to the US and then returned to Germany in 1897 – the rest of the family fell foul of bureaucratic absurdities and were ultimately murdered. Affidavits were sent and resent, bonds promised and re-promised, passage aboard ships booked, cancelled and booked again, but always something went wrong: first one needed a visa to book a ticket, then one needed to show a ticket to acquire a visa. 'These days one has to try everything,' wrote Felix Frühauf on 23 July 1941. But they were out of luck.[63]

Inclusion and Exclusion

Violence, as we have seen, was terrifying for its victims. But it also affected the perpetrators: at the same time as it demonstrated in the clearest terms to Germany's Jews that they were no longer considered people to be treated with decency (indeed, perhaps already no longer considered as people at all by the end of 1938), violence also produced a sense of community for those on the perpetrator side.[64] The perpetrators were not just those who actively took part in the pogroms but all those who benefited from them, knowingly or not. 'Aryan' Germans, whether they had supported the Nazis or not, increasingly came to feel that the Nazi rhetoric of creating a racial community (*Volksgemeinschaft*) was becoming reality by the end of the 1930s. When Walter Tausk encountered a crowd surrounding a smashed-up Jewish-owned liquor store in Breslau during the November pogrom, he came across a work colleague who told him: 'If I'd gone with I would have helped with both arms to take stuff for the Winter Aid like they've taken stuff away for the Winter Aid!' As Tausk realized, the Jewish businesses had been 'quite simply stormed and robbed', but, as his colleague's words reveal, the logic of the community provided cover and justification for the crime, even when it came with a nod and a wink.[65] The logic of 'revolution in the name of order' which gave rise to full employment, clean streets and a supposed breaking down of class barriers meant that even those Germans who wanted to resist Nazism found themselves living a Nazified life.[66]

That squeezing of identities, so that anti-Nazi Germans had ever-fewer chances to lead an authentic life, becoming increasingly coordinated with the regime just by living their daily lives, also applied in reverse. The concepts of Jew and Aryan were of course categories defined and imposed by the Nazis. This is sometimes forgotten by historians, especially when they write about the victims and their responses, although some historians do talk about 'Jews' in inverted commas in order to emphasize that in this context we are talking not about people who self-identified as Jewish, although many did, but people identified as Jews by the Nazi regime.[67] Jews did not make up a homogeneous community and they occupied all places on the political and religious spectrum. But Nazi legislation also defined racial Jews as people who were not merely assimilated but who had no association with Judaism whatsoever. Often they were Christians descended from Jewish grandparents. As assimilated Jews were forced to retreat to Jewish community institutions for aid during the 1930s, non-Jewish 'Jews' did not even have this solace and were excluded from both 'Aryan' and 'Jewish' society. This is why there were churches in the Warsaw ghetto.[68] Since they were not really Jewish, these 'Jews' often do not feature in the records of Jewish organizations yet they numbered several tens of thousands; their stories still need to be investigated.[69]

In her remarkable novel *The Seventh Cross*, written in the late 1930s and published in Mexico in 1942, Anna Seghers shows how German workers who had been opposed to the Nazis had learned to keep their heads down and their thoughts to themselves, and how easily ordinary Germans adapted to the regime's requirements of social surveillance and conformity, with its system of block wardens in apartment blocks and ideological supervision at work.[70] As Jews were stripped of their rights and separated from the Aryan Germans, especially through the boycott and the exclusion from local clubs and organizations, local Nazi officials 'could transform the social, cultural, and political order of the community'.[71] As community aliens (*Gemeinschaftsfremde*) were sent for re-education in concentration camps, so Aryan Germans were forced to become increasingly familiar with barracks and camps of all sorts, from the Hitler Youth and League of German Girls to labour camps which aimed to break down class boundaries, creating in their stead a National Socialist consciousness. Thus, when anti-Nazi trainee lawyer Sebastian Haffner was sent to a labour camp for ideological training, he and his fellow articled clerks went unenthusiastically along with what was required of them – singing, marching, attending ideological instruction sessions – until he had to admit that by doing so, no matter how reluctantly, they had been changed. 'By acceding to the rules of the game that was being played with us,' he honestly wrote, 'we automatically changed, not quite into Nazis, but certainly into usable Nazi material.' They had become, like Seghers' workmen, ensnared in the 'trap of comradeship'.[72]

No institution represents the radical exclusion on which the Nazis' racial community was based more forcefully than the concentration camp. 'There are people whose look speaks of the fear of death when they open their lips. Dread resonates in their words when they are able to free their hearts from experiences that are almost impossible to render in human language. They are prisoners released from German concentration camps.'[73] In fact, this report, one of about 350 by German-Jewish émigrés taken by the Wiener Library, then based in Amsterdam, is a remarkable source of information on the pre-war concentration camps in general. Noting that 'several things' were published about German concentration camps in the first year or two after the Nazis came to power, but that the world 'gradually went silent' about them, the report proceeds in an admonitory style:

One thought that with the consolidation of National Socialist power this worst form of terror had slowly liquidated, one accepted that with the successes of the Hitler government internally and externally and with its stabilization, those elements would be gradually eradicated on whose account the inhumane incidents of the years 1933-35 had been made. This belief is erroneous![74]

The unnamed reporter went on to note the opening of Buchenwald and Oranienburg (Sachsenhausen, near Berlin) and the rapid expansion of the concentration camps in 1938. He was also at pains to emphasize what a mistake it had been to believe that the element of terror would slowly diminish: 'The concentration camp means sentence of death without prosecutor and without judge, slow, agonising, mental and physical destruction full of horrible orderliness, compared to which the implementation of the death penalty of a murderer by gallows, axe or the electric chair is humane.'[75] Offering considerable detail on the torture that constituted all aspects of 'life' in the camps, the report noted the special venom that was reserved for Jewish veterans:

One persecuted them in particular out of the instinctive feeling that one had to justify the relentless antisemitism for oneself, because one refuted such men in comparison with oneself in one's wrongfulness and senselessness. One hated particularly those Jews who had been distinguished by their bravery in the face of the enemy, their *Eiserne Kreuz* [Iron Cross] or *Verwundetenabzeichen* [decoration for the war-wounded] was already ripped from the jacket upon their arrival in the camp, trodden upon, they were ridiculed, cursed and mistreated.

The primitive torturers in their black SS uniforms were
unaware that they were simultaneously besmirching
German *Soldatenehre* [military honour]. They lacked any
understanding of it.[76]

The report goes on to describe the endless hours of backbreaking forced labour, the absence of decent food and drink,
the lack of hygiene facilities, the spread of diseases, the beat-
ing and vicious, random ill-treatment by the guards, and all
the other tortures which characterized the Nazi concentration
camps. 'It is no wonder, then,' the report went on, 'that the few
allowed to leave the concentration camp come out as people
broken in body and soul, who require months of care and recovery, which the pressures of imminent emigration hardly
allow.'[77] Yet in retrospect, these were the 'lucky' ones; before
the war the majority of concentration camp inmates, including Jews, were released; the Jews, following the November
pogrom, on condition that they left the country swiftly.[78] Most
did not need to be told twice and left as soon as they could,
despite the loss of their possessions, facilitated by the establishment of the Reich Central Office for Jewish Emigration
in early 1939. After the November pogrom, the total amount
taken by the so-called Reich Flight Tax – essentially a measure
to fleece Jews of their property before they left the country –
amounted to 342.6 million RM.[79] Nearly 130,000 Jews had already left Germany by the end of 1937; in 1938 between 33,000
and 40,000 emigrated, and in 1939 that number jumped to between 75,000 and 80,000.[80] As an SS secret report put it, in the
wake of the pogrom: 'what can be ascertained is that Jewry –
at least with respect to those Jews who are state subjects and

stateless Jews – has been completely excluded from communal life in Germany, so that the only option left for Jews to secure their existence is to emigrate'.[81] The number who did would have been even higher were it not for the fact that the Nazis' contradictory measures – encouraging emigration but depriving Jews of the means to emigrate – meant that many Jews decided or felt that they had no option but to stay.

In 1939, Martha Dodd, the daughter of the United States' ambassador to Germany, warned in print that 'If Hitler is allowed by his own people and by the people and leaders of the world to remain in Germany, I fully believe that eventually there will be no Jews in Germany.' She went on to explain that 'the Jews should recognize, once and for all time, that Fascism, no matter what its local colour or brand, is bent on the extermination of their people'.[82] Even if half the Jewish population had left by the start of the war, and even if the remainder – the majority of them women and the elderly – did not look like the vanguard of a world conspiracy, it was hard to refute Dodd's claims. 'True,' she wrote, 'they are not all dead, exiles, or refugees; not all of them have been lucky. Some of them are forced to stay on in Germany, professions closed to them, all privileges and rights as members of the human race denied them, their children taunted and humiliated, their people defiled, their lives in constant danger of violence or starvation.'[83] For the German and Austrian Jews it was too late. Those who remained in Nazi Germany became increasingly desperate to leave, until that option was completely denied them with the banning of all Jewish emigration on 23 October 1941. By that point, emigration was no longer the aim of the Nazis' Jewish policy; as we will see in the next chapter, they had already turned to mass murder.

Before the 'Final Solution'

Long before war broke out, upon Germany's invasion of Poland, it was clear to contemporary observers that it was coming. Hitler's 'strange pacifism', as German émigré S. Erckner put it, had paved the way inexorably, as Germany had left the League of Nations (1933), reintroduced conscription (1935), reacquired the Saarland (1935), remilitarized the Rhineland (1936) and embarked on a massive rearmament and remilitarization programme in contravention of the Treaty of Versailles. What the Nazis had presented as 'national defence' was in fact a 'pseudo-idyll', not just for the German people, whose post-1933 rebuilding was about to be destroyed, but for the rest of Europe's peoples, who were about to discover what it meant that the Nazis had 'restored the old organic relation between war and the nation':

> The real idyll is the aggressive war, which must be
> prepared for by putting the whole economic system into
> a 'state of alarm', the mobilization of everything, gas-
> shelters in every house, life in underground concrete
> vaults, constant thinking in terms of war ideas, the
> hundred per cent infection of the nation with plague-
> rat ideology, cruelty as the most humane weapon – the

preparation of the appalling end – the 'twilight of
the gods'.[1]

Erckner, the pseudonym of a former staff officer in the
German army, wrote these words before the Anschluss with
Austria, before the occupation of the Sudetenland, the demands over Danzig and the Polish corridor and, the last
straw for appeasement, the occupation of the Czech lands
in March 1939. Yet he was already clear about the direction
of travel: Hitler's 'will to catastrophe' meant that everything
was 'being done to make a nation numbering millions ready
for the organised act of madness'.[2]

What Erckner meant by 'the organised act of madness'
was of course the war, which did indeed result in the deaths
of tens of millions of people, vast destruction of infrastructure, extraordinary waste of resources and huge environmental cost. But today it is the murder of the Jews of Europe that
stands out, within the broader context of the Second World
War, as an organized act of madness. The November pogrom
had already witnessed an unleashing of a kind of controlled
outburst, with carnivalesque scenes accompanied by rigid
rules about which buildings could be destroyed and which
people could be harmed. The continent-wide scale of the
Nazi genocide that followed can be seen as a form of organized
transgression insofar as – when it reached its height late in the
war at Auschwitz – it was undoubtedly bureaucratically organized. But the Nazis also set in motion a licence to transgress and
sparked a shared sense of elation that pervades every aspect
of the killing process. Rousing Nazi speeches produced similar emotions to the heightened feelings of terror and corporeal

threat set in motion, in the first wave of mass shootings, by proximity to corpses, which in turn led to further killings. The Nazis, that is to say, unleashed a generalized *excess*. After the start of the war, the spread of this licence and the increased air of madness which surrounded the killing of the Jews became ever more marked as the war itself grew more widespread, more disastrous, more all-consuming.[3] Far from being undertaken as a cool, rational, quasi-industrial enterprise, the continued hunt for and deportation of Jews from remote corners of Europe such as Corfu or southern France, at a point in time when it was obvious that Germany would lose the war, suggests that a frenzied need to kill the Jews was an essential part of the Nazis' self-understanding. The same applies to the increasing shrillness of the Nazi propaganda towards the end of the war, threatening the German people with the Jews' retribution, when most of Europe's Jews were already dead.

For the Jews of Germany, the period between the November pogrom and the invasion of Poland was one of desperation. As the regime became increasingly fanatical, so the noose around the Jews' necks was correspondingly tightened. As of the end of 1938, Jews were supposed to move into houses inhabited only by Jews: 'Jew houses'. They were excluded from pharmacy, dentistry and veterinary medicine in early 1939, and the rules on *Mischlinge* were tightened. Jews were forbidden from driving motor vehicles and owning weapons, excluded from dining and sleeping cars, forbidden from attending cultural events, and compelled to hand over valuables to the state, including jewellery and precious metals. Unemployed Jews were subjected to forced labour, for example in the construction of Autobahns and dams, and in quarrying, a measure which was regarded as a 'substitute for military service', from which Jews had also been excluded, as Bernhard Lösener, the Interior Ministry's 'Jewish expert' put it.[4] The Jewish Assets Tax added to an already substantial burden being imposed on Jews in order to impoverish them. On 8 November 1938, the day after vom Rath's shooting, Himmler delivered a speech to SS leaders from the elite SS-Standarte 'Deutschland' unit, at which he assured his listeners that: 'In Germany the Jew will not be able to maintain himself; it is only a matter of years.' By way of explanation, he added: 'We will force them out with an unparalleled ruthlessness.'[5] In light of the welter of measures forced upon them, one must also add that Jews were not only being forced out of Germany; they were being made to pay for their own expulsion.[6]

Not that it was easy for German and Austrian Jews to find somewhere to go. Although about half of all German Jews and slightly more than two-thirds of all Austrian Jews (over 126,000 of 180,000) did leave by the end of 1941, many of them (perhaps 55,000 in the case of the Austrians) finding refuge in European countries that were later occupied, from where they were rounded up and deported to their deaths.[7] German and Austrian Jews did manage to get to North Africa, South America, China, Australia, New Zealand and elsewhere but by the late 1930s options were running out. Still, those who made it out of the Reich were fortunate, even if it did not seem that way at the time. One Viennese Jew, Tobias Farb, arrived in Shanghai in early 1939 and spent the war there. His shock on arrival is palpable:

Since February 22nd I have been in Shanghai, and feel wretched. The first impression on arrival and the journey through the war shelled area to our camp was depressing beyond words. The conditions we are faced with, the deplorable economic circumstances and consequently the hopelessness of getting a job, the remoteness of the world, the difficulties to get away from here some day and the dread of spreading diseases, these each in turn add to inexpressible despair and drive us, who had to go through inhuman hardships already, to a complete breakdown. We keep ourselves upright as yet, as we are newcomers but are aware of sufferings on end to come.[8]

On the other side of the world, Eduard Cohn, a refugee in Paraguay, was writing to the American Jewish Joint Distribution Committee (the 'Joint') to ask for help in getting his wife and children, who were in Uruguay, to join him in Asunción. The immigration authorities would only permit them to enter on payment of 1,500 pesos oro; given that 'my wife has no possibility to raise the said amount in Montevideo, a perfect strange city, and that my income as a worker on a mill will not enable me to send her the required sum, we have to realise that we have to remain separated for the time being'.[9] The German and Austrian Jews were spread to the four winds, ultimately taking visas to whichever country would issue them. Only in retrospect can Farb's and Cohn's trajectories be seen as fortunate; for those living through those years, the experience of being made homeless and then being shunted across the world, with no sense of what would happen next, understandably threw them into despair.

This was why President Roosevelt proposed a meeting of representatives of the 'free world' to discuss the matter of emigration from Nazi Germany shortly after the Anschluss.

When the meeting finally took place, in Évian-les-Bains on the shores of Lake Geneva, in July 1938, it was already clear that concern would not be translated into action. Roosevelt's original plan to hold the meeting in Geneva had been vetoed by the Swiss; the UK declared itself unwilling to budge on its immigration rules either with respect to Britain itself or, more pressingly, from the World Jewish Congress's point of view, Palestine; and the US, despite having called the conference, had already announced, in the hope of getting other countries to attend, that it would not be asking any government to relax its rules, as it would not be doing so itself. Besides, the language used at the conference was carefully phrased so as to avoid talking about Jews. All the talk was of 'political refugees' and the 'refugee problem'. The conference's 'achievement' was the creation of a new body, the Intergovernmental Committee for Political Refugees from Germany; visas and other such practical assistance were not, however, forthcoming. The WJC's statement that 'The Jewish refugee problem cannot be discussed without taking into account the immense possibilities of Palestine as an outlet for Jewish immigration' was simply ignored.[10]

No wonder that the *Völkischer Beobachter*'s headline of 13 July trumpeted 'No One Wants to Have Them', that Hitler, in a speech in September, lambasted the hypocrisy of the 'democratic empires' or that the *Daily Express* carried a cartoon illustrating the would-be refugees' plight (see figure 2), making it plain that there was nowhere for them to go. Indeed, the attendees feared that if they were generous with assistance to German Jews, governments such as Poland's, which were also beginning or planning to implement

EUROPEAN CROSS ROADS

Figure 2
Cartoon in the *Daily Express*, 17 October 1938.

antisemitic measures, would demand that the US and UK open their borders to even greater numbers of Jews.

On the sixth anniversary of the 'seizure of power' – one of the Nazis' typical euphemisms – Hitler delivered a speech in front of the specially recalled Reichstag, which was otherwise no longer functioning. In what was perhaps the most famous speech of his whole career, over two and a half hours, Hitler reviewed the history of the National Socialist movement and attacked the British critics of appeasement and their Jewish wire-pullers. Then he turned to the Jews. Now Hitler's 'ever-present ideological obsession' received 'paroxysmic expression':

> And on this day – one that is perhaps memorable not only for us Germans – I would like to add one more thing: In my lifetime, I have very often been a prophet and have mostly been ridiculed for it. In the period of my struggle for power, it was primarily the Jews who laughed off my prophecies that I would one day assume leadership of the German state and the entire German *Volk* and that the Jewish problem would be one among the many I would finally solve. I believe, however, that German Jewry is now choking on its resounding laughter.

And then came the chilling threat:

> Today I will be a prophet again and say, if international finance Jewry in and outside Europe succeeds in plunging nations into another world war, then the end result will not be the Bolshevization of the planet and thus the victory of the Jews – it will be the annihilation of the Jewish race in Europe.[11]

The mismatch between the vast conspiracy imagined by Hitler aimed at destroying Germany and the depressing reality of destitution which was now the lot of Germany's remaining Jews could hardly have been starker. There is no clearer example of what the historian Saul Friedländer calls 'classic Nazi thinking', in which the seriousness of what is being described is totally divorced from reality.[12] Yet, as we will see, this paradox only became more marked as the war progressed, until the point at which, with most of Europe's Jews dead or quaking in fear, Nazi propaganda was becoming ever more shrill in denouncing the 'international Jew' and threatening the Germans with the Jews' retribution. 'Who drives the Russians, English and Americans into the fire, and sacrifices the masses of foreign lives in a hopeless struggle against the German people?' Goebbels asked in an editorial in *Das Reich* on 21 January 1945. The answer: 'The Jews!'[13]

In January 1939, however, Hitler's 'prophecy' speech also had another function: to warn the Americans to stay out of the war – this was the implication of Hitler's reference to 'another world war'.[14] After the 'victories' in achieving the Anschluss with Austria and annexing the Sudetenland, Hitler was sending out a message to the world's statesmen not to interfere. But the crucial point is that Hitler regarded the real rulers of the free world as the hidden hand of international Jewish finance. The link between continued German expansionism and the threat to it from the Americans was inseparable in Hitler's mind from the role played by the Jews. Hitler was not merely thinking about Germany's military capabilities and how they would be diminished in the event of a world war involving the US; he also saw America and 'the

Jew' as one and the same. Hence the threat to annihilate the Jews as a way of keeping the US at bay.

The New Territories

The situation of the German Jews was mirrored in the regions acquired by Nazi Germany in 1938 and 1939. In Austria, in fact, the policies put in place following the Anschluss had a direct and swift impact on the treatment of Jews in the *Altreich* (Germany in its pre-1938 borders), especially with respect to their financial expropriation. Austria became a testing ground for Jewish policy, with the Vienna model setting the Nazi standard for exploitation and dispossession. As soon as the Anschluss took place, in March 1938, violence against Jews was unleashed, markedly more severely than in January 1933, when the Nazis obtained power in Germany. Himmler and Heydrich flew to Vienna to coordinate the Austrian police, and Gestapo headquarters were opened on 15 March. On that same day, Adolf Eichmann, an Austrian born and bred who had been sent to Vienna by the Security Service in Berlin, began ordering Jewish leaders to appear before him and he set about creating the organization that would be responsible for stripping the Jews of their possessions as it processed them for emigration; the Zentralstelle für jüdische Auswanderung (Central Office for Jewish Emigration) became renowned in Nazi circles as the 'Vienna model' and was later emulated in Berlin, Prague and Paris.[15] In 1939 it became part of the Reich Security Main Office (RSHA), by which point its 'division of labour' approach, which forced the cooperation of the Jewish community in terms of administration and financing the operation, had been extraordinarily 'successful': 'the greater the distress of the Jewish population, the greedier the authorities became', as one historian puts it.[16] By the start of the war, 126,481 Austrian Jews had left the country, but only after being robbed first.[17] The combination of forced labour, stringent taxation measures designed to plunder the Jews and coordinating bureaus to accelerate the emigration process would be used elsewhere; it also established Eichmann's credentials as a key player in Nazi Jewish policy.

In the Sudetenland, Jews started to flee, mostly for unoccupied Bohemia, as soon as Germany took over control. Some 15,000 made this escape, only to fall into the hands of the Germans when rump Czechoslovakia was occupied a few months later. They were also immediately subjected to the Aryanization measures that the German regime had established in Austria. Those who remained were treated like the German Jews, except that what took five years to realize in Germany was implemented in days in the Sudetenland. The Jews of the Sudetenland 'were stripped of their rights, crowded into "Jew houses", and plundered to the point of total poverty; all persons capable of work had to perform forced labour'.[18] And all of this with immediate effect.

Thus by the time that German soldiers marched into Prague, sealing the German occupation of Bohemia and Moravia, Jews across Europe were able to observe what would befall them should they find themselves under Nazi control. This was the zenith of Hitler's pre-war success, at which point the post–Great War settlement had been revised entirely in Germany's favour, the Great Powers had been bamboozled by Hitler's claims to want only peace and national self-determination for ethnic German minorities, and appeasement, though it bought time for the British and French to catch up with Germany on the rearmament front, met all of Hitler's demands without him having to go to war. Nevertheless, the booming German economy – which won so many ordinary Germans over to the Nazi regime, at the same time as they were seduced by the seemingly unstoppable foreign policy successes – was taking Germany towards war, since it was a boom based wholly on preparation for war, as Erckner and others pointed out at the time, and as many historians have shown since. Hitler's drive for expansionism was not matched by the resources that the country had; the result was a drive to war which, paradoxically, only made this economic deficit worse. In the hope of obtaining land and resources which would compensate for Germany's economic weaknesses, Hitler explained that the economy's role was 'to secure the inner strength of the people so it can assert itself in [the] sphere of foreign policy'.[19] Rearmament thus dominated the Third Reich's economic recovery.[20]

When Germany invaded Poland on 1 September 1939, it was with the intention of obtaining *Lebensraum*, using the 'Danzig question' and the rights of the German minority as a pretext. Attentive readers of *Mein Kampf* knew that Hitler regarded Poland as nothing more than a corridor to Russia, populated by backward savages who would need to be tamed, much as colonial settlers dealt with 'natives' in North America.[21] It was obvious that, however much he might protest, Hitler would not remain content with occupying Poland. Nevertheless the Hitler–Stalin Pact, which divided Poland between the Nazi and Soviet empires, drew the wool over the eyes of many contemporaries who were shocked and wrong-footed by this alliance of ideological enemies.

Poland's 3.5 million Jews comprised about 10 per cent of the population in 1939. Although the initial attack on Poland was not conceived as a war against the Jews, the onslaught on Polish civilians affected Polish Jews disproportionately, perhaps a result of the relentless propaganda which portrayed Polish Jews as the embodiment of the *Stürmer*-style stereotype: backwards, superstitious, dirty and devious. Many of them, in the knowledge of what had happened to the Jews of Germany, fled to the east, into the Soviet-occupied zone. The Wehrmacht shot some 16,000 civilians between early September and the end of October 1939, which was when it handed over control of occupied Poland to civilian authorities. By the end of the year the German Security Police, with the help of local ethnic German auxiliary groups, had killed as many as 50,000 civilians, among them at least 7,000 Jews, as the Germans sought to liquidate Polish elite groups such as the clergy, academics and politicians.[22] They had soon created out of rump Poland the so-called General Government, the area that was not incorporated directly into the Reich (as was, for example, the so-called Wartheland, which contained Łódź, renamed Litzmannstadt, or East Upper Silesia, which contained Oświęcim, or Auschwitz), which was to be used as a 'racial dumping ground' for Jews and uprooted Poles. From the very start of the occupation of Poland German policy towards civilians was harsh. The treatment meted out to Catholic Poles left them brutalized and, for the most part, too preoccupied with their own survival to be able to offer assistance to the even more beleaguered Polish Jews.

Because it was so brief (Poland was crushed within five weeks), this initial wave of killings in Poland was not the same as the systematic *Einsatzgruppen* shootings that char-acterized the invasion of the Soviet Union. Nevertheless, the killing squads terrorized the general population and did result in some Jewish communities being wiped out at a very early stage of the war.[23] In the small town of Ostrów Mazowiecka, in north-eastern Poland, for example, the population of 20,500 included 7,600 Jews before the war. By the spring of 1940, they were all dead.[24] Even these numbers – relatively small in the wider context of Holocaust history – disguise the terrifying reality of what happened to the Jews of Ostrów. On 10 September, for example, all Jewish men between sixteen and sixty were ordered to assemble on the marketplace in front of the town hall. This is what happened next:

> The waiting crowd was escorted in the aftermath to the yard of the Polish secondary school, where they were made to sit down. Around six o'clock, one of the Germans took the floor and announced that the town would be destroyed if any Germans were shot. No Jew could walk through the streets after six o'clock. He then ordered the crowd to go home. As people got up to obey the orders, they were fired upon. Some witnesses reported that on their way home, they ran into an unknown army group that had just arrived, which immediately opened fire on them. Panic-stricken people tried to run for safety and evade the attackers. It remains unclear how many people lost their lives that day, but according to reports, the numbers vary between twenty-one and three hundred victims.[25]

Then in November the remaining Jewish inhabitants of Ostrów, including the elderly, women and children, were shot into pits just outside the town that had been prepared for that purpose by men from Police Battalion 91. Although this sort of procedure was not yet the normal course of action for the German occupiers, it was a crucial test for the policemen involved and it established a way of operating that would become the default position in the Soviet Union just a year and a half later. Indeed, some of the perpetrators at Ostrów would continue their careers as mass murderers in the Soviet Union. When the celebrated historian Emmanuel Ringelblum referred in his diary, written in Warsaw, to 'the famous killing in Ostrów', it was not only clear that news of what had taken place there had spread but that the event's implications were beginning to be felt by Jews elsewhere in Poland.[26]

As these events suggest, the radical nature of the war in the Soviet Union was prefigured in the war against Poland.[27] As Richard Bessel notes, 'if the Polish campaign appeared a conventional war to the near-sighted, the nature of the German occupation quickly revealed itself as part of something far more sinister'.[28] Goebbels' diary reference to the Jews he saw in Łódź on his visit in November 1939 – 'These are not human beings, these are animals. Therefore it is not a humanitarian operation but a surgical one' – is widely cited, but major deportations took place not only of Jews (who at this stage were being ghettoized and deported to the General Government) but of Catholic Poles, hundreds of thousands of whom were deported. At the same time as he described Jews as animals, Goebbels summed up the Polish streets as 'Asia' and envisaged 'radical action against the Poles'.[29]

The experience of rapid victory in Poland – and, of course, in Western Europe in 1940 – shaped Nazi expectations vis-à-vis the Soviet Union. Poland in particular paved the way for what would happen further east, for it was in Poland that the *Einsatzgruppen* were first used, that Himmler (who was appointed Reich Commissar for the Strengthening of Germandom, RKFDV, on 7 October 1939) really came to the fore in the Third Reich's internal struggle for power, that the newly created RSHA, forged out of the merger of the SD, SS, Gestapo and Criminal Police, began operating under Heydrich, and the euthanasia campaign was systematized. The concentration and ghettoization of Jews, which began immediately on the occupation of Poland, and the suppression and deportation of Catholic Poles were vital way-stations on the road to the war of annihilation in the USSR.[30] The occupation of Poland opened up wider vistas for the SS's fantastical visions. For the Wehrmacht too, a more sinister outlook became common: 'Many German military personnel seem to have considered the Polish–German conflict a struggle between competing ethnic groups', writes one historian, who goes on to say that this conception 'facilitated greater overall acceptance of the regime's definition of the war in racial-biological terms'. The result, he suggests, was that the war 'provided a fitting context for the explosion of attitudes that had been deeply poisoned by prejudice, racism and the exaltation of violence towards Others. In many ways, therefore, the viciousness of German warfare in 1939 proved a foreshadowing of still greater violence to come, violence that provided a foundation for the war of annihilation and the genocide of the Jews.'[31]

It was not only the brutality of the war in Poland that fuelled the Nazis' genocidal dynamic, however. At the same time as Catholic and Jewish Poles were being massacred, the

Nazi regime had embarked on its first systematic wave of killing in the so-called Euthanasia programme. Codenamed T4 after the office at Tiergartenstrasse 4 in Berlin from where the operation was directed, the killing of the mentally and physically disabled was violently different in its unblinking drive to kill and marked by far the largest eugenics-inspired mass murder of the period.

Eugenics – the science of breeding better human beings – was a widely regarded belief and practice across the world in the first half of the twentieth century, ever since the term was coined by Francis Galton in England in the 1880s. It gave rise to a slew of sterilization laws: Indiana was the first US state to introduce forced sterilization in 1907, but they spread to countries across the world. Critics of eugenics had mocked its aspirations from before the time of the Great War, whether from a religious perspective, as in the writings of G. K. Chesterton, or from an ethical, social and scientific point of view. Some, such as Bernard Shaw, had scoffed at the eugenicists, claiming that they wished to erect 'lethal chambers' to do away 'painlessly' with the unfit.[32] Legislation based on eugenics was never passed in the UK, however, perhaps because a social reform agenda predominated, which showed that slum clearances and the provision of sewers improved the lives of the poor, thereby undermining the eugenicists' argument that 'unfitness' was hereditary and unalterable. But whereas hard-line hereditarian eugenics gradually gave way in most of the world, especially as genetics began to reveal that the science behind heredity was more complex than eugenics allowed, in Germany the opposite proved to be the case. Eugenics, or racial hygiene as it was known in Germany, was a contested field; in the interwar period there were socialist and Jewish eugenicists, just as there were elsewhere. But the growing right-wing trend of the Weimar years was also mirrored in science, and leading geneticists such as Eugen Fischer, Otmar Freiherr von Verschuer and Felix von Luschan advocated a reconciliation of science with Nazism.[33]

When the Nazis came to power, eugenic legislation was immediately brought forward. The Law for the Prevention of Hereditarily Diseased Offspring (14 July 1933), the so-called sterilization law, was merely the legal instrument that enforced a large-scale attempt to change German cultural attitudes towards the disabled, with children being educated at school about the cost to the state of maintaining such 'social ballast' and the population as a whole subjected to propaganda films designed to re-educate them in values that praised the strong and derided the weak.[34] The law went much further than in other countries (for example in Denmark, which was one of the Nazis' inspirations), by legalizing the sterilization of the blind – not so much because they were considered feeble-minded but because the genetics of blindness, which was considered as an exemplary case of Mendelian laws, lent themselves to the Nazis' claims about the 'validity of heredity to human maladies'.[35] By the start of the war, some 300,000 people had been sterilized, and a further 100,000 by May 1945. This includes 30,000 women who underwent 'eugenic abortions' with compulsory sterilization.[36] Here the Nazis' assumptions about gender intersected most forcefully with their eugenic ideals. Hitler had already proclaimed in *Mein Kampf* that the *völkisch* state 'must see to it that only the healthy beget children' and that, 'conversely it must be considered reprehensible to withhold healthy children from the nation'.[37] With the laws permitting forced abortion (25 June 1935) and the vetting of marriages for genetic suitability (*Ehegesund-heitsgesetz*, 18 October 1935), we see the truth of the claim that fascism regards women primarily not as human beings in their own right but as breeding machines, carriers of the race.[38]

These eugenics-inspired ideas – given an added impetus by economic considerations – quickly led into a programme of killing, beginning with disabled children. It is likely that plans were already under way when the parents of a disabled child wrote to Hitler to request his mercy death, the moment that is usually regarded as the opportunity the regime had been waiting for to set its ideas in motion.[39] Hitler appointed his personal physician Karl Brandt – a charlatan as a medic but a fanatical Nazi and an extremely important figure, one of Hitler's commissars who stood apart from party or state bureaucracies – and Philipp Bouhler, the chief of the Füh-rer's Chancellery, to run the operation. From autumn 1939 to summer 1941 children were murdered in special hospi-tal wards, mainly by being starved to death. Sometimes the reality of what this meant became overwhelmingly clear, as when Christine Weihs, visiting her brother in an asylum in Essen (where he would later die), discovered when she heard a child's cry in the next-door room: 'And then I pushed the door handle and there lay a child, a boy, in the bed,' she said. 'And his scalp had been opened and the brain was gushing out. Of a living body.'[40]

From killing children, the T4 programme soon moved to murdering adults as well. It was aided by the fact that doctors, attracted to Nazism's support for racial biology, were the most highly represented professional group in Nazi structures, with nearly 45 per cent joining the Nazi Party, 25 per cent the SA, and 7 per cent the SS. By contrast, lawyers, the next most Nazified group, were enrolled in the party to the tune of 25 per cent.[41] With the barest of medical checks – often without seeing the patient at all – doctors would indicate on a form that an asylum inmate should be killed. The bewildered and unsuspecting victims would then be taken by truck – 'transported not as human beings but as cattle' – and murdered by gas in remote spots.[42] Later on, they were killed in the gas chambers of six specially selected sites.[43] Shockingly, and despite the claim to be releasing the incurably ill from their suffering, some asylum patients were aware of what was happening. One patient, an epileptic whom we know only as Helene, wrote to her father from the asylum in Liebenau: 'Sadly it had to be. And so today I must send you my words of farewell from this earthly life as I go to my eternal home . . . May God accept my illness and this sacrifice as an expiation for it.'[44]

When the euthanasia programme was officially ended in August 1941 some 70,000 Germans – mostly Aryans considered racially deficient – had been killed. Despite attempts to educate the population about the need to 'release' the disabled from their 'sufferings', T4 gave rise to widespread unease and, to a limited extent, to a backlash against the regime. Most famously, Bishop Clemens August Graf von Galen of Münster sermonized that the logic of extermination being applied to those with 'lives unworthy of life' could soon just as easily be applied to wounded soldiers.[45] The result was that Hitler officially ended the programme and learned an important lesson about leaving his mark on potentially unpopular decisions – this is one reason why no written order from Hitler for the genocide of the Jews has ever been found. In actual fact, the killings continued clandestinely, both in Germany and in the occupied territories, where asylums were brutally emptied of their patients, who were killed to provide space for wounded Wehrmacht soldiers, and in 'action 14f13' (so-called 'wild euthanasia'), which saw the killing of concentration camp inmates.

T4 was thus one vital part of the Nazis' expanding genocidal visions. Nevertheless, the unique place of the Jews in Nazi ideology means that the Holocaust was not simply a logical extension of the euthanasia programme: Jews were not merely regarded as subhumans who needed to be removed for the sake of race progress; they were also considered a racial threat because of their supposed global power. There is not much evidence that race scientists played a significant role in driving or radicalizing Nazi antisemitic policy. They were supportive of and deeply implicated in those policies, but from the point of view of eugenics, the murder of the Roma and Sinti made more sense, since the Nazis believed them to be 'racial pollutants'.[46] But the links between the T4 project in terms of technologies – a term to be used carefully so as not to suggest that the gas chambers of either T4 or Operation Reinhard were sophisticated, which they were not – and personnel means that there was a convenient transition from 'euthanasia' to the Holocaust which proved crucial to the 'success' of the murder of the Polish Jews in Bełżec, Sobibór and Treblinka. Most important, the lack of objection to T4 – von Galen and some other protests notwithstanding – suggests that the euthanasia programme's real significance was in encouraging the Nazis' genocidal mindset. Nevertheless, the euthanasia programme was only one – albeit an important one – of the sources for the rapidly radicalizing nature of the attack on the Jews.

The radicalizing shift in the Nazis' visions is clearly visible in their plans for dealing with the Jews in the period before June 1941, plans which owed little to eugenics or the logic of the T4 operation. In the almost two years between the signing of the Hitler–Stalin Pact and Operation Barbarossa, the furthest reach of the Nazi empire was the River San in south-east Poland. It was here that plans for a *Judenreservat* (Jewish reservation) were drawn up, its main manifestation the so-called Nisko Project – holding deported Jews at a transit camp in Nisko, near Lublin, before transferring them to an unspecified destination further east. The project failed for logistical reasons, but as with the later Madagascar Plan, this 'territorial solution' to the 'Jewish question' proved a significant milestone in the development of the Nazi genocidal imagination. It is clear that by the time of the invasion of the Soviet Union, Nazi Germany's leadership had already made some important mental leaps. Historians agree: the 'origins of the Holocaust', writes one, 'lie in Germany's determination to fight a race war in Poland in September 1939'.[47] Others are even more explicit: 'The failure to realize these plans, combined with the rapid decomposition of normative behavioural constraints in the context of war and a growing belief among the Nazi elite that anything was possible, would eventually open the gates to Auschwitz.'[48]

The Meaning of the War

In March 1941 Alfred Rosenberg gave a speech at the opening of the Institute for the Study of the Jewish Question in Frankfurt, in which he said:

> The present war is a world struggle of the greatest magnitude. Its outcome will determine the fate of nations for centuries . . . The Nuremberg Laws are revolutionary in nature for world history, and it is the task of the National Socialist movement, today and forever, to ensure that a November 9, 1918, can nevermore occur and that even a remotely similar dominance by the Jews can nevermore be established in Germany . . . The war that is being waged today by the German Wehrmacht under the supreme command of Adolf Hitler is therefore a war of enormous transformation. It is not only overcoming the intellectual world of the French Revolution but also directly obliterating all the blood-polluting germs that the Jews and their bastards were able to develop unarrested from amid the European peoples for more than 100 years now. The Jewish question, a task that has been set for the peoples of Europe for 2,000 years and not resolved, will henceforth find its solution, for Germany and for all of Europe, as a result of the National Socialist revolution! . . . For Europe, the Jewish question will only be solved when the last Jew has left the European continent.[49]

By the time Rosenberg gave this speech, Nazi Germany had occupied Poland for a year and a half, splitting the country down the middle with the Soviet Union, and since the spring of 1940 it had also occupied France, Belgium, Luxembourg, the Netherlands, Denmark and Norway. While the treatment of the Jews of Western Europe was crucial for the unfolding of the 'Final Solution of the Jewish Question' in the sense of a continent-wide programme, events in Poland in the autumn of 1939 were most significant as first steps on the road to genocide. Up until that point, German and Austrian Jews had been the victims of Nazi anti-Jewish policies; several thousand Czech Jews were also sent to concentration camps and local prisons after the swallowing up of rump Czechoslovakia in March 1939. After the invasion of Poland, Himmler ordered the rounding-up of all Polish male 'enemy aliens' over the age of sixteen who were living in the Reich, some 2,000 of whom were sent to Sachsenhausen and Buchenwald, where they were held in special blocks and subjected to treatment whose brutality was worse than that experienced by Jews in concentration camps before then.[50]

In Poland itself the experience of the Jews rapidly appeared to justify the decision made by many to flee. Those who remained under German control in the autumn of 1939 – some 1.5 million – quickly found themselves trapped; their lives were to deteriorate very rapidly indeed. In May 1940, Ringelblum noted that 'The victories on the Western front have made a powerful impression. The populace is enveloped in deep melancholy.'[51] With the creation of ghettos, the situation would only get worse.

One of the first things that Himmler did after his appointment as RKFDV was to grant Heydrich maximum space to realize SS plans. To that end, on 21 September 1939, the latter sent a *Schnellbrief*, or express letter, to the chiefs of the *Einsatzgruppen*, ordering the concentration of the Polish Jews in cities, preferably close to railway junctions. It is likely that the contents of the letter were meant less for its addressees than the agencies outside of the SS who received copies, as a way of enforcing their cooperation with policies which were already in motion, and of ensuring their subordination to the SS.[52] Heydrich wrote that 'Distinction must be made between: 1. The final aim (which will require extended periods of time) and 2. The stages leading to the fulfilment of this final aim (which will be carried out in short periods).'[53] The words 'final aim' sound, in retrospect, ominous, and indeed they were, but in September 1939 they did not necessarily mean what 'final solution' came to mean two years later. For the time being, the goal was to concentrate Jews in towns and cities until they could be deported to the east when Germany had won sufficient living space. The *Schnellbrief* did not mandate the creation of ghettos, which emerged thanks to grassroots initiatives in response to Germans' encounters with the Polish Jews, whom they regarded with horror as, in one soldier's words, 'a nest of Jews in the full sense of the word . . . a colony of filth'.[54] Nevertheless, from the outset the ghettoization process should be regarded as murderous; not only were the ghettos themselves death traps, but, even if the 'final aim' changed over time, the initial aspiration to deport Jews east of the Urals was undoubtedly genocidal in its implications. To aid them in their goals, the Nazis set up Jewish Councils (*Judenräte*), whose role was to administer the ghettos so that the Germans did not have to and, in doing the Germans' bidding, to make it look to the ghettos' inhabitants that they were the victims of the Jewish Councils first and foremost.

Closed ghettos – that is to say, enclosing Jews in the places where they already lived ('ghettos') or forcing them to move to locations considered Jewish by the occupiers – were not introduced simultaneously across the board, however, and much depended on local initiatives. Although preparations for a large ghetto in Łódź were set in motion in October 1939 it was only officially announced on 8 February 1940 following debate between different Nazi agencies, and only sealed on 30 April 1940. Other smaller ghettos in the Warthegau, such as Tulisków, Pabianice and Brzeziny, were created between January and April. In the Radom district, the first ghettos were set up in December 1939, whereas in Warsaw the ghetto was only established in November 1940. In Cracow, despite the city being the capital of the General Government, Jews were expelled gradually from the spring of 1940; only in March 1941 was the ghetto in Cracow-Podgorze complete and its inhabitants walled in.[55]

Nazi policy until 1941 was to remove the Jews to the furthest reaches of the Nazi Empire, to at that point what is today the south-eastern corner of Poland, pending their further deportation east of the Urals following the successful prosecution of the war. The prolonged life of ghettos was a result of the fact that the war against the USSR was not concluded as quickly as Hitler wished, and this unexpected longevity gave rise to debates among competing Nazi agencies as to whether the ghettos should be eliminated anyway ('attritionists') or whether the captive Jews should be put to work for the good of the war effort ('productionists').[56]

One should not make too much of this intra-Nazi debate. It is the case that some thousands of Jews survived the war because they were employed working for the war effort, but the vast majority perished irrespective of their potential usefulness. Productionists only ever saw their position as a temporary one, designed to expedite Nazi victory; as soon as victory was assured, the Jews' lives would no longer be required or permitted. As Friedrich Uebelhoer, governor of the Kalisz district, to which Łódź belonged, the man responsible for establishing the ghetto, wrote, 'The creation of the ghetto is, of course, only a temporary measure . . . The final aim must in any case bring about the total cauterisation of this plague spot.'[57] That did not prevent ghettos being exploited as much as possible, nor did it mean that economic considerations played no role.[58] But in the end the debate was academic: even the most successful *Judenrat* chairman, speaking strictly from this 'cost–benefit' point of view, Chaim Rumkowski, who managed to keep a much-reduced Łódź ghetto going until the summer of 1944 by persuading the German civilian authorities of its usefulness, failed ultimately to prevent the liquidation of the ghetto with its remaining 77,000 inhabitants. Almost all of them, including Rumkowski, perished in Auschwitz. Ideology always triumphed.

The ghettos, no matter how they were originally conceived, ended with deportation to death camps. But this is not the end of the matter. While there was no blueprint for genocide in existence when the ghettos were set up, one should note that they were in themselves, as one Nazi official put it, 'death boxes'. If the ghettos were not brought into being as part of a pre-existing plan for genocide, they were genocidal in their consequences – some 500,000 Jews died in the ghettos. The living conditions were unimaginable. Filth and disease reigned, ghetto inhabitants became used to the sight of people dying and dead on the streets, and in Warsaw only the bravery of child smugglers meant that more people did not starve to death. 'Every day', wrote young diarist Mary Berg in Warsaw, 'there were more "dreamers of bread" on the Warsaw ghetto's streets.'[59] 'Who knows,' wrote Warsaw diarist Peretz Opoczynski in 1941, 'some day we ought to erect a monument to the smuggler for his risks, because consequently he thereby saved a good part of Jewish Warsaw from starving to death.'[60] The ghettos turned the Jews into the objects they were portrayed as in Nazi propaganda: lice-ridden, degenerate, living in squalor – though without, of course, their wealth being hidden under the floorboards as the notorious film *Der ewige Jude* (*The Eternal Jew*) suggested was the case. As Opoczynski went on:

> Whoever will endure, whoever will survive the diseases that rage in the ghetto because of the dreadful congestion, the filth and uncleanness, because of having to sell your last shirt for half a loaf of bread, whoever will be that hero, will tell the terrible story of a generation and an age when human life was reduced to the subsistence of abandoned dogs in a desolate city.[61]

When the Polish underground courier, the brave Jan Karski, entered the Warsaw ghetto on one of his missions on behalf of the Polish Government-in-Exile, what he encountered shocked him, to the extent that decades later he had to steel himself to speak about his experiences. He wrote about the ghetto in his book *Story of a Secret State*, published in Boston in 1944, but when interviewed for Claude Lanzmann's film *Shoah* in the 1970s, struggled to describe what he had seen: 'It was not a world. There was not humanity . . . It was some . . . some hell . . . This is apparent that they are subhuman. They are not human,' he stammers out in the film, indicating the extent to which the Nazi dehumanization of the Jews had accomplished its propagandistic aims.[62] Some in the ghettos would have concurred; when historian Emmanuel Ringelblum's clandestine Oneg Shabbat group in the Warsaw ghetto sent questionnaires to leading figures in the ghetto, Israel Milejkowski, the head of the public health and hospital departments of the Jewish Council, wrote:

> At first glance what is most obvious is the benumbed sense of compassion among Warsaw Jews. Without any pity for the desperate plight of thousands of our brethren whom want has forced from their hovels out onto the streets, we pass almost indifferently the barely living unfortunates and the paper-covered corpses of those who died of hunger. Savagery has begun to rule our minds and, accordingly, also our actions.[63]

The ghettos are often remembered in the popular imagination as sites of Jewish culture, where spiritual resistance and shared cultural activities worked to mitigate the Nazis' designs to break the Jewish spirit. They were in fact places of humiliation, where individuals were crushed and solidarity was eradicated. As Josef Zełkowicz, a diarist in the Łódź ghetto, put it, the ghetto was 'the great negator of the civilization and progress that people nurtured for centuries', which 'has swiftly obliterated the boundaries between sanctity and indignity, just as it obliterated the boundaries between mine and yours, permitted and forbidden, fair and unfair'. And, to stress the point, he then added: 'But do not think . . . that this blurring of boundaries has not claimed a price in blood and brains.'[64] What Zełkowicz, a *Judenrat* official, encountered when he visited Jewish homes were people who had lost all sense of decency and shame with respect to clothing and hygiene, people stealing from their own families, who had lost all hope and gone insane.[65]

One can thus understand the agonies of the Jewish Councils, who were tasked by the Germans with administering the ghettos. The councils have been condemned by survivors as leeches, an elite who sought to save their own skins, enjoying a luxurious lifestyle while the masses suffered. It is true that the *Judenräte* established Jewish police forces who rounded up Jews for deportation; one can understand the comment of Emmanuel Ringelblum, historian and director of the Oneg Shabbat secret archive, when he wrote that '[a]n atmosphere of Gestapo seeped from the walls of the Judenrat'.[66] But they also sought to provide welfare in the form of education, medicine and basic hygienic amenities. Some *Judenrat* chairmen, such as the much-admired Elchanan Elkes of Kovno (Kaunas), actively encouraged underground resistance, at great risk to themselves and the Kovno ghetto's inhabitants. Certain figures, notably the megalomaniac Rumkowski, vilified as the King of the Jews, clearly felt at home in the position of illusory power. But one should always remember that the councils were caught in what literary scholar Lawrence Langer calls choiceless choice. They acted under the aegis of the Germans because they had no choice, and in the probably correct belief that by carrying out the Nazis' orders themselves they were mitigating the worst effects of Nazi direct rule. Even so, there is something terrible about reading in reports, as in this one from Łódź, that 'It was the Jewish Police that had to tear the children from the mothers, to take the parents from the children.'[67] Historian Dan Diner is right to note that the choices made by the councils are best understood as counter-rational; that is, they were trapped in a framework not of their own making, so that even decisions which seemed logical and rational led ultimately to destruction.[68] Unbeknown to the majority of the ghettos' populations, the councils themselves understood this. In the minute books of the Białystok ghetto one reads the following comments: 'We are a state without finances, without budgets, without gold reserves ... The matter is difficult. The decisions will not after all be made by the Judenrat, nor by the executive Board. The Germans will settle things.'[69]

The ghetto was liquidated in August 1943.

While tens of thousands were starting to die in the ghettos of Łódź and the General Government, the German Foreign Office was preparing its own solution to the Jewish Question: the so-called territorial solution. The first plan was to deport the Jews to the Nisko region in south-eastern Poland, but as already noted this failed because of difficulties in Germany (notably Goering's objections) and in the General Government, where Governor Hans Frank protested about his territory being used as a racial 'dumping ground'. This was replaced by the ambitious and seemingly improbable idea of deporting the Jews to the French colony of Madagascar, a large island off the east coast of Africa. Actually, the idea of deporting Europe's Jews to Madagascar was, like so much about Nazi ideology, not new, but had been a stock antisemitic fantasy since the nineteenth century. The British antisemitic writers Henry Hamilton Beamish and Arnold Leese had both promoted the idea in the interwar years, as had some other European politicians, such as Romanian Prime Minister Octavian Goga in 1938. It was taken seriously enough by certain elements in the Third Reich for Franz Rademacher in the Foreign Office and Himmler to devote considerable effort to it. In 1940 Himmler wrote to Hitler promoting the deportation of the Jews 'to Africa or some other colony' in order to avoid the 'Bolshevist method' of physical extermination, which, 'from inner conviction', he considered 'un-German and impossible'. But the Madagascar Plan collapsed in September 1940 once Hitler failed to defeat Great Britain, a necessary precondition for sailing across the British navy-controlled Indian Ocean in order to get to the island.

As a result both of its short life and its promotion primarily by the Foreign Office rather than the SS, historians have often regarded the Madagascar Plan as an irrelevance. But in 1940 it was the goal of Nazi Jewish policy. One should not overlook the fact that, as with ghettoization policy, the plan to deport millions of Jews to an island with no infrastructure to accommodate them was itself genocidal. Its failure constituted a psychological ice-breaker for genocide in the east.

Preparing the War of Annihilation

The historian Saul Friedländer writes:

> One way or another, through every available channel, the regime was convincing itself that the Jews, as helpless as they may have looked on the streets of Germany, were

a demonic power striving for Germany's perdition . . .
Thus, alongside and beyond obvious tactical objectives,
some other thoughts were emerging on the eve of the war.
No program of extermination had been worked out, no
clear intentions could be identified. A bottomless hatred
and an inextinguishable thirst for a range of ever-harsher
measures against the Jews were always very close to the
surface in the minds of Hitler and of his acolytes. As both
he and they knew that a general war was not excluded, a
series of radical threats against the Jews were increasingly
integrated into the vision of a redemptive final battle for
the salvation of Aryan humanity.[70]

Not Bolshevism as such but the Jewish unleashing of Bolshevism as a degenerative poison; and not war solely as a
means of acquiring living space but the acquisition of living
space in order to destroy the Jew who was seeking to prevent Germany from flourishing, were at the heart of the war
and the murder of the Jews. Historians who have seen the
Holocaust as a by-product of the war or as a consequence of
a hatred of Bolshevism have things the wrong way around:
the war was a war of annihilation in which Bolshevism had
to be destroyed insofar as it was one way – perhaps the most
threatening – that 'the Jew' sought to destroy Aryan Germany.[71] And the need for living space presupposed the eradication of the Jews as – although they were a small population
group who owned little land – in the Nazis' eyes they were
the masters of national disintegration. By the time of the invasion of the Soviet Union the Nazi regime had already embarked on indiscriminate attacks on specific groups of Jews.

But now the war of annihilation would mark yet another step-change, this time to wholesale mass murder of entire Jewish communities.

Scholars have described in detail the Nazi occupation of the USSR, with the result that one cannot separate the war for *Lebensraum* from the Holocaust.[72] The destruction of 'Judaeo-Bolshevism' went hand in hand with grand schemes to expel Slavs in their tens of millions to make way for the German paradise envisaged by Himmler. If it was the thrill of rapid victory in Poland that gave a frisson of anticipation to the racial fantasies of 1941, the discovery that the Soviet Union would not capitulate quite so readily made the Nazis readier to realize them.[73]

What we see in the build-up to the Final Solution is thus not just that the territorial solution was taken seriously by the Nazi leadership, being far more than a way of diverting the Foreign Office's *Judenreferat* from discovering the more radical steps being taken by the SS. Additionally, it has become clear that one should not draw too much of a distinction between earlier policies of deportation to reservations and later policies of extermination, since both were genocidal. The problem with making this distinction is that one thereby 'misses the core of the plans of Nazi administrators of Jewish policy', because 'the "territorial solution" was always conceived as a "final solution", for it was ultimately directed at the physical destruction of the great majority of the Jews'.[74] In fact, the Madagascar Plan, which, 'like a spectacular meteor . . . blazed across the sky of Nazi Jewish policy, only to burn out abruptly', was 'an important psychological step toward the road to the Final Solution'. Although the circumstances of the war – the failure to secure the sea routes across the Indian Ocean – meant that the plan died a rapid death, it seems clear that 'had the Nazis carried out the plan as they intended, it would have been a murderous operation'.[75] As Himmler wrote, 'The very concept "Jew" I hope to see completely extinguished by creating the possibility of large-scale emigration of Jews to Africa or some other colony.'[76] What the Madagascar Plan reveals is the drive to find a quick solution to the Jewish question in 1940; it was but a short step from a plan that was 'genocidal in its implications' to genocide implemented in situ in Nazi-occupied Europe.[77] What changed in 1941 was the overall conception of a genocidal plan rather than a more limited policy in which genocidal intent was still to some extent veiled, perhaps unconsciously.

CHAPTER 4
War of Annihilation

'Sometimes I think that Heaven is void, because how else can you explain maxims about loving one's neighbour and the purity of the soul while people who utter these phrases turn into haters of mankind?

All religious beliefs are devilish inventions that never lead to a positive resolution. Man is the cruellest of all animals. There were even instances when the murderers shot women in labour. Man is evil by nature.'
— Baruch Milch[1]

On 6 October 1941, a senior lance-corporal (*Obergefreiter*) in the 12th Company of the 354th Infantry Regiment recorded in his diary how he took part in a mass execution of Jews in a village called Krupka (Krupki, Belarus), in the district of Orsha. Recording that he readily volunteered when his lieutenant asked for fifteen men with strong nerves, he then noted what happened:

There were about a thousand Jews in the village of Krupka and they were all supposed to be shot today . . . At seven precisely all Jews had to appear at the assembly place – men, women and children. The lists were read out and then the whole formation marched out in the direction of the nearest swamp . . . As we arrived at the swamp, they all had to sit facing the direction from which we had come. Fifty metres away was a deep trench full of water. The first ten had to place themselves next to this trench and undress to the waist, then they had to get into the water and the firing squad, that's to say we, were standing over them. We had a lieutenant and an NCO with us. Ten shots, ten Jews brought down [*umgelegt*]. It kept going until we had finished them all. Only a few managed to keep their composure. Women clung to their men and children to their mothers. It was a spectacle that we won't forget quickly.

A few days later, when the same soldier was in Cholopenichi, he helped with another execution, 'but here there was no swamp, just some sandy ground. So we "inserted" the Jews there in the sand.'[2]

The war in Poland was brutal, and by the time that Germany and its allies Italy and Romania invaded the Soviet Union on 22 June 1941 many thousands of Catholic Poles had been killed, and the Nazis' plans to reduce the Polish population to the level of slaves were well under way, with forced removals, university closures, looting of national treasures such as libraries and art collections, destruction of monuments and persecution of leading figures all the norm. As Hitler explained to Hans Frank, the Governor General, in October 1940:

The Führer must emphasize once again that the Poles may only have one master – a German. Two masters cannot and must not exist side by side; and that is why all the representatives of the Polish intelligentsia must be murdered. That sounds cruel but it is the law of life. The General Government is a Polish reservation, a great Polish labour camp.[3]

For the Jews of Poland who had been unable to flee to Soviet-occupied eastern Poland, things were even worse: crammed into ghettos, where they were starving to death with no sense of what would happen to them, they found that everything that had characterized their lives before the war had been turned upside down. This difference was clearly spelled out by Frank; in a meeting on 23 April 1940, attended by Herbert Backe, Minister of Food and Agriculture, Frank explained that the Ukrainians in the General Government would be fed to the extent necessary to sustain them and keep them able to work. Poles would get what was left and would have to fend for themselves if they needed more. This left the Jews, and here Frank was explicit: 'The Jews are on the bottom rung, the military and civil servants on top. The majority of the Polish people will still be treated significantly better than the Jews. We have no interest in the Jews.'[4]

Yet if what had happened since September 1939 in Poland was shocking, what would take place in the Soviet Union after June 1941 was of another order still. Frank's stance was harsh but it was nevertheless not enough for the SS, which, under Himmler's leadership, was fast developing into a significant powerbase and regarded itself as the avant-garde of the Nazi worldview, especially with respect to the implementation of racial policy. Hans Frank's headquarters in Cracow became increasingly irrelevant as the SS took charge of Jewish policy; with the invasion of the Soviet Union, this bold takeover was soon plain to see. In the short period between the invasion of the Soviet Union and spring 1942 the Third Reich moved from persecuting Jews through ad hoc, if massive, violence and ghettoization, as in Poland, to full-scale, face-to-face killing in huge numbers and, by mid-1942, to a continent-wide programme to exterminate the Jews of Europe. The process by which this occurred has been the subject of immense debate among historians, and it is indeed in many ways complex, especially when one considers the different, competing German agencies involved and the ways in which persecution and murder took place at different rates in different places, depending on local circumstances, especially the military situation, the type of occupation regime put in place, the relative strength of the SS, and the roles played by collaborating elites and/or independent or quasi-independent regimes allied to Germany. Yet two things quickly become clear: whether there was a Hitler order or a series of unspoken authorizations given by Hitler to his subordinates who were competing for his attention (what the historian Ian Kershaw called 'working towards the Führer'[5]), it is unquestionable that Hitler was the prime mover in the murder of the Jews. The architects of the policy, Himmler and his deputy, Heydrich, were continually attentive to what Hitler wanted and demanded and would have done nothing at this stage without his say-so. Second, whether the decision, if one can talk of 'the decision' rather than a series of steps, to murder the Jews of Europe as a whole was taken in a moment of euphoria at the first wave of victories in the Soviet Union in September–October 1941 or whether it was taken later after the US entered the war (thus precipitating, as in Hitler's 1939 'prophecy', a world war which would end in the annihilation of the Jewish race in Europe) and in rage at setbacks in the war against the Soviet Union, by mid-1942 all necessary agencies, from the Reichsbahn (German railways) to the civil service were informed and involved.[6]

Looking back from the vantage point of 1942, it must have seemed remarkable to anyone on the perpetrator side (by which is meant not just the SS but all other the agencies involved too: civil and local government, industry, research institutions) that they were now party to a vast programme of mass murder.[7] This was a fantastic vision which mushroomed in scope as the Third Reich's leaders' megalomaniac dreams of world domination seemed to become achievable. But we should not be deceived by this apocalyptic language, the Wagnerian grandiosity of the Nazis' vision, or even the huge numbers killed, into thinking that the genocide of the Jews took up a significant amount of German manpower or resources; in fact, it had no impact on the Germans' ability to wage war. Further, not only did Auschwitz's German garrison at its height contain no more men than a single Wehrmacht regiment,[8] but the camp itself was built on bartered material and pre-existing structures. In other words, the amount of the Third Reich's resources that was used to carry out the Holocaust was minuscule. Furthermore, these resources were used for the most part before they became scarce; as historian Peter Hayes notes, 'three-quarters of the Jews murdered in the Holocaust died before the German surrender at Stalingrad'.[9] Hayes calculates, in a remarkable statistical analysis, that the number of Jews transported to death camps on deportation trains (some 2.5 million in 1942–3) is less than 0.5 per cent of the more than 6.6 billion passengers carried by the Reichsbahn in that period; if one takes 1944 into account, the percentage of deported Jews becomes 0.3 per cent. The number of trains involved in taking Jews to their deaths from outside the General Government is reckoned at 821, meaning that the total number of wagons used in three years, at 24,317, is 16.3 per cent of the total number of wagons used *every day* by the Reichsbahn in 1942–4 (149,200).[10] The Holocaust had almost no bearing on German resources, least of all on its railways.

With the invasion of the USSR, the war against the Jews merged with the military war, since in the eyes of the Nazis 'Judaeo-Bolshevism' was synonymous with the Soviet system, representing the antithesis of everything the Nazis stood for. In terms of the persecution of the Jews, a new and far more bloody stage than anything that had gone before now took place: the so-called Holocaust by bullets, during which the SS's *Einsatzgruppen* shot some 1.5 million Jews. This was still not a Europe-wide project but was fast becoming one: the first Operation Reinhard death camps (Bełżec and Sobibór) were already being planned to eliminate the Jews of Poland before the Wannsee Conference, where Heydrich set out the Final Solution to a range of SS, Nazi Party and civil service representatives, took place on 20 January 1942; gas vans in Serbia and the extermination camp of Chełmno were already carrying out mass murder without involving face-to-face shooting; the total eradication of Estonia's small Jewish population of about 1,000 (three-quarters of the prewar population had fled or were deported to Russia) was fast completed; in Latvia, with considerable assistance from the Wehrmacht and the collaborationist Arājs commando, about 69,000 of the country's 75,000 Jews were murdered by the end of 1941 (the remainder were sent to concentration camps, the majority to Kaiserwald Riga); and preparations for deportations in France were also under way before Heydrich and the SS wrested full control over Jewish policy away from Goering, Frank, Rosenberg and other competing parties. That said, in the autumn and winter of 1941 the bulk of the SS's attention was on murder in the Soviet Union and beginning the attack on the huge Jewish communities in Poland, the largest in Europe.[11] What we now know as the Final Solution was arrived at through a series of steps, not a single decision. Although it was probably substantially in place in the autumn of 1941, it culminated in spring 1942, at which point we can see that the programme was fully formed and operational.

To give one important example, some historians have argued that the entry of the US into the war in December 1941 was the key moment in the decision-making process, since the Jews were no longer useful as hostages to prevent the Americans from joining. This is the meaning of Hitler's reference to 'world war' in his speech of 30 January 1939: Hitler believed that the Americans – run by the hidden hand of international Jewry – might not enter the war if the fate of the Jews was at stake. Yet the idea is paradoxical; if the Jews were as powerful as Hitler believed, why could they not prevent the US's entry into the war and/or save the lives of the Jews under Nazi occupation? Besides, it could not have been the moment when the decision was taken, not least because Hitler and other leading Nazis had been making statements about the extermination of the Jews for some months already.[12] On 22 July 1941, Hitler told the head of the Croation army Slavko Kvaternik that 'If there were no Jews left in Europe the unity of the nation states would no longer be disturbed. Where the Jews are to be sent, whether to Siberia or to Madagascar, is irrelevant.'[13] And on 28 November 1941, he told the Grand Mufti of Jerusalem, Haj Amin al-Husseini, that 'Germany is determined to press one European nation after the other to solve the Jewish problem.' In his major speech entitled 'The Jews Are Guilty' of 16 November 1941, Goebbels stated that 'The Jews wanted war and now they have it . . . The Jews must be removed from the German community for they endanger our national unity.' Referring specifically to Hitler's 'prophecy' of 30 January 1939, Goebbels was quite explicit: 'We are seeing the fulfilment of this prophecy . . . World Jewry erred completely in its calculation of the forces at its disposal for instigating this war and now is gradually experiencing the process of annihilation that it planned for us and would have carried out without a second thought it if had possessed the ability.'[14] Hitler had clearly given the order to murder the Jews of Europe before December 1941, for otherwise statements such as Goebbels' would have been unthinkable. What we see between autumn 1941, when the tone became more radical in the context of what Goebbels called Hitler's 'exuberantly optimistic state of mind',[15] and spring 1942, when the overall programme was in place (in theory, if not always in practice, due to logistical constraints), is a process of coordination, enlisting the co-operation of all necessary agencies both inside Germany and among its allies, a process, in other words, of disseminating decisions already taken. The question for German officials had changed; it was 'no longer why the Jews should be killed, but why they should *not* be killed'.[16]

At this point, Jews were still not very relevant to the SS's camp system, since they were being killed in face-to-face shootings in 'the east' or in death camps in Nazi-occupied Poland. The key year was 1942: in March of that year, some 75–80 per cent of the Holocaust's victims were still alive, whereas by mid-February 1943, some 80 per cent of the Holocaust's victims were dead.[17] The Operation Reinhard camps had consumed the Jews of Poland, and Birkenau (Auschwitz II) was, by late 1942, in full swing as a killing centre. In the first stage (1941–2) the victims were primarily religious Eastern European Jews, and, starting in the autumn of 1942, more assimilated Central and Western European Jews were being deported, from Slovakia, France, the Netherlands, Belgium and the occupied Czech lands. Their struggles to comprehend what was happening to them are vitally important for showing how just as there was not one form of persecution, so different people among the victim groups in different places responded in different ways to the attacks on them, as we will see.

Jews in Germany and the Protectorate

With emigration banned as of 23 October 1941, the remaining German Jews were now trapped. The Jews left behind in Germany were mostly women, the elderly and those in 'mixed' marriages. Hertha Feiner, for example, divorced from her non-Jewish husband, was allowed to remain in Berlin because of her two *Mischling* daughters, even though she and her ex-husband had arranged for them to be schooled in Switzerland, where they survived the war. She sought to shield her daughters from the reality of her increasingly restricted life but, in her letters to them, her anguish came through. 'It's true that we haven't seen each other for a long,

long time,' Hertha wrote to her daughter Inge in January 1941, 'but I hope the time will soon come when we can talk about everything in detail.'[18] That time would not come; after losing her job and making ends meet by working for the beleaguered remnant of the Berlin Jewish community, Hertha was finally deported on a transport from Berlin to Auschwitz in March 1943. She committed suicide in the train, swallowing a poison capsule that she had been given by a friend.

Absurdly, throughout this period Jews in Germany, some of whom were already being deported to their deaths from October 1941, were still being subjected to petty legislation aiming at circumscribing their lives even further. A law of 15 May 1942 forbade Jews from keeping pets and another of 17 July forbade blind and handicapped Jews from wearing disabled armbands. When one considers not just that German Jews were being deported but that the Jews of the General Government were being exterminated en masse in the Operation Reinhard death camps at this point, the bizarreness of this legislative onslaught is startling. At the same time, Jews were being held in internment camps in Italy and in Vichy France, or were adjusting to refugee life in the Dominican Republic, Shanghai and elsewhere.

In the Protectorate of Bohemia and Moravia (rump Czechoslovakia), the Jews were similarly trapped. Subjected to a slew of life-degrading legislation like being forced to give up typewriters, bicycles, musical instruments, fur coats and radios, they were excluded from public sites such as swimming pools, parks, cinemas and trams, prevented from buying many food items and, as of February 1941, restricted to shopping between 3 and 5 p.m. In the second half of 1941, shortly after Heydrich's arrival as *Reichsprotektor*, deportations from the Protectorate began, to Łódź and Theresienstadt, the ghetto on the site of a former Austro-Hungarian garrison town about 60 kilometres north of Prague. The Jewish community was terrified, but the Nazis worked hard to persuade them that they were merely being resettled, although unlike the elderly German Jews, they were not obliged to hand over their life savings for the purchase of retirement home contracts, which supposedly guaranteed their end-of-life care in Theresienstadt.[19] However, the ways in which Nazi propaganda advertised Theresienstadt contrasted markedly with what Central European Jews were hearing about what was happening further east, leaving them scared and confused.[20] Marie Bader, a fifty-four-year-old widower, wrote a series of letters to her new love, her second cousin Ernst Löwy, who had fled to Thessaloniki in northern Greece. Throughout their correspondence Marie put on a brave face and, having received the summons to leave for Theresienstadt in April 1942, she tried to reassure Ernst, and herself, that what she had heard was true:

> My future place of residence represents a sort of ghetto, it has the advantage that, if one obeys all the rules, one lives in some ways without the restrictions one has here. Up to 3,000 people live in one barrack and the men can visit the women from time to time. Women up to the age of 55 work, according to their abilities and achievements, the old people go into an old people's home or an infirmary, the children in a children's home . . . What particularly pleases me is that the women can take care of their bodies, wash, etc., even in Theresienstadt, and one hears that there is

a nice, friendly social life with informative lectures, both serious and amusing ones, in the evenings, so people – at least some – know how to create some light hearted moments even there.[21]

In fact, Theresienstadt was a much harsher environment than Marie envisaged, although she was perhaps seeking to reassure her correspondents as much as herself. Despite her confidence that friends would assist her, she had the misfortune to arrive when Siegfried Seidl, the commandant, had ordered four extra transports, each of a thousand people, to leave for Poland in a week. Three days after her arrival at Theresienstadt, Marie was deported for Izbica, a small, isolated and, before the war, almost entirely Jewish town, where conditions were appalling. Many there died of starvation or typhus; most of the men were relocated to do forced labour in Lublin and housed in Majdanek, but most of the Jewish women, children and elderly were sent from Izbica to Bełżec or Sobibór, where they were killed. It is not known where Marie died but after her arrival at Izbica she was never heard from again.[22] The same thing happened to Henriette Pollatschek, a sixty-nine-year-old widow, when the Nazis occupied Prague, where she had already fled from northern Bohemia. Despite the pleading of her son, who had already left for Switzerland, and later Cuba, to join him, she did not wish to leave all that she knew until it was too late. In May 1942, with deportation looming, Henriette wrote: 'I keep asking myself how I will continue to bear this life. It has gone on too long; the nerves no longer hold out.' And she added: 'I will let you hear from me as long as I can, but that cannot last very much longer.'[23] Indeed it did not: Henriette was deported to Theresienstadt on 13 July 1942 and from there to Treblinka on 19 October 1942, where she was murdered.

Those who escaped this fate were extremely lucky or, like Hans Neumann, both lucky and courageous. Judging his best chance of evading the deportations from Prague to be to deposit himself in the lions' den, Hans took the train to Berlin with false papers in May 1943 and there, disguised as the Aryan Czech Jan Šebesta, found work as a paint technician at a firm supplying the German military, Warnecke & Böhm. With remarkable coolness and hiding in plain sight, Hans realized that the Nazis 'could not recognise their own ridiculousness or indeed appreciate the absurdity of anything. Without imagination they were predictable. This realisation enabled me to take calculated risks. I figured that by acting in an unexpected manner or in any way that ran contrary to their expectations, I could increase my chances of survival.'[24] He survived the war and built a new life for himself after it in Venezuela.

The War and the Holocaust

A realistic assessment of the war would have concluded as early as the end of 1941 that the Nazis' failure to take Moscow before the onset of winter meant a protracted and difficult war. Even though Wehrmacht officials knew that the plan for German soldiers to feed themselves off the land made their survival much harder given the likelihood of that failure, and despite the fact that German military strategists could have predicted at the same time that, especially once the US had entered the war in December 1941, the Germans were outpowered and outnumbered in terms of materiel and troops, self-deception and 'thinking with the blood' remained the rule. The true believers simply could not contemplate anything other than a German victory. And it was a victory based on unlimited cruelty: the German leadership 'viewed the bombing of cities and the starvation of the civilian population as war aims in themselves', writes one historian, who then adds: 'This destructive energy was directed in particular against the Jews.'[25] In 1942, for example, the Heidelberg political scientist Giselher Wirsing argued that it was now impossible for Russia to revive and become a threat to German domination in Europe, and that Roosevelt's dream of 'Anglo-Saxon world domination under American leadership' was equally unrealizable since it would require defeating not only German-dominated Europe but also the Japanese–Far Eastern power bloc: 'A vast German-European sphere of control now stretches from the Atlantic Ocean to the near shores of the Caspian Sea, with truly inexhaustible and mutually complementary economic riches.'[26] Even in 1942, the height of the Nazi domination of the continent, when the Allies were hard pressed, such statements were absurd. At the end of the war, when instructional texts paraded 'our strongest weapon – our fanatical belief in victory', the surreal nature of this Nazi faith which continued to perpetrate very real horrors until the last moment was crystal clear.[27]

This fanaticism suggests that the Second World War should not be regarded as a typical military conflict, a fight for control of territory or trade or the assertion of might in a regional power struggle. It was rather, from the Nazis' perspective, a philosophical struggle, a fight for racial life or death, a *Vernichtungskrieg*: a war of annihilation.[28] For the Nazis, the invasion of the Soviet Union meant the opportunity to acquire

Lebensraum, as Hitler had set out in *Mein Kampf*. Hitler said that he would provide a definition of *Lebensraum* after the war: 'When this war is over we want to be masters of Europe ... Then at last we will belong to the "have" nations, we will possess raw materials and then we will have a large colonial empire.'[29] By which he meant a large colonial empire *in Europe*. But inseparable from this aspiration, and from the understanding of the nature of the Soviet system which accompanied it, was a belief in the need to eradicate the Jews. Acquiring living space in Russia meant defeating communism, and since communism was in their eyes a Jewish creation, the war aims had to include 'defeating' the Jews. The murder of Europe's Jews developed on an ad hoc basis, as numerous historians have shown.[30] But even if the Nazis' original plan was to defeat the USSR and then to deport the European Jews somewhere 'east of the Urals', there was always a planned reckoning with the Jews of one sort or another. This was so not because hatred and fear of communism led to a hatred and fear of Jews, but vice-versa. It was the desire to eradicate 'the Jew' which led the Nazis to aim to destroy 'Judaeo-Bolshevism.'

In this crusade, the SS was by no means the sole agency which attacked Jews. Historians have long since demolished the notion, so popular for many years after the war, especially in West Germany, of the 'clean Wehrmacht', and today no serious historian disputes the fact that ordinary soldiers and policemen, as well as many other agencies, were involved in killing Jews. Before the war, the military's leaders made it clear that the Wehrmacht would be involved. Field Marshal von Reichenau set out the following in his 'orders for conduct in the East':

The fear of German countermeasures must be stronger than the threats of the wandering Bolshevistic remnants. Regardless of all future political considerations, the soldier has to fulfil two tasks:

1. Complete annihilation of the false Bolshevist doctrine of the Soviet state and its armed forces.
2. The pitiless extermination of foreign treachery and cruelty and thus the protection of the lives of military personnel in Russia.

This is the only way to fulfil our historic task to liberate the German people once and for all from the Asiatic-Jewish danger.[31]

And shortly before the invasion, OKW, the army high command, issued the following 'directives for the behaviour of the troops in Russia', which is especially noteworthy for being issued not to special forces such as the SS but to the regular army:

1. Bolshevism is the deadly enemy of the National Socialist German people. Germany's struggle is directed against this subversive ideology and its functionaries.
2. This struggle requires ruthless and energetic action against Bolshevik agitators, guerrillas, saboteurs, and Jews, and the total elimination of all active or passive resistance.[32]

The stage was set for mass murder way beyond anything required from a strictly military-strategic standpoint.

Eastern Europe

These apocalyptic aspects of Nazi thinking soon manifested themselves in the treatment of the Jews in Eastern Europe. Regarding the Soviet Union as the kernel of Judaeo-Bolshevism, the Nazis saw the Jews who lived there as dangerous natives. Thus, while they represented an all-powerful global conspiracy on the one hand, the Nazis subjected the Eastern European Jews to the sort of colonial treatment experienced by 'inferior races' in the European overseas empires. The unrelenting ferocity with which the Nazis treated the Jews in Eastern Europe is a result, therefore, of 'the fact that the Nazis viewed them as natives in the classical colonial sense and as pernicious colonizers of supposed ancestral German land. The Jew thereby incarnated both the native other and the colonizing other, combining contempt and fear in a lethal cocktail.'[33]

The drive to eliminate the Jews also helps to explain how so many disparate agencies and groups – from the civil service to the military to the SS, and many others besides, such as nurses, teachers and farmers – could come together: 'Antisemitism was a unifying force among divergent Nazi colonizer groups, each of which pursued its own variant of the colonial mission of building *Lebensraum* in the East.'[34] In light of the notion, put forward by historian Dirk Moses, that the genocide of the Jews was – from the Nazis' perspective – a subaltern genocide, that is to say, an act carried out to free Germany from colonial subjugation by the Jews, carried out by a 'national liberation movement', the idea that Eastern European Jews could be both regarded as primitive and feared as master manipulators of global affairs does seem to account for the viciousness with which they were attacked.[35]

That viciousness was nowhere instantiated more clearly than in the actions of the SS's *Einsatzgruppen*, the four action squads, comprising no more than 3,000 men in total, which followed behind the Wehrmacht as it advanced, and carried out a first sweep of face-to-face shootings of Jews across the whole region, from the Baltic in the north to the Black Sea in the south.

On 5 October 1941, the police secretary Walter Mattner, an administrator in the SS and police headquarters in Mogilev, described his participation in mass murder in a letter to his wife:

> One more thing I have to write to you. I was actually also there the other day in the big mass death. With the first truckload my hand shook somewhat as I shot, but one gets used to it. At the tenth truckload, I already aimed calmly and shot straight at the numerous women, children and infants. I was mindful that I also have two infants at home who would have been treated by this horde exactly the same, if not ten times worse . . . Infants flew through the air in high arches, and we did them in already in midair before they [fell] into the pit and into the water . . . Hitler's words are becoming true when he said at the beginning of the war: if Judaism thinks to instigate another war in Europe, then this war will not be its victory but the end of Judaism in Europe . . . Mogilev lost again [Jews equal to] a number with three zeroes, but this is not a big thing here. I am actually happy, and many

here say, that when we are back in the Heimat it will be the turn of our local Jews.[36]

One wonders what it would mean to treat people ten times worse than this, for it is not a description of military necessity or the ordinary killing of enemy combatants. A combination of indoctrination, a routinized brutalization and a sense of obligation to comrades, superiors and the nation facilitated turning family men into mass murderers.

In fact, it is not hard to find out what Mattner's words meant for the victims. Long after the war, one of Nobel Prize–winning Svetlana Alexievich's interviewees broke down as she described what had happened in Belarus:

> We started living under German rule . . . There were a lot of Jews in our village: Avram, Yankel, Morduch . . . They rounded them all up and took them out to the *shtetl*. They'd brought their pillows and blankets, but they were all killed right away. They rounded up every Jew in the district and shot them all in a single day. Tossed them into a pit . . . thousands of them . . . Thousands . . . People said that for three days afterwards, their blood kept rising to the top of the pit . . . Like the ground was breathing . . . it was alive . . . Now there's a park there. A place of recreation. You can't hear anyone from beyond the grave. No one can scream . . . So, that's what I think . . . [*she cries*].[37]

The savagery of the war in Belarus has still not properly registered in the English-speaking world. Very far from exemplifying what people think of as the Holocaust – mass murder in gas chambers – the local killing in Belarus exemplifies better

121

the Nazis' utter disdain for what they regarded as a backward and primitive region, akin perhaps to how the Belgian colonial regime thought of the Congo. Another of Alexievich's interviewees discusses the Minsk ghetto and what the war meant for Jews directly. Miraculously surviving the shooting of the Jews of the ghetto – the Germans 'tossed all the little kids into one of the pits' and 'looked down into the pit and laughed' – and being allowed to run off by the man who found him, the unnamed interviewee describes the brutality of the partisans with whom he found sanctuary and then hiding from the Germans in the forest. 'One night,' he says, 'three of us were left behind as the rear guard. We cut open the belly of a dead horse, tossed everything out of it, and climbed in.' After two days, they 'climbed out, covered in blood, guts, and shit . . . half-insane.' After the war, at the age of fifteen, he was unable to talk about what had happened as he faced prejudice that was impossible to complain about openly in the Soviet Union when those who had stolen his family's apartment had 'gotten used to the idea that us Jews were gone for good . . .'[38]

At the start of the war, Himmler created the four *Einsatzgruppen*, which accompanied the Wehrmacht and massacred Jewish populations in each place the army occupied. Formed from SS members and led by fanatical Nazis, notably with theologians and lawyers among them (Walter Stahlecker, head of Einsatzgruppe A, had a doctorate in jurisprudence, as did Hermann Hubig, commander of *Einsatzkommando* 1b and Walter Blume, commander of *Sonderkommando* 7a), these 3,000 men were responsible for killing some 1.5 million Jews in two sweeps in the first year of the war. In a huge arc from north to south, these men proved, in Paul Celan's famous words, that death was a master from Germany. They were not, however, alone. After many years in which the ordinary soldiers of the Wehrmacht and police battalions were depicted as untainted by the SS's criminal actions, it is now beyond dispute that the number of men (and some women) involved in perpetrating mass murder by shooting and other atrocities on the eastern front in the early stages of the war in the Soviet Union was huge.

The most important such units were the Order Police (Ordnungspolizei, or Orpo), which comprised the forces required for regular law enforcement such as fire brigades and the coastguard. Although by 1941 they were – like all German police agencies – under the control of Himmler's RSHA, they were not part of the SS, although they were led by SS men. Under the leadership of Kurt Daluege, the Orpo was militarized and made ready for the war in the Soviet Union. As Christopher Browning showed in his path-breaking book *Ordinary Men* (1991), even the least likely among them, like a group of middle-aged policemen from 'red' Hamburg, rapidly turned into hardened killers. Furthermore, as other historians have shown since, their numbers were far greater than those of the *Einsatzgruppen* and thus, as the backbone of the killing operations, they killed more people than the *Einsatzgruppen*. Even more remarkable, they exemplify the process whereby ordinary men became killers quickly and with apparent ease.[39]

That a majority of soldiers and policemen trod this path was not simply a result of a culture of comradeship or a sense of peer pressure. These situational factors were important, but behind them stood a tacit ideological framework, one which did not always need to be articulated because it was widely understood. Numerous texts instructed the SS that the war against the Soviet Union was 'a war of world views' which required the Germans, as 'Europe's leading Volk' to destroy the 'world enemy', the Jews.[40] The leadership of the Wehrmacht – not the SS, it is worth repeating – clearly felt after a certain point that such words no longer needed to be said. A command issued in 1938 set out the purpose of ideological education for the troops: 'It is a given that the officer, in every situation, acts according to the ideology of the Third Reich, and furthermore, does so when such ideologies are not explicitly expressed in official regulations and decrees or in orders while on active duty.'[41] Murdering Jews was simply understood. Nevertheless, when mass murder became policy, this was sometimes communicated directly and in a simple language that surprises those who think that the Nazis dealt only in euphemisms. In December 1941, the Order Police's training journal spoke frankly:

> The word of the Führer [in his speech of 30 January 1939] that a new war, instigated by Jewry, will not bring about the destruction of antisemitic Germany but rather the end of Jewry, is now being carried out. The gigantic spaces of the east, which Germany and Europe have now at their disposition for colonization, also facilitate the definitive solution of the Jewish problem in the near future. This means not only removing the race of parasites from power but its elimination [*Ausrottung*] from the family of

European peoples. What seemed impossible only two years ago, now step-by-step is becoming a reality: the end of the war will see a Europe free of Jews.[42]

The men involved had, despite what they usually claimed after the war, the choice not to participate in the shootings. In a cross-examination of 1962, one former member of *Einsatzkommando* 3, known only as Friedrich W., made this plain:

> At one of the executions in Minsk in which I took part, Kommando leader Dr Bradfisch gave a speech. Among other things, he stated in it: we have been stationed here on the orders of the Reich Main Security Office [RSHA], so as to fulfil the Führer's order to annihilate the Jews [*um auf Führerbefehl die Juden zu vernichten*]. This would be a hard task but we could not oppose the order. However, anyone who could not reconcile taking part in the shootings with his conscience should report to him. He would understand. No one should feel burdened by taking part since – as the Führer had said – the Jews should no longer be regarded as human beings. This speech was familiar to all members of the Kommando.[43]

Nor were German policemen the only non-SS to take part in the killings. Across the occupied areas of the western Soviet Union, local collaborators willingly took part. Some did so out of hatred for the Jews, wrapped up in the anti-communist belief in 'Judaeo-Bolshevism' – though again, it should be stressed that this was a form of antisemitism first and foremost, since one did not need to hate Jews to be an anti-communist, but the combination of these two hatreds

made a ferocious synthesis. One of the most famous examples is the so-called 'death dealer of Kaunas', who beat Jews
with an iron rod in Kaunas as onlookers stood and watched
the rivers of blood run higher. The report of an astonished
German soldier who photographed the scene is instructive:

> A young man – he must have been a Lithuanian – . . . with
> rolled-up sleeves was armed with an iron crowbar. He
> dragged out one man at a time from the group and struck
> him with the crowbar with one or more blows on the back
> of his head. Within three-quarters of an hour he had beaten
> to death the entire group of forty-five to fifty people in this
> way . . . The behaviour of the civilians present (women and
> children) was unbelievable. After each man had been killed
> they began to clap and when the national anthem started
> up they joined in singing and clapping.[44]

Others did so out of avarice, a sense that, since they owed no
social obligation to the Jews, their removal was an opportunity for self-enrichment, even if of the most meagre sort. As
the Polish journalist Kazimierz Sakowicz noted: 'For the Germans 300 Jews are 300 enemies of humanity; for the Lithuanians, they are 300 pairs of shoes, trousers, and the like.'[45]

Whatever the reason, the end result was the same. And it
involved the same brutality, whether the killers were German
or Lithuanian, whether the Jews were shot into shallow
graves or beaten to death in town squares. Over a two-year
period, Sakowicz documented the murder of the Lithuanian
Jews on the outskirts of the town of Ponary, where they were
shot into huge pits. At the beginning of September 1941, for

example, he records the murder of some 4,000 Jews, 'exclusively women and many babies', shot by drunk Lithuanian collaborators. Men were in fact shot too, but the high number of women and children in this shooting was a result of the fact that many of the Jewish men of Vilnius had already been murdered. This *Aktion* was carried out ostensibly in reprisal for an attack on two German soldiers in Vilnius; neither was injured but the opportunity presented itself for the Germans, in Sakowicz's words, to carry out 'a punishment for the bogus shooting at German soldiers'. His description reveals the intricate connection between German-inspired mass murder, locally directed ethnic hatreds and the local economy: 'The way they shot, the group stood on the corpses. They walked on the bodies! . . . On September 3 and 4 there was a brisk business in women's clothes!'[46]

A sense of the shocking nature of the face-to-face killings carried out by the *Einsatzgruppen* and the Orpo cannot be found in the reports sent to Berlin on a daily basis from the front. These are bureaucratic, emotionless, statistical summaries, couched in a self-exculpatory and occluding language which thinly disguises the transgressive exudation of the mass murders with 'rational' excuses such as 'security measures'.[47] By contrast, the testimonies of witnesses and survivors are explosive in their ability to render the scene. In Tłuste in eastern Galicia (today in Ukraine), several murderous 'actions' took place in 1942, witnessed by a local Jewish doctor, Baruch Milch. His descriptions of the murders are blood-curdling, but what follows is even more terrible for understanding the devastation the Nazis wrought:

In the afternoon of May 28, my wife, my brother-in-law, and I went to the Jewish cemetery, following the victims' road to death. We could not cry any more. The path was strewn with photographs, papers, hunks of hair, clothing, pools of blood . . . and empty cartridge cases. Three huge pits in the cemetery loomed over the old graves. There was a pile of bodies on one side, as corpses were still being brought in from the town and the fields. Some people were searching among the heap of bodies for loved ones or friends, and if they identified someone, they dug a fresh grave.

I had no way of knowing in which pit my family was buried. Beside every pit, the murderers had left the bloodstained plank. There were many cartridge cases here, too. I took one for a souvenir. We went home.[48]

Those who survived initial executions and ghettoization in the Soviet Union knew what would happen to them, as surviving letters attest. Sof'ia Ratner wrote to her children from the Vitebsk ghetto on 6 September 1941, saying that 'It would be better to die' than to continue to suffer in the ghetto, and finishing by saying that 'We are still alive. Our ghetto has been surrounded with barbed wire. We are doomed to death by starvation.'[49] From Vinnitsa, Tumer Gonchar wrote to her sons on 15 April 1942, saying: 'There are no words to express our desire and urge to live but, evidently, that is not to be.'[50]

Nazi Germany was certainly responsible for initiating the programme to kill the European Jews, and the killings occurred within this overall framework. But at the local level, the ways in which the killings often took place were quite different from the factory-line extermination associated with the death camps, not least because many locals participated:

> for the Jews living in these East European villages, towns and cities, who had coexisted with their Christian neighbours for centuries, the fact that their acquaintances, colleagues, classmates, and friends had turned against them, hunted them down, or delivered them to the Nazi murderers, meant that they experienced the Holocaust not just as a murderous invasion by a foreign enemy but also as a series of communal massacres in a once familiar but now lethally hostile environment.[51]

Indeed, historian Omer Bartov's example of the town of Buczacz in eastern Galicia (today Buchach in Ukraine) shows how the murder of the Jews was by no means a random, one-off event but part of a long-term cycle of violence that began with the rise of Polish and Ukrainian (or Ruthenian) nationalism during the days of the Austro-Hungarian Empire and worsened in the wake of the First World War, the rise of Zionism, communism and fascism, and the increasingly violent clashes of these mutually exclusive visions for the land that each of the three groups called home.[52]

As well as being local – unlike the Jews of Western and Central Europe, the Jews of Eastern Europe were not deported but were murdered near their homes – the Holocaust in the east was massive.[53] While the image of factory-line genocide still prevails in public understanding, it is easy to forget that vast numbers of people were shot in the utmost brutal and degrading circumstances in close proximity to their homes.

The most famous and shocking of all of these massacres – and the largest single massacre carried out by the Germans in the Holocaust – took place at Babyn Yar (Babi Yar), on the outskirts of Kiev, on 29–30 September 1941. The occasion for the massacre was the series of bombings in Kiev that took place after the German occupation, bombs planted by the NKVD before the Soviet retreat, which killed a number of high-ranking German officers. The Germans – and many Ukrainians – blamed the Jews. They were destined to die sooner or later anyway, and the bombings, with which the Jewish population of course had nothing to do, probably hastened their murder. On 29 September, sections of Einsatzgruppe C, assisted by Ukrainian militia, drove the Jews of Kiev to Babyn Yar, with the route there being guarded by regular Wehrmacht soldiers. When they arrived, the Jews were ordered to undress and then, in an operation lasting two days, they were shot into the ravine. The driver Fritz Höfer reported that he was 'so astonished and dazed by the sight of the twitching blood-smeared bodies that I could not properly register the details' but that he saw how the Jews were forced to lie down in layers to be shot and that then packers, Ukrainian militiamen, would lay the next layer on top to make the killing process easier for the shooters.[54] One of the shooters, Kurt Werner, testified after the war how 'I still recall today the complete terror of the Jews when they first caught sight of the bodies as they reached the top edge of the ravine. Many Jews cried out in terror. It's almost impossible to imagine what nerves of steel it took to carry out that dirty work down there. It was horrible . . .'[55]

At the same time as the Jews of the western Soviet Union were being massacred by the *Einsatzgruppen*, Jewish communities in Bucharest, Zagreb, Belgrade, Transnistria and Bulgarian-occupied Thrace and Macedonia were being attacked too, by indigenous fascist regimes as well as by German forces. In fact, the Bucharest pogrom preceded the invasion of the Soviet Union by five months. Striking in its brutality, it was an intense outburst of violence against the Jews which occurred in the context of the struggle between the Iron Guard (also known as Legionnaires, after the Legion of the Archangel Michael) and the government of Ion Antonescu. The World Jewish Congress reported on the attacks, deeply shocked by the 'sadism and barbarism of the odious acts committed':

> Wild animals bite and kill, but never think of defiling dead bodies, as was the case for all these innocent beings. Tongues cut out, eyes plucked out, fingers and hands chopped off, skin torn from still-living bodies, bodies mistreated, hacked and wounded, hung on slaughterhouse hooks with a label attached marked 'kosher', heads cut off, and organs torn out – this is the balance sheet of the Legionnaires' heroism.[56]

About 120 Jews were killed in the Bucharest pogrom, including 79 who were shot in the forests of Jilava, having been taken there by truck from the Romanian capital.[57]

In Croatia, under the Nazis' ally Ante Pavelić, head of the Independent State of Croatia, Jews were harassed and dispossessed, and quickly deported to camps run not by Germans but by Croats. As one report, aiming to summarize the rapid onset of the persecution of Croatia's Jews, noted:

'Trustees' were installed in Jewish firms and shops;
the Jews had to leave their homes; all of their property,
first the movable goods and then the real property, was
confiscated; the deportation of the Jews to the camps
began. Numerous Jews were shot in Maksimir Park, in the
eastern part of town. The only possible means of escape
was leaving the country immediately or fleeing to one of
the Italian-occupied areas of Yugoslavia. Robbed of all their
possessions, even these refugees were usually unable to
escape with anything but the clothes on their backs.[58]

It is easy to add atrocity story to atrocity story when recounting the history of the *Einsatzgruppen* and the early phase of the Holocaust. It is harder to reflect on what it means. As Saul Friedländer notes, 'There is something at once profoundly disturbing yet rapidly numbing in the narration of the anti-Jewish campaign that developed in the territories newly occupied by the Germans or their allies. History seems to turn into a succession of mass killing operations and, on the face of it, little else.'[59] Extending the scope of the story beyond Germany and France to encompass places such as Romania, Greece or Croatia, which are rarely brought into mainstream narrative accounts of the Holocaust, only adds further accounts of atrocity. Even if one does not rely only on sources created by perpetrators or, as in Sakowicz's case, bystanders (albeit someone who ran a considerable risk by documenting the crimes he witnessed), and even if one makes use of reports produced by Jewish aid organizations, one is left with a harrowingly repetitive sequence of stories of persecution, dispossession and murder. These sources need to be supplemented by others which can give us some sense of how the victims experienced what was happening to them.

In the Łódź ghetto, Irene Hauser wrote in her diary of the reaction of the ghetto's inhabitants to the deportations in September 1942:

> At 4am the roundup of children continues with help from the military, since it was going too slowly . . . let's just rely on God, no people can help us because there are none. Since 6am they've been standing and waiting for bread in spite of the curfew and shop closures, nobody's at work and we are a hundred thousand cowardly people and don't move a muscle.[60]

Attempting to hide in the fields near Buczacz, Aryeh Klonicki wrote in his diary of the hopelessness of his and his wife's situation:

> All the odds are against us. Is there any hope for us to continue living without money, surrounded by robbers? To the peasant the Jew is not a human being, but merely a source from which to extract money and valuables. All our efforts are in vain, I feel, and there is little sense in continuing our struggle for existence.[61]

And in the ghetto of Djurin in Transnistria, nineteen-year-old Mirjam Korber wrote in her diary of how she was losing the will to continue: 'What I write is pointless. None will read, and I, if I survive this, will be more than happy to throw into the fire everything regarding the cursed time I spent in Djurin.' Five months later, she again wrote of her 'lethargy' and called on Providence to explain the hardships to which she and her family had been condemned: 'For what sins this punishment? For what fault? The uncertainty with which we live is harsher than any death sentence.'[62]

Most of these letters and reflections are encompassed by the statement of Anna Grasberg-Górna, writing from the Warsaw ghetto to a friend, Maria, in September 1942. The latter was sheltering Anna's infant daughter Erika and, following the decision that women would no longer be allowed to work at the factory in the ghetto where she had been working, she now asked for help with finding a place for her to hide on the Aryan side so that she could be with her daughter: 'We have nothing to lose. Would you or one of your relatives or friends be able to help me, or rather us? For, ultimately, what will become of a child of such tender age who is deprived of a mother? And one would so very much like to live a little bit longer.'[63]

Yet, even if we can show that, to a greater or lesser extent, the Nazis' victims were able to comprehend and articulate what was happening to them, they remained in despair. No doubt it is right to say that there is something numbing about recounting a seemingly endless sequence of atrocities; it is also a reflection of what happened, leaving the victims numb. And sometimes it is important to tarry with a tiny atrocity – tiny in the grand scale of the murders but the whole world to those who were affected. In Baruch Milch's account of his time in hiding with his wife, sister, brother-in-law and their son during the war, he recounts how, when the noise made by the nine-year-old boy Lunek led to the group being threatened with expulsion by the man hiding them, his father strangled him. The description is matter-of-fact:

We all sat down again, withdrawn into ourselves, and Lunek went wild again. Unable to calm him, we thought we would go mad. Suddenly, as though struck by lightning, my brother-in-law bolted from his seat and wrapped a hand around his son's tender neck as if to stifle his cries. Instead, the boy's eyes rolled in their sockets, his tongue protruded, and he fell silent. His father knew exactly where to squeeze; he, like me, was a doctor . . . When he finally let go of his son's throat, the boy was lifeless. I took his hand and felt no pulse. His father left him, covered his son's face with a blanket, seated himself in a corner, and began to tear his hair. 'I am forever accursed as the murderer of my son,' he mumbled, 'but I spared him much more suffering. At least I didn't let him die at the hands of the murderers.'[64]

The Turn West – and Back East

Although Himmler's initial aim had been to 'comb' Europe from west to east (as Heydrich expressed it at the Wannsee Conference), in fact the mass murder of the Jews began in the east and then spread to the west. By the time the process of deporting Jews had started in Western Europe, the Final Solution, as opposed to the local or regional solutions imposed on the Jews of the Soviet Union or Poland, was largely in place. And like the Jews of the ghettos in Poland, headed by their beleaguered Jewish councils, the Jewish councils in Vienna and elsewhere in Central and Western Europe were put in positions of authority by the Nazis but were without power of their own.

By the spring of 1942 the Final Solution was in place. Before that point, the *Einsatzgruppen* had killed well over a million Jews in the Soviet Union; Jews from the Reich were deported to Riga in November 1941; the first mass killings by gas had begun at Chełmno, and construction had started on the death camp at Bełżec in December 1941. On 23 October 1941, the Nazis forbade all emigration of Jews from occupied Europe and around the same time, the first experimental gassings of Soviet POWs took place at Auschwitz. Whatever the precise order of the decision-making process, it is clear that by the end of 1941 the Nazis were working towards a comprehensive plan of mass murder.[65]

For all the detail that historians have added since – for example with respect to the creation of the Reinhard camps, the link between the euthanasia programme and the killing of the Jews or the role played by local planners in occupied Eastern Europe – it seems clear that the Nazis were turning localized mass killings into a continent-wide genocide by the end of 1941. The direction of travel was clear; following the initial success of Operation Barbarossa, Hitler gave the go-ahead for the first deportations from the Reich and from the Protectorate, and Goering transferred his control over Jewish policies to Heydrich, in his 31 July 1941 authorization, where he wrote: 'I hereby charge you with making all necessary preparations in regard to organisational and financial matters for bringing about a total solution of the Jewish question in the German sphere of influence in Europe', a letter which was perhaps written to save face, as de facto recognition of the SS's unstoppable rise to prominence.[66] Nowhere is this process clearer to see than in the infamous Wannsee Conference.

It took place in a beautiful villa along the shores of the Wannsee just outside Berlin on 20 January 1942, having been postponed from 9 December 1941 because of the Japanese attack on Pearl Harbor and the entry of the Americans into the war. It was chaired by Heydrich, with his deputy Eichmann taking the minutes, and sitting around the conference table were fifteen senior officials representing most of Nazi Germany's important ministries and RSHA agencies. Friedländer argued that at Wannsee Heydrich presented the outline of the Final Solution to the invited representatives of various ministries and SS agencies and that the 'establishment of extermination camps in the General Government in the following months eliminates any possible remaining doubt or vagueness about what was meant at Wannsee'.[67] His claim has since been backed up many times by historians who agree that the 'main purpose of the Wannsee Conference . . . was to provide notice that the SS, under the leadership of Reinhard Heydrich and Heinrich Himmler, intended to organize deportations on a European-wide scale'.[68]

Nevertheless, the precise role played by the Wannsee Conference remains disputed. Clearly it cannot have been the site where the Final Solution was decided upon, as historians sometimes used to claim; that makes no sense in the context of a narrative which maintains that the Nazis had always intended to kill the Jews and it seems especially unlikely given that neither Himmler nor Hitler was present. Furthermore, as some of the SS representatives who had arrived fresh from the Baltic states were happy to confirm, they had already begun making 'their' regions free of Jews (*judenrein*), Estonia and Latvia especially. It seems much more likely that the meeting was partly about coordination but primarily about stamping the SS's control on Jewish policy and creating a situation whereby other agencies, especially those belonging to the state (the civil service) rather than the Nazi Party, would be rendered complicit in the project. In the words of Mark Roseman, author of the standard work on the Wannsee Conference, the meeting 'was part of a concerted, coordinated campaign by Himmler and Heydrich to assert their supremacy'. The latter's 'major aim' was 'to achieve unity and common purpose among the participants, and above all to secure acceptance of the RSHA's leading role'.[69] This explanation seems much more persuasive when one considers that the discussion was short on detail and focused more on general principles and grandiose aspirations, with the only detailed discussion being reserved for the 'problem' of how to deal with different grades of *Mischlinge*.[70]

The reason why Wannsee was long thought of as the moment when the Final Solution was launched is largely serendipitous: the discovery of the one surviving copy of the record, or 'protocol' of the meeting – which the recipients had been instructed to destroy – by Robert Kempner, a former German-Jewish lawyer and civil servant, in 1947, when he was working as US assistant chief counsel in the Nuremberg trials. The document is, as Roseman says, 'probably the closest the Nazis ever came to writing down their overall plan of genocide'.[71] In that sense, the meeting did indeed mark a kind of turning point, from more or less ad hoc mass killings to the systematization of a process which ended in continent-wide genocide. If it was not where the decision was taken but more of an echo of a previously made decision, Wannsee did capture the midway point in the 'transition from quasi-genocidal deportations to a clear programme of murder'.[72] Besides, for all the debate and the euphemisms, 'the genocidal implications were totally and unmistakably clear'.[73] As Eichmann testified at Jerusalem, 'these gentlemen were standing together, or sitting together, and were discussing the subject quite bluntly, quite differently from the language which I had to use later in the record. During the conversation they minced no words about it at all . . . they spoke about methods for killing, about liquidation, about extermination.'[74]

Wannsee is not just important as one of the key moments in the unfolding of the Nazis' genocidal mindset, however. When one pictures the fifteen leading Nazis sitting around the table in the sumptuous villa that Heydrich planned to claim for himself after the war – which we can easily do, as the site is now a museum and the setting of the film *Conspiracy*, one of the few largely convincing historical reconstructions of the Nazi period – it becomes clear that the optics and aesthetics of the meeting were equally significant. The meeting looks, in retrospect, like an exemplary scene in the Nazis' staging of their own myth as the master race. These smug, self-satisfied men, sure of their own superiority, discussed, while being fed fine food and wine, the intricacies of mass murder and the legal problems that arose from them. They laughed and joked, argued and fell into line – and the massive disjunction between their self-performance and the reality of what it all meant is devastating.

Whatever the precise timing, in the months after Wannsee the deportation trains started to roll across Europe. Until then, Jews had been shot in Eastern Europe in huge numbers, they had been gassed in vans in Chełmno, and the Operation Reinhard camps were being readied to receive and kill the Jews of the General Government. Some Jews had been deported from Germany to Minsk, Riga, Izbica and elsewhere, but not in very large numbers and not in a very systematic fashion. Now the Jews of the Protectorate, Slovakia and Western Europe were targeted for deportation and murder, and they would be joined, soon after, by the Jews of Greece, Norway, Croatia and other countries. In Romanian-occupied Transnistria, the vicious brutality of the Iaşi and Bucharest pogroms was being replaced with systematic deportations, if not to death camps in the Nazi fashion (because the Germans refused to take them in autumn 1941), then to death by massive neglect, abandonment to the elements and large-scale massacres. Although Auschwitz was not, as popular memory has it, the place where the majority of the Holocaust's victims were killed, it became the killing centre for Jews from across Europe and, as we will see, the centre of a vast slave labour operation.

By the end of 1941 leading Nazis began to speak openly of what was now a continent-wide programme. On 15 November 1941 Himmler met Rosenberg; three days later, the latter told the German press that 'In the east some six million Jews still live, and this question can only be solved in a biological eradication of the entire Jewry of Europe.' According to Goebbels, at a meeting on 12 December 1941 in his private apartment in Berlin, Hitler told the assembled Reichsleiter and Gauleiter (i.e. some of the regime's leading officials) that 'The world war is here, the destruction of the Jews must be the inevitable consequence.' And Hans Frank, the Governor General, told his underlings on 16 December that 'We must put an end to the Jews, that I want to say quite openly . . . Gentlemen, I must ask you, arm yourselves against any thoughts of compassion. We must destroy the Jews, wherever we encounter them and wherever it is possible, in order to preserve the entire structure of the Reich.'[75]

In this process, we see for the first time the vital role played by the cooperation of the Nazis' allies. In Eastern Europe, huge numbers of Ukrainians, Lithuanians and Latvians took part in the killing of Jews carried out by the *Einsatzgruppen*, as the Nazis rapidly created auxiliary police forces from the local populations. These Hiwis (*Hilfswillige*, or volunteers), as they were known, played an essential role in not only identifying Jews but in murdering them too. Many men from these countries went on to become camp guards, especially the infamous Trawniki men, named after the training camp where they were brought into the perpetrator fold.[76] Over the year 1942, the number of locals in the occupied Soviet territories (Ukraine, Belarus and the Baltic states) recruited to work under the Order Police rose nearly tenfold, from 33,000 to about 300,000.[77] A little later, faced with the choice of signing up or dying an agonizing death through starvation in Nazi captivity, some 800,000 Russians joined the so-called Vlasov Army and fought on the side of the Wehrmacht, mostly as cannon-fodder. The auxiliaries, in the words of one historian, provided proof that with minimal German input the Third Reich could realize its 'destiny': the Trawniki men 'not only served as foot soldiers of the Final Solution; they also represented prototypes for the enforcers of the world that the Nazis intended to construct'.[78]

Western Europe, however, was not unimportant in this process. It is not simply the case that the killings began in the east and then spread to the west. Rather, the deportations of

Jews from Western Europe were undertaken in the full knowledge of the killings in the east, while the latter were still ongoing. In other words, the decision-making process for the Final Solution was shaped by the occupation of Western Europe too. The postwar statement given by Eichmann's deputy Dieter Wisliceny, for example, indicates that Western Europe was always conceived of as part of the final solution.[79] Werner Best, formerly Heydrich's representative and legal adviser to the SS and then head of the SD in France between 1940 and 1942 before becoming German Commissioner in Denmark, remarked in March 1941 – the date is worth stressing – that 'Germany's interest lies in progressively relieving all European countries from Jewry with a goal of a completely Jew-free Europe.'[80] The rapid intensification of the killings in Eastern Europe gave the green light to those in the occupied west who favoured radical action. Otto Abetz, for example, the German ambassador in Paris, argued to Himmler in September 1941 that lack of space for arrested Jews – in fact, a lack which the Nazis contrived – meant that the Jews should be transported from France to the east, a request to which Himmler eagerly agreed.[81] There were, in other words, processes at work in the countries of occupied Western Europe which fed the radicalizing dynamic of the unfolding Final Solution, processes which paralleled and fed off those occurring in the 'wild east'.

In Western Europe, the extent of collaboration varied from country to country and depended on the nature of the occupation regime imposed locally by the Germans. In the Netherlands, where the penetration of the SS was deep, in a country with a topography which hardly facilitated hiding, and where the Jewish population was heavily concentrated in one city, Amsterdam, in a few districts there the death rate was 75 per cent – far higher than in France, where the proportion of Jews killed was 25 per cent. Yet in Marshal Pétain's Vichy, France had a regime which was not only collaborationist but eager to show its devotion to the Nazis' antisemitic agenda by taking the initiative on anti-Jewish legislation. In October 1940 Vichy introduced the first Statut des Juifs, defining in strict terms who was a Jew, and in spring 1941 it created the Commissariat Général aux Questions Juives (CGQJ) in order to deal with the 'Jewish problem' in France. As Debórah Dwork and Robert Jan Van Pelt write:

> the Jews in France . . . both native-born and refugee,
> believed that French authorities would seek to safeguard
> them. France was the country of the Rights of Man, of
> asylum, of *liberté, égalité, fraternité*. Those were the founding
> principles of the state. Jews who had fled to France from
> the Nazi regime elsewhere in Europe trusted in the national
> promise of protection. They were utterly betrayed.[82]

Nevertheless, and as we will see in the next chapter, the Pétain regime baulked at deporting French citizens with the result that, when pressed to do so by the Germans in September 1942, as it had previously agreed to do, it held firm. Only a small percentage of the 75,000 Jews deported from France were French citizens, which hardly speaks well for the 'country of asylum' but which does show that genocide is complex and that thinking of actors in terms of fixed roles cannot capture the fluid nature of such a complicated and shifting reality. Vichy contributed to the failure of the Final Solution in France as well as its initiation.[83] The actions of the Vichy regime demonstrate that where legally recognized states continued to function in Nazi Europe, they could both accede to and resist Nazi demands. They could also, as we will see in more detail in the following chapter, initiate the murder process themselves without being pressurized into doing so by the Germans.

For the victims of these murderous policies, which by the spring of 1942 had ensnared most of the European continent's Jewish communities, the result was disastrous. By that point, the Nazis' Final Solution was in place, and Jews across Europe were marked for death. For the different Jewish populations actually to be captured, deported and murdered, however, required a high degree of collaboration across the continent, as we will see in the next chapter. The precise path to genocide differed from place to place, but in the end the outcome was the same. When Baruch Milch commented at the end of November 1943 that 'I am the walking dead', he knew what he was talking about.[84]

A Continent-wide Crime

'What do a Swiss banker and a Polish peasant have in common? The answer to this question, only a slight exaggeration, would be: a golden tooth extracted from the jaws of a Jewish corpse.'
— Jan Gross[1]

The Holocaust was a continent-wide crime with many perpetrators, not just Germans. 'Collaboration' is a highly loaded term, with its wartime connotations of treason, but it is useful so long as one bears in mind that it should not be seen solely through the lenses of the resistance movements, but also as a form of deliberately decided-on behaviour and action by groups of people with specific aims in mind.[2] Collaboration here means in the first instance countries such as France, Norway, Croatia, Slovakia, Hungary and Romania, where persecuting, expelling and killing Jews fitted with long-held nationalist aspirations to create ethnically homogeneous nation-states, whether these views were widely shared, as in Romania, or whether they marked the ascendancy of a particular anti-liberal tradition, as in France. Collaboration also refers to organizations, from the Organization of Ukrainian Nationalists (OUN) in Ukraine, which allied itself for a time with Nazi Germany in the hope of obtaining a Ukrainian state, to Nazi movements such as Norway's Nasjonal Samling or the Dutch Nationaal-Socialistische Beweging (NSB), ideologically aligned groups which believed in the Nazi vision of a racially cleansed Europe and thought that their national interests were best served in a Europe united under German hegemony. It also meant individuals, such as those who signed up to join the Waffen-SS, from Denmark to Bosnia, as well as Ukrainian and Baltic camp guards and, at a local level, so-called *szmalcowniki* in Poland (those who bribed Jews or who betrayed them to the SS) and, especially in the Eastern European borderlands, the Jews' neighbours and – often – friends who took part in mocking, looting and killing them.[3] As Hannah Arendt wrote just after the end of the war, 'One should not forget that even when it was unmistakably clear that it would mean merely a Europe ruled by Germans, the slogan of a United Europe proved to be the Nazis' most successful propaganda weapon.'[4] The shocking extent of collaboration, which took many forms for different reasons – from ideological affiliation to a simple life-or-death decision for Soviet POWs – has become clearer since the end of the Cold War; the *ressentiment* its discovery has bred is all too clear in revived radical right movements today.

In order to bring some of these issues into sharper focus, it is helpful to look in detail at the Holocaust in Romania and the deportation of the Jews of Hungary in spring 1944, as well as the actions of other states' leaders. This way one can gain a sense of how collaborating states enjoyed considerable freedom of manoeuvre (for example, the common description of the Independent State of Croatia as a puppet state does not reflect Ante Pavelić's Ustaša regime's independent input) and allows one to understand how it was possible for the Nazis to deport Jews across Europe as a whole and beyond, from Norway to Crete, Alderney to the Caucasus, the Baltic states to North Africa. The Holocaust did not only happen where the state was destroyed by the Nazis;[5] Poland is the best example of where this was the case, but Romania shows the opposite, that is, that where the heads of a functioning state want to carry out criminal policies on a huge scale and then to halt them, they will find reasons and resources to do so.

The story is thus complicated by the fact that the killing of the Jews was not simply a German affair conducted in every land they occupied. This description does define quite adequately the murder of the vast majority of the Holocaust's victims, in Poland and the western Soviet Union, during the *Einsatzgruppen* campaign and during Operation Reinhard, even taking into account murders carried out by local collaborators in the Baltic states, which were fewer than the Nazis had hoped. It also describes, to a greater or lesser extent, the Holocaust in Greece, although here too the occupying German forces relied heavily on local assistance to deport the 56,000 Jews of Salonika, Europe's largest Sephardi (and Ladino-speaking) community to fall victim to the Nazis, as well as smaller numbers of Romaniots, that is, older Greek Jewish communities on the islands and elsewhere on the mainland. As in Vichy France, the new collaborationist regime under a group of mutinous officers led by Georgios Tsolakoglou claimed to be representing the will of the people and announced the fact that Greece had a 'Jewish problem'. In September 1941 Tsolakoglou stated that although there was 'no question today of taking legislative measures' against the Jews, it was only 'natural, however, that this question will be definitively solved within the framework of the whole New Order in Europe'.[6] By identifying the Jews of Salonika, who had only become Greek citizens in 1912, as outsiders and different from the Romaniots, the Greek government set them apart in a dangerous way. When the Greeks assisted the German occupiers in enlisting Jewish men for forced labour in 1942, it took a step – registering Jews – which facilitated the isolation of Salonika's Jewish population. When the Germans destroyed the huge Jewish cemetery in Salonika, the result was to drive a wedge even further between the Christian and Jewish populations of the city, paving the way for plunder and looting and, as of spring 1943, the deportation and murder of the Jews. Although the Germans were the prime movers of the whole policy, Greek collaborators assisted. 'It was', summarizes one historian, referring to the persecution of the Jews, 'a political price they were willing to pay and dovetailed with the aim of Hellenizing the border areas.'[7]

Likewise in Bulgaria: although the country is remembered for refusing to surrender 'its' Jews to the Nazis, Bulgarian leaders, in particular Alexander Belev, the head of the Commissariat for Jewish Questions, worked with the Germans to arrange for the deportation of the Jews from occupied Thrace and Yugoslav Macedonia. In March 1943, some 7,144 Jews from Macedonia were rounded up, concentrated in Skopje, and then deported to Treblinka – an action undertaken solely by Bulgarian policemen and other administrators.[8]

On the basis of recent research, rather than a tale of German occupation, deportation and murder in death camps, the Holocaust looks more like a series of interlocking local genocides carried out under the auspices of a grand project. In the English-speaking world we have long been accustomed to the history of the German Jews, even though this group made up no more than a few per cent of the Holocaust's victims. The vast majority of the victims were traditional, observant Jews living in small towns, or shtetls, in Eastern Europe. Many of them remain unknown despite impressive attempts by Yad Vashem in Jerusalem and the United States Holocaust Memorial Museum (USHMM) in Washington, DC, to name as many victims as possible, a consequence of entire communities being wiped out in places such as Belarus, where whole regions – and not just the Jews in them – were destroyed.[9]

One consequence of the Holocaust being narrated in the context of German history – which has long been the tradition among British historians – is that insofar as the victims appear at all, they assume a German character, which was the case for only a small minority. There are good reasons why the genocide of the Jews should be narrated in this way: the Third Reich did other things than kill Jews, and the 'National Socialist Revolution', with its attack on democracy and attempts to reshape German culture and society, precipitated the war which was the context in which the Holocaust took place. Yet an overhaul of the social system was not the Nazis' main aim: 'What mattered to them above all else was race, culture and ideology.'[10] At the same time, while German historians provide a wider context for understanding the Holocaust, they tend – given their expertise and areas of focus – to homogenize the very varied experiences of what should be included under the term Holocaust.

Europe, 1942

German Reich with incorporated territories

Territories under German civil administration

German-occupied territories

Italy/Albania

Italian-occupied territories

Allies of the Axis Power

Finnish-, Romanian-, Hungarian-
and Bulgarian-occupied territories

Neutral and non-belligerent

Soviet Union

Trondh

NORWAY

Bergen

Oslo

NORTHERN
IRELAND

Glasgow

NORTH

SEA

DENMARK

Copenhagen

IRELAND

Dublin

Manchester

GREAT
BRITAIN

NETHERLANDS

Hamburg

Hanover

Ber

London

The Hague

BELGIUM

GERMAN
REICH

ATLANTIC

OCEAN

Brest

Cherbourg

Brussels

Cologne

Leipzig

Paris

Alsace
Lorraine

Luxembourg

Prague

Nantes

Prot. Bohem
and Moravia

English Channel

Berne

Munich

V

Vichy

Lyons

SWITZ.

FRANCE

Milan

Porto

Rhône

Genoa

Zara
(Ital.)

Toulouse

PORTUGAL

Madrid

Barcelona

Marseille

Corsica

ITALY

SPAIN

Rome

Valencia

Sardinia

Seville

Gibraltar (Brit.)

Mediterranean
Sea

Messir

Tangier

Spanish
Morocco

Sicily

Rabat

Oran

Algiers

Tunis

MOROCCO
(French)

ALGERIA
(French)

TUNISIA
(French)

MALT

The problem is not only one of a German-centric focus. It is salutary to be reminded that the Holocaust did not take place in English. Especially for readers of English, who are now exceptionally well served with documentary collections and a vast scholarly and popular literature on the subject, it is easy to forget that very few people involved in any way with the events we now bring together under the name of 'Holocaust' could even read or speak English. From Greece to Estonia, Italy to Ukraine, Hungary to Belgium, historians of the Holocaust in fact have to grapple with a wide range of national settings and traditions, different types of occupation or collaborationist regimes and many different languages. No historian can master all of these languages, but it is worth bearing in mind that what might appear to be a narrow focus on the killing of the Jews – as opposed to setting that genocide in the history of the Third Reich more broadly – is in fact an exercise in European history. And the more that historians uncover the pan-continental scale of the Holocaust, especially when it comes to the movements of refugees and survivors' networks, and explain it as a transnational event, the more complex it becomes. When one factors in the responses of the Allies, the Churches and the neutral countries, and the worldwide movement of Jewish refugees both during and after the war, the Holocaust becomes a major phenomenon in world history.

The historian of the Holocaust Raul Hilberg proposed a simple model of the Holocaust in his seminal 1961 book *The Destruction of the European Jews*. In this scheme, which encompassed the definition, expropriation, concentration and finally extermination of the Jews, the Holocaust unfolded more or less mechanically and in a pre-determined fashion;

as he famously wrote, the destruction of the Jews was 'no accident': 'When in the early days of 1933 the first civil servant wrote the first definition of "non-Aryan" into a civil service ordinance, the fate of European Jewry was sealed.'[11] Hilberg's research remains essential, but we now understand the Holocaust as far messier, with violence characterizing the years 1933–9 more than one would imagine in Hilberg's scheme, far more driven by circumstance, especially military circumstance, and far more dependent on the collaboration of others. This collaboration varied massively depending not just on the nature of the Nazi occupation or the Axis regime in question, but on the complex social relations that pertained in a given area. Bessarabia for example, the area acquired by Romania after the First World War, which is roughly equivalent to today's Republic of Moldova, had been subjected to Romanian state-directed antisemitic policies before the war, with the result that many local inhabitants subsequently took part in the killing of Jews during the war; by contrast, their neighbours in Transnistria, who had experienced – at least in theory – civic equality under Soviet rule, were more reluctant to engage in attacking their Jewish neighbours after June 1941 because they were already accustomed to Jews being treated as equal citizens.[12]

The Holocaust was by no means simply the outcome of top-down German action but also depended on local political, social and economic conditions as well as inter-ethnic relations, all of which could be very complex.[13] In the Eastern European borderlands, relations between Belarusians, Russians, Poles, Ukrainians, Lithuanians and Jews, in the different contexts of Soviet and/or Nazi occupation, shaped local responses to the Nazi persecution of the Jews. In Belgium, death rates of Jews varied widely across the country depending on local circumstances. In Romania, the murder of some communities took place while others were spared thanks to local initiatives, elite interventions and changing state policies. That said, the final outcome – the genocide of the Jews – was, with exceptions such as the non-deportation of the Jews of the Romanian Regat and Banat or of the majority of Jewish French, Danish or Bulgarian citizens, remarkably consistent and homogeneous. As we will see, whether one looks at Thessaloniki, Kishinev or Amsterdam, Lvov, Corfu or Bratislava, local circumstances shaped the way in which the deportation and killing of Jews occurred but rarely had any meaningful effect on whether or not the Jews would be killed:

> the 'Final Solution', as it was known in Nazi terminology, combined the political will of mass murder with organisational and logistical rigidity. If and to what extent it could be implemented in the German-controlled countries and territories was not a matter of determination on the German side, which remained adamant and unrelenting. Rather, the implementation of the 'Final Solution' hinged on political and institutional conditions that the Germans, despite relentless efforts, were not always able to control fully.[14]

They could be helped by willing accomplices and frustrated by recalcitrant ones but the essential German role in initiating, directing and overseeing the process should not be forgotten.

Nor should the bigger context, that is to say, the Nazi

vision of a united Europe, which meant a pacified Europe, racially cleansed of Jews and other undesirables, ideologically coordinated and economically aligned in the interests of German hegemony.[15] This vision required collaborators everywhere across Europe, and the Third Reich found them, albeit they subscribed more or less willingly and not all for the same reasons. In the occupied countries of Western Europe, the Nazis generally aimed to retain some semblance of local autonomy, whereas in occupied Eastern Europe they were more radical, especially in Poland, Belarus and Ukraine, lands they regarded as backward and barbarous, infected with Judaeo-Bolshevism. That did not prevent many individuals and some organizations, such as the Organization of Ukrainian Nationalists (OUN), headed by Stepan Bandera, from working with the Nazis on the basis of their anti-communism and anti-semitism, nor its armed wing, the Ukrainian Insurgent Army (UPA), from taking part in the killing of Poles and Jews on a large scale in Belarus, eastern Galicia and Volhynia.[16] Indeed, it is misleading to think of the Holocaust in Ukraine – as elsewhere – as a solely German affair, when local actors were involved to a considerable degree.[17]

Yet the Nazis' different attitudes towards their conquered states did not always produce the desired results, especially when it came to the murder of the Jews. In the Netherlands, Reich Commissioner Arthur Seyss-Inquart harped on optimistically about the 'common will for order' that the Dutch – an 'Aryan' people – supposedly shared with the Germans, yet far fewer Dutch volunteered for the German armed forces than either the Nazis or the local Dutch fascists, the NSB, expected.[18] But when it came to the Jews, the percentage of

Dutch Jews deported and killed was, at 75 per cent (*c.*104,000 people) the highest in Western Europe, comparable to the Eastern European countries and a much higher death rate (as a percentage of the Jewish population) than for Germany. The reasons are many: the high concentration of the Jews in Amsterdam, the lack of hiding places in a small, flat country, the extent of SS penetration in the country, which was deeper than in France or Belgium, the obedience of the *Joodse Raad,* or Jewish Council.[19] Above all, however, the German 'success' at deporting the Dutch Jews was a result of the 'professional' functioning of the Dutch civil service, that is to say, its employees' willingness to fulfil the tasks they were set without considering the moral implications of their actions. Without the civil service's continued functioning, it would have been far harder for the German occupiers to round up the Jews.[20] No wonder that Dutch civil servants were the group perhaps most vociferously averse to the postwar purges, arguing that they had merely done their duty, and that 'their only fault was that they had taken pride in their administrative duties'.[21] In Norway, despite considerable resistance to Nazi rule – again, a surprise to the Germans, who considered the Norwegians 'kindred racial stock' – the arrest and deportation of the country's small Jewish population took place swiftly, with few escapes. On 26 November 1942, for example, 532 Jews in Oslo were rounded up not by Germans but by Norwegian plain-clothes policemen, who drove them in taxis to Oslo harbour, where they were put on board a German ship, the *Donau,* sailed to Germany and then sent by freight train to Auschwitz. Most were gassed on arrival.[22]

Nazi Germany's allies were no more predictable. In the

case of Vichy France, 'the very same actors who radicalised the persecution of the Jews a short time later went on to contain it'.[23] In Italian-occupied south-eastern France the same was true; here the deportations were blocked by the Italians 'not despite the fact but precisely because fascist Italy was Hitler's closest ally'.[24] In other words, where Nazi Germany's allies decided not to cooperate with the plans to murder the Jews, the Nazi authorities yielded, on the basis that a temporary delay to their plans could be tolerated in the larger interest of maintaining the Axis. They assumed that, with German domination complete after the war, these postponed actions could be implemented later. These events did not result from capricious decision-making on the part of the actors involved, but from 'rational political strategies that led to compromises':

> The German side was willing to make concessions
> when it came to French gains in prestige in questions of
> administrative competences and political symbolism, and
> the French side was willing to make concessions when such
> gains could only be had at the cost of supporting the aims
> of the German occupation policy. The Germans defined the
> 'Final Solution' as such an aim.[25]

Thus, however powerful the French antisemitic ideologues were, to take another example, their freedom to manoeuvre was circumscribed by the larger framework of collaboration and the need to maintain the delicate balance between the French elites, the Wehrmacht and the SS. When important figures in the French clergy spoke out against the deportations, this equilibrium was disturbed. The same figures in the Catholic establishment who had supported Pétain and the persecution of the

Jews now reversed course; the effect was to force the Vichy regime to roll back its approval for the planned revocation of Jews' citizenship (those who had been naturalized as French since 1927) and thus to put the Nazis' plans on hold.

The most prominent person to speak out against the deportations was Archbishop Jules-Géraud Saliège. Deportations began in France following the round-ups of July 1942 and the herding of the Jews in the infamous Vélodrome d'Hiver (Vel' d'Hiv, or Winter Velodrome) near the Eiffel Tower or in the makeshift transit camp set up in a former housing project at Drancy, near Paris, before being transported to their deaths, mostly in Auschwitz. Saliège's pastoral letter was read from the pulpits of most of the churches in Toulouse on 23 August 1942 and included the following key passage:

> There is a Christian morality and there is a human morality that imposes duties on us and recognises rights. These rights and duties correspond to human nature. They come from God. One can violate them but no mortal has the right to suppress them. That children, women, men, fathers, and mothers are being treated like a herd of cattle and are being carted away to an unknown destination – it has been reserved for our era to witness this sad spectacle . . . The Jews are men and women, just as the foreigners are men and women. One cannot do anything one pleases to these men, to these women, to these fathers and mothers. They also belong to the human race; they are as much our brothers as the others. A Christian must not forget this.[26]

By impugning Pétain's moral authority as the head of a Catholic, conservative regime – even though he did not regard it as a personal attack on Pétain – Saliège, one of the pillars of the regime, effectively torpedoed Vichy's continued collaboration in the murder of the Jews.[27] The mass round-ups 'were the clearest indication that the term "Free" was illusory when applied to the Unoccupied Zone' – they were 'the price Vichy paid for an appearance of sovereignty'.[28] By the same token, the reversal of course was tolerated by the German occupiers for the same reason: to maintain the illusion of French sovereignty. It remains the case that this reversal 'brings no credit to Vichy France'. Indeed, 'It is misleading to ask why three-quarters of the Jews of France survived the German occupation. Given the many opportunities for protection and escape, we must ask rather why so many perished.'[29] Stressing the 'rescue' of 75 per cent of France's Jews means tending to overlook the extent to which the heirs of the anti-Dreyfusard, anti-republican tradition in France succeeded in implementing their vicious ideas, pre-empting the Germans' demands to deport Jews.

Although deportations later resumed, this was in a situation akin to that of the period of Arrow Cross rule in Hungary, that is, when the established collaborationist regime had been overthrown (in the case of Horthy) or bypassed (as in the case of Vichy). The majority of the deported French Jews were sent off in the summer of 1942. Deportations continued after that point but only in small numbers, a result of the fact that Eichmann's plans were put on hold as the French authorities hesitated to deport Jews who were French citizens.

The comparison with Hungary is instructive. Although Hungary had been at the forefront of antisemitic policies in the interwar period, when its political culture was dominated by irredentism and antisemitism, while it remained an independent ally of the Third Reich the Hungarians refused to deport 'their' Jews. Hungary introduced the first post–Great War antisemitic legislation in Europe, with the so-called *numerus clausus* law of 1920, restricting the number of Jews in higher education. But between then and 1944, despite the alliance with the Third Reich and increasingly antisemitic appointments in government, Hungary under Miklós Horthy mistreated the Jews, forced men into labour battalions and did send Jews to be killed in a major killing action in Kamenets-Podolski in August 1941 in which 23,000 were murdered but, with this exception – admittedly a major one which pointed to what would come in 1944 – it did not surrender the Jews to the Germans, as the latter repeatedly asked them to do. Only once Prime Minister Miklós Kállay tried to extricate Hungary from the Axis, precipitating the German occupation of March 1944, was the fate of the Jews sealed (the Germans did not want a repeat of what happened in Italy after Mussolini's fall, when the new government joined the Allies). Nevertheless, for all that the deportation of the Jews of Hungary to Auschwitz required the German occupation, the foremost historian of the Holocaust in Hungary notes that 'the *decisive factor* in the destruction of Hungarian Jewry was the wholehearted cooperation of the [Döme] Sztójay government, which was appointed on March 22, 1944, with the consent of Miklós Horthy, the regent of Hungary'.[30]

The German occupation was designed first and foremost to prevent Hungary from siding with the Allies. But in its wake Eichmann and his team of 150–200 men followed and immediately set about creating the architecture that had been applied elsewhere for deporting the Jews. With the urgency of the situation and with the expertise the perpetrators had acquired in the previous years they telescoped a series of processes that had taken months, even years, elsewhere into a matter of weeks. The first ghetto was set up on 16 April, and by the start of June, more than 170 ghettos were holding over 400,000 Jews. Only the Jews of Budapest were not yet ghettoized.[31] That the Germans were so 'successful' was not only because Eichmann, Reich Plenipotentiary Edmund Veesenmayer and a few hundred men had extraordinary organizational skills. To the contrary, the recently discovered calendar of László Endre, the newly appointed Secretary of State of the Interior Ministry, reveals that the deportations began – with the assistance of some 20,000 Hungarian gendarmes – only after an important meeting on the night of 22 April at which Eichmann and German officials came to an agreement with Endre.[32] The combination of these two men 'embodied perfectly the two forces that caused the deaths of almost two-thirds of the Hungarian Jews'.[33] In other words, the deportation of the Jews accorded with German dreams of a 'world without Jews' on the one hand and long-held local fantasies of creating an ethnically pure 'Greater Hungary', from which not only Jews (though Jews above all) but also Ukrainians, Romanians, Serbs and Romanies were to be excluded on the other.[34] Such visions acquired purchase under wartime conditions, in which different communities which might previously have lived together with greater or lesser degrees of harmony or conflict, were brutally set against one another in a competition for resources and, above all, belonging, especially in the borderlands of Eastern Europe. Genocide is a societal endeavour. Local hatreds became enmeshed in geopolitical, even (in the case of the Jews) metaphysical, aspirations and fantasies, with horrific consequences.[35]

Perhaps the best proof that the Holocaust in Hungary owed at least as much to local initiative as to German demands and organization is the fact that Horthy had the power to stop the deportations, which he did on 7 July 1944, under international pressure and out of fear for his own reputation. The corollary of that evidence – which was used by Horthy's defenders to rehabilitate him in Cold War émigré circles and now in post-communist Hungary – is the fact that the vast majority of the nearly 500,000 Hungarian Jews who died during the Holocaust were murdered during Horthy's reign and not when the Arrow Cross under Ferenc Szálasi was in power, that is to say, not during the 'wild' interregnum of fascist rule between mid-October 1944 and the Red Army's occupation of Hungary in April 1945, vicious though that period was.[36] Deportations to Auschwitz began fifty-six days after Eichmann and his *Sonderkommando* arrived in Budapest; another fifty-six days sufficed to deport 437,000 people, almost all the Jews of Hungary, with the partial exception of most of the Jews of Budapest. They were saved because of Horthy's decision to halt the deportations and because the Jews from the provinces – recognizably more alien – had been targeted first, primarily for logistical reasons. Of the 1.1 million people murdered at Auschwitz, 1 million were Jews; one in three of them was from Hungary, and they arrived and were killed there in fifty-six days, between 15 May and 9 July.[37] Were it not for the deportations in spring 1944, the most infamous Nazi death camp would have been dwarfed in terms of the number of its victims by Treblinka. The infamous images of Birkenau – the railway spur running into the camp, the 'Jewish ramp' where selections for murder or for labour took place, the photographs of the selection process from the so-called *Auschwitz Album* – all come from the period of the Holocaust in Hungary. This huge and rapid deportation process would not have been possible without the role played by Hungarian gendarmes and police in rounding up and deporting the Jews.

The Jewish leadership in Hungary has also come in for much criticism, for being complacent about the community's chances of survival and, after the German occupation, for not telling the Jewish masses the truth about where they were being deported. In his memoir, Menachem Mendel Selinger, who escaped from Poland to Hungary, recalls how he pleaded with members of the Jewish Council in Budapest to reveal what was happening, telling them: 'Gentlemen, you are playing a fraudulent game. Resign your positions and dissolve the Judenrat. We Polish refugees have seen it before and I believe you too have intuited what kind of job you are being asked to do: to aid and abet the murderers of our people.' To their response that doing this would result in chaos, Selinger replied: 'it is precisely chaos that might be the solution! . . . Do not get on the transportation trains, let yourselves be killed on the spot if you have no other choice. Chaos is our only hope of salvation!'[38] He was, of course, ignored. Whether Seligman's assessment was correct or not, we have no way of knowing; but we should not forget that, whatever the merits of the *Judenrat*'s position, responsibility for the murder of the Jews of Hungary rests with the Germans and their Hungarian accomplices. We are also rightly reminded that the murder of the Jews of Hungary was anomalous in the history of the Holocaust, since the majority of victims were not deported across Europe but were murdered where they lived in the borderlands of Eastern Europe, in face-to-face shootings, in ghettos, or in the Reinhard camps.

The case of Mussolini's Italian Social Republic (RSI), better known as the Salò Republic, presents many similarities to what happened in Hungary. Although the extent to which Italian Fascism was free of antisemitism has been greatly overstated, Mussolini's regime did not hand over Italian Jews to the Germans; indeed, it went further and protected Jews (French or other) who were able to make their way into the region around Nice occupied by the Italians. In Hungary, mass deportations began when the Germans occupied the country; so in Italy the Jews were only deported after the surrender of August 1943 and the creation in the north of the RSI, that is to say, a German puppet regime. Nevertheless, the way had been paved for the deportations at the start of the war, when Mussolini ordered that 'dangerous' or foreign Jews be interned in concentration camps and imposed forced labour on Italian Jews in the summer of 1942. These measures were never fully implemented because of Mussolini's fall, but their existence made the later cooperation with Nazi genocidal plans easier. As one historian notes, 'many Fascists in the RSI favoured anti-Semitic policies no matter how much the Salò government reeled from German highhandedness'.[39]

As soon as the RSI was created, Fascist ideologues began to call for a definitive solution to the Jewish question in Italy: 'Let us confiscate *all* their property . . . burn out their lairs . . . drive them from the country, *now!*' demanded the *Popolo di*

Alessandria on 4 October 1943.[40] The order for the general arrest of Italian Jews was made by minister Buffarini Guidi on 30 November 1943, and the Italians and Germans soon agreed a plan for Jews arrested by the Italians to be handed over to the Germans. The main transit camp where Jews were held prior to deportation was Fossoli, near Modena; the most infamous round-up took place in Rome on 16 October 1943, in which Italian policemen worked together with German forces to round up over 1,000 Jews; and once the Germans directly occupied the Adriatic Littoral (Adriatisches Küstenland), the only extermination camp to operate on Italian soil was opened at a former rice mill, the Risiera di San Sabba in Trieste. Furthermore, this camp, 'though established and run by the Germans, could not have operated without local Italian support'.[41] Some 7,495 Jews were deported from Italy between 1943 and 1945, of whom 610 survived; additionally, 10,000 Jews were saved in hiding. Campaigners did not know where the deported Jews were taken, although they had strong suspicions; in a letter from the Colonia Libera Italiana (Free Italian Colony) in Lausanne to the ICRC in the same city, pleading for Red Cross help, Luigi Zappelli, the colony's president, wrote:

> People have said that the deportees were put to work on behalf of the public good. But if this may appear plausible for men of sound health, the same hypothesis may not be applied in the case of the elderly (including some over the age of ninety), women, and children. We may thus infer that the truth is much more terrible than one thinks and that extermination is the only end that awaits them.[42]

The RSI, though hardly an independent state, was an entity based on the longstanding, most radical antisemitic trends in Italian Fascism. Whether deporting Italian Jews to be murdered by the Germans would have been harder without the RSI's support can be debated; what cannot is that such help was forthcoming.

In the cases of both Hungary and Italy, the deportations relied on substantial local help, more so in Hungary than in Italy, although it is certainly the case that 'the Italian Fascists and police forces provided crucial help for the realization of the Nazi project to exterminate the Jews, so much so that in Italy, as elsewhere in Europe, it would not have reached the scale it did without their collaboration'.[43] Although Salò is closer in many ways to the Arrow Cross period in Hungary (after Szálasi took power), the crucial point is that the Jews in states which were allied to Nazi Germany but retained some independence were more dependent on the attitudes of the local regime than on the Germans. This could veer from resistance to German demands for deportation (as in Finland or Italy before 1943) to outright hostility.

The latter – outright hostility towards the Jews – is best represented by the fascist regimes in Slovakia and Croatia, where, as in Vichy France, Jozef Tiso's and Ante Pavelić's antisemitism led them to pre-empt the Germans' demands. The designation of these countries as 'puppet states' has led historians to underestimate their room for manoeuvre; the ways in which they implemented policies which were not just slavishly following German demands but realizing long-held dreams of ethnic 'purification'. In Slovakia, the rise to power of the Hlinka Slovak People's Party after the

Munich Agreement was accompanied by anti-Hungarian, anti-Czech and anti-Jewish riots and pogroms. Just as Jews were blamed for the loss of territory in Hungary in 1918, so they were blamed for Slovakia's loss of territory to Hungary after the First Vienna Award of 1938. The Slovak Republic, under Tiso's leadership, was established on 14 March 1939. Tiso immediately announced that the 'Jewish Question' would be handled 'without hatred, non-violently in a Christian manner' and on 18 April, the government issued a decree defining who was considered a Jew and beginning the process of 'Aryanization'. With the radicals Vojtech Tuka (Prime Minister) and Alexander Mach (Minister of the Interior) now in important posts, over 10,000 Jewish-owned businesses were liquidated and 2,300 'Aryanized' by the end of October 1941, as was all Jewish domestic property. The logic of these measures was clearly expressed by Nazi Germany's *Judenberater* (Adviser on Jewish Questions) in Slovakia, Eichmann's deputy Dieter Wisliceny: 'Depriving 90,000 inhabitants of Slovakia of income and property will create a Jewish problem, which can be solved only by emigration.' The deportations which followed were sent primarily to Auschwitz, but some were killed in Majdanek, Sobibór, and elsewhere. Over 70,000 Slovak Jews were deported, of whom more than 60,000 were murdered.[44] Although the Slovak state persecuted the Jews because the Germans expected them to, the onslaught of legislation, expropriation and physical attacks flowed from the Hlinka Slovak People's Party's vision of an ethnically pure state; the Germans did not intervene directly in Slovak Jewish affairs until August 1944. In fact, on 26 March 1942, Mach stated quite plainly that 'We have also obtained help from the Germans on this Jewish question. We want to rid ourselves of the Jews with the help of Germans.'[45]

It is no surprise that in Bohemia and Moravia, which had been incorporated into the Reich, all institutions of government were involved in the expropriation and deportation of the Jews.[46] In Slovakia, which was a quasi-independent state, the persecution of the Jews was driven as much by Slovak as by German demands. When Rabbi Abraham Frieder of Nové Mesto and five other communal leaders tried to intercede with the Education Minister Jozef Sivák in February 1942, he learned that the entire Jewish population of Slovakia was due to be deported,

> and I was forced to realise that the Jews of Slovakia were utterly lost. I burst into tears during this meeting. The Minister himself was very moved and wished he could help, but unfortunately the matter was under the jurisdiction of the Minister of the Interior, who completely shared the opinion of Prime Minister Tuka: Slovakia must be cleansed of Jews.[47]

Thanks in part to Frieder's 'Working Group', deportations from Slovakia were halted in October 1942, after twenty trains had taken nearly 52,000 Jews to the death camps; Slovakia's remaining Jews were deported in 1944 only once the Germans took full control of the process after invading the country in the wake of the Slovak National Uprising.

In Croatia, the Ustaša regime aimed at the 'cleansing' of Croatia not just of Jews but of all non-Croat groups, especially Serbs. As of May 1941, laws were introduced, such as the Nuremberg Laws, establishing 'race membership' in Croatia, forbidding Jews and Gypsies from marrying Aryan Croatians and forcing Jews to wear a Ž (*Židov*) mark on their front and back, identifying them as Jews.[48] 'The Croatian nation', wrote one newspaper in the wake of these laws, 'must be like any other ethical movement if it wants to protect its racial purity, to protect the purity of its blood, if it wants to accomplish its historical mission. We have to protect our blood from Jewish, Gypsy and non-Aryan manifestations because this is one of the basic prerequisites of the construction of a new Croatia.'[49] This was a view fully in accord with the Pavelić regime's: 'This is a Croat land and nobody else's,' wrote government minister Milovan Žanić on 6 June 1941, 'and there are no methods that we would not use to make this land truly Croat and cleanse it of all Serbs.'[50] Indeed, the regime moved against the Serbs in a genocidal campaign which ended with more than 300,000 killed, from a prewar Serb population in Croatia of about 1.9 million. Indicating the close link between religion and racial purification in Croatian fascism, Andrija Artuković gave a speech announcing the founding of the Croatian Orthodox Church on 24 February 1942, during which he also stated that the Croats would deal with the Jews more radically than the Nazis, and that with 'healthy and decisive action' the Independent State of Croatia would destroy the 'insatiable and poisonous parasites'.[51]

Croatia, in fact, ran what has been called 'the only non-Nazi extermination centre active during the Holocaust', the Jasenovac camp.[52] It was actually a complex of five camps located on the Una and Sava rivers 100 kilometres south-east of Zagreb, and modelled on the Nazi example. More than 70,000 people were killed there, the majority of them Serbs but also between 12,000 and 20,000 Jews and about 15,000 Romanies.[53]

The deadliest part of the complex was Jasenovac III, known as the 'brickyard' (*Ciglana*), built on a former industrial complex. Here at least 57,000 people were tortured and murdered in the most brutal way.[54] One survivor, Duro Schwarz, wrote an account of his eight months in Jasenovac (August 1941– April 1942) in 1945; his description of the flogging of a group of inmates speaks to the transgressive, sexualized nature of the violence in the camp, depicting an atmosphere which is far removed from the notion of industrial murder: 'The Ustashis fight among themselves for the right to administer the floggings. Here are the Modrič brothers and the rest of the "elite". Miloš breathes hard, pants, becomes possessed and starts hitting with all the strength he can muster. The blows land with a dull thud. They keep on striking as if possessed, until they draw blood.'[55] No wonder that an anguished Schwarz concluded of the guards: 'To me it seems that these people, lazy by nature, found the job of torturing prisoners to be the fulfilment of their desires – entertainment and satisfaction of their needs.'[56]

Most of Croatia's Jews had been deported either to Jasenovac or another Croatian concentration camp or into the hands of the Nazis by the summer of 1942 – the peak period of the Holocaust. For those deported, the experience was a shocking rending of their world. The Jewish community in Zagreb soon realized what it meant if they had no response to the letters and parcels they were sending to deportees in Jasenovac and other camps: 'Anyone who did not write for three or four months in a row was eliminated from our card index, on the assumption that the writer was no longer alive, which unfortunately proved to be true almost without exception.'[57]

Nowhere is this independent course with respect to the

Nazis' Final Solution clearer than in Romania, which veered from enthusiastic participation, indeed implementation of its own killing measures without German involvement, to refusing to deport large Jewish populations. In the first instance, Romania's fascist regime's antisemitism – an antisemitism deeply rooted in Romanian culture and religion, and entrenched at national level since the creation of the Kingdom of Romania in 1859, further heightened after the 1878 Congress of Berlin, which required the Romanians to grant civic equality to the Jews, which they failed to do, and notably spread in intellectual and youth circles in the interwar period – led it to seize the opportunity offered by the war on the Soviet Union to acquire 'lost' territory and to attack the Jews. As Romania's leader Ion Antonescu said:

> if we do not take advantage of the current national and European situation to purify the Romanian people, we will miss the last opportunity history offers us . . . I can bring Bessarabia back and Transylvania too, but if we don't cleanse the Romanian people we will have done nothing, because it is not borders that make the strength of a people, but the homogeneity and purity of its race. And this is my first aim.[58]

Antonescu was not quite as obsessed with the Jews as a world-historical enemy as Hitler but he came close. The connection in his mind between the Jews and Romanian national 'purification' is evident in the fact that the first groups of Jews targeted for deportation were the communities of Bukovina and Bessarabia, that is to say, mostly traditional, Yiddish-speaking communities in regions which had been incorporated into Greater Romania following the peace treaties after the First

World War, notably including Cernăuți (Czernowitz) and Chișinău (Kishinev). His namesake, Deputy Prime Minister Mihai Antonescu, explicitly spoke of deporting 'the whole Jewish population in Bessarabia and Bukovina', arguing that there was 'no moment in our history more favourable . . . for a complete ethnic unshackling, for a national revision and purification of our people'.[59] Many locals agreed, especially in Bessarabia, taking part in a vast looting spree which, in their minds, rebalanced the region's economic situation and foreshadowed the state's 'Romanianization' policies.[60] Nevertheless, there was no single 'decision' to murder the Jews of Romania but a series of more or less coordinated deportations, from different regions.[61]

The experience of the Romanian Jews deported to Transnistria in the autumn of 1941 was far removed from what, in the English-speaking world, we think of as the Holocaust.[62] They were not deported to death camps but, following the failure of negotiations between the Romanians and the Germans to send the Romanian Jews to the east because the war in the Soviet Union had not gone according to plan, they were instead dumped in Transnistria. They were abandoned in makeshift camps and ghettos, most of which were open spaces close to the River Bug, the border with German-occupied Ukraine, which provided no shelter or other resources. In the middle of winter 1941–2, they were left to fend for themselves, often living in animal barns and pigsties, with the result that tens of thousands died of exposure, starvation and disease; having bartered their clothes for food, most were clothed in newspapers and rags, in temperatures as low as minus 40° Celsius. The Romanians' approach to the 'Jewish problem'

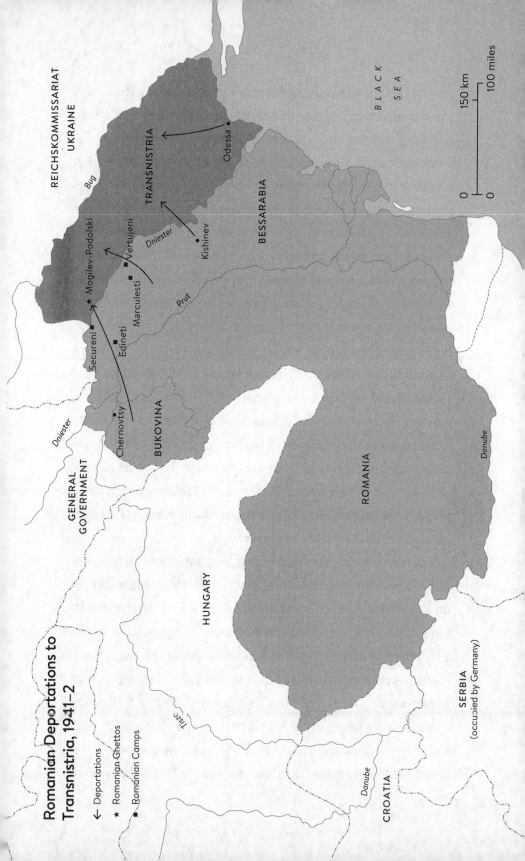

Romanian Deportations to Transnistria, 1941–2

→ Deportations
★ Romanian Ghettos
■ Romanian Camps

REICHSKOMMISSARIAT
UKRAINE

Bug

TRANSNISTRIA

Odessa

BLACK
SEA

0   150 km
0   100 miles

Dniester

Mogilev-Podolski
Vertujeni
Marculesti
Edineti
Secureni

Kishinev

BESSARABIA

Prut

Chernovtsy

BUKOVINA

Dniester

GENERAL
GOVERNMENT

ROMANIA

Danube

HUNGARY

TISZA

Danube

CROATIA

SERBIA
(occupied by Germany)

was to isolate the Jews, refuse to provide them with any of the resources necessary to sustain life and drive them into unpaid or minimally paid forced labour.[63]

Some of the Jews in Transnistria survived because their labour was used; in Moghilev-Podolski, for example, the local economy depended on the ghetto, as the Jews were set to work in the *turnatoria* (foundry), which provided essential power for local industries. Over 10,000 survived.[64] But the Romanians did sometimes murder the Jews directly, usually using the spread of epidemics in the places where Jews were most densely concentrated as the reason for doing so – obviously failing to note that their own policies were responsible for causing those outbreaks. The shared fear of the Romanian authorities and of the Germans east of the River Bug (the demarcation line between Transnistria and German-occupied territory) that they too would be infected proved to be a murderous combination. At Domanovka, some 18,000 Jews were shot; at Acmecetka, 5,000. The Jews of Odessa – which had a prewar Jewish population of 233,000 and even after the sea evacuations at the start of the war about 150,000 – were, in a clear parallel to events at Babyn Yar, subjected to 'punishment' following an assassination attack in which 46 Romanian and German soldiers and officials were killed. In the resulting massacre, which took place on 23 October 1941, between 18,000 and 25,000 Jewish civilians were shot by Romanian soldiers and *Sonderkommando* 11b, a subunit of Einsatzgruppe D. A further 20,000 were shot in nearby Dalnik.[65] Following further deportations and massacres, in the summer of 1942 Odessa was declared '*judenfrei*'.[66] In the single largest massacre of the Holocaust, at Bogdanovka from 21 December 1941 to mid-January 1942, as many as 48,000 mostly Soviet Ukrainian Jews (therefore the most feared for their 'Judaeo-Bolshevism') were massacred, burned alive and shot by Romanian gendarmes, Ukrainian auxiliaries and local ethnic German militia. Modest Isopescu, the prefect of Golta county, in which Bogdanovka was situated, was furious when he learned that an additional 40,000 Jews were to be sent to his county. Writing to the Governor of Transnistria, Gheorghe Alexianu, Isopescu complained that he had already had to find space 'for 11,000 Yids in the state farm pigsties, where there was not sufficient space for 7,000 pigs'. He pleaded with Alexianu not to allow another 40,000 Jews to arrive in Golta, asking him 'not to infest it through new convoys of Yids'.[67] Quite apart from the ritual humiliation of 'housing' Jews in pigsties, the huge overcrowding and lack of sanitary facilities meant that the Romanians created the situation in which it then 'made sense' to them to exterminate the Jews like pests.

The numbers are staggering and far outnumber any massacres that took place in Western or Central Europe, and are larger even than the massacres at Babyn Yar or Operation Harvest Festival, which saw 18,400 Jews killed in Majdanek on 3 November 1943 following the inmate uprising at Sobibór. More Jews were murdered in massacres in Transnistria than were deported from the Netherlands to the Nazi death camps, yet in Western Europe these places still remain largely unknown. As has rightly been noted, 'The Holocaust did not mean only the gas chambers of Auschwitz, but also the reserves set up by Hitler and his allies for other methods of mass extermination. Transnistria was among them.'[68]

Yet by the summer of 1942, Antonescu and his advisers

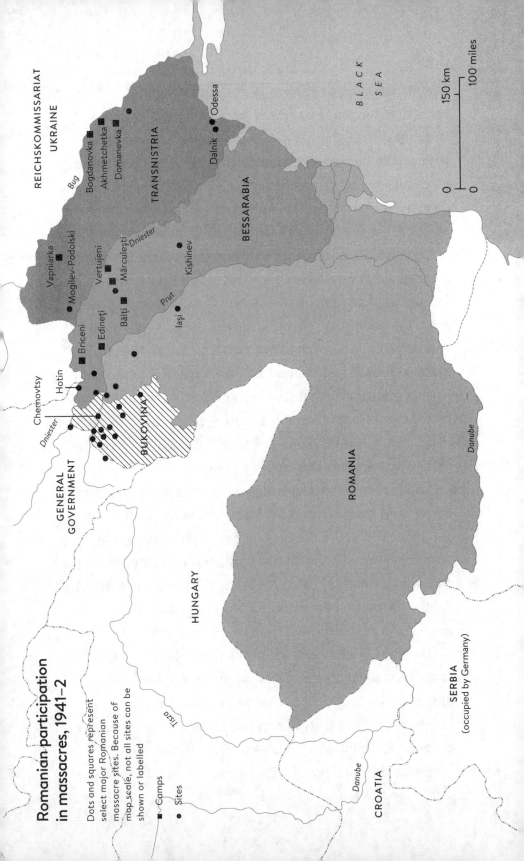

Romanian participation in massacres, 1941–2

Dots and squares represent select major Romanian massacre sites. Because of map scale, not all sites can be shown or labelled

■ Camps
● Sites

BLACK SEA

150 km
100 miles
0
0

REICHSKOMMISSARIAT UKRAINE

Odessa
Dalnik

TRANSNISTRIA

Bogdanovka
Akhmetchetka
Domanevka

Bug

BESSARABIA

Vapniarka
Mogilev-Podolski
Vertujeni
Mărculeşti
Dniester

Kishinev

Briceni
Edineţi
Bălţi
Prut
Iaşi

Hotin
Chernovtsy
Dniester

BUKOVINA

GENERAL GOVERNMENT

ROMANIA

HUNGARY

Danube

CROATIA

Danube
Tisza

SERBIA
(occupied by Germany)

were beginning to have second thoughts about deporting the remaining Jews of Romania, still one of the largest Jewish population groups in Europe. This was a choice made by an independent state which had previously enthusiastically murdered Jews – not so much participating in the German-led Holocaust as using the opportunity to execute a Holocaust of its own. Antonescu's decision to halt deportations to Transnistria, made in October 1942, indicated the same degree of autonomy and was made partly because of the pleas of Jewish leaders, notably Wilhelm Filderman, the head of the Federation of Jewish Communities; a police report of 16 October 1942 noted that Jewish circles in Bucharest regarded Filderman's intervention with Antonescu as crucial.[69] Their supporters too, especially representatives of the Orthodox and Catholic Churches, influenced Antonescu's decision. But the decisive cause was Antonescu's perception that the war would end with Germany's defeat and that posing as a saviour of Jews would bring him benefits in the post-war world.[70] 'Obviously', wrote the German ambassador Manfred von Killinger to the German Foreign Office on 5 October 1942, 'the Jews of Transylvania and the Banat reacted against the deportations in such a way that they set in motion the most varied forms of intervention. They were served by formerly leading democratic and liberal politicians, who for their part spoke with leading Romanian government representatives in favour of the Jews.'[71] But it was not only such people who made these intercessions on behalf of the Jews.

In many cases, local grandees also raised objections to the deportation of the Jews from the Banat. Their objections were founded less on love of their fellow citizens or abstract notions of human rights than on a fear of what would happen to their businesses and to the local economy; according to von Killinger, the chamber of commerce in Timişoara wrote to the ministry of economics to note: 'that with the resettlement of the Jews, the Jewish businesses would fall into the hands of the Swabians and Saxons, and the Romanian economy cannot withstand such an expansion [*Ausbreitung*] of the German element. If such an expansion takes place, they would threaten the economic role of the Romanians.'[72]

Nevertheless, the end result in this case was that the Jews of Banat, as well as most of the Jews of Romania's *regat*, or 'old kingdom' (the pre–First World War borders), including most of the Jews of Bucharest, were not deported. For the Germans, the continued alliance with Romania, which meant access to oil and other resources, was, for the time being, more important than forcing the Romanians' hands. Since Romania did not switch sides until August 1944, it was then too late, unlike in the case of Hungary five months earlier, for the Germans to invade and occupy the country. When Abba Kovner, the famous Jewish partisan, arrived in Romania with the soldiers of the Jewish Brigade, he was astonished to find not just isolated survivors but 'a living Jewish community': 'We were confronted by the dank cellar smell of a Jewish community living as if nothing at all had happened, as if before the Flood, as if there had never been a Flood.' It was hard for him to take, and his joy was mingled with resentment: 'while we initially rejoiced at meeting so many Jews, our hearts turned to stone with wonderment and pain at the sight of a surviving Jewish community living thus, not far from the mass grave, not far from Treblinka and Majdanek, on the edge of the abyss (which just by chance had failed to engulf the whole of Rumania as well)'.[73]

We now know a great deal more about the Holocaust in Romania than was the case a few years ago, but Hilberg's words from sixty years ago remain true: 'No country, besides Germany, was involved in massacres of Jews on such a scale.'[74] What we also see, in the cases of Romania and France, is that a power-sharing arrangement, such as in France, or an alliance such as Romania's with Nazi Germany, did not necessarily put limits or a brake on forces of persecution. 'On the contrary', what we often observe is that 'rivalry and competition among power centres might unleash even more destructive energy than might hierarchy and authoritarian fiat.'[75]

The 'Free World'

In many ways, this extensive collaboration remains mysterious. It is clear that across Europe, there were considerable constituencies – often those representing existing elites – who were to a greater or lesser extent ideologically aligned with Nazism. Anti-communism, dreams of national and racial homogeneity or territorial revision, as well as pure and simple venality or just a belief that the Third Reich was the strongest power in Europe and should or could not be resisted, all drove collaboration. On the other hand, we should not forget the resistance to Nazism which existed, even (perhaps especially) in Germany. Anti-fascist émigré author Paul Hagen, who throughout the war years published the *Inside Germany Reports*, put it most succinctly. 'The Nazis', he wrote, 'exalt their New Order as the beginning of a new epoch.' The reality, however, was quite different:

Oppressed, dismembered, played off against each other, plundered to the limit, starved and frozen, lacerated and bleeding from a thousand wounds, under the yoke of slave labour, their fathers and sons conscripted for work in the Reich and forced into Hitler's armies, they suffer but for one purpose – to feed the insatiable war machine and fill the pockets of the Nazis. Like swarms of locusts, the armies of occupation have settled down on rich countries and on poor countries and stripped them bare. That is Europe today. The living space of the Nazis has become the dying space of Europe, and at the same time the dying space of the German people.

He concluded that 'the Nazis have carried out the greatest mass plunder in the history of the world'.[76] That despite the reality of the Nazi 'new order', there was nevertheless enthusiastic and widespread collaboration until the end, or close to it, across Europe, says something not just about opportunism but about the deep affinity many, especially leaders of states who dreamed of 'national purification', felt for the principles of Nazism.

This massive Europe-wide crime met something of a weak mirror-image in the response of the 'free world'. The declaration of the Atlantic Charter setting out joint British and American war aims, the creation of the United Nations and, later, the War Refugee Board (WRB) show how, despite their best intentions, the Allies' responses hardly matched the scale of the crime which precipitated these bodies' establishment. This inability to quite take the measure of Nazism was an echo of prewar appeasement and a failure, even in 1943, to believe that the Nazis meant what they said in their apocalyptic rhetoric. Recognizing this mismatch helps to explain why the Allies, despite the existence of a large literature on Nazi camps since the 1930s and an insightful intelligence network, were unprepared for what they found in the final stages of the Holocaust.

The WRB exemplifies these problems. Created in January 1944 after years of campaigning by some segments of the Roosevelt administration to do more to aid the Jews of Europe, it appears, on the face of it, to illustrate how the US did all it could to save Jews. Yet apart from being, as many historians have noted, 'too little, too late' – though, as has been noted, 'perhaps as early as it could make any difference to people's fates'[77] – the WRB was hampered by its small size, relatively modest funds (primarily provided by the American Jewish Joint Distribution Committee (JDC) and other Jewish organizations) and lack of cooperation on the part of crucial segments of the administration, not least Roosevelt himself, who seems to have been somewhat indifferent to the organization. According to one historian, the WRB 'revealed years of systematic antisemitism on the part of the US State Department'.[78] The WRB ran operations in many countries (Raul Wallenberg, for example, was funded by the WRB and was said by the Swedish Foreign Office to feel 'that he, in effect, is carrying out a humanitarian mission in behalf of the War Refugee Board'), and its energetic and devoted employees went to great lengths to help those Jews they could access, in Hungary and in neutral countries (liberated countries were the domain of the Intergovernmental Committee on Refugees and the United Nations).[79] It also provided the Red Cross with the trucks and food parcels that it delivered to concentration camp inmates in the final weeks of the war, primarily at Ravensbrück. But it came up against the reluctance and sometimes outright hostility of the State Department, the War Department and the Office of War Information to its projects.[80] The idea that America did all it could to help the Jews or, in the reverse argument, that America failed to help because it did not care is too simplistic.[81] The War Refugee Board shows that some in the Roosevelt administration cared a great deal and that others did not.

Whether saving Jews was considered a priority or not, in 1943 it was not hard to find out quite a lot about what was happening to them. 'Jews were and are, of course,' wrote American academic Frank Munk in 1943, 'target area number one of German population policies. The Nazis' publicly avowed aim is complete extermination of the Jews, "with a little torture thrown in", and it is succeeding very well.'[82] As if admonishing his readers for not paying attention to the readily available information, Munk went on, saying that although 'not till the winter of 1942 did the Nazis publicly announce that all the Jews of Europe would be completely and irrevocably exterminated', it was clear that the Nazis meant what they said. 'Extermination is not a threat; it is a stark and naked fact, visible to anybody who does not close his eyes.'[83]

This clear-sighted appraisal was part of the background to the War Refugee Board's creation and it was the reason why Europe's neutral countries – primarily Sweden, Switzerland, Portugal, Spain and Turkey – were involved in the final stages of the Holocaust. Those countries had always been involved, of course; they could hardly withstand the pressures created by the rise of Nazism and the war, and most had hedged their bets by appeasing the Third Reich as much as was expedient in terms of their diplomatic and economic advantage (and in the case of Spain and Portugal especially, out of cautious ideological affinity with Nazism, especially its anti-communism), but also sought to curry favour with the Allies where it seemed advantageous. This was particularly the case after Stalingrad, when the tide of the war turned, and the neutral countries could be more confident that they would not be invaded by Germany and increasingly feared that their policies of supplying Germany with raw materials or deporting 'illegal' Jewish refugees would be regarded unfavourably by the Allies.

Portugal under the Salazar dictatorship, though an authoritarian regime, was not marked by antisemitism in the manner of the fascist dictatorships, and Jewish refugees who were able to get to Lisbon were generally well treated by the population, including the local Jewish community. Lisbon became, in the early years of the war, a crucial hub for Jewish emigration from Europe.[84] The policies of other neutral countries changed over the course of the war, sometimes resistant to allowing Jewish refugees, even returning them. Switzerland, for example, though its record is generally positive, did return Jewish refugees trying to cross its border at certain points in time; a famous case is that of historian Saul Friedländer's parents. Having left him in the care of a monastery in France, thinking that would be best for all three of them, Friedländer's parents then tried to cross the border into Switzerland in a group of fifteen Jews. At 3 a.m., as they crossed over to the Swiss side of the street which marked the border in the village of Saint-Gingolph, some youngsters coming out of a bar spotted them and called the police. The entire group was arrested. The next morning parents with small children were allowed to stay in Switzerland (a very brief exception) while my parents and another couple without a child were kept overnight and, on the following day, delivered to the French police in Saint-Gingolph, then sent to the French camp of Rivesaltes, followed by Drancy, followed by Auschwitz.[85]

Spain's record is similar, the Franco regime operating under what it felt were the constraints of its diplomatic relations with Nazi Germany on the one hand (it had troops fighting on the eastern front) and the Allies on the other. Sweden's record is perhaps the best; although it traded lucratively with Germany, providing it with iron ore from late 1942 onwards, the Swedes made a startling about-face where the Jews were concerned. Sweden first informed the Germans that it would offer asylum to the remaining Jews in Norway, irrespective of their citizenship, and in October 1943 they facilitated the mass escape of the Jews of Denmark, offering asylum and provisional passports to those who made it across the sound. Nevertheless, in general the neutrals were indifferent to the fate of the Jews until, diplomatically speaking, their fate directly concerned them.[86] This it did in the latter years of the war.

From autumn 1942, the German Foreign Office began issuing ultimatums to its allies to repatriate 'their' Jews (that is, Jews with Spanish, Portuguese, etc. citizenship) from Germany itself and countries under German rule. For example, on 4 February 1943, the German Legation in Lisbon informed the Portuguese government that, 'in the interest of German military security', Jews with Portuguese citizenship, if not repatriated, would, from 1 April, be included in 'the provisions in force concerning Jews, including their identification, internment, and later expulsion'. The Salazar government vacillated, possibly with the result that many of the Jews of Salonika who could have been rescued perished, although a handful of Jews interned in Belsen were rescued in July 1944.[87] That said, it was not easy to 'repatriate' Jews who, in many cases – such as large numbers of the Sephardi Jews of Salonika – had never lived in the country of which they could legally claim citizenship. In fact, the ultimatum was, as has rightly been noted, 'a form of scarcely disguised diplomatic extortion by Nazi Germany'. The ultimatum 'forced the respective governments to choose to either deliver their Jewish citizens to the Germans, making themselves accomplices to German war crimes, or to "take their Jews back", meaning essentially to agree to their forced removal'.[88]

In light of these ultimatums and especially following the German occupation of Hungary, the War Refugee Board wrote to the neutral countries' governments, warning them not to collaborate in the Nazi persecution of the Hungarian Jews and advising them to assist in taking Jews who might be released through any negotiations. Their response was, for the most part, favourable, even if the number of Jews who could be saved was small. Sweden was again most forthcoming, issuing *Schutzpässe* (protective documents akin to temporary passports) in their thousands and, on 3 July, a message from King Gustav V to Horthy which was crucial in persuading him to halt the deportations on 7 July. The neutral countries were trapped between their desire to retain their sovereignty and the need to walk a careful path between Nazi Germany and the Allies; it is no surprise that their attitudes towards the Jews changed over time. As Hayes notes, 'the fate of the Jews of Europe was always a matter of secondary importance to everyone but themselves and the regime that wished to kill them'.[89]

Conclusion

According to resistance fighter Abba Kovner, 'Only a handful of sadistic S.S. men were needed to hit a Jew, or cut off his beard, but millions had to participate in the slaughter of millions. There had to be masses of murderers, thousands of looters, millions of spectators.'[90] Kovner's claim is overstated: there were tens of thousands of committed Nazi ideologues, RSHA bureaucrats and SS killers; tens of thousands of German civil servants, Reichsbahn employees, German businessmen, bankers, local civilian officials, secretaries and functionaries of all sorts, from local Party cell leaders to Gauleiters; there were millions of Wehrmacht soldiers involved in the killings too. But it is clearly the case that without the support of millions of non-Germans (or Austrians) across Europe, the pace of the Holocaust would have been slower and its extent less comprehensive.

Why so many people across Europe chose to participate in the persecution of the Jews remains perhaps an unanswerable question. But several key factors stand out: venality, opportunism, fitting in, obedience, hatred. One did not need to be a committed antisemite who believed that the murder of the Jews would bring about the salvation of the 'Aryan race' to take part in the Holocaust. The opposite is also true: probably not many who regarded themselves as friends of the Jews are to be found among the ranks of the perpetrators. The disturbing fact remains – and this is true of all cases of genocide in the twentieth century – that many perpetrators appear to have taken part because they enjoyed doing so. Photographs of locals laughing as German Jews are deported from provincial towns are no less shocking than the descriptions of participation that survivors' insights offer, such as this passage from the memoir of Françoise Frenkel, the Polish-Jewish woman who ran Berlin's first French bookshop until 1939, when she fled to France. She was writing just after the war:

> Police and gendarmes were on the hunt, displaying
> inexhaustible levels of skill and energy. They implemented
> the Vichy regulations strictly and inexorably. These
> subservient men harboured a violent anger accumulated
> in the wake of the defeat, and it was as if they wanted to
> take it out on those weaker, less fortunate than themselves.
> There was nothing heroic about these agents of authority,
> not their job nor their approach.[91]

She is talking about Vichy France, but the same themes of humiliation, shame, rage and violent masculinity could be applied everywhere across wartime Europe.

As this chapter has shown, Jews were not safe anywhere in Europe during the Second World War. Although Jews in Axis countries were, paradoxically, more likely to survive than their coreligionists in Nazi-occupied lands because the regimes under which they lived were keen to display their autonomy vis-à-vis the 'Jewish Question', ultimately most countries allied to Nazi Germany saw 'their' Jews drawn into the Final Solution. Countries such as Croatia and Slovakia

took the opportunity offered by the war and the Nazis' genocidal policies to realize longstanding dreams of eliminating
minorities, Jews and Roma especially. Others, such as Bulgaria and France, deported some Jews but not others, baulk-
ing at the murder of Jews with citizenship of their countries,
especially once the tide of the war had turned. Romania
under Antonescu exemplifies these changes: a radically antisemitic regime that engaged in horrific deportation and
murder policies in 1941–2, which then declined to deport any
further Jews, meaning that Romania had the largest Jewish
population still alive at the end of the war. Hungary, by contrast, shows that Germany's allies could resist the pressure
to deport Jews, for here the Holocaust was implemented only
once the country was occupied, in 1944. Yet Horthy's actions
show that his regime also shared the Nazis' attitudes toward
Jews; his putting a halt to the deportations reveals the extent
to which Hungary retained control of the process, as well as
the Germans' need for local collaboration for the policy to
succeed. Although there were exceptions to the deportation
and murder process, Denmark being the most celebrated, in
the end there was nowhere in Nazi-occupied or Axis Europe
where Jews were safe. Only the vagaries of the war, the Nazis'
and their allies' willingness to devote resources to hunting
down Jews, and the mobilization of limited support by the
Churches and other elites late in the war, were able to mitigate the ferocity of the Final Solution. One of the few things
that kept Jews alive late in the war was the Nazis' need for
labour, as we will see in the next chapter.

CHAPTER 6
Camps and the Mobile Holocaust

'Roll-call was their sacred act, an inebriation with an
unquenchable thirst on the magnitude of their power.
To say that roll-call had a religious meaning for them
and that the muster ground was their temple is not being
metaphorical.'
— Abel Herzberg[1]

On 25 August 1942, a group of Jews was deported from
the Warsaw ghetto to the Treblinka death camp, located
in a sparsely populated spot about 50 miles north-east of
Warsaw on the railway line to Białystok. Over 100 people
were crammed into a boxcar, driven in by Lithuanian guards.
'When the door shut on me,' wrote Abraham Krzepicki, 'I felt
my whole world vanishing.' And indeed, the experience of deportation alone was shattering: 'It's impossible to imagine the
horrors in that closed, airless boxcar. It was one big cesspool.'[2]
One of the few selected to work at the camp, Krzepicki lived,
as he put it, 'in terror': 'We knew well that the execution of
our death sentences had been put off only for a short time.'[3]
Despite saying that he did not want to describe the horrors
he witnessed at Treblinka, Krzepicki's account is in fact full
of them. What shocked him, indeed began to drive him crazy,

was the relentless killing of so many innocents: 'Herds of human beings like herds of oxen, herds of sheep, driven to the slaughter, with the only difference that oxen and sheep don't know what will happen to them until the last minute, while in the case of humans, even the youngest children understand the situation sooner and can see and sense what's coming.'[4] Krzepicki was one of the very few escapees from Treblinka and one of the small number of survivors. After making his way back to the Warsaw ghetto, he was killed during the ghetto uprising in April 1943. His writing and that of other survivors and witnesses makes plain that Treblinka was not, as the Nazis liked to believe, tucked secretly away, but could be sensed for miles around. The smell of burning which came from the camp could be felt day and night and was ubiquitous and unavoidable; it 'was in my nose, in my ears, in my clothes, everywhere. I was soaked in it', said Edward Sypko, at the time an inmate in Treblinka I, the small slave labour camp that was part of the Treblinka complex. The stench reached as far as nearby towns; in Małkinia, 5 miles from Treblinka, one German guard grumbled that 'It stinks so damned bad, one cannot eat', and one local Pole, Jerzy Królikowski, stated that because of the smell, people in the town suffered from an 'extreme nervousness . . . [that] bordered on a mental breakdown'.[5]

In December 1941 and March 1942 gassings began at Chełmno and Bełżec respectively; in May and July, Sobibór and Treblinka also began operating. The Operation Reinhard camps (Bełżec, Sobibór and Treblinka) were built to kill the Jews of Poland, although some Jews from the Netherlands, Czechoslovakia and elsewhere were also murdered at Sobibór and Treblinka. By 1943 they had accomplished their task; Treblinka was dismantled in August and Sobibór, the last to be closed, was dismantled in December 1943. In about eighteen months, somewhere in the region of 1.7 million Jews had been killed at these three camps, with the rate of killing at its height in an extraordinary three-month period from August to October 1942. In this period of intense killing, over 1 million victims were murdered at the Reinhard camps, and, if one adds in those killed by the *Einsatzgruppen* and at Auschwitz at the same time, then these three months saw the murder of approximately 1.47 million Jews, about one-quarter of the total killed in the six years of the war. This rate of murder makes this period of the Holocaust probably the fastest rate of genocidal killing in history.[6]

Under the direction of the vicious, thuggish antisemites Odilo Globocnik, SS- und Polizeiführer (SS and police chief) for Lublin, and Christian Wirth, the first commandant of Bełżec and later inspector of Operation Reinhard, these three camps were staffed by former members of the T4 programme (like Wirth), assisted by Ukrainian and Baltic guards. The lower-ranking staff, men such as Ernst Zierke in Bełżec, threw themselves into their work with commitment.[7] The Reinhard camps were not part of the SS's concentration camp system, that is to say, they were not under the direction of the Inspectorate of Concentration Camps (IKL). The Nazis experimented with killing using gas near Minsk and in Mogilev in September 1941, and, a month later, the T4 'race experts', led by Victor Brack of the Führer's Chancellery, and one of the key organizers of the euthanasia programme, were offering their services to the authorities in the occupied east. Erhard Wetzel, the 'race expert' in Rosenberg's ministry for the occupied east, wrote that '[i]n the present situation, there are no objections to getting rid of Jews who are unable to work with the Brack remedy'.[8] Indeed, Himmler and the SS welcomed the initiative since, as August Becker, one of the SS's 'gassing experts', put it, 'the men in charge of the *Einsatzgruppen* in the east were increasingly complaining that the firing squads could not cope with the psychological and moral stress of the mass shootings indefinitely'.[9] Logistically, it was too complicated to transport the Jews of Poland to Russia, but 'Brack's remedy' was implemented in the General Government instead. As Brack claimed after the war, having received the order to halt the euthanasia programme, 'In order to keep the personnel employed, and also in the light of the need for an EP [euthanasia programme] after the war, Bouhler ordered me – I think it was after a conference with Himmler – to send the personnel to Lublin and place it under the supervision of SS Brigadeführer Globocnik.'[10] Thus began the use of gas chambers in the specially constructed Reinhard camps.

Although the Holocaust still calls to mind concentration camps in the popular imagination, and although Jews were always present in the concentration camps from 1933 onwards, the Holocaust as such (*qua* murder of the Jews) had very little to do with the SS's concentration camp system until the later stages of the war. As we have seen, huge numbers of Jews were shot in face-to-face killings reminiscent of colonial massacres, albeit on a vast scale; in ghettos, where they were starved to death and in which some 500,000 died, in itself a genocidal process; and then in the Reinhard extermination camps. The second sweep of *Einsatzgruppen* killings continued the Holocaust by bullets in the occupied USSR in 1942, especially in what was now designated the Reichskomissariat Ukraine (RKU) and in eastern Poland. At the same time, Majdanek (Lublin) began operating as a combined concentration camp, slave labour camp and extermination camp, serving as the administrative centre and collection point for clothing and belongings stolen from those people murdered in the Reinhard camps. In Transnistria, which at that point was the other major centre of Jewish death, tens of thousands of Jews died from disease and exposure, as well as large massacres. Had it not been closed and dismantled in 1943, Treblinka would perhaps today be remembered in the same way that Auschwitz is; far more Polish Jews, including most of the Jews of Warsaw, were murdered at Treblinka than the total number of Jews from Western Europe killed during the Holocaust.

There were very few survivors of these camps. By the time the first published accounts of Treblinka appeared, the camp was about to be dismantled. An article, 'The Treblinka Slaughter House', published in the New York–based émigré newspaper *Polish Jew*, offered grim reading in its August 1943 issue. Before then the above-cited escapee from Treblinka, Abraham Krzepicki, had provided the historian Rachel Auerbach with an account of the camp, which she transcribed over the winter of 1942–3. But his account was buried in the rubble of the Warsaw ghetto along with other documents from the Ringelblum archive and was only recovered in 1950, first appearing in print in Yiddish in the Jewish Historical Institute of Warsaw's *Bleter far Geshikhte* in 1956.[11] The *Polish Jew* report is remarkable both for the vividness and for the calmness with which it describes what was happening:

On the road between Warsaw and Bialystok, in the vicinity of the main railway line, there is a small village by the name of Treblinka. Near that village, the Germans, with the fiendish ingenuity for which they are noted, have built a huge slaughter house, which is operated as a well-organized factory and even has a railway connection with the main line.

From five to six thousand Jews daily are being executed there. The victims are Jewish men, women and children from Poland and from other occupied countries, such as Holland, Czechoslovakia, France, Greece, Belgium and Norway.[12]

The article then describes the killing process, from the arrival of the transports to the burial of the bodies, sparing none of the gruesome details. This report was then followed up by a second a few months later, by 'a prominent Łódź Jew, well known in the Zionist movement', who escaped from Poland in February 1943 and wrote his account 'somewhere in occupied Europe' before it reached a neutral country at the end of September and was then forwarded to Jewish labour leaders in Palestine. The report was described by the journal's editor as 'the best eyewitness account of the horrors of Treblinka, the Polish "city of death", where hundreds of Jews from all occupied Europe are reported to have been executed in gas chambers in accordance with Hitler's plans for the extermination of all Jews within its borders'.[13] The author, deported to Treblinka in September 1942, saved himself by mingling with the 'work Jews' in the camp, the 'derelict, half-mad individuals' who were directing the Jews along the 'corridor' (*Schlauch*) from the undressing area to the gas chamber. After four days at Treblinka, during which time Jews from Holland,

France, Vienna and Poland were brought to the camp and murdered, the author escaped by hiding in a pile of clothing and, after nightfall, creeping out and digging under the barbed wire fences that surrounded the camp. After several failed attempts, the author made it to an unnamed neighbouring country in February 1943.[14] The vague nature of the report – the anonymity of the author and the report's convoluted passage to the US – lend it both its authenticity and a sense of the journal's urgency. But by the time the report appeared in *Polish Jew*, Treblinka was already dismantled.

Because they were pulled down before the Allies arrived at them, and because they were discovered by the Red Army (Vasily Grossman's account of Treblinka is an extraordinary piece of reportage), because primarily Polish Jews were killed there, and most important, because there were so few survivors, the Reinhard camps have long been obscure in Western Europe and the Americas, although that has changed somewhat in recent years.[15] The decision to close them was partly a response to uprisings at Treblinka and Sobibór, which took place in August and October 1943 respectively. Following the Warsaw ghetto uprising in April 1943, which took the Germans by surprise and which required considerable force to quell, most of the forced labour camps for Jews still in existence in Poland were liquidated. Now, after the extraordinarily brave and, from the Nazis' point of view, utterly unexpected revolts on the part of the small number of 'work Jews' in the death camps, especially in Sobibór, where the Jews in the camp managed to murder eleven members of the camp's SS staff, Himmler took the decision to close the major camps in the Lublin region. Over two days on 3–4 November 1943

the Germans carried out 'Operation Harvest Festival', shooting some 42,000 Jewish slave labourers from Majdanek and
other nearby camps, in particular Trawniki and Poniatow-
ska.[16] The remaining Jewish inmates were also shot at the
Janowska camp in Lvov, an infamous site which functioned
as a combined slave labour camp, transit camp and killing fa-
cility, at which some 80,000 Jews are reckoned to have been
killed by shooting.[17] The other reason the Reinhard camps
were dismantled, however, was because the killing facilities
at Auschwitz-Birkenau were being readied. From the spring
of 1942 onwards, while the Jews of Poland were being killed
at the Reinhard camps, the Nazis began deporting Jews from
Western and Central Europe to their deaths at Auschwitz.

Auschwitz opened in 1940 as a concentration camp for
Polish political prisoners. What we know about its role in
the Final Solution reveals as much as it obscures about the
ways in which the Nazis' decision-making process for that
immense genocidal programme unfolded. When he was held
by the Allies after the war, the commandant of Auschwitz,
Rudolf Höss, wrote that he had been informed about the
Final Solution by Himmler:

> In the summer of 1941, I cannot remember the exact date,
> I was suddenly summoned to the *Reichsführer* SS, directly
> by his adjutant's office. Contrary to his usual custom,
> Himmler received me without his adjutant being present
> and said in effect: 'The Führer has ordered that the Jewish
> question be solved once and for all and that we, the SS,
> are to implement that order. The existing extermination
> centres in the East are not in a position to carry out the

large *Aktionen* which are anticipated. I have therefore earmarked Auschwitz for this purpose, both because of its good position as regards communications and because the area can easily be isolated and camouflaged.[18]

Höss' claim should be regarded with suspicion: although it was already clear that he would be hanged when he wrote these words, Höss was still aiming to minimize his own culpability. The fact that he placed the date of the meeting in the summer of 1941 suggests a desire to lay the blame for the Final Solution at the door of eager ideologues such as Himmler. His claim does have some merit, since this timing more or less coincides with Goering's attempt to save face when, on 31 July 1941, he gave de facto recognition to the SS's increasing power and authorized a transfer of power with respect to *Judenpolitik* to Heydrich:

> As supplement to the task which was entrusted to you
> in the decree dated 24 January 1939, to solve the Jewish
> question by emigration and evacuation in the most
> favourable way possible, given present conditions,
> I herewith commission you to carry out all necessary
> preparations with regard to organisational, substantive,
> and financial standpoints for a total solution of the Jewish
> question in the German sphere of influence in Europe.[19]

As we saw in chapter 4, all of this evidence suggests that a decision by Hitler to murder all the Jews of Europe had been taken in July 1941, although the situation was changing rapidly.[20]

Before Auschwitz became, as it has aptly been called, the

'capital of the Holocaust', its role in the Final Solution is not wholly clear. The town itself was in East Upper Silesia and was thus, as of October 1939, part of the German Reich, now being 'Germanized' in the manner of Litzmannstadt (Łódź) in the Warthegau: 'a German Eden in the German East', as it has been called, a fantasy of German colonial settlement with the Poles, both Jewish and non-Jewish, replaced by Germans.[21] We should also note the separation of the Holocaust from the SS's concentration camp system in general until the late stages of the war; Auschwitz, like Majdanek, was anomalous in that it combined the functions of concentration camp, extermination camp and slave labour camp, with many sub-camps attached to it. Its significance grew once it became clear that the Reinhard camps would not suffice to kill all the Jews of Europe. Yet that must have been obvious long before the dismantling of those camps in 1943. Jews exploited by the work camps in the region (run by Albrecht Schmelt) to the point at which they were no longer able to work were killed at Auschwitz in the autumn of 1941.[22] The first experimental gassings of Soviet POWs in the cellars of Block 11 in the main camp in September 1941, then of Jews in February 1942, in the reconverted morgue of the Auschwitz I crematorium as a gas chamber, quickly led to the development of the camp's gassing installations. Regarded as unsatisfactory because it was close to administration buildings, the new crematorium was transferred to Birkenau, where it was used in the Red House (also known as 'Bunker I'), a reclaimed cottage in the village of Brzezinka that was converted into Birkenau's first gas chamber. Bunker I became operational on 20 March 1942, and the first arrivals were 999 Slovak women on 26 March; the next day, a transport of 1,000 Jews left from soon joined by the White House, or 'Bunker II', and these two 'pretty and tidy-looking farmhouses', both 'dazzlingly white-washed, cosily thatched and surrounded with fruit trees', as SS guard Pery Broad put it, became the makeshift gas chambers where the Nazis carried out their mass murder at Auschwitz during 1942.[23]

The first new purpose-built gas chamber and crematorium in Birkenau did not become operational until March 1943, when the large majority of the Holocaust's victims were already dead. In 1941, some 1.1 million Jews were killed by the Germans and their collaborators; in 1942, they killed a further 2.7 million, some 200,000 of whom were murdered in Auschwitz. In 1943, that number dropped significantly to 500,000, of whom about half were killed in Auschwitz.[24] By June 1943, all four of Birkenau's gas chamber and crematorium buildings were in use. Not only does this history confirm the fact that Auschwitz was low-tech, partly built on scavenged materials, but it also suggests that the decision to carry out mass murder at Auschwitz must have been hatched at around the same time as the decision to construct the Reinhard camps, since the planning process required a lead-in time of months. From architectural blueprints to placing orders for ovens with the firm that supplied them, Topf and Sons, Auschwitz's incorporation into the Holocaust must have been in train since October/November 1941, long before the first gassings in Birkenau actually took place.[25] The architects' and engineers' detailed planning, overseen by the fanatical Nazi and talented engineer Hans Kammler, suggests not that the regime slipped accidentally into genocide but that, once Nazism's inherently genocidal inner dynamic had crossed the line from mass murder by neglect in the ghettos to mass murder by direct commission in the euthanasia programme and the *Einsatzgruppen* shootings, the last step of finding a rapid but, for the perpetrators, less difficult form of killing, made the steps to the Reinhard camps and Auschwitz easier.[26]

As a steady stream of transports to Auschwitz-Birkenau continued over the summer of 1942, so too the Nazis' belief that they ruled over an inextinguishable flow of slave labourers grew, with the result that those registered into the men's or women's camps and not killed on arrival were treated with the utmost contempt. The average life expectancy would be measured in weeks. Birkenau itself expanded in 1943 to accommodate the Gypsy family camp and the family camp for Jews from Theresienstadt, both of which allowed family members to remain together for expedient reasons, the latter in case they were required for a further Red Cross inspection as had already taken place at Theresienstadt. When they were no longer needed, both family camps were 'liquidated', that is to say, their inmates murdered: the Theresienstadt family camp on 10–12 July 1944 and the 'Gypsy family camp' on 2 August 1944.

The number of Jews transported to Birkenau rose only slightly in 1943, but they came from all across Europe. In March of that year, the deportation of the Jews of Greece, predominantly from Salonika, began; some 55,000 would be sent to Auschwitz, of whom only a tiny number survived. And in October, following the creation of the Salò Republic, the Nazis began deporting the Jews of Italy; 7,500 would be shipped to Auschwitz. Transports arrived that year from Poland, the Netherlands, Norway, France, Belgium, the Protectorate of Bohemia and Moravia, Yugoslavia, Germany and

Austria, as well as Greece and Italy. For those who were transported long distances to Auschwitz, the journey was horrific. Simon Umschweif, a Viennese Jew deported to Auschwitz in 1942, had the very rare fate of being selected to work in the *Sonderkommando* (the special squad of men forced to work in the gas chamber and crematorium complex, more on which below) but then, with the assistance of influential friends in the camp, being moved to another work detail, the ramp commando. In his 1958 account, he describes as 'particularly terrible' the arrival of a deportation train from Greece that had taken five weeks to arrive:

> The wagons were sealed and nailed shut. As we opened them, we were presented with a terrible image. Crammed in by the hundreds, the people squatted on their possessions. Since they were unable to get out, their excrement remained in the wagon. Everything was a stinking heap. There was no one alive. The air was so poisoned that comrades in our commando fainted. We had to throw everything – the corpses, the possessions and the filth – into huge pits which burned day and night. The pits were eight metres deep and four metres square. Children up to the age of four, who had arrived on other transports, were also thrown, alive, into these pits.[27]

Only the murder of Jews from Hungary changed Birkenau into the iconic camp of the Holocaust, characterized by the modern efficiency of factory-line murder. The famous images of the ramp and the selection process and the notion, now deeply ingrained in Western culture, of the gassing process as industrial genocide, stem from this final phase of Birkenau's existence. Indeed, they come from a single source: the album of photographs created in the camp by SS photographers and discovered by inmate Lili Jacob at the end of the war, and known today as the *Auschwitz Album*.[28] Murder at the Reinhard camps, with their wooden gas chambers and unreliable motor engines, all controlled by a small group of Trawniki men and an even smaller number of SS, was rampantly violent, about as far from the sanitized image of smoothly functioning genocide as one can get, even if the numbers killed in the summer of 1942 were astronomical. In Auschwitz, the same was true in 1942 while the two bunkers were being used, before the new gas chambers and crematoria were constructed in Birkenau. And even these broke down in 1944 because of the huge numbers of corpses, which then had to be burned in the open, as the four clandestine photographs taken by members of the *Sonderkommando* reveal. In other words, the moment at which the killing process at Birkenau became most streamlined was an exception in the history of the camp and in the history of the Holocaust as a whole.[29]

Because Auschwitz combined several functions, it housed many inmates who witnessed the gassing. Life in Auschwitz, especially in Birkenau, was beyond brutal. It has been spoken of many times by eyewitnesses but still seems to defy description; or at least, the gulf between our daily lives and what took place at Auschwitz means that, if it was not another planet, it shakes our understanding of what everyday life can be. What, for example, could religious observance in the camp look like? One memorial book records a Kol Nidre service (the start of Yom Kippur, the holiest day in the Jewish calendar) in one of the barracks. During the prayer, the rabbi blows the shofar, the ram's horn, breaking the chanting of 'who by fire!': 'The shofar awakens the men as if from a dream. At first it is quiet in the barrack. I hear my heart bang. Soon the whole crowd weeps. The voices of the naked women reach Heaven. The crowd weeps softly.'[30]

Helen (Zippi) Tichauer was among the first group of Jews to be deported from Bratislava to Auschwitz in March 1942. Here is how she describes her arrival:

> The thousand girls who came to the lager saw before
> themselves, before the last block, it was block ten, a crowd.
> We did not know at the first moment whether these are
> girls or women or humans altogether. They stood there
> in old Russian uniforms, their hair shorn bare, wooden
> slippers on their feet. And so they stood and stared at us.
> Then suddenly there were heard some calls. Certain girls
> had recognised girl friends, sisters, or the kind, and after
> long . . . They had arrived a day earlier . . . We could not
> talk much, because we were surrounded by SS, but we
> understood that these are our women neighbours from
> Slovakia, and the conditions in which they find themselves.
> That was enough for us.

After being shorn and given their old uniforms to wear, 'in a few hours we were made equals to the arrivals who preceded us'.[31] Describing the bathing and shaving process to her interviewer, David Boder, was clearly traumatic for Tichauer, as she explains the presence of male SS guards who came in 'to inspect us like cattle'. After being tattooed, Tichauer notes that the women 'did not feel anything any more. Because we were like . . . like transformed into stone.'[32] Men too felt different after going through these rituals of induction into the camp, but the gendered dimension to the women's experience, surrounded by men whose gaze humiliated them further in an already terrifying situation, is clear to see. Now the women knew that they were, as Tichauer put it, 'completely cut off from civilisation, from mankind, and that we were now on the "other side" of life, on an "other side" where, however, people still live'.[33] More important, Tichauer gave Boder a powerful description of the murder process, describing the operation of the white house in 1942 and the gas chambers in the next two years. When Boder asks Tichauer for details of 'life in the lager', the first thing she says is:

> What I, for instance, am unable to forget is the fire by day and night. Four ovens . . . were active day and night. And when the pits which were installed in the year 1944 when the Hungarian transports were arriving . . . rendered a sight which does not yield to description. Because one imagined himself in a living hell. One was encircled all round by fire.[34]

Another survivor, Gertrud Deak, later famous as the author Trude Levi, gave an account of her experiences in several Nazi camps to the Wiener Library in London in 1958. Deak was born in Szombathely in Hungary in 1924 and was deported with her family to Auschwitz in 1944. Like Tichauer, Deak describes the humiliation of being shaved all over by men in the 'sauna' building and then explains the life of those inmates registered to work in Birkenau: at 4 a.m. standing for roll call in the cold for four hours, followed by a ladle of something called 'coffee'; another inspection at 9 a.m.; another roll call at midday, this time in the hot sun, for two and a half hours, when 'lunch' was served (a 'pot with a so-called vegetable was passed round'); at 4 p.m. another roll call and the distribution of two small loaves of bread and some cheese between five women; and at 5 p.m., 'we were herded into the barracks, 1200 of us, and we took up our positions for the night, sitting on the floor, back to back, making up rows and pulling up knees, touching the knees of the person opposite'.[35] Two weeks after arrival, Deak explains how the women were taken to Auschwitz I for a shower. Having to run the distance on sharp stones on the way, she was beaten for stepping out of line. On arrival in the town of Auschwitz, 'we were led through the village into a building, where the showers were, but before they led us there, we were taken into a hall, where enormous heaps of fur, silver and jewellery were lying. They made us look at them and told us, that for those hoarded Jewish things we were suffering.'[36] Here the combination of racial paranoia, sexual violence, plunder and greed, ritual humiliation and what Primo Levi called 'useless violence' come crashing together, exemplifying the realities of Auschwitz: not a death factory in the sense of a site of clean, efficient genocide (as if such a thing could exist), but an abattoir of concentrated genocidal fantasy.

Perhaps the most abject of the inmates were the men of the *Sonderkommando*, the 'special squad' forced to work in the gas chamber and crematorium complex, where they helped the victims undress, led them to the gas chamber, cleared the corpses and cremated the bodies. This unimaginable work was literally soul-destroying, as interviews with some of the few survivors attest. As one, Abraham Dragon, said, 'What happened there will remain in our hearts and souls forever. We will never be able to rid ourselves of the memories of Birkenau.'[37] Outsiders

regarded them with suspicion, even considering them collaborators; two famous escapees from Birkenau, Rudolf Vrba and
Alfred Wetzler, described the *Sonderkommando* men as 'always
filthy, destitute, half wild and extraordinarily brutal and ruthless'.[38] And yet, they were able, thanks to the access to resources
they 'enjoyed', to write and to bury secret documents in the
earth around the gas chambers. Thanks to collaborators in the
Polish underground, they were able to smuggle in a camera and
take some of the most important images from the Holocaust,
of corpses being burned and of women waiting in the birch
forest to be gassed; and thanks to the help of four female slave
labourers from the Union munitions plant at Auschwitz (all
four later hanged), they gained access to the gunpowder that
facilitated the *Sonderkommando* uprising of 7 October 1944,
which destroyed one of the gas chambers.[39] Some of their texts
were discovered after the war, the last in 1980, and they likely
buried more manuscripts which will now never be found, or, if
they are, will be unreadable after so many decades of decay.[40]
Probably the most remarkable is a text written by Zalman Gradowski, a religious Jew from Suwałki in north-eastern Poland,
who was deported to Auschwitz in December 1942. His text is
written in a literary Yiddish, addressing the reader directly to
follow him through the stages of murder. It is hard to imagine how he found the solitude and presence of mind to pen
such a carefully structured and beautifully written text under
such conditions, and yet it is full not just of factual information about the murder process but some of the most profound
meditations on what was taking place and the nature of the
perpetrators. 'Come to me, you, the citizen of the free world,'
he exhorts the reader, 'you whose existence and security are

guaranteed by human decency and the law, and I will tell you how the modern criminals and vile murderers have crushed the decency of life and detached the laws of existence.'[41]

Gradowski is most penetrating when he pinpoints the singularly modern aspect of Nazism, assigning it a dialectical relationship with its crimes. The philosophical astuteness of his remarks, which are akin to the ideas being developed at the same time by émigré scholars Max Horkheimer and Theodor Adorno, living in exile in Los Angeles, is remarkable:

> Tell them that even if your heart turns to stone, your brain to a cold calculator and your eyes to camera lenses, even then, you will never again return to them. They would do better to seek you in the eternal forests, for you will have fled from the world inhabited by men, to seek comfort among the cruel beasts of the field, rather than live among cultured demons. For although even animals have been restrained by civilization – their hooves have been dulled and their cruelty greatly curbed – man has not, but has become a beast. The more highly developed a culture, the more cruel its murderers, the more civilized a society, the greater its barbarians; as development increases, its deeds become more terrible.[42]

Auschwitz, the domain of the 'cultured demons', may not have been the site where most of the Jews killed in the Holocaust died but it marked the apogee of the murder process and is rightly remembered as such.

In late 1943 and early 1944 the killing rate slowed at Birkenau, as the Nazis realized that placing ideology above labour made little sense now, given the parlous state of the war economy and the military situation after Stalingrad. The increasingly desperate needs of the war economy drove the Nazi leadership to reconsider its killing programme – a remarkable fact given the drive to murder Jews that was central to Nazism. From 1943 onwards Jews and others were as likely to end up in slave-labour sub-camps attached to the SS's main camps as they were to be murdered outright. In fact, between 210,000 and 220,000 inmates, the majority of them Jews, were transferred from Auschwitz to other camps, including Auschwitz's sub-camps.[43] The rapid growth in the sub-camp system is something that histories of the Holocaust often fail to explain, but it does not downplay Nazi genocidal plans to show that they were attenuated to a small extent in the final year and a half of the war. Rather, when one considers the ways in which slave labourers were treated, the exact opposite is the case. If one cannot always talk of 'annihilation through labour' (this is a term which does not occur very often in the sources), nevertheless the Nazis' attitude, even when labour needs were acute, was that Jews were expendable and that no effort should be made to ensure that productivity levels could become anything like those for normal labourers.

Even within sites which today appear silent and still, the hubbub of movement on the part of guards, SS, civilians and inmates meant that the camp was 'always in motion'.[44] For the victims, this movement was overwhelmingly bewildering, and sub-camp inmates often did not even know where they were. The fact is, however, that the use of Jews as slave labourers saved the lives of several hundred thousands who would otherwise have simply been killed. Even if their deaths were being deferred, their lives were prolonged as a result of the unexpected flexibility of the Nazis' racial laws from late 1943 onwards in reaction to the desperate needs of the war economy. 'These camps', one historian notes, 'were among the best options available for Jews; for other inmates they were usually the worst. Jews were worst affected, but it would be incorrect to say that their labour ability played no role in their fate under the Germans.'[45]

This flexibility should not be overstated; it was a last-ditch measure, and the survivors were simply fortunate that the war did not last even a few days longer, for otherwise their number would have been even smaller. But the use of Jews as slave labourers was, from the Nazis' ideological point of view, ironic. The vast expansion of the sub-camp system and, especially, the death marches which took place as the camps were evacuated in the face of the Allies' advance (which we will examine in chapter 7) suggest the idea of the Holocaust as an ecological project. The Nazis wanted to 'purify' Europe from the 'non-native' species that was the Jews, with the extermination camp the place where 'the Nazi ecological imperative – to make Germany "judenrein" – will be implemented in full'.[46] From the ghettos – which the Nazis called 'Jew reservations' – to the extermination camps, the victims of the Holocaust testified to the fact that they felt like animals. Naomi Sampson, in hiding in a small underground shelter on a farm in Poland, could see cattle through the cracks in the shelter:

> My eyes nearly popped out watching them chew and drool
> over the food as they were eating. As I felt my tears and
> my saliva dripping onto my cold hands, I licked my hands

without taking my eyes from those animals, 'Lucky animals!' I thought. Why couldn't I be one? (Actually, I felt I *was* an animal in those days – an underprivileged animal.)[47]

Teenage diarist Dawid Sierakowiak put it in the Łódź ghetto: 'We are not considered humans at all; cattle for work or slaughter.'[48] During the round-up in Buczacz in April 1943, ten-year-old Izidor Hecht hid with his family behind a staircase on a farm owned by a Polish-Ukrainian couple, Józef and Barbara Zarivny: 'The feeling of death stomping right above your head is impossible to communicate,' he said. 'You wish you could turn into an ant, you close your eyes and try to hide somewhere deep in the ground.' The next year, when the rest of his family was caught and murdered, only Izidor and his grandmother survived, because they made it to a hiding place in the hayloft in time.[49] A nine-year-old girl hiding with her three-year-old sister told her interviewer after the war how they slept in fields and orchards: 'Shulamit used to say then, "Buzha, do you see what a faithful mother the calf has? Look how she licks its ears. I wish I had been a little calf!" And when she saw the cat on a bed of boards over a stove, she used to say, "I wish I had been a cat!"'[50]

What is ironic then is that, late in the war, when the majority of the Holocaust's victims had been killed and when the Nazis, from an ideological point of view, should have been eradicating the memory of the existence of such a thing as a 'Jewish race', they instead 'contaminated' German soil. Although the Reich had officially been declared *judenrein* ('free of Jews'), by hugely expanding the number of sites in which Jews were held and then, by marching them across Central Europe, killing tens of thousands along the way, the Nazis rendered the notion of a cleansed fatherland utterly void. This world of sub-camps grew up not because the Nazis did not believe in their ideology – the latter was not, as some early commentators suggested, merely a means of seducing the masses – but out of sheer necessity and it was only conceived of in such terms. The Nazis never gave up on their dream of denying the Jews the right to exist, depriving them not only of the right to live in a German environment but of far more: 'They deprived the Jews of their "there is",' as one commentator puts it, emphasizing the Nazis' goal of eliminating the Jews not just from particular places but from the ranks of existence as such.[51] Bearing that in mind helps us to understand how the Nazis could murder hundreds of thousands of Jews from Hungary at the same time, in spring and summer of 1944, as they were extracting the young and fit – a quarter of those who arrived at Auschwitz – in order to put them to work as slave labourers in the arms industry and elsewhere as the German war economy was at its lowest ebb. 'The terrifying truth', one historian says, 'is that Germany contrived to murder so many people so swiftly and still gain some economic benefit.'[52] Following a three-day visit to the Lublin region in July 1942, including to Sobibór in the company of Globocnik, Himmler ordered on 19 July that the 'resettlement of the entire Jewish population of the General Government' should be completed by the end of that year and that Jews should not be used for labour apart from half a million who were to be held in specified assembly camps.[53] In other words, in the competition between labour and annihilation, when it came to the Jews, annihilation took precedence. Yet, towards the end of the war, this rule was bent so that Jews were once again used for labour, albeit temporarily. A few examples suffice.

Jürgen Bassfreund, a young man originally from Trier, was sent to Auschwitz from Berlin in 1943. After surviving until the camp was evacuated, he was sent on a death march (as we will see in chapter 7) until he ended up in Mühldorf, a sub-camp of Dachau, in February 1945.[54] Here he and his fellow inmates, emaciated from the journey, were set to work carrying cement to build an airport. Bassfreund spoke about his experiences after the war, when he was interviewed by the pioneering David Boder, one of the first to use recording equipment to collect accounts of surviving Jews, in the Funkkaserne DP camp near Munich. He told Boder that 'the conditions in Mühldorf were catastrophic. People were covered with lice. We received no underwear to change.' He contracted typhus and was placed in a tent with other dying men. At the end of the camp's existence he claims that an order was given to kill the sick but that the camp commandant was too scared to comply with the Americans so close by, and so Bassfreund survived.[55]

Another survivor, an Orthodox Jewish Hungarian girl named Kornelia Paskusz, was deported with her mother and sisters from Csorna to Sopron in June 1944, and from there to Auschwitz. Within a week, they 'were all defeated in body and spirit, stricken with pain, suffering from exhaustion, hunger, heat and rain'. Then they were suddenly sent off to a new camp in Hessisch Lichtenau, a sub-camp of Buchenwald near Kassel which served a munitions factory run by Dynamit Nobel. As Paskusz notes, the German workers by this time had been drafted to fight on the front, and so 'the Germans had brought the Jewish prisoners here to work as slave labour-ers'. As was common in these sub-camps, the conditions were slightly better than at Auschwitz; nevertheless, 'we were now slated to suffer the punishment of working beyond our physi-cal and emotional limits' in manufacturing cannon powder. Even without the lack of food and decent conditions, the work was itself deadly: 'The powder was yellow and bitter, and the air was so saturated with it that our hair and bodies were constantly yellow. It was dangerous to inhale this poi-sonous powder, and we were given flimsy masks to minimize the hazard. In spite of the masks, two of our workmates, both young girls, died from inhaling the poison.' Paskusz reflected that she and the other inmates would follow in their footsteps: 'Were we prisoners or were we slaves? We could not be prison-ers, because prisoners are not forced to do such hard labour. We could not be slaves because slaves are given a proper meal at the end of the day. We knew only that we were a down-trodden, abused and humiliated people.' The only bright spot was that Paskusz was together with her mother; despite being weak and ill, they survived.[56]

Although most survivors could describe the work they had to do, many had little sense of what exactly they were doing, what or who it was for or what product they were being forced to work on. Often, they barely knew where they were; the fight for survival made such considerations irrelevant. In her report on Mittelsteine, for example, the former inmate Sara Michalowicz explained, in a mixture of Yiddish and German, that: 'Wo war di genaue Lage fun lager Mittelstein kan ich nicht wissen, wajl wir haben ni di frajhejt gezejn' (I cannot know the exact location of the Mittelsteine camp, because we never saw freedom).[57] Nevertheless, survivors could often provide quite detailed descriptions of their living conditions in the camps. Rachel Zolf worked on the production line of the Jumo 004 jet engine in Markkleeberg, a sub-camp of Buchenwald; she could describe her work but, from the Nazis' perspective, there was no need for her to know any more:

> There was a line of machines, and I worked on the first one. It was called *Drehbank* [lathe]. I received a large piece of iron, maybe more than one meter long, and put it in the machine. I was supposed to cut it into pieces, take off the black iron from the top, and drill a round hole in the middle with different knives . . . then they passed it on to the second machine behind me. So it went like a conveyor belt and each woman made a part.[58]

Miriam Givon, a survivor of Zittau, another Jumo engine factory, described the contrast between this camp and Auschwitz, from where she had come:

> We were billeted in a three-storey building and it was a paradise in comparison to Auschwitz. Each inmate got his own bed with a straw mattress and a pillow. We got food and they told us: 'Kinder, you are now in the hands of civilians so have no fear. We will take care of you and everything will be all right. You are going to work and in the evenings you return here and get enough food.' There were baths and a WC with running water. We got dishes and spoons with our numbers (which was not tattooed on us).[59]

Although conditions at Zittau worsened towards the end of the war, most of the inmates survived. The same applies to the women who worked at Christianstadt, a huge complex of factories which comprised one of the Gross-Rosen sub-camps. Arriving from Auschwitz, Miriam Jung said Christianstadt was 'like being on vacation' in comparison, and Věra Hájková-Duxová said that the women 'couldn't get over [their] amazement' when they saw proper bunks with straw mattresses.[60] They soon had to face the reality, which meant brutal work and harsh overseers, with little food and extremely basic hygiene facilities.

Like Kornelia Paskusz, Gertrud Deak, whom we encountered above as she arrived at Auschwitz, was also sent to the sub-camp of Hessisch-Lichtenau at the end of August 1944, in a journey that lasted three days. She was twenty years old. After the experience of Auschwitz, she was amazed by what she saw:

> At the camp there were small barracks, consisting of 6 rooms each, with stripes of beautifully tended grass and trees as well as a beautiful shower-room, which was at our disposal and where we could wash ourselves once a day. We had bunks with straw-sacks to sleep upon and though it was quite warm, there was a radiator in every room and we had central heating. Soap was handed out; again marked, that it was the fat of the Jews. We received a blanket each, and an overcoat and a number on an enormous white square, nearly covering one's back, which had to be sewn on everybody's clothes . . . we had three extremely good meals and the 'Zaehl-Appell' [roll call] twice a day lasting half an hour only in the morning and in the evening.

'Life', as Deak said after the war, 'seemed to be a paradise.'[61] Once work began on the sixth day, however, the true nature of the place was revealed. One working group was sent to a factory producing sulphur products; within two weeks, the skin of the women working there turned yellow, and they began dying in agony from sulphur poisoning. The second group, to which Deak belonged, had to walk 6 kilometres to a munitions factory, where they worked preparing the mixture for grenades and shells. Deak had to pull a wagon loaded with grenades and was lucky not to be crushed by it. She found herself at the receiving end of the foreman's 'unpleasantness' and was often ordered by him to collect the human excrement that was around the factory. As bombardments became more frequent, life in the camp became harsher, with the inmates being made to perform pointless tasks such as moving piles of stones from one place to another. Food became scarcer, the heating only worked intermittently, and the shower-room was closed.[62] With the inmates now increasingly emaciated, a selection took place, with the guards telling the inmates that 200 volunteers were needed for light work elsewhere. Deak was selected, but when the group was counted and found to be one person too many, she was removed, probably because of her rosy cheeks, which made her look healthier than she was. The group was sent to Birkenau and gassed.[63]

The sub-camps may not have been comparable to Auschwitz but they were, as another witness said of Hochweiler, another Gross-Rosen sub-camp, 'still concentration camp-like' (ebenfalls KZ-mäßig).[64] 'We were beaten at work and very poorly accommodated', noted one witness who had been in Gebhardsdorf and St Georgenthal, also Gross-Rosen sub-camps. The same witness, Rosa Rubin, also explained that relations between the different national groups were not bad but also not close and that the Polish and Hungarian women were housed separately. In general, she remembered Gebhardsdorf as being 'a tough camp, we went hungry there, there was no medicine, we were treated badly'; on the other hand, she also noted that she knew of no cases of killing in the camp, with the exception of a Hungarian woman, a doctor, and her daughter, who were transported along with several ill inmates, though she admitted she also did not know for sure what their fate was.[65] As brutal as they were, still, none of these camps was like Auschwitz.

The largest of these camps was Mittelbau-Dora, in the Harz Mountains of northern Germany, where 60,000 inmates were worked to death in the production of secret 'V' weapons (the 'wonder weapons' which were to be used against Britain, Belgium and France in the late stages of the war) in huge subterranean tunnels. Originally a sub-camp of Buchenwald with the code name Dora, created after Allied air raids destroyed the rocket production facilities at Peenemünde on the Baltic Sea, Mittelbau became an autonomous camp in 1944, the last one created in the Third Reich, with its own complex of sub-camps. Until the last stage, most of the inmates were not Jews. The conditions in the underground tunnels, in which the inmates worked for twelve hours a day with little food then slept, breathing in the same noxious fumes, were murderous from the start, and the death rate mushroomed. As more sub-camps were created in a desperate bid to keep arms production going (even though only a minority of the Mittelbau inmates worked on arms production – most worked in mining or construction), a mobile selection process was introduced, in which inmates were moved to ever-harsher commandos until, weakened by their experience, they finally died.[66] In the final phase of the war, at the start of 1945, some 16,000 already dying Jewish inmates from Gross-Rosen and Auschwitz were dumped into the Mittelbau complex, with disastrous results. Some final transports from Mittelbau took place to Belsen and Ravensbrück in the final days of the war, meaning that some of the suffering inmates passed through a handful of sites of horror in the chaos of the collapsing concentration camp system.[67]

The variety of Nazi sites of incarceration was well captured in an intelligence report from early 1945 produced by Supreme Headquarters, Allied Expeditionary Forces. Giving a remarkably well-informed overview of the Nazi camp system and distinguishing between the different sorts of camps and grades of prisoners, this report explains in some detail how the sub-camps were understood by the Allies just before the end of the war.[68] Using the example of Natzweiler and its 'Aussenlager (Subsidiary Labour Camps)', which had been liberated in the autumn of 1944, the report explains how these camps were successfully evacuated, 'allowing the Germans to retain much-needed manpower and machinery and denying this, along with possible sources of information, to the Allies'.[69] With respect to the sub-camps, the report noted that 'Recent reports have claimed greater leniency towards the inmates of concentration camps, despite the fact that executions are still taking place (especially of potential collaborators) and the death rate in camps is abnormally high.' Although somewhat incredulous, the author then went on:

Recent documentary evidence corroborates these reports. However, it must be stated that this change of heart on the part of the SS is not due to any suddenly developed humanitarian feelings, and the new policy is in fact entirely due to the fact that they have now discovered the potential value of the labour force provided by concentration camp inmates at a time when manpower is extremely short. One feels entitled to say that if the inmates are not considered 'the property of the Führer' they are now at any rate considered HIMMLER's property and a source of income to the SS.[70]

This was a remarkably accurate assessment. Although there had always been some Jews working as slave labourers both before and during the war, including some of those still alive when ghettos were liquidated, the sub-camp system developed rapidly at the end of the war. A quarter of the Jews sent to Auschwitz from Hungary in the spring of 1944 were selected for labour, and by 1945 there were more inmates in sub-camps than in main camps.[71] At the start of the war there were six main camps in existence; by the end of 1943 that had become 260 main and satellite camps; by July 1944 almost 600, and by January 1945 more than 730. A list compiled by Polish prosecutor Jan Sehn in 1950 contained 1,050 names of camps, from Abterode in Thuringia, a sub-camp of Buchenwald, to Zwodau in Czechoslovakia.[72] By some reckonings, the number of sub-camps was more than 1,100.[73] That figure had been reached 'despite the fact that the area of German rule had been considerably reduced and numerous camps in both the east and west had been disbanded and their inmates deported back within the boundaries of the Reich'.[74] Indeed, the increased use of slave labour towards the end of the war was a sign of crisis, 'a measure of last resort for a mercilessly overheated armaments industry and in a system whose downfall was ever more likely in view of the hopeless state of the war'.[75] Apart from revealing the complex network of the camp system itself, such figures indicate that by the last stages of the war, 'there was hardly a single town in Germany and Austria without its own satellite camp'.[76] When one considers that these figures refer only to the camps administered by the SS and not to camps run by other agencies such as local councils, firms or private individuals, of which there were at least 1,300 in the Reich and occupied Poland,[77] it becomes clear that it is quite justified to write that the Nazis created 'perhaps the most pervasive collection of detention sites that any society has ever created'.[78] Europe was literally a continent of camps.[79] These camps were not, as Primo Levi rightly noted, a by-product of wartime emergency conditions; rather, they were 'the early seedlings of the New Order'. In this vision, in which a new law would dictate the roles played by master and slave, camps would have been essential: 'If Fascism had prevailed', Levi wrote, 'the whole of Europe would have been transformed into a complex system of forced labour and extermination camps, and those cynically edifying words ["*Arbeit macht frei*"] would have been read on the entrance to every workshop and every worksite.'[80]

It is striking that the existence of and role played by these sub-camps has not been better incorporated into the history and memory of the Holocaust, since very many of the survivors who have written or given spoken accounts of their survival managed to survive precisely because of their passage through them. Indeed, the notion of a mobile Holocaust becomes meaningful at the end of the war, since many camp inmate slave labourers were moved around from one site to another as the war economy demanded. Besides, although being held as slave labourers in the sub-camps saved the lives of tens of thousands of the Nazis' victims, for the Jews among them this fact is a matter of contingency, not policy. Had the Nazis prevailed, there is no doubt that they would have been murdered. And many survived only because they were 'liberated' by the Allies at the last minute; a few days or weeks more and the majority of them, emaciated and despairing, would not have lived. The sub-camps are also an important part of the history of the Holocaust.

The piano-playing murderer has become a cliché of Holocaust film and literature. Yet the juxtaposition of civilization and barbarism continues to offer an insight into the nature of Nazism. In 1944 the composer Gideon Klein was deported from Theresienstadt to Auschwitz, and from there to the sub-camp of Fürstengrube, where he died. One of his fellow deportees later recalled:

> With us, the other prisoners, he was brought for a medical examination and there we all stood and waited, against the wall, naked, under an SS-man guard. In the otherwise empty room stood a piano. To make the waiting easier on himself, the bored SS man asked if someone could play. Klein said he could and, naked like the rest of us, he sat down and played something of his own repertoire.[81]

CHAPTER 7

Great Is the Wrath: 'Liberation' and Its Aftermath

> 'It was just because we knew that liberation was close
> that the German terror became so insufferable. We felt
> like a swimmer approaching the shore and fearing that his
> strength will fail him just before his feet touch land.'
> — Tuvia Borzykowski[1]

Death Marches

Jürgen Bassfreund, as we saw in the previous chapter, grew up in Trier and Cologne. He was deported to Auschwitz from Berlin in February 1943, then sent to Monowitz (Buna) and, at the end of the camp's existence, was sent on a death march to Dachau, which he described as 'the greatest torture of all we had undergone in the camps'. 'En route, many, many people who could not keep up were shot. Those who stopped, everyone who fell on the road, was shot, no matter whether it was a man or a woman.' From Ploetz, Bassfreund was sent by train to Gross-Rosen and then on to Dachau, also by train. The camp inmates were quickly disabused of their assumption that being in a closed car would be preferable because it was so cold: 'It was so terrible that people went

223

crazy during the trip, and soon we had the first death among us.' The train stopped to allow troops to pass, the number of dead soon rose 'and the bodies began to smell . . . without any nourishment, without a drop of water – there was snow outside [but] the SS men gave us nothing – there was a mass of insane and dead people in the car'. After five days and nights in this travelling death camp with no food, Bassfreund arrived at Dachau, where after three weeks he was transported again, to the sub-camp of Mühldorf in Upper Bavaria.[2]

Bassfreund told his story to David Boder after the war. Another of Boder's interviewees was Ludwig Hamburger, who at the age of fourteen was taken from Katowice to Auschwitz with his parents, where he was separated from them and never saw them again. After two months of backbreaking work carrying stones, Hamburger was transferred to the Blechhammer sub-camp. One of the largest of the Auschwitz sub-camps, Blechhammer held about 4,000 men and boys.[3] After two years at Blechhammer, Hamburger was evacuated with most of the rest of the camp on 21 December 1944. Explaining to Boder how they marched day and night in the direction of Gleiwitz (Gliwice) in Silesia, Hamburger's description of 4,000 men being forced into a barn one night left Boder forced to ask for clarifications – this was still an unknown story in 1946:

Hamburger: It was terrible, indeed. The SS men were around. They were strongly armed. They chased us inside. There was very little room, so that one climbed on top of the other. When we came out in the morning, many comrades remained behind.

Boder: What does it mean, 'remained behind'?

Hamburger: We ourselves have trampled them to death.

Boder: Yes. In the barn.

Hamburger: With only . . . with our own feet have we trampled our brothers to death.

Boder: Hm.

By the time they arrived in Gross-Rosen, the 4,000 men who had left Blechhammer had become 280. 'The road from Blechhammer to Gross-Rosen', Hamburger said, 'was strewn with dead. Every ten or fifteen meters, a corpse.'[4]

How can one explain the death marches? Between 17 and 22 January 1945, just days before Red Army troops arrived at the camp complex, some 56,000 inmates of Auschwitz, Jews and non-Jews, were evacuated. Most were marched in the direction of towns fairly close by, especially Gleiwitz (Gliwice) and Wodzisław, before being taken by rail to concentration camps deeper inside the Reich. Among them were small numbers of children aged as young as six.[5] The evacuations occurred in three stages: from April–September 1944, when Majdanek and camps such as Kaiserwald in the Baltic states (then still Reich Commissariat Ostland) were emptied, as well as the camp set up on the ruins of the ghetto in Warsaw after the 1944 uprising; inmates from camps closed at this stage were for the most part moved to sub-camps set up further west; January–February 1945, when Auschwitz and its sub-camps, some of the Gross-Rosen sub-camps and Stutthof were evacuated; and April–May 1945, when just before the end of the war the inmates of other camps, including Mittelbau-Dora, Neuengamme, Sachsenhausen, Mauthausen and

Figure 3
An American soldier stands over the bodies of inmates of
Flossenbürg shot in a forest near Neunburg vorm Wald,
29 April 1945.

Ravensbrück were also evacuated, even as inmates from other camps arrived at some of them. The last camps to be evacuated were Reichenau, Gablonz and Landeshut, sub-camps of Gross-Rosen in the Sudeten Mountains, during the night of 7–8 May 1945, just hours before the area was liberated, and the Theresienstadt ghetto, which the Red Army reached on 9 May.[6] They were sent towards Dachau, Buchenwald, Sachsenhausen, Flossenbürg, Mauthausen and Belsen, and in the very last days of the war from those camps too, where the evacuations were often halted by Allied troops, or found by them abandoned in forests or on railway sidings.

The Jewish camp inmates sent on the death marches have been described as 'the last mass victims of the Holocaust'.[7] But Jews were not the only victims of the death marches, which are perhaps better understood as part of a wider genocidal paroxysm that was undertaken by the camp guards, with the widespread participation of the German population. They were not a deliberately contrived means of continuing a genocidal policy; had that been the case, the Nazis had the means to kill all the inmates.[8] They were nevertheless murderous on a huge and brutal scale, with the weak and dying inmates at the mercy of the guards' rage and bitterness. The latter was heightened by the guards' anxiety about what would happen to them at war's end, in a context of fear, shame and resentment, societal breakdown, large-scale executions of Germans for defeatism and desertion and widespread propaganda insisting that a defeated Germany would be subjected to the vampiric revenge of the 'international Jew'. The death marches have been described as 'walking camps', 'intertwined micro-communities', a 'societal crime', the 'last collective crime of Nazi Germany', the 'last phase of the Final Solution' and the 'final stage of Nazi genocide'.[9] Whatever the case, it is clear that the experience was shattering for the victims. They died in agony, knowing that the end was near, and 'the killings became more intimate through relocation to the space of the moving columns'.[10]

Even today it remains extremely difficult to reconstruct the precise routes taken by the marches. Especially with respect to the larger evacuations, different groups were sent in different directions, sometimes the same group was split and sent on different paths before reconnecting later. The guards destroyed many documents, meaning that a precise record of official instructions cannot be found; for example, Paul Kreutzer, an SS man and member of the administration at Mittelbau, stated after the war that when he was at Belsen for two days he guarded 'two big boxes containing all the documents and receipt forms and also quite a lot of money'. These he took to Heide in Schleswig-Holstein and then, after the capitulation, 'I was ordered to destroy everything and all the documents were destroyed and the money was distributed amongst the men of the whole regiment as a sort of farewell discharge money.'[11] Or, as Abel Herzberg more cuttingly put it: 'Onwards! Where to? They are clearing the camp. The archives are being taken to the crematorium by the cartload, to stoke the fire to burn the corpses. The British are advancing.'[12] It is hardly surprising that when it comes to explaining the death marches, much remains speculative.

Herzberg again provides an ironic commentary on the process:

The death marches, January–May 1945

■ Concentration camp
--- Route on foot
— Route by train

SOVIET UNION

POLAND

Königsberg
Palmnicken
Mikoszewo
Stutthof
Puck
Gdańsk
Pruszcz Gdańsk
Poznań
Warsaw
Łódź
Lublin
Majdanek

Kraków
Płaszów
Mikołów
Auschwitz
Rybnik
Reichenau
Kłodzko
Jelenia
Wrocław
Gross-Rosen

BALTIC SEA

SWEDEN

DENMARK

NORTH SEA

Neustadt
Lübeck
Hamburg
Neuengamme
Bremen
Bergen-Belsen
Hanover
Magdeburg
Berlin
Sachsenhausen

NETHERLANDS

BELGIUM

Düsseldorf
Cologne
GERMANY
Frankfurt
Stuttgart

Mittelbau-Dora
Nordhausen
Buchenwald
Ohrdruf
Weimar
Leipzig
Dresden
Theresienstadt
Prague
Flossenbürg

CZECHOSLOVAKIA

Dachau
Mühldorf
Munich
Kaufering
Landsberg

Linz
Gusen
Mauthausen
Gunskirchen
AUSTRIA
Vienna

Graz
Graz-South

HUNGARY
Budapest

FRANCE

SWITZERLAND
Bern

ITALY

Natzweiler-Stutthof

0   100   200   300 km
0   100   200 miles

We meet endless convoys of prisoners who are being brought to Bergen-Belsen from the east. Why? Only someone who knows what is *Organisation* understands that. 'When the enemy advances from the east, retreat to the west.' That is *Befehl*. 'When the enemy advances from the west, retreat to the east' – that is also *Befehl*. That they must meet somewhere no one has thought about. For if one did think about such things, the entire *Organisation* would be superfluous. The convoys greet one another: 'Where are you going?'

'We don't know.'

'Where are we?'

'In Bergen-Belsen.'

'What's the food like?'

'Marvellous, every day potatoes with goulash.'[13]

A map of death marches to Belsen illustrates the distances that camp inmates marched or were transported, the variety of sites from which they came, and helps to explain visually why it was that Belsen was in such a state of disarray by April 1945. That was, of course, the fault of the commandant and the concentration camp system but the scenes described by the Allied soldiers on arrival there make more sense when we consider the large number of inmates who were dumped in the camp in its last weeks of operation.

Such a broad analysis runs up against the horror experienced by the victims, whose accounts confirm the picture of relentless death and murder. Sarolta Mittelmann, a Hungarian Jewish woman from Ungvár, was one of a group of inmates evacuated from Mauthausen to its sub-camp of Gunskirchen, some 60 kilometres to the south-west, at the end of April

Transports to KZ Bergen-Belsen,
December 1944 to April 1945,
from the sites shown on this map

■ Main concentration camps
■ Sub-camps
• Other sites

FRANCE

BELGIUM
• Brussels

NETHERLANDS
• Amsterdam

SWITZERLAND

Wilhelmshaven
Bremen-Farge
Hamburg-Langenhorn
Hamburg-Eidelstedt
Hamburg-Fuhlsbüttel
Hamburg-Sasel
Hamburg-Tiefstack
Pölitz
Hornburg
Bremen
Obernheide
Uphusen
KZ Neuengamme
Lübberstedt

Hannover-Mühlenberg
Hannover-Stöcken
Hannover-Ahlem
Lerbeck
Hildesheim
Eschershausen
Lippstadt
Dortmund
Bad Salzgitter-
Duderstadt
Hessisch-Lichtenau
Allendorf
Klein-Bodungen
Grosswerther
Mühlhausen
KZ Bergen-Belsen
Unterlüss – Hambühren
Hannover-Misburg
Hannover-Limmer
Braunschweig
Magdeburg
Drütte
Watenstedt
Wolfen
Ellrich
Harzungen
Wöffleben
Nordhausen
KZ Mittelbau-Dora
Leipzig
Markkleeberg
Taucha
Tröglitz
Altenburg
Oederan
Dresden
Elsnig

Cologne
Frankfurt
Leonberg
Stuttgart
Echterdingen
Kaufering
Schömberg
KZ Natzweiler
KZ Dachau
• Munich

KZ Buchenwald
Ohrdruf
Neustadt
Plauen
Helmbrechts
KZ Flossenbürg
Leitmeritz
Theresienstadt
Prague
Altenburg

KZ Sachsenhausen
• Berlin
KZ Ravensbrück

Guben
Schertendorf
Halbau
Schleisiersee/Grünberg
Kurzbach
Christianstadt
Birnbaumel
Dyhernfurth
Hochweiler
KZ Gross-Rosen
Gräben
Falkenberg
Wüsteglersdorf

PROTECTORATE OF
BOHEMIA
AND MORAVIA

SUDETENLAND

AUSTRIA
KZ Mauthausen
• Vienna

SLOVAKIA

HUNGARY
• Budapest

WARTHELAND
• Warsaw

GENERAL
GOVERNMENT

EAST
PRUSSIA
KZ Stutthof
• Danzig

• Kraków
• Tschenstochau
KZ Auschwitz

0   100   200   300 km
0   100   200 miles

1945. They had only arrived there on 15 April, having already endured Auschwitz, the Gross-Rosen sub-camp of Zillerthal-Erdmannsdorf, Walldorf (Frankfurt), Morgenstern (another Gross-Rosen sub-camp), Mittelbau, and the Mittelbau sub-camp of Grosswerther (where the women were held in two requisitioned dance halls). They were moved swiftly from place to place as the Allies advanced or, in the case of Mittelbau and Grosswerther, as they bombed the area around the town of Nordhausen. The women still alive at this point were evacuated with the other Mauthausen inmates:

> We were marched off together with the men. On departure we got food for one day. We marched off. On the way we had very little to eat. Hunger was terrific. The men plucked out grass and herbs, which we boiled. Sometimes we managed to dig out a few potatoes, but whoever was caught was bumped off. Nevertheless, we dared it, so badly were we famished. Of course not many could stick it out, and many sat down on the roadside worn out. The SS officer rode by bicycle all along the road and shot everybody to death who he saw sitting. Once we sat down totally exhausted. The SS man noticed it and pulled his gun on us. Quickly we jumped up, and so he spared our lives.[14]

Reska Weiss, a middle-aged woman also from Ungvár, was initially transported to Latvia, where she experienced a number of camps. At one, near Dvinsk (Daugavpils), in June 1944, she was forced to work as part of a group covering a pit of corpses; when the job was done the SS shot the group into another pit, but Weiss and another woman miraculously survived unscathed and, the following morning, surreptitiously joined the next group that had been sent to cover the pit she had climbed out of. She was then sent to Stutthof, from where the inmates were evacuated in the direction of another part of Nazi-occupied Poland. In the snow and freezing cold, the women could barely keep up:

> Had weeks or months elapsed since we started on this death march? Neither, just a few days. But we could measure time only by the number of our dead. The living were constantly dwindling, and the racing row, running at whatever speed it could summon up, had already become pathetically short . . . We were really no longer human beings in the accepted sense. Not even animals, but putrefying corpses moving on two legs . . . But the dead were no concern of ours. We still wanted to survive.[15]

And she did survive, after hiding in a haystack one night, after which she received help from locals and wandered the area until, after the liberation, she made her way to Cracow and finally back to Ungvár, where her two sons also returned, ill but alive. Not all evacuations took place on foot, however. The inmates of Hessisch-Lichtenau, including Gertrud Deak, whom we encountered in chapter 6, were sent out from that camp as the US army was approaching Kassel. They were loaded into wagons and told they were going to be sent to Buchenwald. The train was bombed and the engine destroyed; by the time a replacement arrived, they were told that since Buchenwald was now under American control, they would be going elsewhere.[16] Two days later they arrived in Leipzig and were surprised to be placed in what had previously been an SS officers' camp, which was clean, with showers and decent food. When it was bombed, they were marched to the Buchenwald sub-camp of Leipzig-Thekla and then, on 7 April 1945, out again, as the whole sub-camp was evacuated.

When Auschwitz was evacuated, Thomas Buergenthal, not quite eleven years old, was among the inmates. On the first night of the march, they were allowed to sleep on the side of the road. 'By that time', Buergenthal recalls, 'some of the marchers had already died. Those who could not go on and either sat down by the side of the road or simply collapsed were shot by the SS guards, who kicked their bodies into the nearest ditch. Over the next two days many more would die in this manner. After a while I would no longer flinch when yet another shot was fired.'[17] After three days walking to Gliwice, Buergenthal and the other marchers were then placed in open railcars and sent, in a journey that lasted ten days, to Oranienburg, near Berlin. There he was sent first to the Heinkel aircraft factory and then to Sachsenhausen concentration camp. Seven decades later, Buergenthal reflected:

In January 1945 Germany was fighting for its survival and yet the Nazi regime was willing to use its rapidly dwindling resources – rail facilities, fuel and troops – to move half-starved and dying prisoners from Poland to Germany. Was it to keep us from falling into the hands of the Allies or to maintain Germany's supply of slave labour? The insanity of it all is hard to fathom, unless one thinks of it as a game concocted by the inmates of an asylum for the criminally insane.[18]

If insanity is generally not a useful analytical term for trying to explain Nazi Germany, with respect to the death marches it seems hard to avoid.

'Liberation'

As the camps in the heart of Germany were being evacuated, so inmates from camps further east were arriving at them. The result was administrative chaos, the collapse of the concentration camp system and, for the inmates, a devastating situation of overcrowding, starvation, and the rapid spread of diseases such as typhus and dysentery. Statements such as this have been written many times in numerous history books and survivors' accounts. But what they really mean remains almost unbearable to read. The killing process of the Holocaust, from the face-to-face shootings to the gas chambers of Auschwitz, is hard to take in. The descriptions of the 'liberation' are, if it is possible, even more shattering, a result of the fact that the living were mingled in with the dead in Belsen, Buchenwald and other camps, and the absurd futility of the unnecessary deaths so close to the end of the war. All deaths in the Holocaust were unnecessary, of course, but the fate of those killed on the death marches or who died just before or – as occurred in many cases – after the Allied troops arrived on the scene is intolerable, and the mind rebels against it. The fact that small children were among those who died adds to the sense of incomprehensibility, as Herzberg implies: 'Next to us, among the Greeks, a child of two is dying. Croup. It takes a long time. People whisper. When it is over, a wild wailing breaks forth. It is not even heartrending any longer. It is no longer possible for one person to feel compassion for another. All he feels is tired-ness. He is sleepy.'[19]

The soldiers involved in uncovering evidence of massa-cres committed on the death marches were shocked by their discoveries. They swiftly rounded up local German civilians, forced them to disinter the bodies, often with their bare hands, then make coffins for them and participate in services which gave the dead a decent burial.[20] Those soldiers liber-ating the camps were even more astonished by what they found; nothing had prepared them for the experience. James Creasman, for example, an army reporter for the *Rainbow Reveille*, the journal of the division that liberated Dachau, wrote of his comrades that:

> Seasoned as they were to stark reality, these trained
> observers gazed at the freight cars full of piled cadavers, no
> more than bones and skin, and they could not believe what
> they saw . . . Riflemen, accustomed to witnessing death,
> had no stomach for rooms stacked almost ceiling-high with
> tangled human bodies adjoining the crematorium furnaces,
> looking like some maniac's woodpile.[21]

With respect to the confusion between the living and the dead, Lieutenant George Moise wrote of Nordhausen that:

> The camp was literally a charnel house, with the distinction
> that a small proportion of the bodies therein were not
> quite dead. As the camp was cleaned out the living and
> the dead were found intermingled indiscriminately, and in
> some cases bodies had to be carefully examined by medical
> personnel to ascertain whether they contained life or not.

Those that were living were in such advanced stages of starvation, and frequently tuberculosis, that there was little hope for them.[22]

Or as Isaac Levy, the senior Jewish chaplain in the British army, wrote after being taken to see the 'horror camp' of Belsen, 'At first sight it was impossible to distinguish between the barely living and the dead, for those who still had the barest trace of life looked lifeless.'[23]

The Red Army liberated Majdanek in July 1944, although its reports, including Constantine Simonov's searing account, were treated with suspicion in the West.[24] The Red Army then arrived at Auschwitz on 27 January 1945, just days after most of the inmates had been forcibly evacuated, leaving behind some 7,000 of the sick and dying. As the Red Army then pushed westwards, it liberated Sachsenhausen and Ravensbrück in April, Stutthof, Gross-Rosen and, finally, Theresienstadt in May. The Soviets also overran the sites of the Operation Reinhard death camps, and although there was little there to see by then, not least because they had been picked over by local Poles who had been hunting for 'Jewish treasure', they were able to uncover many of the details of what had transpired there.[25]

After the liberation of Natzweiler in Alsace in November 1944, it fell to the western Allies to discover the largest number of surviving concentration camp inmates, including Holocaust survivors who had been marched westwards, when they liberated Buchenwald, Mittelbau-Dora, Flossenbürg, Dachau and those camps' sub-camps, and Bergen-Belsen in April 1945, then Neuengamme and Mauthausen and their sub-camps, including the horrific Ebensee and Gusen, in May. Not all Holocaust survivors were liberated in camps; many were freed from death marches, including after being abandoned by the Germans in train carriages and left for dead at sidings or on the tracks; emerged out of hiding; or – the largest number – returned from the Soviet Union, where they had spent the war as refugees. This last group, almost exclusively Polish Jews, in fact made up the majority of Jewish DPs by the summer of 1946, as we will see.

Derrick Sington, one of the first British soldiers to enter Belsen with the 63rd Anti-Tank Regiment, said afterwards: 'I had tried to visualise the interior of a concentration camp, but I had not imagined it like this. Nor had I imagined the strange simian throng, who crowded to the barbed wire fences, surrounding the compounds, with their shaven heads and their obscene striped penitentiary suits, which were so dehumanising.'[26] And that was apart from the thousands of corpses which filled the camp.

Sington, despite his shock at what he saw, was nevertheless among those who, on talking to the inmates, understood that the majority of the inmates had not been there for long:

By the end of our second day in Belsen we had been able to find out the nationality groups in the camp. About 25,000 out of the 40,000 inmates were women, and of these some 18,000 were Hungarian, Polish, Rumanian, Czech and German Jewesses. They were a large part of the survivors of European Jewry, hastily piled into Belsen as the advance of the Allied armies from East and West forced the Germans to evacuate the extermination camp of Auschwitz-Birkenau in Poland and the scores of slave-labour camps in Silesia and North East Germany. The greater part of these Jewish women were sole survivors of families who had perished in the gas chambers of Birkenau and Treblinka.[27]

In the wake of what the British (and some Canadian) troops who entered Belsen following its surrender on 15 April 1945 found – Belsen was the only camp surrendered in a war zone rather than discovered following the German retreat – the army supply and medical corps rapidly got to work, re-establishing the water supply, finding food and organizing the burial of the dead in mass graves. They also called for medical assistance, whereupon a team of ninety-six University of London medical students who had originally been destined for the Netherlands were diverted to Belsen instead, arriving on 30 April. It was a training none of them would forget. Together with volunteers from other charitable bodies, notably Quakers, the United Nations Relief and Rehabilitation Administration, the Red Cross and, later, the London-based Jewish Relief Unit, they tried to save as many inmates as possible in what rapidly, thanks to the work of the 32nd Casualty Clearing Station, became the largest hospital in Europe, established in the 'lavishly equipped' nearby Wehrmacht barracks.[28]

The challenge was immense; Lieutenant Colonel M. W. Gonin noted that there were 'at least 20,000 sick suffering from all the diseases known to man, all of whom required urgent hospital treatment and 30,000 men and women who might die if they were not treated but who would certainly die if they were not fed and removed from the horror camp'. The problem was: 'What we had not got was nurses, doctors, beds, bedding, clothes, drugs, dressings, thermometers, bed-pans or any of the essentials of medical treatment and worst of all no common language.'[29] Although the Allies – the British at Belsen and the Americans at Dachau, Buchenwald and Mauthausen – have been criticized for implementing the wrong feeding regimes and allowing too many survivors to die after the liberation, in fact such criticism (not wholly unjustified given the military intelligence on what was going on in the Nazis' concentration camps) largely fails to appreciate the complexity of the situation and the unprecedented nature of what was found in April and May 1945. 'We start to feed the poor wretches,' wrote Major Charles Philip Sharp, 'but many of them are too far gone to eat.' Anita Lasker-Wallfisch, nineteen years old on her liberation at Belsen, but feeling, as she said, 'like 90', states that 'What the British Army had to cope with was simply mind-boggling.' And Brigadier Hugh Glyn Hughes, Chief Medical Officer of the 2nd Army and the man responsible for organizing the medical relief at Belsen, explained at the Belsen trial in September 1945 that:

> I appreciated that of the inhabitants 70 per cent required hospitalisation, and that of these at least 10,000 would die before they could be put in hospital. There were 10,000 corpses in the camp when we arrived there. Every form of disease was prevalent, but the ones mainly responsible for the frightful conditions were typhus, starvation and tuberculosis. The cause of the disease was the privation and suffering which they had gone through.[30]

After all that has been written and said about Belsen, Robert Collis' conclusion from 1945 remains true today: 'It is a complete understatement. No words can describe the stench of decaying faeces, rotting bodies, and burning rags, which in the first weeks one could begin to smell miles from the camp.'[31]

Such statements can be easily multiplied. Reports from Dachau, Buchenwald and Mauthausen, and their numerous sub-camps, all testify to the terrible conditions, the dreadful state of the surviving inmates and the callousness of the guards and local population. Max Garcia, a Dutch survivor of Ebensee, summed up the encounter between the inmates and the Allied soldiers in unflinching terms, deliberately recalling Nazi terminology:

> Soldiers in unfamiliar uniforms gaped in frank amazement from the top of their tanks at a mass of shrunken, ghastly scarecrows in filthy, striped rags, a reeking mass with their heads shaved except for a stripe in the middle. The soldiers stared at us and we stared at them . . . The silence of the first shock of our encounter was broken now, the gates somehow were opened, and we drew back to allow the roaring tanks and their small escort to roll slowly into the middle of our roll call square. Prisoners swarmed around the tanks, as the engines were switched off. The soldiers in and off their tanks seemed to be afraid. They looked as if they did not want to come down and mix around with us. Perhaps they just came from the latest battle, but we seemed to be too much for them. These sunken faces and skeletal bodies. These stinking subhumans. Us.[32]

The soldiers, medics and charity workers who strove to help the survivors performed extraordinary work in unforgiving circumstances, and many later reflected with not unjustified pride on what they had done. Yet the survivors themselves were left bewildered and shocked. Although they were nursed back to physical health, it took many of them years, if not decades, to feel whole again, if they ever did. Most testified not just to feeling joy at having unexpectedly outlived the Nazi regime but to an 'infinite loneliness within ourselves' that left them isolated and enervated.[33] Many did not know how to respond.

Michał Głowiński, hidden as a child in a convent in Turkowice, near Hrubieszów, had become so used to being alone and unable to think of the future that, when he was told at the end of the war that his mother had arrived to collect him, he did not know how to respond. In searingly honest words, he wrote, some half a century later, about his behaviour:

> I should have been mad for joy – an indescribable good fortune had come to me – and yet I was not capable of rejoicing, happiness transcended the repertoire of my behaviour. I was so taken by surprise, so unable to absorb what was happening, that I was incapable of wresting from myself anything that would express it . . . I made no gestures appropriate to such an extraordinary situation. I didn't throw my arms around her. I didn't know how to extract from myself so much as a single sentence that would have been spontaneous and, at the same time, appropriate in such circumstances.

As he goes on to say, 'A mother's first encounter with her son after the most terrible of catastrophes ought to be sublime. Yet it was not so.'[34]

The effects of persecution, as is evident in Głowiński's words, did not suddenly come to a halt after liberation. As

Isaac Goodfriend, a child who was in hiding with a Polish farmer along with eight other Jews, said at a meeting of survivors, military liberators and medical personnel in 1981, 'We whispered – we didn't talk, even though there were no neighbours around. We whispered even after the war. After I was liberated, I could not get back to normal; I kept on whispering for two months after the war.' Besides, as Goodfriend recalled, he rejoiced at the arrival of the Russians and the end of the war, yet, as he was about to leave his protector's house, the farmer called him over and said: 'You are free. You can go, but where? There is nobody waiting for you out there. This little child – I don't know how, how a little child would survive. The men? You work, maybe. But now you're free. But where will you go?'[35] Or, as another survivor put it in an interview in 1946, where he described returning to Poland after the war and having to leave again:

> Any Jew who still owns anything in Poland, then it is better that he . . . that he leaves, because if he remains, then death threatens him, and it was too painful for me when I saw strange people who have . . . have my property, live in my flat. But the most terrible was that I found no one any more. From a family which had numbered seven persons, I alone had remained.[36]

The survivors were traumatized and, above all, lonely.

Displaced Persons – Refugees – Survivors

Seeking some escape from this existential loneliness no doubt partly accounts for why the Jewish DP camps became hives of activity. Survivors from Western Europe were able to return home, albeit slowly – Primo Levi's journey, recounted in his memoir *The Truce*, was convoluted and took months – and, although they faced many difficulties, as we will see, they were nevertheless home. For the majority of Jews from Eastern Europe, by contrast, home no longer existed. Nine days after the liberation of the camp, Abraham Ahubia, a survivor of Buchenwald, wrote in the diary he was keeping:

> The Frenchmen and the Belgians are going *home*. Yes indeed, they are going *home*, to their relatives, families and neighbours. They go to those whom they love and who return their love. They are returning to their former lives. And I – where will I go? Where shall I seek my home? Where shall I find my family and relatives? I have neither.[37]

People such as Ahubia ended up in DP camps in, ironically, occupied Germany and Austria, with a small number in Italy. This was so because many of the Jews who were liberated in the camps in Germany at war's end were in no fit state to travel or to be moved elsewhere and so were treated where they were found. It followed that as Jews emerged from hiding or discovered that they were no longer welcome in their former homes in Eastern Europe, they moved westwards to be under the care of the occupation authorities in the western zones of Germany, in the 'assembly centres' established by the United Nations Relief and Rehabilitation Administration (UNRRA), which rapidly became known as displaced persons camps. Most headed for the American zone, for there the Jewish DPs received the best treatment.

In fact, the returnees from the Soviet Union were not, strictly speaking, DPs, since they were not on German

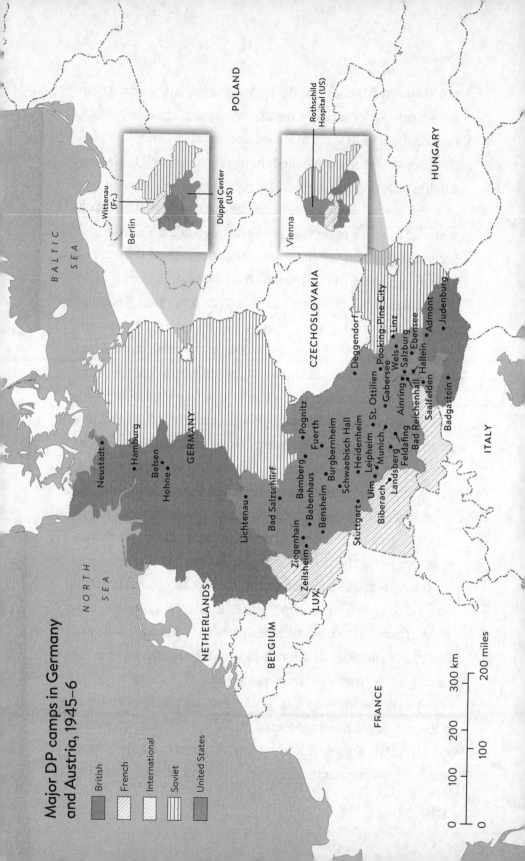

Major DP camps in Germany and Austria, 1945–6

British
French
International
Soviet
United States

BALTIC SEA

POLAND

Berlin
Wittenau (Fr.)
Düppel Center (US)

Vienna
Rothschild Hospital (US)

HUNGARY

CZECHOSLOVAKIA

GERMANY

NORTH SEA

• Neustadt
• Hamburg
• Belsen
• Hohne
• Lichtenau
• Bad Salzschlirf
• Ziegenhain
• Zeilsheim
LUX.
• Bamberg
• Babenhausen
• Bensheim
• Pognitz
• Fuerth
• Burgbernheim
• Schwaebisch Hall
• Heidenheim
• Deggendorf
• St. Ottilien
• Leipheim
• Munich
• Pocking-Pine City
• Wels
• Linz
• Gabersee
• Ainring
• Salzburg
• Ebensee
• Feldafing
• Bad Reichenhall
• Hallein
• Admont
• Saalfelden
• Judenburg
• Badgastein
• Stuttgart
• Ulm
• Biberach
• Landsberg

NETHERLANDS

BELGIUM

FRANCE

ITALY

0   100   200   300 km
0   100   200 miles

territory at war's end. The British were reluctant to grant them DP status but eventually treated them as if they were DPs, but the Americans were more welcoming. The occupation authorities nevertheless labelled them 'infiltrees', as if their continuing suffering and demand for refugee status was some sort of nefarious or illicit migration. Their arrival was the reason why the number of Jewish DPs grew considerably from the summer of 1945, when there were about 53,000, to the start of 1947, when there were 250,000. It was a small number given the total number of about 7 million DPs in total in Germany in the spring and summer of 1945, but by the autumn of that year, when some 6 million DPs had been repatriated, the Eastern European Jews made up a notable proportion of the 'hard core' of DPs who could not go back to where they were from. As a result of being rejected by their countries of origin, they in turn rejected their citizenship (Hungarian or Polish, for example), but found that they could not go where they wanted. Entry into the US or British-controlled Palestine was denied them, except for very small groups of special cases, such as unaccompanied children sponsored by certain charitable schemes or on the basis of the tiny quota that allowed 1,500 Jewish immigrants a month to enter Palestine. They were thus obliged to remain in Europe, either in the DP camps or, as a minority chose, to become 'free livers' in Germany (that is to say, to live outside the DP camps), and to try and rebuild the destroyed German-Jewish communities.

The DP camps were first and foremost places of rumour, hope and despair. Before the arrival of the Polish-Jewish refugees from the Soviet Union, among whom were family groups, most DPs were alone, the sole survivors of their families.

They set off to find relatives at the slightest suggestion that a loved one had survived. Evelyn Le Chêne, a French survivor of Mauthausen, reports that 'Many people died because they left the camp before they were strong enough. The Americans warned them against doing so and encouraged them to stay on, but the pull of their homelands was too powerful.'[38] Aid workers were amazed by this urge to find relatives and were at a loss to explain how the DPs managed to circumvent the restrictions on travel:

> How these people manage to move about at all in this heavily guarded country is indeed difficult to understand. A young man (he appeared to be about 30) with his arm slung round a woman (who looked about 40 or 45) told me with a beaming face: 'I fetched her from Poland. I heard here in the camp [Föhrenwald] that she was there, so I went to bring her along here.' They go forward and backward to Poland, to Czechoslovakia from camp to camp wherever they believe they may find some member of their family, and we here are not even able to go from one camp to another without travelling papers, and without being checked time and again.[39]

Nothing speaks to the loneliness of the survivors more than this desperate and dangerous search for loved ones.

DP camps could be large, as in the case of Belsen (strictly speaking now called Hohne, although the DPs liked to retain the name Belsen because it suggested their continued suffering under British control), Feldafing, Föhrenwald, Zeilsheim or Landsberg in the American zone. Often such camps were repurposed army barracks. But they were sometimes small, consisting of no more than a few requisitioned apartment blocks, schools, hotels or garages. Jews were initially housed alongside non-Jews, a threatening situation, since this meant Holocaust survivors living with their tormentors. Only after several outbursts of antisemitic violence and considerable protest from Jewish DPs did this policy change, faster in the American than in the British zone, where Jews and 10,000 non-Jewish Poles who refused to be returned to Poland were not separated in the Belsen DP camp until August 1946.

The catalyst for this change in policy was the Harrison Report. It was in response to the tensions between different DP population groups and between DPs and the army that in June 1945 President Truman commissioned Earl G. Harrison, the Dean of the University of Pennsylvania Law School, to visit the DP camps and to produce a survey of conditions in them. This he did in August, accompanied by Joseph Schwartz, the head of the JDC in Europe. Harrison's report was explosive, taking the Jewish DPs' view at every turn.

Harrison criticized UNRRA's inability to run DP camps as well as its resistance to allowing charities to assist. More significant, he noted of the surviving Jewish victims of Nazi persecution that:

Up to this point they have been 'liberated' more in a military sense than actually. For reasons explained in the report, their particular problems, to this time, have not been given attention to any appreciable extent; consequently, they feel that they, who were in so many ways the first and worst victims of Nazism, are being neglected by their liberators.

And he went on, in a famous passage:

> As matters now stand, we appear to be treating the Jews as the Nazis treated them except that we do not exterminate them. They are in concentration camps in large numbers under our military guard instead of S.S. troops. One is led to wonder whether the German people, seeing this, are not supposing that we are following or at least condoning Nazi policy.[40]

Knowing full well the implications of his position for Anglo-American relations, Harrison added that the only solution, as far as he could see, was to allow the Jewish DPs to emigrate for Palestine.

This option, however, remained blocked; the British would not permit entry to more than the 1,500 Jews per month that it already allowed. The consequence was that, as Jews tried to escape via the underground channel known as *brichah*, many ships (often hastily repurposed merchant ships) which sailed from ports such as Brindisi or Constanța were intercepted en route to Palestine and their passengers incarcerated yet again, this time in refugee camps on British-controlled Cyprus. Here, either in Caraolos or Xylotymbou, tens of thousands of Jewish refugees, at least 60 per cent of them migrants from the DP camps of Europe, were within touching distance of Palestine and regarded Cyprus as *erev Eretz Yisrael*, or 'on the eve of Israel'. Though psychologically painful for those detained there, the Cyprus camps undoubtedly provided powerful propaganda for the Zionist cause, with the British accused of imprisoning concentration camp survivors in the same way that their Nazi tormentors had done.[41]

Once the DPs – as 'survivors' had now become – were

physically well enough, the DP camps became vibrant places of activity. Surviving texts, documents, photographs, films and material objects all testify to a remarkable outpouring of energy, as Jewish DPs sought to rebuild their lives. This was not an unfettered positive; many were desperate for contact and entered into unsuitable marriages; many took up training in trades that prepared them for life as pioneers in Palestine when they might have been better suited to other careers. Reports of religious ceremonies like circumcisions and weddings are unmistakably tragic as well as celebratory. 'Tears flowed quite freely and it was obvious that not all the tears were tears of joy', wrote Rabbi Max B. Wall of a wedding he performed in October 1945 in a hotel in Altötting (Bavaria).[42] And of course the ubiquitous presence of the dead was unavoidable, as the report of one memorial service held at the Föhrenwald DP camp makes plain:

> The assembled rise in honour of the martyrs. The cantor intones the memorial service . . . When the cantor recites the words 'the souls of the murdered who relinquish their souls for the sanctification of God's name', the assembled see the souls of their dear ones in the burning candles, and their hearts fill with tears; the assembled cannot restrain themselves, and the hall erupts in a wailing lament by all the assembled. The assembly of bereavement is over, [but] the people cannot move, tears gush, the heart is in pain. *Great is the wrath.*[43]

Reports such as this were written up in the newsletters and journals rapidly established by the survivors. They edited newspapers, set up tracing services such as the International

Information Office at Dachau, began gathering material for the first *yizker-bikher* (memorial books) and took down the first survivors' accounts of what had happened during the Holocaust, primarily at this stage either with the aim of contributing to the memorial books or with the aim of establishing facts that could be used in prosecuting perpetrators – the idea of collecting survivor testimony for its own sake was not yet part of the landscape. In fact, the DPs wrote so much that as early as 1946 authors started to preface their works by noting that many works had already appeared.[44]

Among many topics, the DPs reported on the failings of postwar German justice; in May 1947, for example, two of the three judges who gave six-year sentences to two brothers, Wilhelm and Ernst Bering, for the murder of Heinrich Rosenblum during the November pogrom, were, according to *Unzer Sztime (Our Voice)*, the main journal of the Jews in the British zone, former members of the Nazi Party.[45] They reported on the ways in which Jews in Germany were accused of controlling the black market, especially in Munich's infamous Möhlstrasse; on the celebration of Jewish festivals such as Purim; on attacks on Jews, such as occurred in Hanover when thirty hooligans hospitalized two Jews they encountered at the train station; and they reported on conferences held by the central committees representing the DPs.[46] The Central Historical Commission, set up by survivors in Munich in November 1945, created branches across the American zone of occupation and sent out its activists to document the recent past. For them, this was a holy duty: 'Do not forget that every document, picture, song, legend is the only gravestone which we can place on the unknown graves of our murdered parents, siblings and children!' stated one call to the public:

> Therefore, help the historical commission in its work!
> Describe the economic, social and cultural life of the
> destroyed Jewish community from which you come.
> Describe the activity of the society or organization you
> used to be a member of before the war. Eternalize how the
> Jews have lived, fought, and were murdered during the
> Nazi regime. Eternalize all expressions, legends and stories
> of the bygone tragic days. Write down the songs sung in
> ghettos, camps, and among the partisans during the Nazi
> era. Hand the material over to the historical commission,
> which is collecting and preserving this material for the
> generations to come! Do not refuse your help when the
> historical commission turns to you![47]

Such early postwar responses to the murder of the Jews – not yet called the Holocaust – from the survivors themselves set the tone for later scholarship, even though, as we will see in chapter 8, it was forgotten in some scholarly quarters for decades thereafter.

As this outpouring of ink suggests, the DP camps rapidly became sites of cultural activity. Sport was very important, with football especially highly regarded for encouraging a team spirit and building up young survivors physically as well as mentally in preparation for their new role as pioneers in Palestine. Theatre too was popular, with some startling works performed that took the audience – and the actors, themselves survivors – close to the edge of their experiences. This too was regarded as a holy duty, as Norbert Horowitz, one of the founders of the Minchener Yiddisher Teater (Munich Yiddish Theatre), explained a few years after the war:

> After the liberation, they come together, weak and suffering from typhus, barely alive, still they gravitate to the Yiddish theatre. Singing teachers, a dance master, amateur actors, amateur and professional musicians all assemble – *and as if by magic – a Yiddish theatre is created*. They have no tools for such work: no makeup, no costumes, no paint for decoration, and not a single printed Yiddish word.
>
> Memory dictates the script, and after six years of inhuman suffering Jews, fugitives from death, can once again look upon a Jewish stage and hear a Jewish word, a Jewish song. The Katzet Theatre discharged a holy obligation.[48]

The success of some of the troupes was such that the Katzet-Teater group founded by Sami Feder in Belsen DP camp was invited to tour France, Belgium, Sweden and England, although it only actually made it to the first two countries. The theatre sometimes helped Jewish survivors nostalgically to retreat briefly into their past lives, delighting them with Yiddish classics. More often, it recreated their recent experiences on the stage. With plays like *The Mother*, starring survivor Sally Katz, or *Shoes from Majdanek*, starring Sonia Boczkowska, audiences willingly chose to be confronted with their own trauma, as one journalist explained:

> They play just like they write: with tears and blood, utter devotion and love. There has never been a theatrical phenomenon such as this in the history of our theatre.

The actors don't need to identify with their parts; they lived them in the desolate reality of Nazi camps, ghettos and forests. They don't have to learn their parts – learn in the ordinary sense of the word – because they've already 'studied' them in blood and tears in past years . . . Neither did they have to refresh their memories: what they experienced as Jews they'll never forget . . . I attended two performances of the same play – I was moved to the deepest of depths. It was a new universe for me, a new theatrical reality, a new art.[49]

Unsurprisingly, the powerful emotions described here also spilled into and fuelled Jewish DPs' politics. Although with gradual physical recovery came a revival of the multiplicity of political positions held before the war by Jews, especially in Eastern Europe, where the Bundist (Jewish socialist) tradition had been so strong, in the DP camps politics was unmistakably stamped with a Zionist hue. The Harrison Report recognized this reality, as did the subsequent Anglo-American Committee of Inquiry (AACI) report, even though it had been convened by the British Government to alleviate some of the tension that the former report had generated between the two allies. In February 1946 this group of six Americans and six Britons visited several DP camps, with the result that, as Richard Crossman, the Labour MP and member of the AACI, set out, they came to realize why it was that 'policies which seemed sane enough in the White House or in Downing Street struck these wretched people as sadistic brutality'. After Ernest Bevin, Britain's Foreign Minister, remarked at a press conference that 'the Jew should not push to the head of the queue', Crossman pointedly observed: 'that might go down in Britain; in Belsen it sounded like the mouthing of a sadistic anti-Semite'.[50]

The Jewish DPs' self-designation as the *she'erit hapletah* or 'saved remnant' (a reference to, among other places in the Bible, Ezra 9:14–15: 'Would you not be angry with us until you consumed us, so that there should be no remnant, nor any to escape?') was a statement of national self-determination, forcing a recognition on the part of the occupation authorities that Jews, especially survivors from Eastern Europe for whom the idea of Jews as a nation marked a longstanding difference from their Western European co-religionists, would not be categorized according to their previous nationalities. While, before the war, Jewish politics was remarkably varied, in the DP camps Zionism prevailed. This was not, for most, a well-thought-out political philosophy but, as one historian says, 'an instinctive "gut" Zionism rooted in a loss of faith in the European emancipation and the profound sense of humiliation that [the Jews] felt during the years of destruction'.[51]

This gut Zionism clashed with the British position on Palestine. Along with the tensions that characterized relations between the Jewish DPs and the local German population, the DPs felt under increasing strain, no matter how many weddings took place or what vocational training they received. The establishment of kibbutzim on sequestered German farms fostered this sense of embattlement, as their members prepared for an emigration which they could not foresee. As Shea Abramovicz, a charity worker at Föhrenwald, keenly noted at the end of 1945, 'The Palestine question and the Bevin policy have a great effect on daily life.'[52] Six months later he was beginning to despair: 'If the people have to stay here very much longer,' he wrote, 'their nerves are bound to get even more strained and then we can expect anything . . .'[53]

And yet most of them were required to stay for several years yet. Their continued incarceration confused and angered the Jewish survivors, especially when they saw Polish, Baltic and Ukrainian DPs admitted to Britain and the US in large numbers to fill labour shortages. The Zionist cause was given a shot in the arm by British intransigence, as the DPs were not slow to point out. Speaking at the second congress of She'erit Hapletah in the American zone in February 1947, Samuel Gringauz, the Landsberg DP spokesman, stated:

> We must proclaim that keeping the camps going is a slow form of genocide . . . the selfsame crime which the International Military Tribunal at Nuremberg tried. The camps are destroying our readiness to return to life in the same way as the concentration camps destroyed our lives.[54]

Only once the state of Israel came into being in May 1948 did a majority leave. The fact that not all did, however, indicates that Zionism was not a universally held position among the DPs; nor did all of them have their hearts set on leaving Germany. By the late 1940s a minority of Jewish survivors had established themselves in Germany, with businesses, spouses and other reasons to stay. And a large proportion of Jewish DPs wanted first and foremost to get into the US, which some did by going first to Israel and then emigrating again once the Americans amended the DP Act in 1950 to make it easier for Jewish DPs to enter – with the reasoning being that since most had left for Israel already, the influx would be relatively small. Still, by 1952 over 80,000 Jewish DPs had emigrated to the US.

This large-scale emigration from Germany was not the end of the story, however. By September 1948 there were still 30,000 Jewish DPs in Germany, down from 165,000 in May. In 1951 the Federal Republic took over control of the DP camps, renaming them Government Transit Camps for Homeless Foreigners. The Jewish DPs were transferred to Föhrenwald, which became the last remaining camp. Those in them were the 'hard core' of DPs, who would not or could not leave, including many who were too ill to move or be admitted to a new country. A decade after the war, this small number, many of them still traumatized by their experiences and scared of the German authorities, had been unable to find new homes. Föhrenwald did not shut until February 1957, when its inhabitants were rehoused in newly built apartments.

The experiences of those who did return home should not be forgotten, however, for it would be wrong to assume that they had an easy time. Jacqueline Mesnil-Amar, one of the most clear-sighted of postwar commentators, summed up the situation after the war in France when she condemned those who remained silent about the persecution of the Jews during the war but who suddenly showed up to offer 'help' in the aftermath. Her bitter invective speaks volumes:

> Worst of all was the deafening silence, which started at
> the highest level and permeated the whole of France,
> reaching as far as the welfare organisations at whose doors
> we so frequently knocked in vain, the cautious silence
> even of the Red Cross, whose ladies looked so pretty in

their uniforms, and so brave at the wheel of their lorries and inside the prison camps, and who maintained their serenity even when faced with our frantic appeals. It wasn't a malign silence, and one could detect an almost cheerful optimism regarding the fate of the deportees on the part of some of the Red Cross officials, who appeared not to have noticed in the course of their polite inspections, the red glow of the crematoria, or the stench of charred bones, the smell of Germany. The people who were so bizarrely optimistic then, are the same ones who have been pouring into France since January 1945 checking on the fate of 'the poor German prisoners'. A worldwide conspiracy of silence surrounded a tragedy which was unknown until then, and not one cry of protest was heard.[55]

Those who were able to return to their prewar homes in Western Europe were no less traumatized than those who stayed in the DP camps, waiting for a new life in Palestine, the US, or one of the other countries (such as Canada, South Africa or Australia) which took in some thousands of survivors. They faced the fear of those who had not been deported, and their stories were subsumed into official narratives of resistance, patriotic sacrifice and national solidarity which kept them silenced.[56] In Auschwitz, Primo Levi dreamed of being at home in Turin, starting to recount what had happened to him, and his relatives looking away in embarrassed silence. It is no surprise that if, after the war, the survivors were not silent, they largely spoke to each other.

Conclusion

Although it is painful to accept, the fact is that survival for most Jews was a matter of chance. Various factors mitigated that chance: connections, linguistic abilities, looks, age and health all played a role. Being elderly or a young child meant almost no chance of survival, and it is no surprise that the majority of survivors were young, healthy single men and women aged between fifteen and thirty.[57] Above all, however, class – in particular wealth, privilege and status – was, despite being largely overlooked by historians in recent decades, probably the most significant factor. The so-called 'Diamond Jews' of Amsterdam who were housed in Belsen, for example, were there because the Germans thought they might prove useful, with their wealth and their international connections; Jews who survived on the 'Aryan side' in Warsaw or in hiding anywhere in Europe often had to pay their hosts, which meant those without means were unable to do so.[58] The ability to bribe one's way out of trouble, such as an encounter with a *szmalcownik* who would otherwise hand Jews over to the Gestapo, depended on having possessions and money. This is not to say that everyone who survived came from a wealthy background or had some sort of 'privileged' position as a kapo or other type of prisoner functionary in a camp, but proportionally speaking such was the case. That said, even power and privilege was, for the vast majority of the Nazis' victims, an insufficient guarantee against the force of the Nazis' racial logic. As Michał Głowiński, himself able to survive as a child because of his family's connections, puts it:

When I think now about my time in hiding on the Aryan side, about the flight from death, I'm overwhelmed by the great role played by chance – chance that was auspicious or at times seemingly auspicious or seemingly inauspicious, chance deciding survival or extinction, chance deciding life or death, chance sudden and not only unforeseen (such is always the case), but also bewildering, irrational, and contrary to all rules of probability, chance that was all the more incalculable for materializing in a world governed by draconian determinism – after all, one did not decide for oneself whether or not one was a Jew. So often it was precisely chance that determined life or death. It weighed upon human fate to a much greater degree than in calmer times, when determinisms did not operate with such forcefulness.[59]

The interest in survivor testimony in recent years – and the worry on the part of many about how the Holocaust will be remembered once the last survivors are dead – has obscured the fact that survival was the exception, death the norm. Those who reported on the death marches and on the liberation were a small minority of the Holocaust's victims, most of whom could by definition never speak about what had happened to them. On 'liberation', survivors quickly found out, with rare exceptions, that their families and communities had been decimated; they were alone in the world. There is much to be learned about the aftermath of the Holocaust by looking at the survivors' experiences of medical care, DP camps and searching for relatives, but the history of the Holocaust was, for the overwhelming majority, not one of survival. The genocidal logic of the Holocaust – the Nazis' intent to destroy the Jewish people in Europe – was accomplished all too well. Pockets of Jewish communities survived, some quite large, in Budapest, Bucharest and Paris, and in Switzerland and other lands of escape and refuge, most importantly in the Soviet Union. Tiny numbers of Jews survived in Sweden, Finland, Albania, Bulgaria and elsewhere. But most of the major Jewish population centres in Europe, in Vilnius, Warsaw, Czernowitz, Kishinev, Lvov, Łódź, Breslau, Frankfurt, Berlin, Prague, Amsterdam, Salonika, and smaller but ancient communities in Crete, Rhodes, Belgium, Croatia, Slovakia, Italy and everywhere across Europe were destroyed for ever. There was a good reason why David Boder titled his 1949 book of interviews with survivors *I Did Not Interview the Dead.*

CHAPTER 8
Holocaust Memory

'Many a person had left his soul and senses at home together with everything else that had ever been dear to him, and although he recognised himself in the camp, it was like recognising himself in a photograph. What he now calls "memory" is a dialogue between his soul, that he left behind at home, and his shadow that returned. That is why it is so difficult sometimes to explain "how it really was", as difficult as describing a dream accurately.'
— Abel Herzberg[1]

In early 2021, two Polish historians of the Holocaust, Barbara Engelking and Jan Grabowski, were taken to court in Warsaw. In her chapter of their co-edited book, *Dalej jest noc* (*Night without End*), Engelking mentions one Edward Malinowski, a village elder from the Podlasie region who, according to eyewitness testimony, betrayed scores of Jews to the Germans, who later killed them. The man's eighty-year-old niece, Filomena Leszczyńska, supported by the government-backed NGO, the Polish League against Defamation, sued the two historians, arguing that they had denied Ms Leszczyńska her 'right to one's national pride and identity', following a law of 2018 which made it a criminal offence to accuse Poles of being complicit in the Nazi murder of the Jews ('defaming the Polish nation'). In its judgment of 9 February 2021, the district court of Warsaw ordered Engelking and Grabowski to issue an apology. It is inconvenient for the ruling Law and Justice Party that its strategy of presenting Poles purely as victims of the Second World War and rescuers of Jews on a huge scale runs up against the fact that, in Grabowski's estimation, some 200,000 Polish Jews who fled the ghettos during the period of their liquidation (1942 onwards) were denounced or murdered by Polish civilians. Yet the campaign against Engelking and Grabowski, and other historians such as Jan Tomasz Gross, suggests that a communist mindset which thinks that the ruling party can control the past still exists in post-communist Poland. In the age of the internet, this is obviously absurd; but it is not absurd for the historians involved, for anyone who wants to tell the complex truth of what happened in wartime Poland (in which Poles were indeed victims – but that is not the whole story) or for Poland's political health. 'It strikes', Grabowski said, 'at the heart of what I as a historian do.'[2] Selective Holocaust memory is being put at the service of criminalizing scholarship. Although in August 2021 Grabowski and Engelking's appeal succeeded, with the Warsaw Appellate Court dismissing the case against them, this is not the end of the matter. Zbigniew Ziobro, the Polish Minister of Justice, tweeted after the result that:

> According to the Appellate Court the authors of the book 'Night without End' are academics, so they can lie without punishment. They can transform a hero into a criminal, and a Pole who helped the Jews into someone who was

co-responsible for their deaths. It not only brings shame to the court, it is a judicial coup d'etat against justice itself.

As Grabowski notes, 'a small battle has been won but the war is not over. The authorities want to see the decision of the Appellate Court set aside. We should not delude ourselves – independent historians of the Shoah continue to face today, in Poland, the full might and wrath of the state.'[3]

In 2020 the British government, represented by the Minister for Education Gavin Williamson, mandated that universities should adopt the International Holocaust Remembrance Alliance (IHRA) working definition of antisemitism, a move which saw considerable pushback on the part of academics, even as Jewish student organizations advocated in favour of doing so. Part of the problem is that IHRA's working definition of antisemitism is vague – 'a certain perception of Jews, which may be expressed as hatred toward Jews' – but more concerning for many commentators is that of its eleven examples of antisemitism, seven of them concern or include reference to Israel, giving the impression to many that the definition's aim was at least as much about heading off anti-Israel criticisms as of protecting Jews (and thus, ironically, of doing what the examples seek to highlight as antisemitic, that is to equate Jews with the state of Israel).

A number of universities quickly adopted the definition, but many others either stalled or actively defied the government. In its report on the matter, University College London's working group argued that the College should retract the adoption of the IHRA working definition because 'the IHRA working definition is not appropriate for adjudicating complaints of antisemitism in a proscriptive manner'. It argued that the definition 'potentially conflates statements critical of the State of Israel with antisemitism', 'risks undermining academic freedom' and potentially 'creates a rift between various groups on campus that is not helpful for communal cohesion at UCL'.[4] British universities already have a legal obligation to permit free speech and of course have to abide by laws against racial harassment, such as the 2010 Equality Act. UCL's argument was not that work to fight antisemitism on campus should not be done – indeed, it stated unequivocally that more should be done to use the tools that it already has at its disposal for combating harassment – but that the IHRA working definition was an insufficiently effective instrument for doing so. This is a sober and measured assessment. It begs the question, however – if the working definition has so many problems – of why the government took this unusual step of mandating universities to adopt it. The suspicion arises that in this case Holocaust memory is being leveraged for outing pro-Palestinian scholars, a kind of deliberate generation of a culture war which, while not as aggressive as in the Polish case, nevertheless aims at forcing scholars into line with an approved point of view.

When fascist thugs attacked the Capitol in Washington, DC, on 6 January 2021, one was spotted wearing a t-shirt emblazoned with the logo 'Camp Auschwitz' on the front, and 'Staff' on the back. Much ink has been spilled over whether the events at the Capitol were encouraged by Donald Trump, whether they should be termed an insurrection or a failed coup, whether the rioters were harbingers of a coming American fascism or were simply letting out a disorganized howl of protest at being Trump's most fanatical losing supporters. Historians are divided, with some warning that the events constituted a kind of pre-fascism that should set alarm bells ringing, others countering that the vocabulary from the first half of the twentieth century is inadequate for explaining what was happening in contemporary America.[5] Irrespective of one's view, the sight of Holocaust references in the context of an attack on the most potent symbol of American democracy was at the very least inflammatory, a reminder that the Holocaust continues to inform today's clashes over the meaning of democracy, the nation and security.

The Holocaust is not just a historical event occurring between 1939 and 1945. It names a transnational crime committed in Nazi-occupied Europe by the Third Reich and its allies, whose after-effects are felt to this day in the spheres of politics and culture in many, often unexpected ways. In the 1990s questions about Swiss gold laid bare aspects of the transnational economic dispossession of the Jews; the creation of the International Task Force (now International Holocaust Remembrance Alliance [IHRA]) in 2000 marked a shift towards transnational commemoration of the Holocaust; the number of Holocaust memorials and museums being redesigned or built from scratch across the world; and Holocaust-related cultural production such as films, family memoirs, exhibitions, websites and online resources testify to the worldwide reach of 'Holocaust culture'. Today, Holocaust memory is ubiquitous and conspicuous, a fixed part of the culture.

There is, so to speak, a 'progressive' story of Holocaust consciousness: the genocide of the Jews was more or less not understood or was overlooked by most of the world (even if survivors spoke and even if one can find glimpses of Holocaust references in postwar culture)[6] but then gradually became more prominent until the point at which 'Holocaust consciousness' became globalized, with Auschwitz standing as a symbol for evil and the memory of the Holocaust doing service for combating human rights abuses across the world.[7] It is this narrative of 'progress' that we will consider first.

Memory as Progress

In 1991 two French survivors of Buchenwald, both former political prisoners, retraced the steps of the death march they had been on forty-six years earlier.[8] For Robert Deneri and François Perrot, this was a matter of personal memory; but the impetus to make the journey and the fact that it occurred to them to do it owed much to a renewed interest in such matters in the 1980s and the immediate aftermath of the Cold War, a period of rapidly growing 'Holocaust consciousness'. Theirs was just one of many such pilgrimages, the desire to follow in the footsteps of former concentration camp inmates just one example of the ways in which the generations born after the Second World War were seeking to understand the most horrific crimes committed during that war. Their example stands as a kind of symbol, in this case an active remembrance, of the ways in which the Holocaust entered into the wider consciousness of the Western world in the 1990s.

Holocaust memory is often described as having developed in stages: silence in the postwar period; a 'discovery' of the Holocaust in the wake of the trial of Adolf Eichmann in Jerusalem in 1961–2 and the Frankfurt Auschwitz trials in 1963–5; the beginning of widespread 'Holocaust consciousness', following NBC's *Holocaust* TV series in 1978, which was seen by an estimated 120 million viewers in the US and 20 million in West Germany, and broadcast in more than two dozen countries in 1979, including most of Europe;[9] and the worldwide focus on the Holocaust following the success of Steven Spielberg's film *Schindler's List* (1993), the fiftieth anniversary of the liberation of Auschwitz in 1995 and the 1990s debates about Swiss gold. This story has much to recommend it.

Yet there were other staging posts along the way. The publication of Anne Frank's *Diary* (in English) in 1952 was a worldwide phenomenon, although in the first years after the war her father had found little interest among publishers, and at the time of the book's publication the Anne Frank House was under threat of demolition, to be replaced by an office block.[10] The Nuremberg trials had brought to light the persecution of the Jews, even if they failed adequately to conceptualize what we would now recognize as the Holocaust. The Israeli War of Independence, hard on the Jewish terrorist attacks on British forces in Palestine, left an ambivalent attitude prevailing towards Jews and their suffering in the UK. The publication of middlebrow books such as Leon Uris' *Exodus* or *Mila 18* probably did more to bring the Holocaust to the attention of a wide public than did the first works of historians.[11]

In West Germany scandals over former Nazis in senior posts rocked Konrad Adenauer's government in the early 1960s, in the wake of the GDR's publication of the so-called *Brown Book*, in which these men were outed. Theodor Oberländer, the Minister for Refugees and Expellees, was revealed to have a Nazi past; and Hans Globke, Adenauer's chief of staff in the chancellery, was exposed as the author of the guide for implementing the Nuremberg Laws. Both were tried in absentia in the GDR and, despite Adenauer's support, forced to resign. Their exposure constitutes just one example of many of how 'the process of coming to terms with the past' was thrust into the public sphere in West Germany. Nor was this by any means a straightforward process; even in the 1980s, it was still possible to talk about the Nazis' victims in the abstract but very problematic to name the names of perpetrators. Exemplifying the problem was the fact that the Central Office for the Investigation of Nazi Crimes, founded in Ludwigsburg in 1958 in the wake of the trial in Ulm of former *Einsatzgruppen* members, was woefully underfunded.[12] When Ronald Reagan visited Bitburg cemetery in May 1985, where, it was discovered, SS men as well as Wehrmacht soldiers were buried, in what was supposed to be an act of reconciliation, there was international uproar. The same was true when it was revealed that Kurt Waldheim, previously the Secretary General of the UN and running to be the Austrian president, was implicated in Nazi war crimes in the Balkans – this at a time when Austria was still maintaining its official li(n)e that the country was 'the first victim of National Socialism'. His election to the presidency in June 1986 led to him being placed on the US's watch list – barring him from entry to the US as a private citizen – and to a belated focus on Austria's wartime past in Austria and in the international press.[13]

Typical of the strained attempts to grapple with the Nazi past in the 1980s was the speech given by the Federal Republic's President Richard von Weizsäcker on 8 May 1985, commemorating the fortieth anniversary of the end of the war in Europe. On the one hand, von Weizsäcker was open about the centrality of antisemitism to the Nazi worldview and called the genocide of the Jews 'unparalleled in history'. On the other hand, his verbal contortions illustrate perfectly the ways in which German politicians and commentators struggled to face up to what this insight really meant. 'The perpetration of this crime', claimed von Weizsäcker, 'was in the hands of a few people. It was concealed from the eyes of the public, but every German was able to experience what his Jewish compatriots had to suffer, ranging from plain apathy and hidden intolerance to outright hatred.' The majority, in other words, had shunned their responsibility and looked away.[14] This was an honest and anguished attempt to face up to the Holocaust, but it completely failed to reckon with the involvement and complicity of not just the German population at large but (and this would have been remarkable in 1985) the Third Reich's collaborators across Europe.

Von Weizsäcker's speech was delivered just as the major debate in West Germany's 'coming to terms with the past' in the 1980s was starting to play itself out in the country's press: the *Historikerstreit*, or Historians' Debate. In 1980 the conservative historian Ernst Nolte, noted at that point as a scholar of fascism, wrote that 'the so-called annihilation of the Jews by the Third Reich was a reaction or a distorted copy [of the Gulag] and not a first act or an original'.[15] A few years later, in a West Germany where questioning the uniqueness of the Holocaust was considered scandalous, Nolte's conspicuously inappropriate words were echoed in speeches produced for Chancellor Kohl by the historian Michael Stürmer; the question of the Holocaust's singularity suddenly became politically charged. The issue of the Holocaust's comparability was part of a determined effort to control the past as a contribution to the German conservative turn of the 1980s (the so-called *Tendenzwende*). As Stürmer put it, echoing Orwell: 'in a land without history, the future is controlled by those who determine the content of memory, who coin concepts and interpret the past'.[16]

In the political climate of West Germany of the 1980s, those who objected to Nolte's and Stürmer's project of making the Holocaust appear like any other mass crime, in particular those committed by Stalin's Soviet Union, reinforced their belief in the Holocaust's 'uniqueness'. For liberals such as philosopher Jürgen Habermas, who countered Nolte's arguments in the national press, holding to this notion of uniqueness was crucial for maintaining the Federal Republic's stability, decency and 'constitutional patriotism'. Leaving aside for the moment the notion that comparing the Holocaust to the Gulag – which was not exactly a happy story – hardly plays down the significance of the genocide of the Jews, it is striking that Habermas' argument made 'Auschwitz' central to the self-identity of West Germans, for fear that were that not to be the case, the country would slide into forgetting the past: 'The unconditional opening of the Federal Republic to the political culture of the West', he wrote, 'is the greatest intellectual achievement of our postwar period . . . This event cannot and should not be stabilised by a kind of NATO philosophy coloured with German nationalism.' Even more important, he pleaded for Germans not to ignore the memory of those murdered at German hands, for otherwise 'our Jewish fellow citizens, the sons, the daughters, the grandchildren of the murdered could no longer breathe in our country'.[17]

Habermas' asphyxiation metaphor, his emphasis on German perpetrators and his reference to NATO all remind us that he was writing in the 1980s, when the Cold War was still ongoing (Gorbachev had just come to power as the Historians' Debate was getting started), and when the majority of countries across Europe had not yet faced their own involvement in what was assuredly a German-led project but was by no means only carried out by Germans. With the end of the Cold War, all this was to change.

'Bitburg history' – the irruption of the past in the present, the confusion of perpetrator and victim and a failure to pin down responsibility for past crimes – was already a feature of Western European political culture in the 1980s. The rise of the radical right in Belgium, Italy, Norway and Austria all attest to a nostalgia, which could not be articulated openly in the first thirty years after the Second World War, entering the public sphere. In other words, moments of scandal, introspection and anguished soul-searching in West Germany were echoed elsewhere, most notably in France.

In the home of the Revolution and the rights of man, the postwar period was marked by a Gaullist narrative of the Second World War which emphasized French unity in opposition to the Germans. Its strongly nationalist flavour meant political deportees were lauded as emblems of the Resistance, whereas racial deportees (that's to say, Jews) were largely overlooked.[18] Starting in the 1960s with the film *The Sorrow and the Pity*, this veneer of unanimity started slowly to crack. By the 1980s, a similar phenomenon was occurring in France as – more noticeably – in West Germany: the radical right was on the rise as parties of the right and left began dismantling the postwar social contract; Holocaust consciousness grew, with Claude Lanzmann's epic film *Shoah* (1985) its key way-station; former Vichy officials such as Maurice Papon and Paul Touvier were eventually brought to trial or at least threatened with prosecution; and a drive to grapple with Vichy came alongside a failure to see connections between what happened in France during the Second World War and what happened in the French colonies, especially in Algeria. Indeed, France's war of decolonization in Algeria (1954–62) was referred to not as a war but as an internal police matter, since Algeria had been incorporated into metropolitan France and was split into three departments. During the war the actions of the French military were widely supported even by those on the left, who regarded the Algerians' rejection of French civilization with bewilderment; lone voices such as Jean-Paul Sartre, Frantz Fanon and, notably, Nazi camp survivors such as Germaine Tillion, arguing that the army was behaving like the Gestapo, failed initially to break through this unanimity. Only after many years of soul-searching over Vichy have the French begun to work through what happened in Algeria and the connections between the two. These are not only empirical (the role, for example, of police chief Maurice Papon in wartime Bordeaux and Paris in 1961); they exemplify the ways in which the Holocaust was never solely a German project but a crime in which Europeans from across the continent were implicated.[19]

All of these scandals notwithstanding, the arc of the story seems to be heading towards greater openness about the Holocaust and a gradual acceptance of its importance for Western self-identity. This direction of travel is most evident in the United States. From the 1970s interest in the Holocaust in the US developed rapidly; by the start of the 1990s, Holocaust Studies as an academic discipline was being shaped, and monuments and museums, especially the USHMM, were being built. Many of the moments mentioned above, such as Bitburg or the Waldheim affair, had worldwide ramifications either because they involved America directly or because they were taken up in the US as legitimate causes. That process of becoming involved with issues occurring in Europe does not mean, as a popular notion from the end of the twentieth century had it, that there exists a 'Holocaust industry' which cynically manipulates popular sentiment in order to deflect criticism of Israel and to extort huge sums of money out of Germany, Switzerland and private firms.[20] Certainly, Jewish groups in the US promoted this agenda for various reasons, but the take-up of Holocaust consciousness among the American public at large should not be explained as a Jewish conspiracy.[21] Even as governments and international organizations took up the idea of Holocaust Memorial Day, for example, as a simple and effective way of appearing to be promoting liberal values, the resonance of such programmes with the wider public suggests that the Holocaust should be a problem for thinking people everywhere.

By contrast, the UK was an outlier in this process. It came late to Holocaust consciousness but, when it did so in the 1990s, it happened with a bang with the creation of

Holocaust Memorial Day, first in the UK and then internationally. The result was that Holocaust consciousness was, so it seemed, a permanent fixture of Western political culture by the end of the twentieth century.[22]

But there are other trajectories. Much of the rest of the world might not have wanted to hear about the genocide of the Jews, but survivors were far from silent. From the historical commissions set up in the DP camps to projects run by the Contemporary Jewish Documentation Center (CJDC, Paris), the Jewish Historical Institute (ZIH, Warsaw) or the National Committee for Attending Deportees in Budapest (DEGOB), survivor historians and their helpers collected survivors' accounts, published numerous studies – the first works in Holocaust history – published lists of survivors, produced numerous *yizker-bikher*, or memorial books, commemorating the prewar lives and wartime deaths of Jewish communities across Eastern Europe, and helped to formulate some of the key postwar architecture of international human rights law.[23] The 'forgetting' of this literature was mainly thanks to language: most were written in Yiddish (with the major exception of the DEGOB collections in Hungary) and published in Tel Aviv, Buenos Aires and New York. But few people were left who could speak the language. Additionally, they were inaccessible, as many of these collections fell behind the Iron Curtain during the Cold War and could not be read by specialists. Their rediscovery, however, is not only a legacy of the end of the Cold War. It is first and foremost a reflection of a change in sensibility, away from thinking about genocide only from the perspective of the perpetrators. A new focus on the victims of the Holocaust means that the writings of survivors, especially the survivor historians and the survivor accounts that they helped to collect, are newly in the sights of scholars, curators and educators.[24]

Thus, as historians have gradually shifted their focus to consider the victims as well as the perpetrators, the sources they use have become more varied. Where early Holocaust historians relied almost exclusively on Nazi documents captured at war's end and collated for the Nuremberg trials, now historians recognize that documents produced by the victims, from letters to diaries to petitions to applications for assistance, are equally important for understanding the Holocaust. As a result, they have also realized that after the war survivors put pen to paper to a great extent and that what we now call Holocaust memory has existed in different places among different communities at different times. If today there is a (sort of) worldwide Holocaust consciousness, promoted by the United Nations and other global or regional institutions, most notably the European Union, this has also led to some unpredictable mnemonic effects.[25] Holocaust memory was always implicated in geopolitics, as for instance in Israeli–Turkish relations in the 1970s and 1980s, or West Germany's relations with the US as it sought to assert itself as a normal, independent, sovereign state on the world stage.[26] But since the end of the Cold War, it has come into competition and conflict with the memories of communism, slavery and other cases of genocide, in often unseemly but instructive ways.[27] It has led in unexpected directions, as for example the building of the United States Holocaust Memorial Museum on The Mall in Washington, DC, which provided an impetus to create the National Museum of African American History and Culture.[28]

For all that there is no straight line of progress leading from silence to worldwide commemoration, the story of growing Holocaust consciousness has much to recommend it. It is certainly true that, no matter how much survivors, scholars, archivists, clinicians, international lawyers and psychologists spoke about the Nazi murder of the Jews (not yet 'the Holocaust') in the 1940s and 1950s, there was no widespread and shared Holocaust consciousness. The term 'Holocaust' began to change from an occasionally used metaphor for atrocity to refer specifically to the genocide of the Jews in the 1960s and by the late 1970s had become synonymous with it. By the 1980s the Holocaust was widely taught at American universities and, with the slow exception of the UK, was being taken up in other English-speaking countries, especially Canada, South Africa and Australia, which were also discovering that their wartime experiences were part of the history of the Holocaust. In Israel the Holocaust had always been present, of course, but Yad Vashem's international reach as a research institution was growing; and across Western Europe, Holocaust films, trials, monuments – if not yet surviving Holocaust sites – were garnering attention. Important survivor testimony collection projects were established, notably the Fortunoff Archive at Yale, but also a plethora of similar, often small, local, oral history projects that have been largely forgotten. The 1990s witnessed an explosion of interest which has continued to this day.

Memory in the Post-Truth Age

If, by the 1990s, Holocaust consciousness seemed destined
to be channelled in favour of human rights, cosmopolitanism and progressive ideas, in the twenty-first century this
confident narrative has been derailed. The use of Holocaust
memory to further nationalist agendas, to facilitate geopolitical alliances on the far right or to 'expose' progressive
thinkers for their supposed antisemitism or anti-Israel bias
is now a familiar part of the landscape. At the same time, the
notion of the Holocaust survivor as the universal witness,
standing metonymically for victims of oppressive regimes
everywhere, in an echo of the way that Auschwitz stands for
evil everywhere, leads, in some estimations, to the forgetting of the specific suffering of the Nazis' victims.[29] Holocaust memory, far from being a comfortable place to inhabit
for the liberal-minded, is now highly contested, confusing
and not a little disorienting. We see that this memory cannot
guarantee a turn to universal human rights; it might instead,
in a salutary warning for those who promote Holocaust education and commemoration, lead to a '"calamatization" of
politics', that's to say, bitter contests in the public sphere in
which genocidal rhetoric might end up perpetuating hatreds
rather than overcoming them.[30] As Herzberg wrote after returning to the Netherlands:

> After several detours, we are back from Bergen-Belsen and
> already everything belongs to the past. The memory of it
> is beginning to fade; a dull spot is forming in my mind. It
> is hardly surprising. It is not very agreeable always to think
> of atrocities and to talk about them constantly also has its

objections. For it is not true that cruelty only repels. It also attracts. Cruelty is contagious. It is important therefore *how* one writes about the camps. With this in mind, it is most important that one should not only know what happened, but also try to understand it.[31]

We witnessed this effect in Rwanda and Yugoslavia in the 1990s as histories of past genocides or other group violence were instrumentalized to justify pre-emptive strikes to 'prevent' supposedly genocidal threats. In both cases, Holocaust imagery was present and mobilized, albeit marginally so in Rwanda, where the Hutu Power regime has been likened to 'tropical Nazism'. But in Yugoslavia there was much discourse in Croatia – ironically, the country which committed genocide against Serbs and Jews in the Second World War and at the time of the Yugoslav wars governed by a Holocaust denier, Franjo Tudjman – about how the Croats were the 'new Jews', under threat of genocide committed by the Serbs. In Serbia too, a Holocaust rhetoric was spread abroad, evoking the memory of the Second World War in order to justify Serbia's 'pre-emptive strike' against the other Yugoslav republics, Croatia especially.[32] We have seen, and continue to see, similar rhetoric in many places around the world since. In other words, the 'uplifting' version of the Holocaust memory has, unfortunately, come to an end. In the twenty-first century the terrain is more complex, rapidly changing and contested.

This is not a question of Holocaust denial. That particular idiocy has a history which stretches back to the war itself, with the Nazis' attempts to cover up their crimes, and was taken up by former Nazis and their sympathizers – especially

in France – immediately after the war. Despite the easy proliferation of Holocaust denial of various guises (from outright
negationism to 'softer' versions which question particular aspects of Holocaust history, such as the numbers killed) in the
digital age, it remains a marginal phenomenon. Even though
Holocaust denial has been promoted in countries where it
has traditionally been a marginal concern – notably Iran,
where President Ahmedinejad sponsored a well-publicized
conference on the topic – Holocaust denial per se is less
of a concern than the bundle of far-right narratives which
it usually comes wrapped up in. These include the sorts of
issues highlighted by far-right terrorists such as Anders Brei-
vik, who murdered seventy-seven people, mostly children, in
Norway in 2011: not just historically familiar antisemitic conspiracy theories but especially their currently most notable
manifestation, the 'great replacement theory'. This narrative
asserts that 'liberals' – that is to say, Jews – are plotting to
destroy the 'white race' by importing migrants to Europe, especially Muslim migrants, with a view to 'diluting' the white
population and undermining 'Christian' civilization.[33]

Rather, this is a problem of Holocaust memory in the post-
truth age. It is certainly the case that, as Herzberg said, it is not
pleasant always to dwell on atrocities. But one way of not doing
so is to beautify the history of the Holocaust, focusing only on
the 'positive' aspects. This was the strategy of the Polish government from 2015 to 2023, the flip side of whose attack on
those who air the nation's dirty laundry in public is to promote a narrative of Poles as rescuers. In several well-funded
museums and in the projects of the government-funded Pi-
lecki Institute, for example, we can learn about programmes

Polish embassy staff to provide false passports to Jews, thus enabling them to escape deportation to the death camps. At the same time, a subtle form of Holocaust distortion is being supported. It is clearly the case that some Catholic Poles – in quite large numbers, actually – helped their Jewish compatriots. There are many survivor accounts which detail the assistance from non-Jews, at considerable risk to themselves and their families. But this was by no means the standard experience, and the number of Poles who were involved in betraying Jews to the German occupiers, or robbing or killing them themselves, dwarfs the number of rescuers.

A similar, if better intentioned, form of Holocaust distortion is being promoted by the German government. In Germany, perhaps for understandable reasons, it is considered scandalous to point to non-Germans as being to blame for the Holocaust. But this principled position has unfortunate consequences. As this book has shown, without the impetus provided by the Nazi regime, the Holocaust would not have happened. But without the active support of willing collaborators across Europe, the Germans' programme to murder the Jews of Europe would have been far less successful. When Germany objects to anything that ostensibly detracts from German guilt, it serves to exculpate those others.

This problem is especially notable given that since the end of the Cold War most countries in Europe, especially in the former communist bloc, have conducted commissions of inquiry into their roles during the Holocaust. All of them have shown that local participation was considerable, driven by greed, nationalist aspirations and ideological affinity with Nazism.

Perhaps the most troubling form of Holocaust distortion has arisen in response to these commissions. Although the ideas on which the objections draw have a very long history, those in Eastern Europe who regard the stories of their country's participation in the Holocaust as a form of humiliating obeisance to the European Union or to a Western European memory template are responding in the first instance to the commissions' findings. They object to the idea that the Holocaust was the defining evil of the twentieth century and especially to the sense that by having to emphasize the Holocaust in order to gain an entry ticket to Brussels, the region's much longer experience of communist dictatorship is downplayed.[34] Hence we see the emergence of the double genocide theory in Eastern Europe. In this narrative, there is an entirely reasonable core proposition: that the history of the evils perpetrated by communism deserves to be investigated and commemorated. Unfortunately, by framing the case as a competition with Holocaust memory, the claim easily slips into antisemitic conspiracies, in particular that of 'Judaeo-Bolshevism'. At its most egregious, the double genocide argument not only suggests that communism was a 'Jewish' ideology and that Jews 'brought communism' to their country (there were no non-Jewish local communists, of course, since they were all good patriots), it also implies that the murder of the Jews was a justifiable response to their betrayal of their host country – even if it was carried out by Germans, not by local antisemites – and, furthermore, that the 'genocide' experienced by Eastern Europeans under foreign communist rule was longer lasting and therefore more destructive than that experienced by the Jews under Nazi rule. It is a narrative of 'pure victimhood' which, at its worst, offers an inversion exercise in which the victims are vilified and the perpetrators are refigured as heroes.[35] This is the world in which former Lithuanian Jewish partisans such as Rachel Margolis or the Israeli historian Yitzhak Arad can be threatened with prosecution for war crimes, and in which a fascist leader such as Ferenc Szálasi can be portrayed as the victim of communist repression, as in Budapest's Terror House museum. It is an emotionally fraught and politically dangerous 'debate', promoting as it does a zero-sum game in which reconciliation or shared memories and narratives of the past are unattainable.

Even those who are critical of the double genocide rhetoric are not immune from charges of Holocaust distortion. Eastern European scholars who detect a certain 'smugness' in Western European narratives of the war and the Holocaust are unsurprised that Eastern Europeans find having to accommodate themselves to that perspective objectionable. But can one say that a scholar who makes this point is guilty of Holocaust distortion? There is a tendency for all involved in this field to be very quick to take offence at others' positions, not always taking the time to think them through and to see that they are not necessarily revanchist or, worse, antisemitic.[36] In 2005, Tony Judt could claim that 'As Europe prepares to leave World War Two behind – as the last memorials are inaugurated, the last surviving combatants and victims honoured – the recovered memory of Europe's dead Jews has become the very definition and guarantee of the continent's restored humanity.'[37] One wonders how much longer this will be the case. In September 2016, on receiving the Man of the Year

Award from the Polish Prime Minister, Beata Szydło, Viktor
Orbán said:

> The Central European nations must preserve their
> identities, their religious and historical national identities.
> These are not just outdated clothing that one should
> discard in the modern era, but armour, which protects
> us . . . The communities which will be successful, survive
> and be strong are those with strong identities: religious,
> historical and national identities . . . I regret to say that
> we must protect [these virtues] from time to time not
> only against the faithless and our anti-national rivals, but
> also from time to time we must do so against Europe's
> various leading intellectual and political circles. But we
> have no choice . . . there will be no room for us under
> the sun.[38]

What happens to Holocaust memory in Orbán's vision of
struggle for European values?

This problem of memory confusion is clear too in recent
debates concerning how the Holocaust should be placed in
world history, debates which have become quite ugly both
within academia and in the public sphere.[39] How does the
Holocaust fit into world history, alongside other atrocities
such as slavery, colonial violence and the many other genocides that have scarred the modern world? The risk of comparison spills over from the world of scholarship into the
public domain all too easily, giving rise to feelings of being
slighted, of communities being neglected or their experiences belittled. This has been especially obvious in the ways
in which New World slavery was placed in competition with

the Holocaust in the 1980s and 1990s. Some of these debates drove an unfortunate wedge between African Americans who regarded the emphasis on the Holocaust as a form of Eurocentrism and Jews who found the comparison misplaced and the criticism offensive.[40] Here we see different groups' traumatic experiences vying for attention in an understandable but often unappealing way.

Echoes of these earlier arguments resound quite loudly today, in the context of debates about racism, colonialism and the Black Lives Matter movement. In the 1950s the Martiniquan poet and politician Aimé Césaire wrote, in his startling *Discourse on Colonialism*, one of the major works of anti-colonial literature, that the problem for the 'very Christian bourgeois of the twentieth century' is that 'he has a Hitler inside him, that Hitler *inhabits* him' and that, if he 'rails against him' he is being inconsistent, because

> at bottom, what he cannot forgive Hitler for is not *crime* in itself, *the crime against man*, it is not *the humiliation of man as such*, it is the crime against the white man, and the fact that he applied to Europe colonialist procedures which until then had been reserved exclusively for the Arabs of Algeria, the coolies of India, and the blacks of Africa.[41]

These words constitute a serious challenge to the idea of the Holocaust's unprecedentedness. Although Césaire takes too much for granted – until the postwar period, Jews were not quite considered 'white', for example, and he underestimates the differences between colonial atrocities, even colonial genocide, and the Holocaust – what he says merits careful consideration.

His words have come back to haunt us in the 2020s in quite complex ways. In Germany in 2020, for example, a scandal erupted when there were calls to disinvite the Cameroonian scholar Achille Mbembe from speaking at the Ruhr Triennial festival in Bochum. Mbembe has made several statements attacking the Israeli treatment of Palestinians, saying that the situation is 'far more lethal' than in South Africa under Apartheid. Although some scholars defended Mbembe's right to speak out, the German press and public sphere was far more reserved; it seems that criticism of Israel is still – for understandable historical reasons – under a *Verbot* in Germany. According to one author, this silence on Israel and Palestine serves to maintain a kind of German 'moral supremacy', whereby only the Holocaust counts as the 'universalised standard for human suffering'.[42] Mbembe, a scholar of worldwide renown and a winner of several prestigious German literary prizes for his work on postcolonial theory, suddenly found himself beyond the pale, a victim of targeted civil assassination. Although the festival was cancelled because of the Covid-19 pandemic, Mbembe was officially disinvited because of his alleged demonization of Israel and support for the BDS (Boycott, Divestment and Sanctions) movement. Thanks to the Bundestag's May 2019 decision to pass a resolution branding the BDS campaign as antisemitic, the German attempt to, in Habermas' words, create a country in which Jews can breathe has the consequence of shutting down debate about Israel. A well-intentioned ethical position which seeks moral repair with Jews ends by equating Jews as such with Israel, in the fetishized manner of both hardline Zionist and anti-Zionist thought – a particularly unfortunate result when one is trying to create an atmosphere for making Jews feel at home. As one legal scholar argues, the problem is trying to impose the German 'moral' position on everyone else:

> The critique starts with the special responsibility of the Germans for the Holocaust and postulates a resulting specifically German view, a German narrative, a German identity and a German responsibility. It ignores the particular origin of this view and turns it into a universalism. The critique then imposes this universalism on everybody, including those who do not share in the particular German experience and responsibility. But since this universalism derives from German responsibility, Germans remain in control of the debate.[43]

Germany has undoubtedly done far more than most other perpetrator nations to grapple with its own crimes. But contrary to those who argue that the rest of the world should look to Germany with admiration, we might note a certain German smugness in its own soul-searching, which results in some problematic blind spots. The German identification with Israel is echoed in the widespread refusal to countenance including non-Germans among the perpetrators of the Holocaust. Symbolized by the Memorial to the Murdered Jews of Europe in Berlin, finally dedicated in 2005 after years of debate over its size and role, the German position has been criticized particularly by historians who are struggling with the Polish government's threat to criminalize those who point to the actions of Polish perpetrators. One goes so far as to suggest that this position is 'in danger of leading to the distortion, even falsification, of the history of the Holocaust'.[44]

What is striking is the extent to which Holocaust memory has become a more febrile, contested phenomenon. During the Historians' Debate in the 1980s, comparing the Holocaust with Stalinist crimes was the agenda of the conservative right, seeking to show that the Nazi genocide of the Jews was not a singular crime after all and that the Germans could be a 'normal' nation. Those who advocated the uniqueness of the Holocaust were largely progressive thinkers, represented by Habermas, who feared that any other position would give rise to renewed antisemitism in Germany and a loss of the grounds for the 'constitutional patriotism' that he advocated, in favour of ethnic nationalism. In recent years the stakes in the act of comparison have been reversed. In scholarly debates concerning the place of the Holocaust in world history, comparison is now advocated by, broadly speaking (the labels are imprecise), progressive thinkers, while a defence of the Holocaust's uniqueness – now implying also unwavering support for Israel – is the preserve largely of the conservative right. And this is because the comparison is now no longer solely between the Holocaust and Stalinism. Instead, the focus now is on colonial crimes, especially those committed by Germany in German South West Africa (today Namibia), and the involvement of Black German critics in opening up a discourse that includes the history of slavery, colonial atrocity and anti-Black racism in Germany, making the field much more complex, and giving it much more of a contemporary feel, than a focus solely on the Gulag might do. The conservative position, now the opposite of what it was during the 1980s, makes sense when one sees that it aims to 'avoid additional forms of ethical and political implication' and to absolve Germany of involvement in colonial crimes.[45] The progressive one seeks to expand the discussion beyond the national frame, placing Holocaust memory in dialogue with other massive and contested histories of race and colonialism. What both perhaps overlook is that the history of the Holocaust itself is far more than a German affair. The trans-European dimension of the genocide of the Jews, which can itself be understood as part of the fallout from the earlier collapse of the European empires and thus necessarily connected to wider histories of imperial rule and decline, both in Europe and overseas, also throws up questions of responsibility, race and the role of the state. These mnemonic connections may no longer be quite as predictable as they were but they should not lead us to overlook the complexity of the Holocaust itself, nor the fact that the horror of it is just as telling as that of other varieties of race-based atrocity. In contemporary debates over racism, antisemitism sometimes gets inadvertently left out. It would be ironic if Holocaust memory were to be siloed as somehow 'Eurocentric', when in fact it provides one of the clearest examples of where race thinking or 'security paranoia' can lead under conditions of crisis.[46]

The Challenge of Memory

What, if anything, does the Holocaust tell us about the modern world?[47] The Holocaust was not the logical conclusion of means–ends rationality but rather the consequence of a modern world that creates and canalizes deep passions that have no obvious outlet. Many thinkers have stressed the 'modernity' of the Holocaust; yet, as we have seen, whether in terms of technology or administration, there was nothing that marks the Holocaust as peculiarly modern beyond the fact that it took place in the twentieth century and the perpetrators availed themselves of techniques that epitomized their age. Rather, the radical nature of the Holocaust lay in the way in which modern characteristics such as science, bureaucracy or railways were used to intensify and make manifest a form of non-rational fantasy thinking that underpinned Nazism and was itself a product of the modern age.[48] In principle there is nothing wrong with Holocaust education or Holocaust commemoration. But we should be willing to face the radical conclusions to which these activities should lead us: that the Holocaust was a deeply traumatic event for its victims; that the aftermath of the Second World War had not only positive consequences (the creation of a democratic Germany, the absence of war in most of Europe since 1945) but also incubated a dark legacy, a deep psychology of fascist fascination and genocidal fantasy that people turn to instinctively in moments of crisis – we see it most clearly in the alt-right and the online world, spreading into the mainstream, of conspiracy theory; and that the Holocaust not only reveals the fragility of the modern nation-state and the 'pillars' which support it (rule of law, the military, religion, ruling elites) but calls their very organization and functioning into question. The Holocaust shows that the state, although it can provide universal health care and guarantee citizens' rights, need not do so. In fact, seen historically, and looking at the direction of travel today across the world, we see that the state is more likely to circumscribe the rights of the individual and, when those who control it feel threatened, use the tools at their disposal to carry out programmes of 'purification' in any way they deem necessary.

At the end of the war, one sharp commentator observed that 'Hitler has been vanquished rather than repudiated, most of those who opposed him reacted against the application of his concepts to them. They have still to disavow his conception.'[49] The truth of this claim became obvious during the wars of decolonization that followed hard on the heels of the world war: notions of racial supremacy, of the right to territorial expansion, of the dismissal of minorities' rights to hospitality and membership in the polity in which they live.[50] Many rejected Nazism because they regretted the choice of the targets of its hatreds rather than because they regarded hatred of other groups as such as unacceptable. Race hatred in particular continues to plague the world. It is not sufficient on its own to bring about genocide but in moments of crisis it can be operationalized, set to work in ways that remain threatening.

Over thirty years after the war, this fear of Nazism, this rejection of it without facing its meaning head on was once again explained by a philosopher: 'one does not dare think out Nazism because it has been beaten down like a mad dog, by a police action, and not in conformity with the rules accepted by its adversaries' genres of discourse (argumentation for liberalism, contradiction for Marxism). It has not been refuted.'[51] If in the 1980s, when these words were written, one might justly have argued that they were overstated, today they have acquired new force. How can we argue that Nazism and what it means have been refuted when we witness the rise of the far right across the world, from Brazil to Poland, the shocking slide of America's Republican Party into fascism and the triumph or threat of authoritarian politics in many countries, from Myanmar to Georgia? It seems that, to the extent that Nazism was refuted in the decades after 1945, it was so only among certain sections of the population. Thus, for all that Holocaust education is now entrenched in many countries' school curricula and national commemorative calendars, in times of perceived crisis fascism offers a style, a vocabulary and a simple set of answers to which some people seem instinctively to turn. What does this mean for understanding Holocaust memory, that is to say, the ways in which the Holocaust has been commemorated, remembered, legislated and contested in the public sphere in the decades since the end of the Second World War?

These issues have been summed up well, if polemically, by the Romanian-Jewish author Norman Manea, a survivor of the horrors of the Romanian Holocaust in Transnistria who now lives in the US. In his autobiography, *The Hooligan's Return*, which movingly recounts the circumstances of his exile to the US and his return trips to Romania since the ousting of Ceauşescu, Manea offers some provocative thoughts: 'Public commemorations have transformed horrors into clichés, which have been worked over until they have become petrified, thus fulfilling their function, followed, of course, by fatigue and indifference.'[52] Later he adds, with even greater invective:

The trivialization of suffering . . . mankind's endless enterprise. Only when it becomes a cliché does tragedy find a home in the collective memory. Memory must keep watch so that the horror is not repeated, we have been told over and over. We must hold on to identity, shared memory, race, ethnicity, religion, ideology. Having finally landed on the planet of pragmatism, you thought you might escape your past and your identity and become just a simple entity, as Gertrude Stein, the American in Paris, dreamed – only to find that Thursday's atrocities have become grist for the mottoes on Friday's T-shirts, an instantly marketable product for the collective memory.[53]

The duty to remember and the need to commemorate are here seen as empty, complacent rituals that serve only to pacify the past, making it safe for the present to ignore.

But the past has a way of returning. In January 2018, Yannis Boutaris, the mayor of Thessaloniki, gave a brave speech to mark Holocaust Memorial Day. In it he noted that Thessaloniki's past 'pursues and haunts us', silent but ever present. The huge Jewish cemetery of Salonika may have been destroyed, but its tombstones built the front yard of the Agios Demetrios church, they are laid out in front of the army headquarters and the Royal Theatre, they were used to construct roads and pavements and they were displayed in stacks in front of the city's famous White Tower and the grounds of the International Expo until December 1948. The Ahepa Hospital and the Aristotle University are built on the grounds of the cemetery. The Holocaust is woven into the fabric of Thessaloniki, as its residents increasingly recognize.[54]

But the past does not only return in places where it has not been discussed, or has been hushed up for many decades, as in Greece. Across Europe the scandal of continent-wide collaboration, so stunningly revealed in the numerous commissions that were produced in the early years of the twenty-first century, has opened new questions. The Holocaust was not only a German affair – even if it undoubtedly emanated from Germany and was led by the Germans – and it is no coincidence that the return of the radical right has come at the same time as these revelations about pan-European involvement. Commemorating with ceremonies whose template involves heads of state, a few victim testimonies and children's poems is insufficient to change the ways in which fascism is interwoven into the deep memory of Western culture. The challenge remains: will the Holocaust be understood?

Conclusion

'Historical order turns out to be nothing more than the order of dying.'
— Marek Edelman in conversation with Hanna Krall[1]

'Even if we admit that every generation has the right to write its own history, we admit no more than that it has the right to rearrange the facts in accordance with its own perspective; we don't admit the right to touch the factual matter itself.'
— Hannah Arendt[2]

In her remarkable novel *Swastika Night* (1937) Katharine Burdekin showed that an unexpected setting could provide keen insights into the nature of the Third Reich. Burdekin's book imagines the world seven centuries after a German victory in which two empires, the German and Japanese, have divided the globe, destroyed all trace of pre-Nazi culture and subjected women to a 'Reduction' which has left them housed in cages and treated as animals, to be used by men for breeding purposes. In a tightly regulated and controlled world, only small groups of Christians live outside of the Nazis' structures, left alone as outcasts. When the novel's protagonist, the Englishman Alfred, tries to explain the history of the Christians to his German friend Hermann, he notes that: 'They persecuted and humiliated the Jews for nearly two thousand years, and then the Germans took on the persecution and made it racial, and after a time killed all the Jews off.'[3] Later in the book, the Knight von Hess, who reveals to Alfred his possession of an ancient book – a highly dangerous, illegal possession, for all books save for a handful of technical books have been banned and obliterated – also tries to give the Englishman a potted account, on the basis of his garbled knowledge, of what came before the Nazi triumph. When Alfred says he doesn't understand about Jesus and asks where the Jews came from, the exchange goes as follows:

> 'They were an Eastern Mediterranean people, not black, but dark, and I gather a little like Arabs to look at.'
>   'But where are they now?'
>   'They don't exist. They were either absorbed into other nations or wiped out. There were a few left in von Hess's [the Knight's predecessor's] time. The Palestine Jews were killed, massacred to the last man and the last child, when the Imperial German Army took Jerusalem. The German Jews were killed in various pogroms both during and after the Twenty Years' War. The Jews in other countries were harassed first by the anti-Semitic authoritarian war governments of those countries, before Germany conquered them, and were much reduced in numbers, and then were harassed over again by the German armies of occupation.'[4]

These discussions about Jews take place almost in passing; seven centuries after their disappearance the group has left no trace, and only a few rare enquiring individuals have any sense of who they might have been – and in Burdekin's Nazi empire, such knowledge was strictly to be kept hidden. It was easy for Burdekin to imagine a future without Jews; she understood that Nazism's logic led to the elimination of Jews as a people.

This book has not argued that the Holocaust followed inevitably from the anti-Jewish position first articulated in the Nazi Party programme of 1920 or in *Mein Kampf*. The path to the Holocaust was twisted, and policy was made as competing agencies vied for control of Jewish policy in the context of population policies more broadly. It was further circumscribed by military necessity, technical and personnel resources, the degree of willing displayed by collaborating regimes to deport or kill 'their' Jews and by sheer serendipity. But interpretations which stress only the ad hoc nature of Nazi policy-making and the disorganized and unsystematic ways in which Jews were persecuted in different parts of Nazi- and Axis-occupied Europe fail to explain why it was the Jews who were being targeted in the first place.

The danger in focusing solely on ideology is that it tends to suggest that the perpetrators were simply 'mad'. But as French journalist Jacqueline Mesnil-Amar wrote shortly after the end of the war:

It's easy to appear indignant in the face of the crimes committed by these brutes, to exclaim that 'these people are monsters', and then go back home for a peaceful dinner and sleep with a clear conscience. For there to have been that many monsters, there must have been something unusually propitious for the gestation and growth of monsters, something complex which exists at some level in all of us, and in which each and every one played a part. Across the entire German nation Nazism produced a strange desire to destroy their world and, in a sort of collective intoxication, bordering on madness, to allow another to arise in its place, a world of death, a dark, repugnant bloody and sadistic medieval world.[5]

Although she also stresses a kind of 'madness', she rightly observes that the strange outburst which was Nazism drew on reserves of affect which can be found in all societies in crisis. In the German case, the crisis allowed for the appeal to and operationalization of myths of Teutonic belonging, Aryan racial superiority and the threat posed by the 'international Jew'. It suffices only to think of the levels of European collaboration seen above, however, from Croatia to Romania, France to Norway, Ukraine to Latvia, to see that Europe as a whole was susceptible to the 'collective intoxication' of Nazism. It remains so, as we see when radical right protestors give Hitler salutes on marches purportedly called to 'defend' statues of the likes of Churchill, who, whatever his faults, was no Nazi sympathizer. We see it in the incel culture of the manosphere, in which gender-based complexes merge into fantasies of sexual and racial annihilation.[6] We see it in the 'anti-woke' response to attempts to do away with structural forms of racism. And we saw it when radical-right Trump supporters, living in their fantasy world of a stolen election, stormed the Capitol in Washington, DC.

Ideology, however, as this book has shown, needs to be

placed in context. The fact that Hitler wrote down some of his fantasies in *Mein Kampf* does not explain the Holocaust. In fact, the contexts of the war, of massive forced population movements and the extraordinary killing that took place across Europe, especially in the east, during the Second World War, makes the genocide of the Jews more, not less, noteworthy (as some historians who dislike any attempt to think about the Holocaust alongside other Nazi crimes fear). Likewise, the context of the social crises brought about by the war which led to fear, polarization and collaboration on a massive scale suggests that participation in the Holocaust, even when driven by venality, a desire to be on the 'winning side' or simply falling into line, was nevertheless something that Europeans could consider in ways which indicate that hatred of Jews, or at least indifference to their fate, rooted in ancient stereotypes, could be easily mobilized. The Holocaust was heavily influenced by circumstances such as the role played by the perpetrators of the T4 programme, the type of occupation regime in place, the degree of collaboration offered by different regimes and the Nazis' and their allies' access to Jewish population groups afforded by the military situation – all of these things shaped the number of Jews that the Nazis could put their hands on and the size of the death rates in particular locations, from Thessaloniki to Amsterdam, Oslo to Rome. They explain why the Nazis could kill more Jews from Warsaw than the whole of Western Europe, or why the Jews of the western Soviet Union could be shot in huge numbers in 1941 but the Jews of Hungary could only be deported to Auschwitz in 1944. Yet these factors are not on their own explanations for why the Nazis targeted the Jews, or why so many Europeans joined them in their genocidal enterprise. Only an emphasis on ideology, albeit ideology tempered by contingency, can do so.

In 1995 Lawrence Langer observed a contradiction in Holocaust commentary, noting: 'what we appear to have is, on the one hand, a historical consciousness determined to distort or at least alleviate the harshest truths of the Holocaust, and, on the other, a historical consciousness resolved to confront its implications wherever they may lead'.[7] This book has, of course, positioned itself with the second of Langer's alternatives, in the hope of showing that in many ways we have failed unflinchingly to face the terrible reality of the Holocaust. But I do not pretend that a short book such as this can bring to light all of the facts or shift longstanding cultural attitudes. As Langer and many other critics have observed, the nature of history-writing tends towards order, imposing coherence on events which were fundamentally – even in their organization – chaotic, especially for their victims. History needs supplementing with fiction, film, testimony, theatre, poetry, art, performance, law, philosophy, anthropology, sociology, music – and there is no shortage of such powerful work dealing with the Holocaust. Nevertheless, the historian's critical approach can contribute to an understanding of the Holocaust that brings to light the truly appalling nature of what happened. It can challenge us today to consider whether we have done enough to resist apocalyptic visions and movements when they reoccur, as they already have done and will continue to do in a world convulsed by global warming, mass migration of climate and war refugees, pandemics and xenophobia, and shaped, more and more often, by a perverse delight in the apocalypse that is to come. The Romanian-French fascist philosopher E. M. Cioran wrote, in one of his suavely provocative and cheerfully glib end-of-time pronouncements, that: 'Our capital of misery remains intact throughout the ages; yet we have one advantage over our ancestors: that of having invested our capital better, since our disaster is better organized.'[8] Can we say with certainty that he was wrong?

Notes

INTRODUCTION: WHAT IS THE HOLOCAUST?

1. Abel Jacob Herzberg, *Amor Fati: Seven Essays on Bergen-Belsen* (Göttingen: Wallstein Verlag, 2016 [Dutch orig. 1946]), 68–9.
2. *Trial of the Major War Criminals before the International Military Tribunal, Nuremberg, 14 November 1945–1 October 1946* (Nuremberg: International Military Tribunal, 1947), vol. 1, 34 (henceforth IMT).
3. Hanna Lévy-Hass, diary entry for January 1945, in *Diary of Bergen-Belsen, 1944–1945* (Chicago: Haymarket, 2009), 103.
4. Isaiah Spiegel, 'In the Dark' (1941), in *Ghetto Kingdom: Tales of the Łódź Ghetto* (Evanston: Northwestern University Press, 1998), 15.
5. Ovidiu Creangă, 'Acmecetca' and 'Peciora', in Joseph R. White and Mel Hecker (eds.), *United States Holocaust Memorial Museum Encyclopedia of Camps and Ghettos 1933–1945*, vol. 3: *Camps and Ghettos under European Regimes Aligned with Nazi Germany* (Bloomington: Indiana University Press, in association with the United States Holocaust Memorial Museum, 2018), 588 (Acmecetca), 742 (Peciora). See my review article, 'A Continent of Camps and Collaboration', *Yad Vashem Studies*, 46:2 (2019), 217–28.
6. See Terence Des Pres, 'Excremental Assault', in *The Survivor: An Anatomy of Life in the Death Camps* (New York: Oxford University Press, 1976), ch. 3.
7. Hannah Arendt to Karl Jaspers, 17 December 1946: 'Perhaps what is behind it all is only that individual human beings did not kill other individual human beings for human reasons, but that an organised attempt was made to eradicate the existence of the human being.' *Arendt/Jaspers Correspondence 1926–1949*, ed. Lotte Kohler and Hans Saner (San Diego: Harcourt Brace, 1992), 69.
8. Lawrence L. Langer, *Holocaust Testimonies: The Ruins of Memory* (New Haven: Yale University Press, 1991), 171.

9. See Jan Grabowski's important article, 'Germany Is Fueling a False History of the Holocaust across Europe', *Haaretz* (22 June 2020); and Götz Aly, *Europe against the Jews 1880–1945* (New York: Metropolitan Books, 2020).

10. Aomar Boum and Sarah Abrevaya Stein (eds.), *The Holocaust and North Africa* (Stanford: Stanford University Press, 2019); Aomar Boum, 'Redrawing Holocaust Geographies: A Cartography of Vichy and Nazi Reach into North Africa', in Simone Gigliotti and Hilary Earl (eds.), *A Companion to the Holocaust* (Hoboken, NJ: Wiley, 2020), 431–48; Yvonne Kozlovsky-Golan, 'Childhood Memories from the Giado Detention Camp in Libya: Fragments from the Oeuvre of Nava T. Barazani', *Shofar*, 38:1 (2020), 1–37.

11. Susan Rubin Suleiman, 'Paradigms and Differences', in Boum and Stein (eds.), *The Holocaust and North Africa*, 217–18.

12. Mark Edele, Sheila Fitzpatrick and Atina Grossmann (eds.), *Shelter from the Holocaust: Rethinking Jewish Survival in the Soviet Union* (Detroit: Wayne State University Press, 2017); Markus Nesselrodt, *Dem Holocaust entkommen: Polnische Juden in der Sowjetunion 1939–1946* (Berlin: De Gruyter, 2019).

13. Maria Tumarkin, 'Epilogue', in Edele, Fitzpatrick and Grossmann (eds.), *Shelter from the Holocaust*, 275–9.

14. Simone Gigliotti, *On the Trail of the Homeseeker: The Holocaust and the Cinema of the Displaced* (Bloomington: Indiana University Press, 2023).

15. Diane F. Afoumado, 'France/Vichy', in White and Hecker (eds.), *United States Holocaust Memorial Museum Encyclopedia of Camps and Ghettos 1933–1945*, vol. 3, 96.

16. See especially Christian Gerlach, *The Extermination of the European Jews* (Cambridge: Cambridge University Press, 2016); and David Cesarani, *Final Solution: The Fate of the Jews 1933–49* (London: Macmillan, 2016).

17. Des Pres, *The Survivor*; Langer, *Holocaust Testimonies*; Lawrence L. Langer, *Admitting the Holocaust: Collected Essays* (New York: Oxford University Press, 1995); Amos Goldberg, *Trauma in First Person: Diary Writing during the Holocaust* (Bloomington: Indiana University Press, 2017).

18. Alon Confino, *A World without Jews: The Nazi Imagination from Persecution to Genocide* (New Haven: Yale University Press, 2014).

19. See especially Cesarani, *Final Solution*.

20. Dan Stone, 'Race Science, Race Mysticism, and the Racial State', in Devin O. Pendas, Mark Roseman and Richard F. Wetzell (eds.), *Beyond the Racial State: Rethinking Nazi Germany* (New York: Cambridge University Press, 2017), 176–96; Johann Chapoutot, *The Law of Blood: Thinking and Acting*

as a Nazi (Cambridge, Mass.: The Belknap Press of Harvard University Press, 2018). Aurel Kolnai's 1938 book *The War Against the West* (London: Victor Gollancz, 1938) remains one of the most clear-sighted assessments of this Nazi race obsession; for an analysis, see Wolfgang Bialas (ed.), *Aurel Kolnai's 'War Against the West' Reconsidered* (London: Routledge, 2019). See my essays on this subject in *Fascism, Nazism and the Holocaust: Challenging Histories* (London: Routledge, 2021).

21. See, for example, Anton Weiss-Wendt and Rory Yeomans (eds.), *Racial Science in Hitler's New Europe, 1938–1945* (Lincoln: University of Nebraska Press, 2013); Marius Turda (ed.), *The History of East-Central European Eugenics, 1900–1945: Sources and Commentaries* (London: Bloomsbury, 2015); Marius Turda and Paul J. Weindling (eds.), *Blood and Homeland: Eugenics and Racial Nationalism in Central and Southeast Europe, 1900–1940* (Budapest: Central European University Press, 2007).

22. Thomas Kühne, *Belonging and Genocide: Hitler's Community, 1918–1945* (New Haven: Yale University Press, 2010).

23. See, for a well-made example of this argument, William W. Hagen, 'The Three Horsemen of the Holocaust: Anti-Semitism, East European Empire, Aryan Folk Community', in Helmut Walser Smith (ed.), *The Oxford Handbook of Modern German History* (Oxford: Oxford University Press, 2011), 548–72.

24. Peter Hayes, 'Profits and Persecution: Corporate Involvement in the Holocaust', in James S. Pacy and Alan P. Wertheimer (eds.), *Perspectives on the Holocaust: Essays in Honor of Raul Hilberg* (Boulder: Westview Press, 1995), 64.

25. Jürgen Matthäus, 'Anti-Semitism as an Offer: The Function of Ideological Indoctrination in the SS and Police Corps during the Holocaust', in Dagmar Herzog (ed.), *Lessons and Legacies*, vol. 7: *The Holocaust in International Perspective* (Evanston: Northwestern University Press, 2006), 116–28; Frank Bajohr, 'Vom antijüdischen Konsens zum schlechten Gewissen. Die deutsche Gesellschaft und die Judenverfolgung 1933–1945', in Frank Bajohr and Dieter Pohl, *Massenmord und schlechtes Gewissen: Die deutsche Bevölkerung, die NS-Führung und der Holocaust* (Frankfurt am Main: Suhrkamp Taschenbuch Verlag, 2008), 34–45; Jeffrey Herf, *The Jewish Enemy: Nazi Propaganda during World War II and the Holocaust* (Cambridge, Mass.: The Belknap Press of Harvard University Press, 2006), ch. 2: 'Building the Anti-Semitic Consensus'.

26. Dan Stone, *Goodbye to All That? The Story of Europe since 1945* (Oxford: Oxford University Press, 2014); Emma Kuby, *Political Survivors: The*

Resistance, the Cold War, and the Fight against Concentration Camps after 1945 (Ithaca: Cornell University Press, 2019).

27. Shirli Gilbert and Avril Alba (eds.), *Holocaust Memory and Racism in the Postwar World* (Detroit: Wayne State University Press, 2019); Michael Rothberg, *Multidirectional Memory: Remembering the Holocaust in the Age of Decolonization* (Stanford: Stanford University Press, 2009); Bashir Bashir and Amos Goldberg (eds.), *The Holocaust and the Nakba: A New Grammar of Trauma and History* (New York: Columbia University Press, 2018).

28. Harold Marcuse, 'The Revival of Holocaust Awareness in West Germany, Israel, and the United States', in Carole Fink, Philipp Gassert, and Detlef Junker (eds.), *1968: The World Transformed* (Cambridge: Cambridge University Press, 1998), 421–38; Sebastian Gehrig, 'Sympathizing Subcultures? The Milieus of West German Terrorism', in Martin Klimke, Jacco Pekelder and Joachim Scharloth (eds.), *Between Prague Spring and French May: Opposition and Revolt in Europe, 1960–1980* (New York: Berghahn Books, 2011); Michael Schmidtke, 'The German New Left and National Socialism', in Philipp Gassert and Alan E. Steinweis (eds.), *Coping with the Nazi Past: West German Debates on Nazism and Generational Conflict, 1955–1975* (New York: Berghahn Books, 2006), 176–93; Christoph Schmidt, 'The Israel of the Spirit: The German Student Movement of the 1960s and Its Attitude to the Holocaust', *Dapim: Studies on the Shoah*, 24 (2010), 269–318.

29. Cited in Hans Kundnani, *Utopia or Auschwitz: Germany's 1968 Generation and the Holocaust* (London: C. Hurst & Co., 2009), 145. See my discussion in *Goodbye to All That?*, ch. 3, and Jan-Werner Müller, 'What Did They Think They Were Doing? The Political Thought of the (West European) 1968 Revisited', in Vladimir Tismaneanu (ed.), *Promises of 1968: Crisis, Illusion, and Utopia* (Budapest: Central European University Press, 2011).

30. Norbert Frei, *Vergangenheitspolitik: Die Anfänge der Bundesrepublik und die NS-Vergangenheit* (Munich: C. H. Beck, 2012); Jacob S. Eder, *Holocaust Angst: The Federal Republic of Germany and American Holocaust Memory since the 1970s* (New York: Oxford University Press, 2016); Carole Fink, *West Germany and Israel: Foreign Relations, Domestic Politics, and the Cold War, 1965–1974* (Cambridge: Cambridge University Press, 2019); Eldad Ben-Aharon, *The Geopolitics of Genocide in the Middle East and the Second Cold War: Israeli–Turkish–American Relations and the Contested Memories of the Armenian Genocide (1978–1988)* (PhD thesis, Royal Holloway, University of London, 2020).

31. Dan Stone, 'On Neighbours and Those Knocking at the Door: Holocaust Memory and Europe's Refugee Crisis', *Patterns of Prejudice*, 52:2–3 (2018), 231–43.

32. David Motadel, 'Veiled Survivors: Jews, Roma and Muslims in the Years of the Holocaust', in Jan Rüger and Nikolaus Wachsmann (eds.), *Rewriting German History: New Perspectives on Modern Germany* (Houndmills: Palgrave Macmillan, 2015), 288–305.

33. Anson Rabinbach and Jack Zipes (eds.), *Germans and Jews since the Holocaust: The Changing Situation in West Germany* (New York: Holmes & Meier, 1986); Geoffrey Hartman (ed.), *Bitburg in Moral and Political Perspective* (Bloomington: Indiana University Press, 1986). On the *Historikerstreit* see especially Charles S. Maier, *The Unmasterable Past: History, Holocaust, and German National Identity* (Cambridge, Mass.: Harvard University Press, 1988).

34. Gavriel D. Rosenfeld, *Hi Hitler! How the Nazi Past Is Being Normalized in Contemporary Culture* (New York: Cambridge University Press, 2014).

35. Carolyn J. Dean, 'Recent French Discourses on Stalinism, Nazism, and "Exorbitant" Jewish Memory', *History & Memory*, 18:1 (2006), 43–85; Sarah Gensburger and Sandrine Lefranc, *Beyond Memory: Can We Really Learn from the Past?* (Houndmills: Palgrave Macmillan, 2020); Wulf Kansteiner, 'Censorship and Memory: Thinking Outside the Box with Facebook, Goebbels, and Xi Jinping', *Journal of Perpetrator Research*, 4:1 (2021), 35–58.

36. See, for example, Maria Mälksoo, 'A Baltic Struggle for a "European Memory": The Militant Mnemopolitics of *The Soviet Story*', *Journal of Genocide Research*, 20:4 (2018), 530–44; Aline Sierp, '1939 versus 1989 – A Missed Opportunity to Create a European *Lieu de Mémoire?*', *East European Politics and Societies and Cultures*, 31:3 (2017), 439–55.

37. István Rév, 'Liberty Square, Budapest: How Hungary Won the Second World War', *Journal of Genocide Research*, 20:4 (2018), 607–23.

38. Memories of the radical right are understudied by historians. See, for example, Madeleine Hurd and Steffen Werther: 'Go East, Old Man: The Ritual Spaces of SS Veterans' Memory Work', *Culture Unbound*, 6:2 (2014), 327–59; 'Retelling the Past, Inspiring the Future: Waffen-SS Commemorations and the Creation of a "European" Far-Right Counter-Narrative', *Patterns of Prejudice*, 50:4–5 (2016), 420–44.

39. See Geoff Eley, *Nazism as Fascism: Violence, Ideology and the Ground of Consent in Germany 1930–1945* (London: Routledge, 2013), ch. 7; Stone, *Goodbye to All That?*; Dan Stone, 'The Return of Fascism in Europe? Reflections on History and the Current Situation', in Eleni Braat and Pepijn Corduwener (eds.), *1989 and the West: Western Europe and the End of the Cold War* (London: Routledge, 2020), 266–84.

40. Robert Gerwarth and John Horne (eds.), *War in Peace: Paramilitary Violence in Europe after the Great War* (Oxford: Oxford University Press, 2012).

41. Peter Viereck, *Meta-Politics: The Roots of the Nazi Mind*, rev. edn (New York: Capricorn Books, 1965 [1941]), 313.

42. Hannah Arendt, 'Fernsehgespräch mit Thilo Koch' (1964), in Arendt, *Ich will verstehen: Selbstauskünfte zu Leben und Werk*, ed. Ursula Ludz (Munich: Piper, 1996), 40.

43. Kim Wünschmann, *Before Auschwitz: Jewish Prisoners in the Prewar Concentration Camps* (Cambridge, Mass.: Harvard University Press, 2015); Christopher Dillon, *Dachau and the SS: A Schooling in Violence* (Oxford: Oxford University Press, 2015).

44. Christopher R. Browning, *Ordinary Men: Reserve Police Battalion 101 and the Final Solution in Poland* (New York: HarperPerennial, 1993), xv.

45. Jochen Böhler and Robert Gerwarth (eds.), *The Waffen-SS: A European History* (Oxford: Oxford University Press, 2017).

46. As Timothy Snyder suggests; see *Black Earth: The Holocaust as History and Warning* (London: The Bodley Head, 2015), esp. ch. 9.

47. Stanislav Zámečník, '"Kein Häftling darf lebend in die Hände des Feindes fallen": Zur Existenz des Himmler-Befehls vom 14./18. April 1945', *Dachauer Hefte*, 1 (1985), 219–31.

48. Jeffrey C. Alexander, 'On the Social Construction of Moral Universals: The "Holocaust" from War Crime to Trauma Drama', in Alexander et al., *Cultural Trauma and Collective Identity* (Berkeley: University of California Press, 2004), 196–263.

49. Zygmunt Bauman, *Modernity and the Holocaust* (Cambridge: Polity Press, 1989). See my discussion in *Histories of the Holocaust* (Oxford: Oxford University Press, 2010), ch. 3.

50. For case studies of research into the 'aftermath' of the Holocaust, see for example Suzanne Bardgett, Christine Schmidt and Dan Stone (eds.), *Beyond Camps and Forced Labour: Proceedings of the Sixth International Conference* (Houndmills: Palgrave Macmillan, 2020). On the ITS, see Susanne Urban, *'Mein einziges Dokument ist die Nummer auf der Hand': Aussagen Überlebender der NS-Verfolgung im International Tracing Service* (Berlin: Metropol, 2018); Henning Borggräfe, Christian Höschler and Isabel Panek (eds.), *Tracing and Documenting Nazi Victims Past and Present* (Berlin: De Gruyter, 2020); Dan Stone, *Fate Unknown: The Search for the Missing after World War II and the Holocaust* (Oxford: Oxford University Press, 2023).

51. Noah Shenker, *Reframing Holocaust Testimony* (Bloomington: Indiana University Press, 2015); Hannah Pollin-Galay, *Ecologies of Testimony: Language, Place, and Holocaust Testimony* (New Haven: Yale University Press, 2018); Sharon Kangisser Cohen, *Testimony and Time: Holocaust Survivors Remember* (Jerusalem: Yad Vashem, 2014); Anika Walke, *Pioneers and Partisans: An Oral History of Nazi Genocide in Belarussia* (New York: Oxford University Press, 2015); Alexandra Garbarini, *Numbered Days: Diaries and the Holocaust* (New Haven: Yale University Press, 2006); Dawn Skorczewski and Dan Stone, '"I Was a Tape Recorder. I Was a Mailing Box": Jan Karski's Interviews', *Journal of Holocaust Research*, 34:4 (2020), 350–69; Madeline White, *A Contextual Analysis of Holocaust Oral Testimony in Britain and Canada* (PhD Thesis, Royal Holloway, University of London, 2021).

52. For example: Michael J. Bazyler and Frank M. Tuerkheimer (eds.), *Forgotten Trials of the Holocaust* (New York: New York University Press, 2014); Norman J. W. Goda (ed.), *Rethinking Holocaust Justice: Essays across Disciplines* (New York: Berghahn Books, 2018); Amos Goldberg and Haim Hazan (eds.), *Marking Evil: Holocaust Memory in the Global Age* (New York: Berghahn Books, 2015); Claudio Fogu, Wulf Kansteiner, and Todd Presner (eds.), *Probing the Ethics of Holocaust Culture* (Cambridge, Mass.: Harvard University Press, 2016).

53. For example: Donald Bloxham and A. Dirk Moses (eds.), *The Oxford Handbook of Genocide Studies* (Oxford: Oxford University Press, 2010); Dan Stone (ed.), *The Historiography of Genocide* (Houndmills: Palgrave Macmillan, 2008); Rebecca Jinks, *Representing Genocide: The Holocaust as Paradigm?* (London: Bloomsbury, 2016).

54. Philip Friedman, *Roads to Extinction: Essays on the Holocaust* (New York: Jewish Publication Society of America, 1980); David Bankier and Dan Michman (eds.), *Holocaust Historiography in Context: Emergence, Challenges, Polemics and Achievements* (Jerusalem: Yad Vashem, 2008); Shmuel Krakowski, 'Memorial Projects and Memorial Institutions Initiated by *She'erit Hapletah*', in Yisrael Gutman and Avital Saf (eds.), *She'erit Hapletah 1944–1948: Rehabilitation and Political Struggle* (Jerusalem: Yad Vashem, 1990), 388–98; Laura Jockusch, *Collect and Record! Jewish Holocaust Documentation in Early Postwar Europe* (New York: Oxford University Press, 2012); Mark L. Smith, *The Yiddish Historians and the Struggle for a Jewish History of the Holocaust* (Detroit: Wayne State University Press, 2019); Christine Schmidt, '"We Are All Witnesses": Eva Reichmann and the Wiener Library's Eyewitness Accounts Collection', in Thomas Kühne and

Mary Jane Rein (eds.), *Agency and the Holocaust: Essays in Honor of Debórah Dwork* (New York: Palgrave Macmillan, 2020), 123–40.

55. It is striking that the Holocaust is not mentioned in a book such as Zoltán Boldizsár Simon's *History in Times of Unprecedented Change: A Theory for the 21st Century* (London: Bloomsbury, 2019), which is mainly concerned with the effect of the anthropocene on understandings of history.

56. Alon Confino, *Foundational Pasts: The Holocaust as Historical Understanding* (New York: Cambridge University Press, 2012), 36.

57. I say 'normally considered' because a few scholars have criticized the dispassionate, minimalist style common to most historians, arguing that rage and scandal are hardly inappropriate when writing about the Holocaust. See especially Carolyn J. Dean, *Aversion and Erasure: The Fate of the Victim after the Holocaust* (Ithaca: Cornell University Press, 2010), chs. 2 and 3; and Karyn Ball, *Disciplining the Holocaust* (Albany, NY: State University of New York Press, 2009).

58. See Dan Stone, 'The "*Mein Kampf* Ramp": Emily Overend Lorimer and Hitler Translations in Britain', *German History*, 26:4 (2008), 504–19.

59. For a study that does this to good effect, see Alex J. Kay, *Empire of Destruction: A History of Nazi Mass Killing* (New Haven: Yale University Press, 2021).

60. Moishe Postone, 'The Holocaust and the Trajectory of the Twentieth Century', in Moishe Postone and Eric Santner (eds.), *Catastrophe and Meaning: The Holocaust and the Twentieth Century* (Chicago: University of Chicago Press, 2003), 81–114, here 95; see also Postone, 'Anti-Semitism and National Socialism', in Rabinbach and Zipes (eds.), *Germans and Jews since the Holocaust*, 302–14, here 313; Postone, 'After the Holocaust: History and Identity in West Germany', in Kathy Harms, Lutz R. Reuter and Volker Dürr (eds.), *Coping with the Past: Germany and Austria after 1945* (Madison: University of Wisconsin Press, 1990), 233–51; Postone, 'History and Helplessness: Mass Mobilization and Contemporary Forms of Anticapitalism', *Public Culture*, 18:1 (2006), 93–110. Holocaust historians have in general not given Postone's insights the credit they deserve.

61. Peter Canning, 'Jesus Christ, Holocaust: Fabulations of the Jews in Christian and Nazi History', *Copyright: Fin de Siècle 2000*, 1 (1987), 177.

62. Saul Friedländer, *Nazi Germany and the Jews*, vol. 1: *The Years of Persecution, 1933–1939* (London: Weidenfeld & Nicolson, 1997), 84.

63. Canning, 'Jesus Christ, Holocaust', 182.

64. Ernst Cassirer, 'Judaism and the Modern Political Myths', *Contemporary Jewish Record*, 7 (1944), 126. See also Cassirer, *The Myth of the State* (New Haven:

Yale University Press, 1946), esp. part 3, for more detailed discussion. For the claim that Nazi antisemitism was one of the Nazis' *arcana dominationis*, or techniques of domination, see Franz Neumann, *Behemoth: The Structure and Practice of National Socialism* (London: Victor Gollancz, 1943 [1942]), 381.

65. Saul Friedländer, *Where Memory Leads: My Life* (New York: Other Press, 2016), 252.
66. See Alon Confino, 'From Psychohistory to Memory Studies. Or, How Some Germans Became Jews and Some Jews Nazis', in Roger Frie (ed.), *History Flows Through Us: Germany, the Holocaust, and the Importance of Empathy* (London: Routledge, 2018), 17–30.

CHAPTER 1: BEFORE THE HOLOCAUST

1. Eric Voegelin, *Collected Works of Eric Voegelin*, vol. 2: *Race and State* (Baton Rouge: Louisiana State University Press, 1997 [1933]), 13.
2. See Boaz Neumann, 'National Socialism, Holocaust and Ecology', in Dan Stone (ed.), *The Holocaust and Historical Methodology* (New York: Berghahn Books, 2012), 107; see also Neumann, *Die Weltanschauung des Nazismus: Raum, Körper, Sprache* (Göttingen: Wallstein, 2010).
3. Thomas Mergel, 'Dictatorship and Democracy, 1918–1939', in Walser Smith (ed.), *The Oxford Handbook of Modern German History*, 424–5.
4. Harry Mulisch, *Criminal Case 40/61, the Trial of Adolf Eichmann: An Eyewitness Account* (Philadelphia: University of Pennsylvania Press, 2005), 99.
5. Neumann, *Die Weltanschauung des Nazismus*, 250.
6. On the origins of Christian Jew-hatred, see R. I. Moore, *The Formation of a Persecuting Society: Power and Deviance in Western Europe, 950–1250* (Oxford: Basil Blackwell, 1990). Joshua Trachtenberg, *The Devil and the Jews: The Medieval Conception of the Jew and Its Relation to Modern Anti-Semitism* (Philadelphia: Jewish Publication Society, 1983 [1943]), writes (168–9) that it was the First Crusade which saw Jew-hatred first given free rein in medieval Europe and that: 'the ancient hostility, generalized and in a measure abstract, underwent a process of elaboration and particularization that produced a host of new-fangled superstitions and accusations, and fastened upon the world a conception of the Jew that has not yet been eradicated'. Norman Cohn, *The Pursuit of the Millennium: Revolutionary Millenarians and Mystical Anarchists of the Middle Ages* (London: Paladin, 1970 [1957]) agreed, arguing (77) that 'the peculiarly intense and

unremitting hatred which in Christendom (and only in Christendom) has been directed against Jewry above all other "outgroups" . . . is the wholly phantastic image of the Jew which suddenly gripped the imagination of the new masses at the time of the first crusades'.

7. Aleksandar Tišma, *Kapo*, trans. Richard Williams (New York: Harcourt Brace & Company, 1993), 194.

8. On the operation of this conspiracy theory, see Paul Hanebrink, *A Specter Haunting Europe: The Myth of Judeo-Bolshevism* (Cambridge, Mass.: The Belknap Press of Harvard University Press, 2018), esp. chs. 3 and 4.

9. Dietrich Eckart, 'Jewishness in and Around Us' (1919); Alfred Rosenberg, 'The Protocols of the Elders of Zion and Jewish World Policy' (1923); 'The Program of the NSDAP' (1921); all in Barbara Miller Lane and Leila J. Rupp (eds.), *Nazi Ideology before 1933: A Documentation* (Manchester: Manchester University Press, 1978), 25, 55, 41 respectively. See also the excerpts from Rosenberg's *Die Spur des Juden im Wandel der Zeiten* (1920), in Jürgen Matthäus and Frank Bajohr (eds.), *The Political Diary of Alfred Rosenberg and the Onset of the Holocaust* (Lanham, MD: Rowman & Littlefield, 2015), 353–63 and in Robert Pois (ed.), *Alfred Rosenberg: Selected Writings* (London: Jonathan Cape, 1970), 175–90.

10. Neville Laski, 'Foreword', in G. Warburg, *Six Years of Hitler: The Jews under the Nazi Regime* (London: George Allen & Unwin, 1939), 7.

11. Ella Lingens-Reiner, *Prisoners of Fear* (London: Victor Gollancz, 1948), 2.

12. See Ishay Landa, 'The Magic of the Extreme: On Fascism, Modernity, and Capitalism', *Journal of Holocaust Research*, 33:1 (2019), 43–63; Federico Finchelstein, 'Fascism and the Holocaust', in Stone (ed.), *The Holocaust and Historical Methodology*, 255–71; Geoff Eley, *Nazism as Fascism: Violence, Ideology, and the Ground of Consent in Germany 1930–1945* (London: Routledge, 2013); Matthew Feldman and Marius Turda with Tudor Georgescu (eds.), *Clerical Fascism in Interwar Europe* (Abingdon: Routledge, 2008).

13. Mergel, 'Dictatorship and Democracy', 445.

14. Saul Friedländer, 'Introduction', in Saul Friedländer, Gerald Holton, Leo Marx and Eugene Skolnikoff (eds.), *Visions of the Apocalypse: End or Rebirth?* (New York: Holmes & Meier, 1986), 3–17.

15. Benjamin Ziemann, 'Germany 1914–1918: Total War as a Catalyst of Change', in Walser Smith (ed.), *The Oxford Handbook of Modern German History*, 393. See also Sven Keller, 'Volksgemeinschaft and Violence: Some Reflections on Interdependencies', in Martina Steber and Bernhard Gotto (eds.), *Visions of Community in Nazi Germany: Social Engineering and Private Lives* (Oxford: Oxford University Press, 2014), 226–39.

16. Mergel, 'Dictatorship and Democracy', 427. See also Mergel, 'High Expectations – Deep Disappointment: Structures of the Public Perception of Politics in the Weimar Republic', in Kathleen Canning, Kerstin Barndt and Kristin McGuire (eds.), *Weimar Publics/Weimar Subjects: Rethinking the Political Culture of Germany in the 1920s* (New York: Berghahn Books, 2010), 192–210.

17. R. G. Collingwood, 'Fascism and Nazism' (1940), in *Essays in Political Philosophy*, ed. David Boucher (Oxford: Clarendon Press, 1989), 194.

18. Cited in Peter Fritzsche, 'The Economy of Experience in Weimar Germany', in Canning, Barndt and McGuire (eds.), *Weimar Publics/Weimar Subjects*, 371.

19. Robert Jan Van Pelt, 'From the Last Hut of Monowitz to the Last Hut of Belsen', in Zuzanna Dziuban (ed.), *Accessing Campscapes: Inclusive Strategies for Using European Conflicted Heritage*, 2 (2017), 12–19.

20. For further discussion, see Dan Stone, *Concentration Camps: A Very Short Introduction* (Oxford: Oxford University Press, 2019), 20–21.

21. Robert Gerwarth and John Horne, 'Bolshevism as Fantasy: Fear of Revolution and Counter-Revolutionary Violence, 1917–1923', in Robert Gerwarth and John Horne (eds.), *War in Peace: Paramilitary Violence in Europe after the Great War* (Oxford: Oxford University Press, 2012), 42.

22. Adolf Hitler, *Mein Kampf*, trans. Ralph Mannheim (London: Hutchinson, 1974), 473, 476.

23. Cathie Carmichael, *Genocide before the Holocaust* (New Haven: Yale University Press, 2009), 124.

24. Stone, 'The "*Mein Kampf* Ramp"'; Detlev Clemens, *Herr Hitler in Germany: Wahrnehmung und Deutungen des Nationalsozialismus in Großbritannien 1920 bis 1939* (Göttingen: Vandenhoeck & Ruprecht, 1996); Neil Gregor, *How to Read Hitler* (London: Granta Books, 2014). There are of course some notable deviations in *Mein Kampf* from what actually later took place, most importantly an alliance between Germany and Britain ('England'), but the advance warning of an invasion of the Soviet Union (requiring the elimination of Poland from the map of Europe) in order to acquire living space could hardly have been advertised more plainly.

25. Hitler, *Mein Kampf*, 568 (italics in original).

26. Harold J. Laski, *Where Do We Go from Here? An Essay in Interpretation* (Harmondsworth: Penguin Books, 1940), 9.

27. Sebastian Haffner, *Germany: Jekyll and Hyde. An Eyewitness Analysis of Nazi Germany* (London: Libris, 2005 [1940]), 5. See also Dan Stone, 'Anti-Fascist Europe Comes to Britain: Theorising Fascism as a Contribution to

Defeating It', in Nigel Copsey and Andrzej Olechnowicz (eds.), *Varieties of Anti-Fascism: Britain in the Inter-War Period* (Houndmills: Palgrave Macmillan, 2010), 183–201.

28. Some of the material in this chapter is taken from my previously published articles: 'Nazi Race Ideologues', *Patterns of Prejudice*, 50:4–5 (2016), 445–57; 'Race, Science, Race Mysticism and the Racial State', in Pendas, Roseman and Wetzell (eds.), *Beyond the Racial State*, 176–96; and 'Ideologies of Race: The Construction and Suppression of Otherness in Nazi Germany', in Gigliotti and Earl (eds.), *A Companion to the Holocaust*, 59–74.

29. Eric Voegelin, *Collected Works of Eric Voegelin*, vol. 2: *Race and State*, trans. Ruth Hein (Baton Rouge: Louisiana State University Press, 1997 [1933]), 181, 206.

30. Voegelin, *Race and State*, 9.

31. Aurel Kolnai, *The War Against the West* (London: Victor Gollancz, 1938), 447. On 458, Kolnai also notes Voegelin's 'refined distance from passionate partisanship'.

32. Kolnai, *The War Against the West*, 438, 445. On *The War Against the West*, see Wolfgang Bialas (ed.), *Aurel Kolnai's* War Against the West *Reconsidered* (London: Routledge, 2019); and Dan Stone, *Responses to Nazism in Britain, 1933–1939: Before War and Holocaust*, 2nd edn (Houndmills: Palgrave Macmillan, 2012), 26–34.

33. Aubrey Douglas Smith, *Guilty Germans?* (London: Victor Gollancz, 1942), 208.

34. See Michelle Gordon, *Extreme Violence and 'The British Way': Colonial Warfare in Perak, Sierra Leone and Sudan* (London: C. Hurst, 2020).

35. See Dan Stone, *Breeding Superman: Nietzsche, Race and Eugenics in Edwardian and Interwar Britain* (Liverpool: Liverpool University Press, 2002).

36. For example: Lothrop Stoddard, *The Rising Tide of Color against White World-Supremacy* (New York: Blue Ribbon Books, 1920); Stoddard, *The Revolt against Civilization: The Menace of the Under-Man* (New York: Charles Scribner's Sons, 1922). For discussion, see Patrick Brantlinger, *Dark Vanishings: Discourse on the Extinction of Primitive Races, 1800–1930* (Ithaca: Cornell University Press, 2003); John S. Haller, Jr, *Outcasts from Evolution: Scientific Attitudes of Racial Inferiority 1859–1900*, 2nd edn (Carbondale, IL: Southern Illinois University Press, 1995); Lee D. Baker, *From Savage to Negro: Anthropology and the Construction of Race, 1896–1954* (Berkeley: University of California Press, 1998); and especially George W. Stocking, Jr, 'The Persistence of Polygenist Thought in Post-Darwinian Anthropology',

in his *Race, Culture, and Evolution: Essays in the History of Anthropology* (Chicago: University of Chicago Press, 1982), 42–68.

37. Paul Weindling, 'The "Sonderweg" of German Eugenics: Nationalism and Scientific Internationalism', *British Journal of the History of Science*, 22:3 (1989), 321–33.

38. Franz Boas, 'Changes in Immigrant Body Form' and 'Instability of Human Types', in George W. Stocking, Jr (ed.), *The Shaping of American Anthropology 1883–1911: A Franz Boas Reader* (New York: Basic Books, 1974), 202–14 and 214–21. See Gregory Claeys, 'The "Survival of the Fittest" and the Origins of Social Darwinism', *Journal of the History of Ideas*, 61:2 (2000), 223–40, on the turn to an emphasis on skin colour when talking about 'race' in the late nineteenth century.

39. William H. Schneider, *Quality and Quantity: The Quest for Biological Regeneration in Twentieth-Century France* (Cambridge: Cambridge University Press, 1990); Andrés Horacio Reggiani, *God's Eugenicist: Alexis Carrel and the Sociobiology of Decline* (New York: Berghahn, 2007); and the relevant chapters in Alison Bashford and Philippa Levine (eds.), *The Oxford Handbook of the History of Eugenics* (Oxford: Oxford University Press, 2010).

40. See George L. Mosse, 'The Mystical Origins of National Socialism', *Journal of the History of Ideas*, 22:1 (1961), 81–96.

41. See Eric Ehrenreich, *The Nazi Ancestral Proof: Genealogy, Racial Science, and the Final Solution* (Bloomington: Indiana University Press, 2007); Robert Gellately and Nathan Stoltzfus (eds.), *Social Outsiders in Nazi Germany* (Princeton: Princeton University Press, 2001); Michael Berenbaum (ed.), *A Mosaic of Victims: Non-Jews Persecuted and Murdered by the Nazis* (London: I. B. Tauris, 1990); Dieter Kuntz (ed.), *Deadly Medicine: Creating the Master Race* (Washington, DC: United States Holocaust Memorial Museum, 2004).

42. Walter Gross, *Heilig ist das Blut: Eine Rundfunkrede von Dr. Gross* (Berlin: Rassenpolitisches Amt der NSDAP, 1935), online at: http://www.calvin. edu/academic/cas/gpa/gross3.htm. On heredity, see Amir Teicher, *Social Mendelism: Genetics and the Politics of Race in Germany, 1900–1948* (Cambridge: Cambridge University Press, 2020).

43. Cited in Claudia Koonz, *The Nazi Conscience* (Cambridge, Mass.: The Belknap Press of Harvard University Press, 2003), 110.

44. Wolfgang Bialas, 'The Eternal Voice of the Blood: Racial Science and Nazi Ethics', in Weiss-Wendt and Yeomans (eds.), *Racial Science in Hitler's New Europe, 1938–1945*, 350.

45. Stark cited in Dirk Rupnow, *Judenforschung im Dritten Reich: Wissenschaft zwischen Politik, Propaganda und Ideologie* (Baden-Baden: Nomos Verlagsgesellschaft, 2011), 292.

46. Koonz, *The Nazi Conscience*, 106, 123.

47. Ibid., 112.

48. Henry Friedlander, *The Origins of Nazi Genocide: From Euthanasia to the Final Solution* (Chapel Hill: University of North Carolina Press, 1995), 12.

49. Ernst Krieck, 'Die Intellektuellen und das Dritte Reich', in Uriel Tal, *Religion, Politics and Ideology in the Third Reich: Selected Essays* (London: Routledge, 2004), 9.

50. Goebbels, *Der steile Aufstieg: Reden und Aufsätze aus den Jahren 1942/43* (Munich: Franz Eher, 1944), 301, cited in Bialas, 'The Eternal Voice of the Blood', 358.

51. Christian Ingrao, *Believe and Destroy: Intellectuals in the SS War Machine* (Cambridge: Polity Press, 2013), 42.

52. For a similar argument on one of Nazi ideology's forebears, see John Nale, 'Arthur de Gobineau on Blood and Race', *Critical Philosophy of Race*, 2:1 (2014), 106–24.

53. Paul Weindling, 'Genetics, Eugenics, and the Holocaust', in Denis R. Alexander and Ronald L. Numbers (eds.), *Biology and Ideology from Descartes to Dawkins* (Chicago: University of Chicago Press, 2010), 213. See also Robert J. Richards, 'Was Hitler a Darwinian?', in *Was Hitler a Darwinian? Disputed Questions in the History of Evolutionary Theory* (Chicago: University of Chicago Press, 2013), 192–242.

54. Hitler, *Mein Kampf*, 364–5. For similar examples from the UK and US, see Stone, *Breeding Superman*.

55. Michael Wildt, *An Uncompromising Generation: The Nazi Leadership of the Reich Security Main Office* (Madison: University of Wisconsin Press, 2009).

56. Peter Fritzsche, *Life and Death in the Third Reich* (Cambridge, Mass.: The Belknap Press of Harvard University Press, 2008), ch 2.

57. Norbert Elias, *Studien über die Deutschen: Machtkämpfe und Habitusentwicklung im 19. Und 20. Jahrhundert* (Frankfurt am Main: Suhrkamp Taschenbuch Verlag, 1994), 500.

58. Bronislaw Malinowski, *Freedom and Civilization* (Bloomington: Indiana University Press, 1960 [1944]), 213. See also R. G. Collingwood on the role of magic in daily life in *The Philosophy of Enchantment: Studies in Folktale, Cultural Criticism, and Anthropology*, ed. David Boucher, Wendy James and Philip Smallwood (Oxford: Oxford University Press, 2005)

and the discussion of Florin Lobonț in *Mind, Philosophy, History, and Psychoanalysis: Essays on Historical Understanding* (Bucharest: Trei, 2014).

59. Malinowski, *Freedom and Civilization*, 211, 213. For discussion, see Dan Stone, 'Nazism as Modern Magic: Bronislaw Malinowski's Political Anthropology', *History and Anthropology*, 14:3 (2003), 203–18.

60. Shulamit Volkov, 'Antisemitism as a Cultural Code: Reflections on the History and Historiography of Antisemitism in Imperial Germany', *Leo Baeck Institute Yearbook*, 23 (1978), 25–46; Volkov, *Germans, Jews, and Antisemites: Trials in Emancipation* (Cambridge: Cambridge University Press, 2006), part 2. Cf. older studies such as Eva G. Reichmann, *Hostages of Civilization: The Social Sources of National Socialist Anti-Semitism* (London: Victor Gollancz, 1950); Paul Massing, *Rehearsal for Destruction: A Study of Political Anti-Semitism in Imperial Germany* (New York: Harper & Brothers, 1949); Peter Pulzer, *The Rise of Political Anti-Semitism in Germany and Austria*, rev. edn (London: Peter Halban, 1988); J. L. Talmon, The *Unique and the Universal: Some Historical Reflections* (London: Secker & Warburg, 1965). On the transformation of older prejudices such as the belief in Jewish ritual murder, into the modern age, see Franz Fühmann's story 'The Jew's Car', in Ritchie Robertson (ed.), *The German-Jewish Dialogue: An Anthology of Literary Texts 1749–1993* (Oxford: Oxford University Press, 1999), 310–18.

61. Friedländer, *Nazi Germany and the Jews*; Friedländer, 'An Integrated History of the Holocaust: Some Methodological Challenges', in Stone (ed.), *The Holocaust and Historical Methodology*, 181–9. See also Richard S. Levy, 'Antisemitism', in Peter Hayes and John K. Roth (eds.), *The Oxford Handbook of Holocaust Studies* (Oxford: Oxford University Press, 2010), 23–38.

62. Lucie Varga, 'Die Entstehung des Nationalsozialismus: Sozialhistorische Anmerkungen', in Varga, *Zeitenwende: Mentalitätshistorische Studien 1936–1939*, ed. Peter Schöttler (Frankfurt am Main: Suhrkamp Taschenbuch Verlag, 1991), 121.

63. Theodore Abel, *Why Hitler Came to Power* (Cambridge, Mass.: Harvard University Press, 1986), 160. Abel's study, first published in 1938, contains citations from autobiographies by National Socialists and remains a powerful tool for understanding the attraction of Nazism in its context.

64. E. Amy Buller, *Darkness over Germany: A Warning from History* (London: Arcadia Books, 2017 [1943]), 216.

65. Eric Ehrenreich, *The Nazi Ancestral Proof: Genealogy, Racial Science, and the Final Solution* (Bloomington: Indiana University Press, 2007), xii.

66. Buller, *Darkness over Germany*, 188.

67. Peter Fritzsche, *Germans into Nazis* (Cambridge, Mass.: Harvard University Press, 1998), 211.

68. Fritzsche, *Life and Death in the Third Reich*, 37. As Fritzsche also writes (4): 'Even as they built up a militarized racial state, which appeared almost unassailable to its opponents, they repeatedly imagined the demise of Germany at the hands of Poles, Bolsheviks, Jews, and other enemies. Figures of Germans threatened with sterilization or exterminated and reduced to ashes littered Nazi propaganda. This embattled vision of history, which Nazis shared with many other Germans, helps explain the fantasies of extreme violence the Nazis harboured.'

69. Thomas Kühne, *Belonging and Genocide: Hitler's Community, 1918–1945* (New Haven: Yale University Press, 2010); Christopher R. Browning, 'The Holocaust: Basis and Objective of the *Volksgemeinschaft*?', in Steber and Gotto (eds.), *Visions of Community in Nazi Germany*, 219, writes: 'Within the world as seen through Nazi ideology, the exclusive, racially pure *Volksgemeinschaft* and Holocaust were intimately connected.'

70. Fritzsche, 'The Holocaust and the Knowledge of Murder', 596. See also the important articles by Hermann Beck, 'The Antibourgeois Character of National Socialism', *Journal of Modern History*, 88 (2016), 572–609; and Amit Varshizky, 'The Metaphysics of Race: Revisiting Nazism and Religion', *Central European History*, 52:2 (2019), 252–88, which argues that the Nazis sincerely believed that 'race' would bring about an 'authentic spirituality' that could counter the disintegrating effects of the 'disenchanted' modern world.

71. Haffner, *Germany: Jekyll and Hyde*, 10, 19.

72. Laski, *Where Do We Go from Here?*, 9.

73. Thomas Rohkrämer, *A Single Communal Faith? The German Right from Conservatism to National Socialism* (New York: Berghahn Books, 2007), 190 ('fatal attraction'). See also Alon Confino, 'Why Did the Nazis Burn the Hebrew Bible? Nazi Germany, Representations of the Past, and the Holocaust', *Journal of Modern History*, 84 (2012), 369–400, for the argument that Nazi practices were based on existing ideas in and the collective memories of German society.

74. Peter Longerich, *Hitler: A Life* (Oxford: Oxford University Press, 2019), 957.

75. Thomas A. Kohut, *A German Generation: An Experiential History of the Twentieth Century* (New Haven: Yale University Press, 2012), 6.

76. Alfred Rosenberg, 'The Folkish Idea of State' (1924), in Miller Lane and Rupp (eds.), *Nazi Ideology before 1933*, 69.

77. Mark Levene, *Genocide in the Age of the Nation State*, vol. 1: *The Meaning of Genocide* (London: I. B. Tauris, 2005), 197. This should not be

over-interpreted: in 1939, when Hitler used the word 'annihilated' – as he also did to threaten Czechoslovakia – he most likely meant that the Jews would be expelled from Germany.

78. Hitler, *Mein Kampf*, 406, 568.

79. Tal, *Religion, Politics and Ideology in the Third Reich*, 178. The notion of the 'authenticity' of monotheism is less important here than the insight into Nazism's links with and overturning of established traditions.

80. Unsent letter by Max Mayer to his grandson, Peter Paepcke, 9 May 1938, in Jürgen Matthäus and Mark Roseman (eds.), *Jewish Responses to Persecution*, vol. 1: *1933–1938* (Lanham, MD: AltaMira Press, 2010), 302–3.

81. R. G. Collingwood, 'Fascism and Nazism', in his *Essays in Political Philosophy*, ed. David Boucher (Oxford: Oxford University Press, 1989), 191–2.

82. Ernst Bloch, 'Amusement Co., Horror, Third Reich (September 1930)', in *Heritage of Our Times*, trans. Neville and Stephen Plaice (Cambridge: Polity Press, 1991), 60. For a more prosaic statement of a similar thesis, see Talcott Parsons, 'Some Sociological Aspects of the Fascist Movements' (1942), in Uta Gerhardt (ed.), *Talcott Parsons on National Socialism* (New York: Aldine de Gruyter, 1994), 203–18.

CHAPTER 2: ATTACK ON THE JEWS, 1933–8

1. Michał Głowiński, *The Black Seasons*, trans. Marci Shore (Evanston: Northwestern University Press, 2005), 173.

2. Kurt Rosenberg, diary entry for 20 August 1933, in Matthäus and Roseman (eds.), *Jewish Responses to Persecution*, vol. 1, 37.

3. Baeumler, *Gutachten* [expert opinion] of 13 December 1940, cited in Tal, *Religion, Politics and Ideology in the Third Reich*, 90.

4. Gross cited in Tal, *Religion, Politics and Ideology in the Third Reich*, 94; ibid., 93.

5. Warburg, *Six Years of Hitler*, 26.

6. Richard J. Evans, *The Coming of the Third Reich* (New York: Penguin, 2003), 433.

7. IMT, vol. 1, 234.

8. Saul Friedländer, *Nazi Germany and the Jews*, vol. 1: *The Years of Persecution, 1933–1939* (London: Weidenfeld & Nicolson 1997), 98.

9. Christoph Kreutzmüller and Jonathan Zatlin, 'Belonging and Belongings: The Dispossession of German Jews', in Mark Roseman and Dan Stone

(eds.), *The Cambridge History of the Holocaust*, vol. 1 (Cambridge: Cambridge University Press, 2023).

10. Ernst Hiemer, *Der Giftpilz: Ein Stürmerbuch für Jung u. Alt* (Nuremberg: Verlag Der Stürmer, 1938), 62. Text reproduced as Doc. 1778–PS, IMT, vol. 28, 304–45, here 344–5.

11. Anon., *The Yellow Spot: The Extermination of the Jews in Germany* (London: Victor Gollancz, 1936), 15.

12. Warburg, *Six Years of Hitler*, 191.

13. Reich Citizenship Law, 15 September 1935, in J. Noakes and G. Pridham (eds.), *Nazism 1919–1945: A Documentary Reader*, vol. 2: *State, Economy and Society, 1933–1939* (Exeter: University of Exeter Press, 1984), 536.

14. Warburg, *Six Years of Hitler*, 194.

15. Law for the Protection of German Blood and German Honour, 15 September 1935, in Noakes and Pridham (eds.), *Nazism 1919–1945*, vol. 2, 535–6.

16. Irene Eckler, *A Family Torn Apart by 'Rassenschande': Political Persecution in the Third Reich* (Schwetzingen: Horneburg Verlag, 1998), 12.

17. Warburg, *Six Years of Hitler*, 212.

18. Lösener's comments at a meeting in July 1934 at the Interior Ministry under the title 'Attacks on the Race', cited in Teicher, *Social Mendelism*, 168.

19. See the editors' comments in 'The Nuremberg Laws and Their Impact', in Matthäus and Roseman (eds.), *Jewish Responses to Persecution*, vol. 1, 184.

20. Matthäus and Roseman, 'The Nuremberg Laws and Their Impact', 191.

21. Cicely Hamilton, *Modern Germanies as Seen by an Englishwoman. With a Postscript on the Nazi Regime* (London: J. M. Dent & Sons, 1933), 180–1. For more on the different understandings of Nazism in pre-war Britain, see Stone, *Responses to Nazism in Britain*.

22. *The Yellow Spot*, 58.

23. Ibid., 59–60.

24. See ibid., 66.

25. See the list, entitled 'The Pogrom of "Verbot"', in ibid., 187–9.

26. Ibid., 105.

27. On small and medium-sized businesses, which made up the majority of Jewish firms, see Christoph Kreutzmüller, *Final Sale in Berlin: The Destruction of Jewish Commercial Activity 1930–1945* (New York: Berghahn Books, 2015).

28. *The Yellow Spot*, 123.

29. Avraham Barkai, *From Boycott to Annihilation: The Economic Struggle of German Jews 1933–1943* (Hanover: University Press of New England, 1989),

128. On the Third Reich as a kleptocracy, see Jonathan Petropoulos, 'The Nazi Kleptocracy: Reflections on Avarice and the Holocaust', and Frank Bajohr, 'Cliques, Corruption, and Organized Self-Pity: The Nazi Movement and the Property of the Jews', both in Herzog (ed.), *Lessons and Legacies*, vol. 7, 29–38 and 39–49; Christoph Kreutzmüller and Jonathan R. Zatlin (eds.), *Dispossession: Plundering German Jewry, 1933–1953* (Ann Arbor: University of Michigan Press, 2021).

30. Beate Meyer, '"Aryanized" and Financially Ruined: The Case of the Garbáty Family', in Beate Meyer, Hermann Simon and Chana Schütz (eds.), *Jews in Nazi Berlin: From Kristallnacht to Liberation* (Chicago: University of Chicago Press, 2009), 66.

31. 'Second Decree Concerning Implementation of the Law on Changes to Family Names and First Names' (17 August 1938), in Anson Rabinbach and Sander L. Gilman (eds.), *The Third Reich Sourcebook* (Berkeley: University of California Press, 2013), 228.

32. Joseph Goebbels, 'The Jews Are Guilty!', speech, 16 November 1942, extracted in Rabinbach and Gilman (eds.), *Third Reich Sourcebook*, 739.

33. Kurt Rosenberg, diary entry for 26 April 1936, in Matthäus and Roseman (eds.), *Jewish Responses*, vol. 1, 261.

34. Michael Wildt, 'Violence against Jews in Germany, 1933–1939', in David Bankier (ed.), *Probing the Depths of German Antisemitism: German Society and the Persecution of the Jews, 1933–1941* (New York: Berghahn Books, 2000), 187.

35. Alan E. Steinweis, *Kristallnacht 1938* (Cambridge, Mass.: The Belknap Press of Harvard University Press, 2009), 24–5.

36. See Wolf Gruner and Steven J. Ross, 'Introduction', in Gruner and Ross (eds.), *New Perspectives on Kristallnacht: After 80 Years, the Nazi Pogrom in Global Comparison* (West Lafayette, Ind.: Purdue University Press, 2019).

37. All cited in Steinweis, *Kristallnacht 1938*, 27.

38. Jeffrey Herf, *The Jewish Enemy: Nazi Propaganda during World War II and the Holocaust* (Cambridge, Mass.: The Belknap Press of Harvard University Press, 2006), 44.

39. Cited in Herf, *The Jewish Enemy*, 45.

40. See Robert Gerwarth, *Hitler's Hangman: The Life of Heydrich* (New Haven: Yale University Press, 2011), 127.

41. Reinhard Heydrich, Telegram to State Police and SA, 10 November 1938, 1:20 a.m., in Rabinbach and Gilman (eds.), *The Third Reich Sourcebook*, 231.

42. Gerwarth, *Hitler's Hangman*, 128.

43. See Gordon J. Horwitz, *In the Shadow of Death: Living Outside the Gates of Mauthausen* (New York: The Free Press, 1990), 29.

44. Reinhard Heydrich, 'The Visible Enemy: The Jews', in Rabinbach and Gilman (eds.), *The Third Reich Sourcebook*, 197, 199.

45. SD Memorandum prepared for Heydrich, 24 May 1934, cited in Gerwarth, *Hitler's Hangman*, 95.

46. Ian Kershaw, 'Hitler's Role in the Final Solution', *Yad Vashem Studies*, 34 (2006), 29.

47. Rudolf Bing, 'My Life in Germany before and after January 30, 1933' (1940), in Matthäus and Roseman, *Jewish Persecution*, vol. 1, 351–2.

48. Wolfgang Benz, 'The November Pogrom of 1938: Participation, Applause, Disapproval', in Christhard Hoffmann, Werner Bergmann and Helmut Walser Smith (eds.), *Exclusionary Violence: Antisemitic Riots in Modern German History* (Ann Arbor: University of Michigan Press, 2002), 151.

49. 'Decree for the Restoration of the Street Scene and Decree Concerning Reparations from Jews of German Nationality' (both 12 November 1938), in Noakes and Pridham (eds.), *Nazism 1919–1945*, vol. 2, 560.

50. 'Stenographic Record (Partial Transcript) of a Conference with Göring, 12 November 1938, on the Jewish Question', Doc. 1816-PS, IMT, vol. 28, 538; Friedländer, *Years of Persecution*, 283.

51. But see, for starting points, the books of George L. Mosse and the document collection, Léon Poliakov and Joseph Wulf (eds.), *Das Dritte Reich und seine Denker* (Frankfurt am Main: Ullstein, 1983). See also, for more recent work in a history of ideas vein: Christopher M. Hutton, *Race and the Third Reich: Linguistics, Racial Anthropology and Genetics in the Dialectic of Volk* (Cambridge: Polity Press, 2005); Neumann, *Die Weltanschauung des Nazismus*; Wolfgang Bialas and Anson Rabinbach (eds.), *Nazi Germany and the Humanities: How German Academics Embraced Nazism* (Oxford: Oneworld Publications, 2007); Susanne Heim, Carola Sachse, and Mark Walker (eds.), *The Kaiser Wilhelm Society under National Socialism* (Cambridge: Cambridge University Press, 2009); Dirk Rupnow; *Judenforschung im Dritten Reich: Wissenschaft zwischen Politik, Propaganda und Ideologie* (Baden-Baden: Nomos Verlagsgesellschaft, 2011); David B. Dennis, *Inhumanities: Nazi Interpretations of Western Culture* (Cambridge: Cambridge University Press, 2012); Andreas Höfele, *No Hamlets: German Shakespeare from Nietzsche to Carl Schmitt* (Oxford: Oxford University Press, 2016); Julien Reitzenstein, *Himmlers Forscher: Wehrwissenschaft und Medizinverbrechen im 'Ahnenerbe' der SS* (Paderborn: Schöningh, 2014); Hans-Christian Harten, *Himmlers Lehrer:*

Die weltanschauliche Schulung in der SS 1933–1945 (Paderborn: Schöningh, 2014); André Mineau, *SS Thinking and the Holocaust* (Amsterdam: Rodopi, 2012); Christian Ingrao, *Believe and Destroy: Intellectuals in the SS War Machine* (Cambridge: Polity Press, 2013); Ingrao, *The Promise of the East: Nazi Hopes and Genocide, 1939–1943* (Cambridge: Polity Press, 2018); Johann Chapoutot, *The Law of Blood: Thinking and Acting as a Nazi* (Cambridge, Mass.: Harvard University Press, 2018).

52. Herwig Hartner-Hnizdo, *Volk der Gauner* (1939), extracted as 'Accident of History or Destiny of the Race?', in Rabinbach and Gilman (eds.), *Third Reich Sourcebook*, 218–20.

53. Fritz Arlt, 'Der Endkampf gegen das Judentum', *Der Weltkampf*, 1 (1938), extracted as 'The Final Struggle against Jewry', in Rabinbach and Gilman (eds.), *Third Reich Sourcebook*, 228–30.

54. Peter Viereck, *Meta-Politics: The Roots of the Nazi Mind*, rev. edn (New York: Capricorn Books, 1965 [1941]), 231. Viereck is writing specifically about Rosenberg in this passage.

55. NSDAP Office for [Ideological] Training, Ideological Report, Lahr, 2 December 1938, in Otto Dov Kulka and Eberhard Jäckel (eds.), *The Jews in the Secret Nazi Reports on Popular Opinion in Germany, 1933–1945* (New Haven: Yale University Press, 2010), 379.

56. Frank Bajohr and Dieter Pohl, *Massenmord und schlechtes Gewissen: Die deutsche Bevölkerung, die NS-Führung und der Holocaust* (Frankfurt am Main: Suhrkamp Taschenbuch Verlag, 2008), 37–45.

57. Fritzsche, *Life and Death in the Third Reich*, 133.

58. Benz, 'The November Pogrom of 1938', 152.

59. Dan Diner, 'The Catastrophe before the Catastrophe: 1938 in Historical Context', in his *Beyond the Conceivable: Studies on Germany, Nazism, and the Holocaust* (Berkeley: University of California Press, 2000), 78–94.

60. G. W. Allport, J. S. Bruner and E. M. Jandorf, 'Personality under Social Catastrophe: Ninety Life Histories of the Nazi Revolution', *Character and Personality*, 10:1 (1941), 14.

61. Report B307 in Ruth Levitt (ed.), *Pogrom November 1938: Testimonies from 'Kristallnacht'* (London: Souvenir Press, 2015), 446. The German terms have been left in to give a sense of the complex bureaucracy.

62. Letter from Gerhard Kann to Heinz Kellermann, 24 October 1938, in Matthäus and Roseman (eds.), *Jewish Responses*, vol. 1, 322–3.

63. Armin Schmid and Renate Schmid, *Lost in a Labyrinth of Red Tape: The Story of an Immigration that Failed* (Evanston: Northwestern University Press, 1996), 55.

64. See Michael Wildt, *Hitler's* Volksgemeinschaft *and the Dynamics of Radical Exclusion: Violence against Jews in Provincial Germany, 1919–1939* (New York: Berghahn Books, 2012).

65. Walter Tausk, *Breslauer Tagebuch 1933–1940* (Leipzig: Reclam, 1995), 164 (12 November 1938) [orig.: 'Wenn ich mitgegangen wäre, mit beiden Armen hätte ich geholfen, für die Winterhilfe wegschaffen, was die für die Winterhilfe weggeschafft haben!']. The Winter Aid was a charity which distributed clothing and other goods, sometimes stolen from the Nazis' victims, to poorer Germans.

66. 'Order in the name of revolution, and revolution in the name of order' is Kevin Passmore's succinct summary of fascism in *Fascism: A Very Short Introduction* (Oxford: Oxford University Press, 2002), 29.

67. See, for example, Tim Cole, 'Constructing the "Jew", Writing the Holocaust: Hungary 1920–45', *Patterns of Prejudice*, 33:3 (1999), 19–27; Frank Caestecker and Bob Moore, 'Refugees from Nazi Germany and the Development of Refugee Policies, 1933–1937', in Caestecker and Moore (eds.), *Refugees from Nazi Germany and the Liberal European States* (New York: Berghahn Books, 2010), 207–43.

68. Katarzyna Person, *Assimilated Jews in the Warsaw Ghetto, 1940–1943* (Syracuse, NY: Syracuse University Press, 2014).

69. I am grateful to Harry Legg for this point about non-Jewish 'Jews'.

70. In one scene, for example, one of the protagonists, Paul Roeder, considers his workmates when he needs a confidant. Although each had opposed the Nazis prior to 1933, and in some cases even after, he now finds that with only one exception he cannot trust them with what he needs to say, and not because they are Nazi fanatics. See Anna Seghers, *The Seventh Cross*, trans. Margot Battauer Dembo (London: Virago, 2019), 302–9. This process of living a Nazified life is also succinctly explored in Wolfgang Staudte's 1949 film *Rotation*.

71. Wildt, *Hitler's* Volksgemeinschaft, 272.

72. Sebastian Haffner, *Defying Hitler: A Memoir* (London: Phoenix, 2003), 221, 230.

73. Report B328 in Levitt (ed.), *Pogrom November 1938*, 494.

74. Ibid., 496.

75. Ibid., 499.

76. Ibid., 504.

77. Ibid., 510.

78. Wünschmann, *Before Auschwitz*, 211–12.

79. Ibid., 213.

80. Wildt, 'Violence against Jews in Germany, 1933–1939', 208.

81. 'Secret Report of the Security Service of the Reichsführer SS: The Actions against the Jews on 9, 10, and 11 November 1938', in Rabinbach and Gilman (eds.), *Third Reich Sourcebook*, 232.

82. Martha Dodd, *My Years in Germany* (London: Victor Gollancz, 1939), 261, 273.

83. Ibid., 261.

CHAPTER 3: BEFORE THE 'FINAL SOLUTION'

1. S. Erckner, *Hitler's Conspiracy against Peace* (London: Victor Gollancz, 1937), 280–1. 'Strange pacifism' is also Erckner's term, 24–8. Erckner's book was first published in German as *Die grosse Lüge* (The Big Lie) (Paris: Éditions du Carrefour, 1936).

2. Erckner, *Hitler's Conspiracy against Peace*, 286.

3. On 'licence', see Aristotle Kallis, *Genocide and Fascism: The Eliminationist Drive in Fascist Europe* (London: Routledge, 2009), esp. ch. 10; on the effects of corpses, see Yehonatan Alsheh, 'The Biopolitics of Corpses of Mass Violence and Genocide', in Jean-Marc Dreyfus and Élisabeth Anstett (eds.), *Human Remains and Mass Violence: Methodological Approaches* (Manchester: Manchester University Press, 2014), esp. 24–7; on the concept of *Rausch*, see Saul Friedländer, 'The "Final Solution": On the Unease in Historical Interpretation', in his *Memory, History, and the Extermination of the Jews of Europe* (Bloomington: Indiana University Press, 1993), 109–10. See also Dan Stone, 'Genocide as Transgression', *European Journal of Social Theory*, 7:1 (2004), 45–65.

4. Cited in Peter Longerich, *Holocaust: The Nazi Persecution and Murder of the Jews* (Oxford: Oxford University Press, 2010), 121.

5. Bradley F. Smith and Agnes F. Peterson (eds.), *Heinrich Himmler, Geheimreden 1933 bis 1945 und andere Ansprachen* (Berlin: Propyläen, 1974), 37–8, cited in Friedländer, *Years of Persecution*, 292.

6. Longerich, *Holocaust*, 120.

7. Doron Rabinovici, *Eichmann's Jews: The Jewish Administration of Holocaust Vienna, 1938–1945* (Cambridge: Polity Press, 2011), 63.

8. Tobias Farb, Shanghai, to an unnamed recipient in the US, 28 April 1939, in Alexandra Garbarini with Emil Kerenji, Jan Lambertz and Avinoam Patt (eds.), *Jewish Responses to Persecution*, vol. 2: *1938–1940* (Lanham, MD:

AltaMira Press in association with the United States Holocaust Memorial Museum, 2011), 58. Farb left China for the US in 1947, where he was reunited with his wife and settled in California.

9. Eduard Cohn, Asunción, to AJDC, New York, 4 June 1939, in Garbarini et al. (eds.), *Jewish Responses*, vol. 2, 65. It is not known whether the Cohns were reunited.

10. Memorandum of the WJC to the delegates of the Évian conference, 6 July 1938, in Matthäus and Roseman (eds.), *Jewish Responses*, vol. 1, 316.

11. Hitler, 'Speech to the Great German Reichstag', 30 January 1939, in Rabinbach and Gilman (eds.), *Third Reich Sourcebook*, 723–4; 'paroxysmic expression' is Friedländer's phrase: *Years of Persecution*, 292.

12. Friedländer, *Years of Persecution*, 307.

13. Joseph Goebbels, 'The Glue of the Enemy Coalition: The Origin of the World's Misfortune', *Das Reich*, 21 January 1945, cited in Herf, *The Jewish Enemy*, 255.

14. See Longerich, *Hitler*, 605.

15. Albert Lichtblau, 'Austria', in Wolf Gruner and Jörg Osterloh (eds.), *The Greater German Reich and the Jews: Nazi Persecution Policies in the Annexed Territories 1935–1945* (New York: Berghahn Books, 2015), 47.

16. Rabinovici, *Eichmann's Jews*, 60; see also Gabriele Anderl and Dirk Rupnow, *Die Zentralstelle für jüdische Auswanderung als Beraubungsinstitution* (Vienna: Oldenbourg, 2004).

17. Lichtblau, 'Austria', 61. See also Bettina Stangneth, 'Otto Adolf Eichmann: Reich Main Security Office. The RSHA's "Jewish Expert"', in Hans-Christian Jasch and Christoph Kreutzmüller (eds.), *The Participants: The Men of the Wannsee Conference* (New York: Berghahn Books, 2017), 40–56.

18. Jörg Osterloh, 'Sudetenland', in Gruner and Osterloh (eds.), *The Greater German Reich and the Jews*, 88.

19. Cited in Peter Hayes, 'The Economy', in Robert Gellately (ed.), *The Oxford Illustrated History of the Third Reich* (Oxford: Oxford University Press, 2018), 189.

20. See Adam Tooze, 'The Economic History of the Nazi Regime', in Jane Caplan (ed.), *Nazi Germany* (Oxford: Oxford University Press, 2008), 168–95.

21. Carroll P. Kakel, III, *The American West and the Nazi East: A Comparative and Interpretive Perspective* (Houndmills: Palgrave Macmillan, 2011), 102–5; Edward B. Westermann, *Hitler's Ostkrieg and the Indian Wars: Comparing Genocide and Conquest* (Norman: University of Oklahoma Press, 2016).

22. Alexandra Garbarini, Emil Kerenji, Jan Lambertz and Avinoam Patt, 'Volume Introduction', in Garbarini et al. (eds.), *Jewish Responses*, vol. 2, xxx, n. 9.

23. See Jürgen Matthäus, Jochen Böhler and Klaus-Michael Mallmann, *War, Pacification, and Mass Murder, 1939: The Einsatzgruppen in Poland* (Lanham, MD: Rowman & Littlefield, 2014).

24. Markus Roth, 'The Murder of the Jews of Ostrów Mazowiecka in November 1939', in Claire Zalc and Tal Bruttmann (eds.), *Microhistories of the Holocaust* (New York: Berghahn Books, 2017), 227.

25. Roth, 'The Murder of the Jews of Ostrów Mazowiecka', 229.

26. Jacob Sloan (ed.), *Notes from the Warsaw Ghetto: The Journal of Emmanuel Ringelblum* (New York: Schocken Books, 1974), 11 (entry for 1 January 1940). At the beginning of December, Ringelblum noted in his diary that 600 Jews from Ostrów were said to have been shot outside the town; see Roth, 'The Murder of the Jews of Ostrów Mazowiecka', 236. See also Aba Gordin and M. Gelbart (eds.), *Memorial (Yizkor) Book of the Jewish Community of Ostrów Mazowiecka* (New York: JewishGen, 2013).

27. Alexander B. Rossino, 'Destructive Impulses: German Soldiers and the Conquest of Poland', *Holocaust and Genocide Studies*, 11:3 (1997), 351–65; Alexander B. Rossino, *Hitler Strikes Poland: Blitzkrieg, Ideology, and Atrocity* (Lawrence: University Press of Kansas, 2003); Klaus-Michael Mallmann and Bogdan Musial (eds.), *Genesis des Genozids: Polen 1939–1941* (Darmstadt: Wissenschaftliche Buchgesellschaft, 2004); Jochen Böhler, *Auftakt zum Vernichtungskrieg: Die Wehrmacht in Polen 1939* (Frankfurt am Main: Suhrkamp, 2006); Doris L. Bergen, 'Instrumentalization of *Volksdeutschen* in German Propaganda in 1939: Replacing/Erasing Poles, Jews, and Other Victims', *German Studies Review*, 31:3 (2008), 447–70.

28. Richard Bessel, *Nazism and War* (London: Phoenix, 2005), 91.

29. Joseph Goebbels, *Tagebücher 1924–1945*, ed. Ralf Georg Reuth (Munich: Piper, 1992), vol. 3, 1340 (entry for 2 November 1939).

30. Phillip T. Rutherford, *Prelude to the Final Solution: The Nazi Program for Deporting Ethnic Poles, 1939–1941* (Lawrence: University Press of Kansas, 2007). Rutherford notes that when dealing with ethnic Poles in the Warthegau, economic rationality took precedence over genocidal ideology, a situation that was reversed in the case of the Jews.

31. Rossino, *Hitler Strikes Poland*, 197, 226.

32. Stone, *Breeding Superman*, ch. 5.

33. Garland E. Allen, 'The Ideology of Elimination: American and German Eugenics, 1900–1945', in Francis R. Nicosia and Jonathan Huener

(eds.), *Medicine and Medical Ethics in Nazi Germany: Origins, Practices, Legacies* (New York: Berghahn Books, 2002), 33; Paul Weindling, 'The "Sonderweg" of German Eugenics: Nationalism and Scientific Internationalism', *British Journal of the History of Science*, 22:3 (1989), 321–33; Weindling, 'German Eugenics and the Wider World: Beyond the Racial State', in Bashford and Levine (eds.), *The Oxford Handbook of the History of Eugenics*, 315–31.

34. Michael Burleigh, *Death and Deliverance: 'Euthanasia' in Germany c.1900–1945* (Cambridge: Cambridge University Press, 1994).

35. Amir Teicher, 'Why Did the Nazis Sterilize the Blind? Genetics and the Shaping of the Sterilization Law of 1933', *Central European History*, 52:2 (2019), 289–309.

36. Gisela Bock, 'Nazi Sterilization and Reproductive Policies', in Dieter Kuntz (ed.), *Deadly Medicine: Creating the Master Race* (Washington, DC: United States Holocaust Memorial Museum, 2004), 62, 80.

37. Hitler, *Mein Kampf*, 367.

38. See Dagmar Herzog (ed.), *Sexuality and German Fascism* (New York: Berghahn Books, 2005).

39. See Udo Benzenhöfer, *Der Fall Leipzig (alias 'Fall Kind Knauer') und die Planung der NS-'Kindereuthanasie'* (Münster: Klemm und Oelschläger, 2008); Ulf Schmidt, *Karl Brandt: Medicine and Power in the Third Reich* (London: Hambledon Continuum, 2007), 117–20; and my discussion in *Histories of the Holocaust*, ch. 4.

40. Allison Owings, *Frauen: German Women Recall the Third Reich* (New Brunswick, NJ: Rutgers University Press, 1995), 416. See also Caterina Pascual Söderbaum's remarkable novel *The Oblique Place* (London: MacLehose Press, 2018).

41. Michael H. Kater, 'Criminal Physicians in the Third Reich: Toward a Group Portrait', in Nicosia and Huener (eds.), *Medicine and Medical Ethics*, 79.

42. Testimony of Sister Reinhildis, 18 November 1948, in Ernst Klee, *'Euthanasie' im NS-Staat: Die 'Vernichtung lebensunwerten Lebens'* (Frankfurt am Main: Suhrkamp Taschenbuch Verlag, 1985), 182. Reinhildis was a sister at the district asylum in Jestetten, Württemberg.

43. Bernburg, Brandenburg, Grafeneck, Hadamar, Hartheim, Sonnenstein.

44. Noakes and Pridham (eds.), *Nazism 1919–1945*, vol. 3, 1030; Klee, *'Euthanasie' im NS-Staat*, 184. Helene was killed in Grafeneck.

45. Beth Griech-Polelle, 'Image of a Churchman Resister: Bishop von Galen, the Euthanasia Project and the Sermons of Summer 1941', *Journal of Contemporary History*, 36:2 (2001), 41–57.

46. Richard F. Wetzell, 'Eugenics, Racial Science, and Nazi Biopolitics: Was There a Genesis of the "Final Solution" from the Spirit of Science?', in Pendas, Roseman and Wetzell (eds.), *Beyond the Racial State*, 165.

47. Fritzsche, *Life and Death in the Third Reich*, 158.

48. Bessel, *Nazism and War*, 93.

49. Alfred Rosenberg, excerpt from 'The Jewish Question as a Global Problem', speech given at opening ceremony of the Institute for the Study of the Jewish Question, Frankfurt am Main, 28 March 1941, in Jürgen Matthäus and Frank Bajohr (eds.), *The Political Diary of Alfred Rosenberg and the Onset of the Holocaust* (Lanham, MD: Rowman & Littlefield, 2015), 371–2.

50. Wünschmann, *Before Auschwitz*, 225–6; Leon Szalet, *Experiment 'E': A Report from an Extermination Laboratory* (New York: Didier Publishers, 1945); Szalet was a rare survivor among the Polish Jews rounded up in Germany and sent to Sachsenhausen in September 1939. Thanks to his daughter's efforts, he was freed on 7 May 1940, and the two of them sailed for Shanghai a few days later.

51. Ringelblum, *Notes from the Warsaw Ghetto*, 40 (entry for 16 May 1940).

52. Dan Michman, 'Why Did Heydrich Write the *Schnellbrief*? A Remark on the Reason and on Its Significance', *Yad Vashem Studies*, 32 (2004), 433–47.

53. Yitzhak Arad, Yisrael Gutman and Abraham Margaliot (eds.), *Documents on the Holocaust: Selected Sources on the Destruction of the Jews of Germany and Austria, Poland, and the Soviet Union*, 4th edn (Jerusalem: Yad Vashem, 1990), 173–4.

54. Dan Michman, *The Emergence of Jewish Ghettos during the Holocaust* (Cambridge: Cambridge University Press, 2011), 72–3.

55. Longerich, *Holocaust*, 160–1.

56. Terms coined by Christopher R. Browning, 'Nazi Ghettoization Policy in Poland, 1939–1941', in his *The Path to Genocide: Essays on Launching the Final Solution* (Cambridge: Cambridge University Press, 1992), 28–56; Browning, *Origins of the Final Solution*, ch. 4.

57. Cited in Browning, 'Before the "Final Solution": Nazi Ghettoization Policy in Poland (1940–1941)', in *Ghettos 1939–1945: New Research and Perspectives on Definition, Daily Life, and Survival* (Washington, DC: USHMM, 2005), 5. See also Gordon J. Horwitz, *Ghettostadt: Łódź and the Making of a Nazi City* (Cambridge, Mass.: The Belknap Press of Harvard University Press, 2008), 27–8, and the discussion in Michman, *The Emergence of Jewish Ghettos*, 81–2.

58. See Stephan Lehnstaedt, 'Generalgouvernement: Ideologie und Ökonomie der Judenpolitik', in Jürgen Hensel and Stephan Lehnstaedt (eds.), *Arbeit in*

den nationalsozialistischen Ghettos (Osnabrück: fibre Verlag, 2013), 159–80; Lehnstaedt, 'Jüdische Arbeit in Generalgouvernement, Warthegau und Ostoberschlesien', in Imke Hansen, Katrin Steffen and Joachim Tauber (eds.), *Lebenswelt Ghetto: Alltag und soziales Umfeld während der nationalsozialistischen Verfolgung* (Wiesbaden: Harrasowitz Verlag, 2013), 210–25.

59. *The Diary of Mary Berg: Growing Up in the Warsaw Ghetto*, ed. S. L. Shneiderman (Oxford: Oneworld, 2006), 39 (entry for 5 February 1941).

60. Peretz Opoczynski, 'Smuggling in the Warsaw Ghetto, 1941', in Lucy S. Dawidowicz (ed.), *A Holocaust Reader* (West Orange, NJ: Behrman House, 1976), 200.

61. Opoczynski, 'Smuggling', 207.

62. And in other testimonies. See Skorczewski and Stone, '"I Was a Tape Recorder"'.

63. Dr Israel Milejkowski in 'Evaluating the Ghetto: Interviews in Warsaw, 1941', in Dawidowicz (ed.), *A Holocaust Reader*, 223.

64. Josef Zelkowicz, *In Those Terrible Days: Writings from the Łódź Ghetto*, ed. Michal Unger, trans. Naftali Greenwood (Jerusalem: Yad Vashem, 2002), 141. And see Amos Goldberg, *Trauma in First Person: Diary Writing during the Holocaust* (Bloomington: Indiana University Press, 2017), 68 for a discussion. Lawrence L. Langer, 'Ghetto Chronicles: Life at the Brink', in his *Admitting the Holocaust: Collected Essays* (New York: Oxford University Press, 1995), 41, writes: 'All the evidence suggests that most ghetto residents faced a constant *dis*integration, through hunger, illness, or despair, of the family and community supports that ordinarily help us to thrive.' See also Michael R. Marrus, 'Killing Time: Jewish Perceptions During the Holocaust', in Shmuel Almog et al. (eds.), *The Holocaust: History and Memory. Essays Presented in Honor of Israel Gutman* (Jerusalem: Yad Vashem, 2001), 10–38.

65. Goldberg, *Trauma in First Person*, 68.

66. Emmanuel Ringelblum, 'Oyneg Shabes', in David G. Roskies (ed.), *Voices from the Warsaw Ghetto: Writing Our History* (New Haven: Yale University Press, 2019), 48.

67. Oscar Singer, 'Notes by a Jewish Observer in the Łódź Ghetto Following the Deportation of the Children', 16 September 1942, in Arad, Gutman and Margaliot (eds.), *Documents on the Holocaust*, 285.

68. Dan Diner, 'Historical Understanding and Counterrationality: The *Judenrat* as Epistemological Vantage', in Saul Friedländer (ed.), *Probing the Limits of Representation: Nazism and the 'Final Solution'* (Cambridge, Mass.: Harvard University Press, 1992), 128–42.

69. 'From the Minute Book of the Bialystok Judenrat', in Dawidowicz (ed.), *A Holocaust Reader*, 278 (20 June 1942) and 282–3 (15 August 1942).

70. Friedländer, *The Years of Persecution*, 314.

71. This was the argument of Ernst Nolte, especially, but also Arno J. Mayer, although they came at it from entirely different starting points. For discussion, see Dan Stone, 'The Course of History: Arno J. Mayer, Gerhard L. Weinberg, and David Cesarani on the Holocaust and World War II', *Journal of Modern History*, 91:4 (2019), 883–904. See also Hans-Christian Harten, *Himmlers Lehrer: Die weltanschauliche Schulung in der SS 1933–1945* (Paderborn: Ferdinand Schöningh, 2014), 459–71, esp. 468, where Harten shows how the Nazis regarded Marxism as a vast system of deceit dreamed up by the Jews to destroy peoples: 'Am Bolschewismus zeigte sich, dass das Wesen des Judentums nicht allein die Gier nach Geld, sondern mehr noch nach Macht und in letzter Konsequenz nach der Weltherrschaft war.'

72. Classic studies include: Robert Koehl, *RKFDV: German Resettlement and Population Policy 1939–1945. A History of the Reich Commission for the Strengthening of Germandom* (Cambridge: Mass.: Harvard University Press, 1957); Alexander Dallin, *German Rule in Russia 1941–1945: A Study of Occupation Policies* (London: Macmillan, 1957).

73. See Fritzsche, *Life and Death in the Third Reich*, 180.

74. Longerich, *Politik der Vernichtung*, 579. See also Longerich, *Hitler*, 700–3.

75. Browning, *Origins*, 88–9.

76. Himmler, 'Denkschrift' (28 May 1940), in *Ursachen und Folgen*, ed. Herbert Michaelis and Ernst Schraepler (Berlin: Wendler, 1976), doc. 2879d.

77. Browning, *Origins*, 89.

CHAPTER 4: WAR OF ANNIHILATION

1. Baruch Milch, *Can Heaven Be Void?*, ed. Shosh Milch-Avigal, trans. Helen Kaye (Jerusalem: Yad Vashem, 2003), 180.

2. Diary of Fritz Siegel, in Hans Dollinger (ed.), *Kain, wo ist dein Bruder? Was der Mensch im Zweiten Weltkrieg erleiden mußte – dokumentiert in Tagebüchern und Briefen* (Frankfurt am Main: Fischer Taschenbuch Verlag, 1989), 100–1 ('Habe mich selbstverständlich freiwillig gemeldet'). For details of what happened in Krupki, see Waitman Wade Beorn, 'Genocide in a Small Place: *Wehrmacht* Complicity in Killing the Jews of Krupki, 1941', *Holocaust Studies*, 16:1–2 (2010), 97–128.

3. Hitler to Frank, 2 October 1940, in Noakes and Pridham (eds.), *Nazism 1919–1945*, vol. 3, 988.

4. Frank, record of meeting, 23 April 1940, in Noakes and Pridham (eds.), *Nazism 1919–1945*, vol. 3, 990.

5. Ian Kershaw, '"Working towards the Führer": Reflections on the Nature of the Hitler Dictatorship', in his *Hitler, the Germans and the Final Solution* (New Haven: Yale University Press, 2008), ch. 1.

6. See Raul Hilberg, 'The Bureaucracy of Annihilation', in François Furet (ed.), *Unanswered Questions: Nazi Germany and the Genocide of the Jews* (New York: Schocken Books, 1989), 119–33; and the essays in Christopher R. Browning, Peter Hayes and Raul Hilberg, *German Railroads, Jewish Souls: The Reichsbahn, Bureaucracy, and the Final Solution* (New York: Berghahn Books, 2020).

7. See, for example, Wolf Gruner, 'The History of the Holocaust: Multiple Actors, Diverse Motives, Contradictory Developments and Disparate (Re)actions', in Christian Wiese and Paul Betts (eds.), *Years of Persecution, Years of Extermination: Saul Friedländer and the Future of Holocaust Studies* (London: Continuum, 2010), 323–41, and Mary Fulbrook, *A Small Town Near Auschwitz: Ordinary Nazis and the Holocaust* (Oxford: Oxford University Press, 2012) for an emphasis on the administrative personnel, including mayors and city officials.

8. A Wehrmacht regiment contained about 2,000 men. Throughout the period 1939–45, about 18 million men fought in the Wehrmacht.

9. Peter Hayes, 'Hilberg, the Railroads, and the Holocaust', in Browning, Hayes and Hilberg, *German Railroads, Jewish Souls*, 123.

10. Ibid., 123–7. See also Simone Gigliotti, *The Train Journey: Transit, Captivity, and Witnessing in the Holocaust* (New York: Berghahn Books, 2009), esp. ch. 1.

11. Donald Bloxham, *The Final Solution: A Genocide* (Oxford: Oxford University Press, 2009), 230.

12. See Richard J. Evans, 'The Decision to Exterminate the Jews of Europe', in Larissa Allwork and Rachel Pistol (eds.), *The Jews, the Holocaust and the Public: The Legacies of David Cesarani* (Houndmills: Palgrave Macmillan, 2020), 127–8. Historians who stress the importance of the US's entry into the war for the 'Final Solution' include Christian Gerlach, 'The Wannsee Conference, the Fate of the German Jews, and Hitler's Decision in Principle to Exterminate All European Jews', *Journal of Modern History*, 70:4 (1998), 759–812; Cesarani, *Final Solution*, 447–9; Yitzhak Arad, *The Operation Reinhard Death Camps: Belzec, Sobibor, Treblinka*, rev. edn (Bloomington: Indiana University Press, 2018), 33.

13. Cited in Longerich, *Holocaust*, 265.

14. Goebbels, 'Die Juden sind schuld!', 16 November 1941, in Gilman and Rabinbach (eds.), *The Third Reich Sourcebook*, 737.

15. Christopher R. Browning, 'The Decision-Making Process', in Dan Stone (ed.), *The Historiography of the Holocaust* (Houndmills: Palgrave Macmillan, 2004), 188. See also Browning, 'On My Book *The Origins of the Final Solution*: Some Remarks on Its Background and on Its Major Conclusions', in David Bankier and Dan Michman (eds.), *Holocaust Historiography in Context: Emergence, Challenges, Polemics and Achievements* (Jerusalem: Yad Vashem, 2008), 413, where he argues that 'in the brief twelve day span between October 13 and October 25 plans to construct camps with gassing facilities emerged not only for Belzec but also for Chelmno, Riga, Mogilev, Birkenau, and possibly Sobibor; and moreover (with the probable exception of Birkenau) that Berlin was centrally involved and not merely reacting to local initiatives'.

16. As Jürgen Matthäus astutely observes in 'Operation Barbarossa and the Onset of the Holocaust, June–December 1941', in Christopher R. Browning, with a contribution by Jürgen Matthäus, *The Origins of the Final Solution: The Evolution of Nazi Jewish Policy, September 1939–March 1942* (London: William Heinemann, 2004), 297.

17. Christopher R. Browning, *Ordinary Men: Reserve Police Battalion 101 and the Final Solution in Poland* (New York: HarperPerennial, 1993), xv.

18. Hertha Feiner to Inge Feiner, 19 January 1941, in Hertha Feiner, *Before Deportation: Letters from a Mother to Her Daughters, January 1939–December 1942*, ed. Karl Heinz Jahnke (Evanston: Northwestern University Press, 1999), 39. Hertha's other daughter Marion went on to establish the Marion Boyars publishing house.

19. On this remarkable act of deception and theft, see Jonathan R. Zatlin, 'The Ruse of Retirement: Eichmann, the *Heimeinkaufsverträge*, and the Dispossession of the Elderly', in Christoph Kreutzmüller and Jonathan R. Zatlin (eds.), *Dispossession: Plundering German Jewry, 1933–1953* (Ann Arbor: University of Michigan Press, 2020), 169–201.

20. See Theresa Walch, 'Just West of East: The Paradoxical Place of the Theresienstadt Ghetto in Policy and Perception', *Naharaim*, 14:2 (2020), online at: doi.org/10.1515/naharaim-2020-2001.

21. Marie Bader to Ernst Löwy, 17 April 1942, in Marie Bader, *Life and Love in Nazi Prague: Letters from an Occupied City*, ed. Kate Ottevanger and Jan Láníček (London: Bloomsbury Academic, 2019), 232.

22. Jan Láníček, 'Epilogue', in Bader, *Life and Love in Nazi Prague*, 241–5. On Izbica, see Steffen Hänschen, *Das Transitghetto Izbica im System des*

Holocaust: Die Deportationen in den Distrikt Lublin im Frühsommer 1942 (Berlin: Metropol, 2018). And on Theresienstadt, see Anna Hájková, *The Last Ghetto: An Everyday History of Theresienstadt, 1941–1945* (Oxford: Oxford University Press, 2020).

23. Henriette Pollatschek to Fritz Heller, 16 May 1942, in *A Thousand Kisses: A Grandmother's Holocaust Letters*, ed. Renata Polt (Tuscaloosa: University of Alabama Press, 1999), 186.

24. Ariana Neumann, *When Time Stopped: A Memoir of My Father, Survival and What Remains* (London: Scribner, 2020), 262–3.

25. Martin Dean, *Collaboration in the Holocaust: Crimes of the Local Police in Belorussia and Ukraine, 1941–44* (Houndmills: Macmillan Press, 2000), 20.

26. Giselher Wirsing, *Der maßlose Kontinent* (Jena: Eugen Diederichs Verlag, 1942), 437–9, extracted in Léon Poliakov and Joseph Wulf (eds.), *Das Dritte Reich und seine Denker* (Frankfurt am Main: Ullstein, 1983 [1959]), 478.

27. Harten, *Himmlers Lehrer*, 478.

28. This is Hitler's term; see his comments of 30 March 1941 at a conference with military leaders, in Noakes and Pridham (eds.), *Nazism 1919–1945*, vol. 3, 1086.

29. Hitler, speech to NSDAP leaders, Vienna, 26 October 1940, in Noakes and Pridham (eds.), *Nazism 1919–1945*, vol. 3, 900.

30. From Karl Schleunes and Uwe Dietrich Adam through David Cesarani.

31. Field Marshal Walter von Reichenau, 'Orders for Conduct in the East', in Rabinbach and Gilman (eds.), *Third Reich Sourcebook*, 741.

32. OKW, 'Directives for the Behaviour of the Troops in Russia', 19 May 1941, in Noakes and Pridham (eds.), *Nazism 1919–1945*, vol. 3, 1090. See also Robert Gellately, *Hitler's True Believers: How Ordinary People Became Nazis* (Oxford: Oxford University Press, 2020), 299.

33. David Furber and Wendy Lower, 'Colonialism and Genocide in Nazi-Occupied Poland and Ukraine', in A. Dirk Moses (ed.), *Empire, Colony, Genocide: Conquest, Occupation and Subaltern Resistance in World History* (New York: Berghahn Books, 2008), 376.

34. Furber and Lower, 'Colonialism and Genocide', 377.

35. A. Dirk Moses, 'Empire, Colony, Genocide: Keywords and the Philosophy of History', in Moses (ed.), *Empire, Colony, Genocide*, 37–9.

36. Extracts from Walter Mattner's letters, in Klaus-Michael Mallmann, Volker Rieß and Wolfram Pyta (eds.), *Deutscher Osten, 1939–1945: Der Weltanschauungskrieg in Photos und Texten* (Darmstadt: Wissenschaftliche Buchgesellschaft, 2003), 28. See also Matthäus, 'Operation Barbarossa and the Onset of the Holocaust', 298, for a slightly different translation of the same letter.

37. Marina Tikhonovna Isaichik, in Svetlana Alexievich, *Second-Hand Time*, trans. Bela Shayevich (London: Fitzcarraldo Editions, 2016), 135.

38. 'A Man's Story', in Alexievich, *Second-Hand Time*, 300, 304, 305.

39. Ian Rich, *Holocaust Perpetrators of the German Police Battalions: The Mass Murder of Jewish Civilians, 1940–1942* (London: Bloomsbury, 2018), 2, 5. 'Backbone' refers to Dieter Pohl, 'The Murder of Ukraine's Jews under German Military Administration and in the Reich Commissariat Ukraine', in Ray Brandon and Wendy Lower (eds.), *The Shoah in Ukraine: History, Testimony, Memorialization* (Bloomington: Indiana University Press, 2008), 60.

40. Harten, *Himmlers Lehrer*, 474–8.

41. 'Geheimer Erlass des ObdH über die Erziehung des Offizierkorps, 18.12.1938', cited in Bryce Sait, *The Indoctrination of the Wehrmacht: Nazi Ideology and the War Crimes of the German Military* (New York: Berghahn Books, 2019), 182 (translation slightly altered).

42. *Mitteilungsblätter für die weltanschauliche Schulung der Ordnungspolizei*, 27 (1 December 1941), cited in Matthäus, 'Operation Barbarossa and the Onset of the Holocaust', 300.

43. 'Vernehmung von Friedrich W., 1941 Angehöriger des Einsatzkommandos 8, v. 3.10.1962 (Auszug)', in Mallmann, Rieß and Pyta (eds.), *Deutscher Osten*, 131.

44. 'Report of a Photographer' (Gunsilius), 11 November 1958, in Ernst Klee, Willi Dressen and Volker Riess (eds.), *'Those Were the Days': The Holocaust as Seen by the Perpetrators and Bystanders* (London: Hamish Hamilton, 1991), 31.

45. Kazimierz Sakowicz, *Ponary Diary, 1941–1943: A Bystander's Account of a Mass Murder*, ed. Yitzhak Arad (New Haven: Yale University Press, 2005), 16 (August 1941).

46. Sakowicz, *Ponary Diary*, 28 (2 September 1941).

47. Dan Stone, 'Modernity and Violence: Theoretical Reflections on the Einsatzgruppen', *Journal of Genocide Research*, 1:3 (1999), 367–78. Edward Weisband, *The Macabresque: Human Violation and Hate in Genocide, Mass Atrocity, and Enemy-Making* (New York: Oxford University Press, 2017).

48. Milch, *Can Heaven Be Void?*, 131–2. On Milch, see also Natalia Aleksiun, 'Daily Survival: Social History of Jews in Family Bunkers in Eastern Galicia', in Wendy Lower and Lauren Faulkner Rossi (eds.), *Lessons and Legacies*, vol. 12: *New Directions in Holocaust Research and Education* (Evanston: Northwestern University Press, 2017), 304–31.

49. Sof'ia Ratner to her children, 6 September 1941, in Arkadi Zeltser (ed.), *To Pour Out My Bitter Soul: Letters of Jews from the USSR, 1941–1945* (Jerusalem:

Yad Vashem, 2016), 47. The Vitebsk ghetto inmates who had not died of starvation were murdered in the Tulovskii Ravine on 8–10 October 1941.

50. Tumer Gonchar to her sons, Vinnitsa, 15 April 1942, in Zeltser (ed.), *To Pour Out My Bitter Soul*, 48. The Jews in Vinnitsa in April 1942 were survivors of the first wave of *Einsatzgruppen* shootings, which took place in September 1941. With the exception of about 1,000 who were selected for work, the remainder were murdered in the Piatnichnyi Forest on 16 April 1942.

51. Omer Bartov, 'The Holocaust', in Robert Gellately (ed.), *The Oxford Illustrated History of the Third Reich* (Oxford: Oxford University Press, 2018), 230.

52. See Omer Bartov's brilliant book *Anatomy of a Genocide: The Life and Death of a Town Called Buczacz* (New York: Simon & Schuster, 2018).

53. See Karel Berkhoff et al., *Basic Historical Narrative of the Babyn Yar Holocaust Memorial Center* (October 2018), online at: http://babynyar.org/en/narrative. They write: '*Massive* and *local* – these were the predominant features of the Holocaust in Eastern Europe' (5).

54. Fritz Höfer, statement, 27 August 1959, in Klee, Dressen and Riess (eds.), *'Those Were the Days'*, 65.

55. Kurt Werner, statement, 28 May 1964, in Klee, Dressen and Riess (eds.), *'Those Were the Days'*, 67.

56. World Jewish Congress (WJC), Geneva, Account of the Pogrom in Bucharest, Romania, 21–23 January 1941, in Jürgen Matthäus with Emil Kerenji, Jan Lambertz and Leah Wolfson (eds.), *Jewish Responses to Persecution*, vol. 3: *1941–1942* (Lanham, MD: AltaMira Press in association with the United States Holocaust Memorial Museum, 2013), 89.

57. Adrian Cioflâncă, 'Masacrul antisemit de la Jilava: Ce ştim în plus (II)', *Revista 22* (17–23 January 2017), 10–11.

58. WJC, Geneva, Report on the Activities of the Jewish Community of Zagreb, Independent State of Croatia, after April 1941, 8 July 1945, in Matthäus et al. (eds.), *Jewish Responses*, vol. 3, 93.

59. Friedländer, *The Years of Extermination*, 240.

60. Ibid.

61. Aryeh Klonicki, diary entry for 18 July 1943, in Emil Kerenji (ed.), *Jewish Responses to Persecution*, vol. 4: *1942–1943* (Lanham, MD: Rowman & Littlefield, 2015), 430. The Klonickis were caught and murdered by the Germans in January 1944.

62. Mirjam Korber, Djurin (Transnistria), diary entries for 15 July 1942 and 20 March 1943, in Kerenji (ed.), *Jewish Responses to Persecution*, vol. 4, 431, 432. Mirjam and her sister Sisi and their parents survived the war.

63. Letter from Anna Grasberg-Górna to 'Maria', Warsaw Ghetto, 6 September 1942, in Kerenji (ed.), *Jewish Responses to Persecution*, vol. 4, 412–13. Maria was caring for Anna's daughter Erika on the 'Aryan side' of Warsaw.

64. Milch, *Can Heaven Be Void?*, 147–8.

65. See Saul Friedländer, 'From Anti-Semitism to Extermination: A Historiographical Study of Nazi Policies Toward the Jews and an Essay in Interpretation', in Furet (ed.), *Unanswered Questions*, 26.

66. Hermann Goering, Order to Heydrich to Begin Preparations for the Final Solution to the Jewish Question, 31 July 1941, in Rabinbach and Gilman (eds.), *Third Reich Sourcebook*, 740. Goering's note, Browning claims, 'should be seen as the authorisation of a "feasibility study" and not the definitive order for the murder of European Jewry'. Browning, 'On My Book *The Origins of the Final Solution*', 410.

67. Friedländer, 'From Anti-Semitism to Extermination', 27.

68. Fritzsche, *Life and Death in the Third Reich*, 207.

69. Mark Roseman, *The Villa, the Lake, the Meeting: Wannsee and the Final Solution* (London: Penguin, 2003), 84. See also Bloxham, *The Final Solution*, 227.

70. For the 'protocol' of the meeting, see Rabinbach and Gilman (eds.), *Third Reich Sourcebook*, 752–7. And on the *Mischlinge*, see Jeremy Noakes, 'The Development of Nazi Policy towards the German-Jewish "Mischlinge", 1933–1945', *Leo Baeck Institute Yearbook*, 34 (1989), 291–354; and Teicher, *Social Mendelism*, esp. 199–200 on Wannsee.

71. Roseman, *The Villa, the Lake, the Meeting*, 103.

72. Ibid., 106. On Wannsee as an echo, see Peter Klein, 'Die Wannsee-Konferenz als Echo auf die gefallene Entscheidung zur Ermordung der europäischen Juden', in Norbert Kampe and Peter Klein (eds.), *Die Wannsee-Konferenz am 20. Januar 1942: Dokumente, Forschungsstand, Kontroversen* (Cologne: Böhlau Verlag, 2013), 182–201. See also Gerhard Wolf, 'The Wannsee Conference in 1942 and the National Socialist Living Space Dystopia', *Journal of Genocide Research*, 17:2 (2015), 153–75 for the argument that Heydrich's pronouncements about the use of Jewish labour made at Wannsee were not purely euphemistic but need to be taken seriously, given the RSHA's ambitions and the lack of sufficient Polish labour.

73. Browning, *Origins of the Final Solution*, 412.

74. Eichmann's testimony, June 1961, in Raul Hilberg (ed.), *Documents of Destruction: Germany and Jewry 1933–1945* (London: W. H. Allen, 1972), 102–3, cited in Browning, *Origins of the Final Solution*, 413.

75. All cited in Browning, *Origins of the Final Solution*, 404 (Rosenberg), 407 (Goebbels), 408–9 (Frank).

76. Peter Black, 'Foot Soldiers of the Final Solution: The Trawniki Training Camp and Operation Reinhard', *Holocaust and Genocide Studies*, 25:1 (2011), 1–99; Black, 'Who Were the Trawniki-Men? Preliminary Data and Conclusions about the Foot Soldiers of "Operation Reinhard"', in Peter Black, Béla Rásky and Marianne Windsperger (eds.), *Collaboration in Eastern Europe during the Second World War and the Holocaust* (Vienna: New Academic Press, 2019), 21–68.

77. Donald Bloxham, *Genocide, the World Wars and the Unweaving of Europe* (London: Vallentine Mitchell, 2008), 155.

78. Black, 'Foot Soldiers of the Final Solution', 45.

79. Dan Michman, 'Täteraussagen und Geschichtswissenschaft: Der Fall Dieter Wisliceny und der Entscheidungsprozeß zur "Endlösung"', in Jürgen Matthäus and Klaus-Michael Mallmann (eds.), *Deutsche, Juden, Völkermord: Der Holocaust als Geschichte und Gegenwart* (Darmstadt: Wissenschaftliche Buchgesellschaft, 2006), 205–19. Wisliceny was responsible for the deportation of Jews from Slovakia, Thessaloniki and Hungary and was tried and executed in Czechoslovakia in 1948. See also Safrian, *Eichmann's Men*.

80. Ulrich Herbert, 'The German Military Command in Paris and the Deportation of the French Jews', in Herbert (ed.), *National Socialist Extermination Policies: Contemporary German Perspectives and Controversies* (New York: Berghahn Books, 2000), 146.

81. Ibid., 149.

82. Debórah Dwork and Robert Jan Van Pelt, *Holocaust: A History* (London: John Murray, 2002), 233.

83. See Wolfgang Seibel, *Persecution and Rescue: The Politics of the 'Final Solution' in France, 1940–1944*, trans. Ciaran Cronin (Ann Arbor: University of Michigan Press, 2016), xv.

84. Milch, *Can Heaven Be Void?*, 198.

CHAPTER 5: A CONTINENT-WIDE CRIME

1. Jan T. Gross, 'Opportunistic Killings and Plunder of Jews by Their Neighbors – A Norm or an Exception in German-Occupied Europe?', in Lower and Rossi (eds.), *Lessons and Legacies*, vol. 12, 26.

2. Tatjana Tönsmeyer, 'Besatzung als europäische Erfahrungs- und Gesellschaftsgeschichte: Der Holocaust im Kontext des Zweiten Weltkrieges', in Frank Bajohr and Andrea Löw (eds.), *Der Holocaust: Ergebnisse und neue Fragen der Forschung* (Frankfurt am Main: Fischer Taschenbuch Verlag, 2015), 281–98, esp. 284–5, notes that 'collaboration' is not a useful term of analysis because of its wartime origins and its suggestion of 'treason'. I sympathize with this viewpoint but hope to show here that the term retains some analytical usefulness because it does to some extent describe the self-perception of 'collaborators' and not just the views of their enemies.

3. Jochen Böhler and Robert Gerwarth (eds.), *The Waffen-SS: A European History* (Oxford: Oxford University Press, 2017).

4. Hannah Arendt, 'The Seeds of a Fascist International' (June 1945), in *Essays in Understanding, 1930–1954: Uncollected and Unpublished Works by Hannah Arendt*, ed. Jerome Kohn (New York: Harcourt Brace & Company, 1994), 150.

5. As Timothy Snyder argues in *Black Earth: The Holocaust as History and Warning* (London: The Bodley Head, 2015), esp. ch. 9.

6. Tsolakoglou, interview with the *Donauzeitung*, reprinted in *Eleutheron Vema*, 7 September 1941, cited in Andrew Apostolou, 'Greek Collaboration in the Holocaust and the Course of the War', in Giorgos Antoniou and A. Dirk Moses (eds.), *The Holocaust in Greece* (Cambridge: Cambridge University Press, 2018), 94.

7. Apostolou, 'Greek Collaboration', 112. On plunder, see in the same volume, Leon Saltiel, 'A City against Its Citizens? Thessaloniki and the Jews', 113–34; and Maria Kavala, 'The Scale of Jewish Property Theft in Nazi-occupied Thessaloniki', 183–207.

8. Kerenji (ed.), *Jewish Responses to Persecution*, vol. 4, 252.

9. See the remarkable late-Soviet-era film *Come and See* (1985, dir. Elem Klimov) for a depiction of the horror wrought in Belarus under Nazi occupation.

10. Richard Evans, *The Coming of the Third Reich* (New York: Penguin Books, 2003), 461.

11. Raul Hilberg, *The Destruction of the European Jews*, rev. edn (New York: Holmes & Meier, 1985), vol. 3, 1044. But see Tom Lawson's important review of the final revised edition of Hilberg's work to see why his argument is 'not monolithic'; online at: *Reviews in History*, 31 March 2004: https://reviews.history.ac.uk/review/394.

12. Diana Dumitru, *The State, Antisemitism and Collaboration in the Holocaust: The Borderlands of Romania and the Soviet Union* (Cambridge: Cambridge University Press, 2016).

13. Omer Bartov, *Anatomy of a Genocide: The Life and Death of a Town Called Buczacz* (New York: Simon & Schuster, 2018); Waitman Wade Beorn, 'All the Other Neighbors: Communal Genocide in Eastern Europe', in Simone Gigliotti and Hilary Earl (eds.), *A Companion to the Holocaust* (Hoboken, NJ: Wiley Blackwell, 2020), 153–72.

14. Seibel, *Persecution and Rescue*, 281–2.

15. Robert Edwin Herzstein, *When Nazi Dreams Come True: The Horrifying Story of the Nazi Blueprint for Europe* (London: Abacus, 1982); Raimund Bauer, *The Construction of a National Socialist Europe during the Second World War: How the New Order Took Shape* (London: Routledge, 2020); Johannes Dafinger and Dieter Pohl (eds.), *A New Nationalist Europe under Hitler: Concepts of Europe and Transnational Networks in the National Socialist Sphere of Influence, 1933–1945* (London: Routledge, 2019); Johannes Dafinger, 'The Nazi "New Europe": Transnational Concepts of a Fascist and Völkisch Order for the Continent', in Arnd Bauerkämper and Grzegorz Rossoliński-Liebe (eds.), *Fascism without Borders: Transnational Connections and Cooperation between Movements and Regimes in Europe from 1918 to 1945* (New York: Berghahn Books, 2017), 264–87.

16. Grzegorz Rossoliński-Liebe, 'Stepan Bandera, der ukrainische Nationalismus und der transnationale Faschismus', *Ost-West: Europäische Perspektive*, 21:3 (2020), 201–9; Grzegorz Rossoliński-Liebe, 'The Fascist Kernel of Ukrainian Genocidal Nationalism', *The Carl Beck Papers in Russian and East European Studies*, 2402 (2015); Per Anders Rudling, 'Rehearsal for Volhynia: Schutzmannschaft Battalion 201 and Hauptmann Roman Shukhevych in Occupied Belarussia, 1942', *East European Politics and Societies and Cultures*, 34:1 (2020), 158–93; John-Paul Himka, 'Ukrainian Collaboration in the Extermination of the Jews during the Second World War: Sorting Out the Long-Term and Conjunctural Factors', *Studies in Contemporary Jewry*, 13 (1997), 170–89.

17. Grzegorz Rossoliński-Liebe, 'Conceptualizations of the Holocaust in Germany, Poland, Lithuania, Belarus, and Ukraine: Historical Research, Public Debates, and Methodological Disputes', *East European Politics and Societies and Cultures*, 34:1 (2020), 134. See also John-Paul Himka, 'Former Ukrainian Policemen in the Ukrainian National Insurgency: Continuing the Holocaust Outside German Service', in Lower and Rossi (eds.), *Lessons and Legacies*, vol. 12, 141–63.

18. Johannes Koll, 'From Greater German Reich to Greater Germanic Reich: Arthur Seyss-Inquart and the Racial Reshaping of Europe', in Dafinger and Pohl (eds.), *A New Nationalist Europe under Hitler*, 64.

19. Laurien Vastenhout, *Between Community and Collaboration: 'Jewish Councils' in Western Europe under Nazi Occupation* (Cambridge: Cambridge University Press, 2022). On the differences in survival rates among the Jews of Amsterdam, showing that the wealthier stood the best chance of surviving, see Peter Tammes, 'Surviving the Holocaust: Socio-demographic Differences among Amsterdam Jews', *European Journal of Population*, 33 (2017), 293–318.

20. Rob Bakker, *Boekhouders van de Holocaust: Nederlandse ambtenaren en de collaboratie* (Hilversum: Verbum, 2020).

21. Ido de Haan, 'Failures and Mistakes: Images of Collaboration in Postwar Dutch Society', in Roni Stauber (ed.), *Collaboration with the Nazis: Public Discourse after the Holocaust* (Abingdon: Routledge, 2011), 77.

22. Arne Johan Vetlesen, *Evil and Human Agency: Understanding Collective Evildoing* (Cambridge: Cambridge University Press, 2005), xii. See also Bjarte Bruland, 'Collaboration in the Deportation of Norway's Jews: Changing Views and Representations', in Roni Stauber (ed.), *Collaboration with the Nazis: Public Discourse after the Holocaust* (Abingdon: Routledge, 2011), 125–37.

23. Seibel, *Persecution and Rescue*, 5.

24. Ibid., 287.

25. Ibid.

26. Cited in ibid., 2, 157–8. See also Friedländer, *The Years of Extermination*, 420–1, who notes that Saliège's letter was 'not only . . . an expression of an impetuous and immediate moral reaction' but was suggested by emissaries from Lyon. Thus, as well as being a personal statement, it allowed the Episcopal Assembly 'to save face: the church of France had not remained silent' (421).

27. See also Paul Webster, *Pétain's Crime: The Full Story of the French Collaboration in the Holocaust* (London: Pan Macmillan, 2001), 169; Susan Zuccotti, *The Holocaust, the French, and the Jews* (Lincoln: University of Nebraska Press, 1999), 146–7; Renée Poznanski, *Jews in France during World War II*, trans. Nathan Bracher (Hanover: Brandeis University Press, 2001), 296; Michael Phayer, *The Catholic Church and the Holocaust, 1930–1965* (Bloomington: Indiana University Press, 2000), 92–3.

28. Poznanski, *Jews in France during World War II*, 302. By 'unoccupied zone' is meant Vichy France's southern zone before the German occupation of the whole country in November 1942.

29. Michael R. Marrus and Robert O. Paxton, *Vichy France and the Jews*, 2nd edn (Stanford: Stanford University Press, 2019), xii.

30. Randolph L. Braham, 'Hungary', in David Wyman (ed.), *The World Reacts to the Holocaust* (Baltimore: Johns Hopkins University Press, 1996), 205. My emphasis.

31. Regina Fritz, 'Inside the Ghetto: Everyday Life in Hungarian Ghettos', *Hungarian Historical Review*, 4:3 (2015), 606–40.

32. See Gábor Kádár and Zoltán Vági, *The Final Decision: Berlin, Budapest, Birkenau 1944* (forthcoming).

33. Zoltán Vági and Gábor Kádár with László Csősz, 'Introduction', in Vági, Csősz and Kádár, *The Holocaust in Hungary: Evolution of a Genocide* (Lanham, MD: AltaMira Press in association with the United States Holocaust Memorial Museum, 2013), xxx.

34. See Raz Segal, *Genocide in the Carpathians: War, Social Breakdown, and Mass Violence, 1914–1945* (Stanford: Stanford University Press, 2016), 15: 'the destruction of Subcarpathian Rus' Jews flowed from the vision of "Greater Hungary" and the designs and initiatives of Hungarian authorities with regard to the treatment of Jews *and* other groups'.

35. An exemplary illustration of this argument is Bartov, *Anatomy of a Genocide*. 'Genocide is a societal endeavour' comes from Edward Westermann, 'Old Nazis, Ordinary Men, and New Killers: Synthetic and Divergent Histories of Perpetrators', in Gigliotti and Earl (eds.), *A Companion to the Holocaust*, 129.

36. Braham, 'Hungary', 224, n. 66 notes that 'the close to 600,000 Hungarian Jews and the approximately 270,000 Romanian Jews were killed during the rules of Horthy and Antonescu, respectively. Neither the Arrow Cross (Nyilas) nor the Iron Guard was in power during the mass deportation.' See also László Karsai, 'The "Jewish Policy" of the Szálasi Regime', *Yad Vashem Studies*, 40:1 (2012), 119–56.

37. Vági, Kádár and Csősz, 'Introduction', xxviii–xxix.

38. Menachem Mendel Selinger, *Wir sind so weit . . . The Story of a Jewish Family in Nazi Europe. Memories and Thoughts 1939–1945*, trans. Robert Burns (Milan: Il Faggio, 2020), vol. 1, 270.

39. H. James Burgwyn with Amadeo Osti Guerrazzi, *Mussolini and the Salò Republic, 1943–1945: The Failure of a Puppet Regime* (Houndmills: Palgrave Macmillan, 2018), 145. Burgwyn nevertheless stresses the different opinions among Italian Fascists where the persecution of the Jews was concerned, writing that 'for opportunistic reasons' Mussolini 'brought his regime perilously close to outright collaboration with the Nazi shoah' (146).

40. Simon Levis Sullam, *The Italian Executioners: The Genocide of the Jews of Italy* (Princeton: Princeton University Press, 2018), 44.

41. Ibid. 52.

42. Letter from Luigi Zappelli, president of the Colonia Libera Italiana, to Max Huber, president of the International Committee of the Red Cross, Lausanne, 28 July 1944, in Leah Wolfson (ed.), *Jewish Responses to Persecution*, vol. 5: *1944–1946* (Lanham, MD: Rowman & Littlefield in association with the United States Holocaust Memorial Museum, 2015), 30.

43. Levis Sullam, *The Italian Executioners*, 49. See also Liliana Picciotto, 'The Shoah in Italy: Its History and Characteristics', in Joshua D. Zimmerman (ed.), *The Jews in Italy under Fascist and Nazi Rule, 1922–1945* (New York: Cambridge University Press, 2005), 209–23.

44. This paragraph relies on Nina Paulovičová, 'The "Unmasterable Past"? The Reception of the Holocaust in Postcommunist Slovakia', in John-Paul Himka and Joanna Beata Michlic (eds.), *Bringing the Dark Past to Light: The Reception of the Holocaust in Postcommunist Europe* (Lincoln: University of Nebraska Press, 2013), 551–6. See also Ivan Kamenec, *On the Trail of Tragedy: The Holocaust in Slovakia* (Bratislava: H&H, 2007); Livia Rothkirchen, 'Czechoslovakia', in Wyman (ed.), *The World Reacts to the Holocaust*, 156–99. By autumn 1941, 'emigration' was already a euphemism for 'murder'.

45. Vanda Rajcan, Madeline Vadkerty and Ján Hlavinka, 'Slovakia', in Geoffrey Megargee (ed.), *USHMM Encyclopedia of Camps and Ghettos, 1933–1945*, vol. 3, 844 (German intervention); 847 (Mach).

46. See Wolf Gruner, 'Protectorate of Bohemia and Moravia', in Gruner and Osterloh (eds.), *The Greater German Reich and the Jews*, 99–135; Gruner, *The Holocaust in Bohemia and Moravia: Czech Initiatives, German Policies, Jewish Responses* (New York: Berghahn Books, 2019).

47. Rabbi Abraham Frieder, Nové Mesto, Slovakia, diary entries for February 1942, in Matthäus et al., *Jewish Responses to Persecution*, vol. 3, 236.

48. Rory Yeomans, *Visions of Annihilation: The Ustasha Regime and the Cultural Politics of Fascism 1941–1945* (Pittsburgh: University of Pittsburgh Press, 2013), 14.

49. *Hrvatski branik*, 10 May 1941, cited in Rory Yeomans, 'Eradicating "Undesired Elements": National Regeneration and the Ustasha Regime's Program to Purify the Nation, 1941–1945', in Weiss-Wendt and Yeomans (eds.), *Racial Science in Hitler's New Europe, 1938–1945*, 208.

50. Yeomans, *Visions of Annihilation*, 15.

51. Ibid., 25–6. See also Ivo Goldstein, 'The Independent State of Croatia in 1941: On the Road to Catastrophe', *Totalitarian Movements and Political Religions*, 7:4 (2006), 417–27.

52. Matthew Feldman, *Politics, Intellectuals and Faith* (Stuttgart: ibidem Verlag, 2020), 181.

53. Alexandra Lohse, 'Croatia', in Megargee (ed.), *USHMM Encyclopedia of Camps and Ghettos, 1933–1945*, vol. 3, 49. See also Alexander Korb, *Im Schatten des Weltkriegs: Massengewalt der Ustaša gegen Serben, Juden und Roma in Kroatien 1941–1945* (Hamburg: Hamburger Edition, 2013).

54. Ivo Goldstein and Mirza Velagic, 'Jasenovac III', in Megargee (ed.), *USHMM Encyclopedia of Camps and Ghettos, 1933–1945*, vol. 3, 61.

55. Duro Schwarz, 'The Jasenovač Death Camps', *Yad Vashem Studies*, 25 (1996), 390.

56. Ibid., 396.

57. Report on the Activities of the Jewish Community of Zagreb, after April 1941, in Matthäus et al., *Jewish Responses to Persecution*, vol. 3, 96.

58. Cited in Victor Neumann, *The Banat of Timişoara: A European Melting Pot* (London: Scala Arts & Heritage Publishers, 2019), 392. See also Viorel Achim, 'The Romanian Population Exchange Project Elaborated by Sabin Manuilă in October 1941', *Jahrbuch des italienisch-deutschen Instituts in Trient*, 27 (2001), 593–617, for the wider picture of the Antonescu regime's ethnic aspirations.

59. Cited in Dennis Deletant, 'Transnistria and the Romanian Solution to the "Jewish Problem"', in Ray Brandon and Wendy Lower (eds.), *The Shoah in Ukraine: History, Testimony, Memorialization* (Bloomington: Indiana University Press, 2008), 161.

60. Diana Dumitru, 'Peasants' Perceptions of Jewish Life in Interwar Bessarabia and How This Became Interwoven into the Holocaust', *Plural*, 1:1–2 (2013), 131–48.

61. Vladimir Solonari, 'A Conspiracy to Murder: Explaining the Dynamics of Romanian "Policy" towards Jews in Transnistria', *Journal of Genocide Research*, 19:1 (2017), 1–21. See also Andrej Angrick, 'The Escalation of German-Rumanian Anti-Jewish Policy after the Attack on the Soviet Union', *Yad Vashem Studies*, 26 (1998), 237–8.

62. For useful overviews of Transnistria, see Ronit Fischer, 'Transnistria: The Holocaust in Romania', in Jonathan C. Friedman (ed.), *The Routledge History of the Holocaust* (London: Routledge, 2011), 278–91; Svetlana Burmistr, 'Transnistrien', in Wolfgang Benz and Barbara Distel (eds.), *Der Ort des Terrors: Geschichte der nationalsozialistischen Konzentrationslager*, vol. 9: *Arbeitserziehungslager, Ghettos, Judenschutzlager, Polizeihaftlager, Sonderlager, Zigeunerlager, Zwangsarbeitslager* (Munich: C. H. Beck, 2009),

391–416; Deletant, 'Transnistria and the Romanian Solution to the "Jewish Problem"', 156–89.

63. See Solonari, 'A Conspiracy to Murder', 16. See also Dalia Ofer, 'Life in the Ghettos of Transnistria', *Yad Vashem Studies*, 25 (1996), 229–74; and Dalia Ofer and Sarah Rosen, 'An Account from Transnistria: The Diary of Lipman Kunstadt, a Social Critic from Within', in Suzanne Bardgett, Christine Schmidt and Dan Stone (eds.), *Beyond Camps and Forced Labour: Proceedings of the Sixth International Conference* (Houndmills: Palgrave Macmillan, 2020), 49–66.

64. Andrej Angrick, 'Transnistrien: Nicht länger der vergessene Friedhof?', in Jürgen Hensel and Stephan Lehnstaedt (eds.), *Arbeit in den nationalsozialistischen Ghettos* (Osnabrück: fibre Verlag, 2013), 305. For a compelling account of the Jews' survival in Moghilev, see Siegfried Jagendorf, *Jagendorf's Foundry: A Memoir of the Romanian Holocaust, 1941–1944* (New York: HarperCollins, 1991).

65. Angrick, 'Transnistrien', 306–7.

66. Ibid., 309.

67. Isopescu, cited in Diana Dumitru, 'Genocide for "Sanitary Purposes"? The Bogdanovka Murder in Light of Postwar Trial Documents', *Journal of Genocide Research*, 21:2 (2019), 162.

68. Neumann, *The Banat of Timişoara*, 392.

69. Direcţia Generală a Poliţiei, report of 16 October 1942, in Ottmar Traşcă (ed.), *'Chestiunea evreiască' în documente militare române, 1941–1944* (Bucharest: Institutul European, 2010), 699.

70. Ştefan Cristian Ionescu, 'Legal Resistance Through Petitions during the Holocaust: The Strategies of Romanian Jewish Leader Wilhelm Filderman, 1940–44', in Thomas Pegelow Kaplan and Wolf Gruner (eds.), *Resisting Persecution: Jews and Their Petitions during the Holocaust* (New York: Berghahn Books, 2020), 92–113, esp. 104–6.

71. Von Killinger to Richter, Auswärtiges Amt, 5 October 1942, in Ottmar Traşca and Dennis Deletant (eds.), *Al III-lea Reich şi Holocaustul din România 1940–1944: Documente din arhivele germane* (Bucharest: Editura Institutului Naţional pentru Studierea Holocaustului din România 'Elie Wiesel', 2007), 533.

72. Traşca and Deletant (eds.), *All III-lea Reich şi Holocaustul din România*, 534. Indeed, German observers complained about the lack of benefit to ethnic Germans of the Romanianization measures; see Hilberg, *The Destruction of the European Jews*, vol. 2, 763.

73. Abba Kovner, 'The Mission of the Survivors', in Yisrael Gutman and Livia Rothkirchen (eds.), *The Catastrophe of European Jewry:*

Antecedents – History – Reflections (Jerusalem: Yad Vashem, n.d. [1976]), 672–3. This is the text of a speech delivered by Kovner in Yiddish on 17 July 1945 in Italy before members of the Jewish Brigade and Jewish partisans.

74. Hilberg, *The Destruction of the European Jews*, vol. 2, 759.

75. Seibel, *Persecution and Rescue*, 285.

76. Paul Hagen, *Will Germany Crack? A Factual Report on Germany from Within*, trans. Anna Caples (London: Victor Gollancz, 1943), 145.

77. Peter Hayes, *Why? Explaining the Holocaust* (New York: W. W. Norton, 2017), 293. See also Yehuda Bauer's review of Rebecca Erbelding's book (see below) in *Yad Vashem Studies*, 47:1 (2019), 243, where he writes that the notion that the WRB was 'too little, too late' is 'completely mistaken – in 1942 and 1943, even less would have been achieved; the Allies had no way to rescue the millions who were exposed to the ideology-driven genocide'.

78. Wolfson (ed.), *Jewish Responses to Persecution*, vol. 5, 15.

79. On the WRB's activities in Hungary, see Rebecca Erbelding, 'The United States War Refugee Board, the Neutral Nations and the Holocaust in Hungary', in International Holocaust Remembrance Alliance (IHRA) (ed.), *Bystanders, Rescuers or Perpetrators? The Neutral Countries and the Shoah* (Berlin: Metropol, 2016), 183–97. The Swedish FO quotation is from this article, 196.

80. Richard Breitman, 'Roosevelt and the Holocaust', in Verne W. Newton (ed.), *FDR and the Holocaust* (New York: Palgrave Macmillan, 1996), 123: 'The institutional climate in the State and War departments, as well as in newer agencies such as the Office of War Information, was strongly opposed to active American assistance to European Jews . . . Europe would always have its problems; the important thing now was to win the war.' In the same volume, Breitman also writes ('The Failure to Provide a Safe Haven for European Jewry', 137) that 'Most of the authors give the War Refugee Board credit for belatedly ending the American government's passivity about the Nazi slaughter of Jews, but there are mixed reviews of the board's effectiveness.' On parcels and other forms of aid to Nazi victims in ghettos and camps, including those organized by the WRB, see Jan Láníček and Jan Lambertz (eds.), *More than Parcels: Wartime Aid for Jews in Nazi-Era Camps and Ghettos* (Detroit: Wayne State University Press, 2022).

81. See Rebecca Erbelding, *Rescue Board: The Untold Story of America's Efforts to Save the Jews of Europe* (New York: Doubleday, 2018) for the former argument.

82. Frank Munk, *The Legacy of Nazism: The Economic and Social Consequences of Totalitarianism* (New York: The Macmillan Company, 1943), 60.

83. Ibid., 62, 63.

84. See Avraham Milgram, 'Portugal and the Jews 1938–1945', in IHRA (ed.), *Bystanders, Rescuers or Perpetrators?*, 101–11; and, especially, Kaplan, *Hitler's Jewish Refugees.*

85. Saul Friedländer, *Where Memory Leads: My Life* (New York: Other Press, 2016), 173. See also the film *When Memory Comes: A Film about Saul Friedländer*, dir. Frank Diamand (2012).

86. Cláudia Ninhos, 'What Was Known in the Neutral Countries about the On-Going Genocide of European Jews?' in IHRA (ed.), *Bystanders, Rescuers or Perpetrators?*, 125–37.

87. Irene Flunser Pimentel and Cláudia Ninhos, 'Portugal, Jewish Refugees, and the Holocaust', *Dapim: Studies on the Holocaust*, 29:2 (2015), 109; Corry Guttstadt, 'Origins of the 1942–1943 German Ultimatum on the Repatriation of Jews with Citizenship of Neutral and German-allied Countries', in IHRA (ed.), *Bystanders, Rescuers or Perpetrators?*, 139–43. See also Rainer Schulze, 'The *Heimschaffungsaktion* of 1942–43: Turkey, Spain and Portugal and Their Responses to the German Offer of Repatriation of their Jewish Citizens', *Holocaust Studies*, 18:2–3 (2012), 49–72.

88. Guttstadt, 'Origins of the 1942–1943 German Ultimatum', 142.

89. Hayes, *Why?*, 296. Examples of *Schutzpässe* can be seen in Vági, Kádár and Csősz, *The Holocaust in Hungary*, 316 and 318.

90. Kovner, 'The Mission of the Survivors', 675.

91. Françoise Frenkel, *No Place to Lay One's Head*, trans. Stephanie Smee (London: Pushkin Press, 2018), 132 [orig. *Rien où poser sa tête* (Geneva: Edition J.-H. Jeheber, 1945)]. See the analysis in Wildt, *Hitler's* Volksgemeinschaft, and, on the violence containing and acting out forms of ritual humiliation, such as laughter, see Martina Kessel, *Gewalt und Gelächter: 'Deutschsein' 1914–1945* (Wiesbaden: Franz Steiner Verlag, 2019).

CHAPTER 6: CAMPS AND THE MOBILE HOLOCAUST

1. Herzberg, *Amor Fati*, 63. See also David Koker, *At the Edge of the Abyss: A Concentration Camp Diary, 1943–1944*, trans. Robert Jan van Pelt (Evanston: Northwestern University Press, 2012), 189 (9 May 1943): 'Roll call is a kind of religious ceremony and, like all religious ceremonies, an empty form

that people see through very clearly.' Koker was writing about Vught in the Netherlands.

2. Abraham Krzepicki, 'Eighteen Days in Treblinka', in Alexander Donat (ed.), *The Death Camp Treblinka: A Documentary* (New York: Holocaust Library, 1979), 79. On the experience of deportation, see Simone Gigliotti, *The Train Journey: Transit, Captivity, and Witnessing in the Holocaust* (New York: Berghahn Books, 2009).

3. Krzepicki, 'Eighteen Days in Treblinka', 108.

4. Ibid., 119.

5. Cited in Jacob Flaws, 'Sensory Witnessing at Treblinka', *Journal of Holocaust Research*, 35:1 (2021), 49 (German guard, Królikowski), 51 (Sypko).

6. Lewi Stone, 'Quantifying the Holocaust: Hyperintense Kill Rates during the Nazi Genocide', *Science Advances*, 5:1 (2019), eaau7292.

7. See Jan Henrik Fahlbusch, 'Im Zentrum des Massenmords: Ernst Zierke im Vernichtungslager Bełżec', in Wojciech Lenarczyk, Andreas Mix, Johannes Schwartz and Veronika Springmann (eds.), *KZ-Verbrechen: Beiträge zur Geschichte der nationalsozialistischen Konzentrationslager und ihrer Erinnerung* (Berlin: Metropol, 2007), 53–72.

8. Wetzel to Hinrich Lohse, Reich Commissioner of Ostland, 25 October 1941, in Noakes and Pridham (eds.), *Nazism*, vol. 3, 1144. In slightly different translation cited in Matthäus, 'Operation Barbarossa and the Onset of the Holocaust', 304. See also Friedlander, *The Origins of Nazi Genocide*, 211; Raul Hilberg, 'Die Aktion Reinhard', in Eberhard Jäckel and Jürgen Rohwer (eds.), *Der Mord an den Juden im Zweiten Weltkrieg: Entschlußbildung und Verwirklichung* (Stuttgart: Deutsche Verlags-Anstalt, 1985), 127.

9. Statement by August Becker, 26 March 1960, cited in Klee, Dressen and Riess (eds.), *'Those Were the Days'*, 69.

10. Statement by Brack, in Noakes and Pridham (eds.), *Nazism*, vol. 3, 1145.

11. 'The Treblinka Slaughter House (A Report from the Underground in Poland)', *Polish Jew*, 3:18 (August–September 1943), 1; Krzepicki, 'Eighteen Days in Treblinka', 77–145.

12. 'The Treblinka Slaughter House', 1.

13. 'Horrors of Treblinka', *Polish Jew* (February 1944), 7; International Tracing Service Digital Archive, Wiener Holocaust Library, London (henceforth ITS DAWL), 1.2.7.2/82170598_1.

14. It is unclear who the author of the report was.

15. See Timothy Snyder, 'Holocaust: The Ignored Reality', *New York Review of Books* (16 July 2009); Snyder, 'Commemorative Casualty', *Modernism/*

Modernity, 20:1 (2013), 77–93; Arad, *The Operation Reinhard Death Camps*; Grossman, 'Treblinka'.

16. Longerich, *Holocaust*, 382; Helge Grabitz and Wolfgang Scheffler, *Letzte Spuren: Ghetto Warschau, SS Arbeitslager Trawniki, Aktion Erntefest. Fotos und Dokumente über Opfer des Endlösungswahns im Spiegel der historischen Ereignisse* (Berlin: Edition Hentrich, 1988), 328–33.

17. Waitman Wade Beorn, 'Last Stop in Lwów: Janowska as a Hybrid Camp', *Holocaust and Genocide Studies*, 32:3 (2018), 445–71.

18. 'Extract from Written Evidence of Rudolf Höss, Commander of the Auschwitz Extermination Camp', in Arad, Gutman and Margaliot (eds.), *Documents on the Holocaust*, 350–1.

19. 'Göring's Commission to Heydrich, July 31, 1941', in Dawidowicz (ed.), *A Holocaust Reader*, 72–3.

20. As Browning notes after 400 pages of careful analysis of the months September 1939 to March 1942: 'the leap from disappearance of the Jews "sometime, somehow" to "mass murder now" was taken in the summer of 1941' (*Origins of the Final Solution*, 433). This would appear to suggest that a decision was taken by Hitler and Himmler in summer 1941 and that the next six to nine months should be understood as seeing the SS work out how to make other agencies required to fulfil the mission fall into line.

21. Debórah Dwork, *Auschwitz and the Holocaust*, Hugo Valentin Lectures, IV (Uppsala: The Uppsala Programme for Holocaust and Genocide Studies, 2007), 15. See also Sybille Steinbacher, 'East Upper Silesia', in Gruner and Osterloh (eds.), *The Greater German Reich and the Jews*, 248; Steinbacher, '*Musterstadt Auschwitz': Germanisierungspolitik und Judenmord in Ostoberschlesien* (Munich: K.G. Saur, 2000); Debórah Dwork and Robert Jan Van Pelt, *Auschwitz 1270 to the Present* (New Haven: Yale University Press, 1996).

22. Steinbacher, 'East Upper Silesia', 252.

23. 'Reminiscences of Pery Broad', in *KL Auschwitz Seen by the SS: Rudolf Höss, Pery Broad, Johann Paul Kremer* (Warsaw: Interpress Publishers, 1991), 131.

24. Dwork, *Auschwitz and the Holocaust*, 27; Franciszek Piper, *Auschwitz: How Many Perished. Jews, Poles, Gypsies . . .* (Cracow: Poligrafia ITS, 1992).

25. See Michael Thad Allen, 'Not Just a "Dating Game": Origins of the Holocaust at Auschwitz in the Light of Witness Testimony', *German History*, 25:2 (2007), 162–91; Steinbacher, 'East Upper Silesia', 259.

26. On Kammler, see Michael Thad Allen, *The Business of Genocide: The SS, Slave Labor, and the Concentration Camps* (Chapel Hill: University of North

Carolina Press, 2002), 140–8. On the links between T4 and the Reinhard camps, see Friedlander, *The Origins of Nazi Genocide*; and my discussion in *Histories of the Holocaust*, ch. 4.

27. Simon Umschweif, 'Sonderkommando Krematorium' (1958), Wiener Holocaust Library, P.III.h. (Auschwitz), no. 768, 3.

28. For the most recent, thorough assessment of the images, see Stefan Hördler, Christoph Kreutzmüller and Tal Bruttmann, 'Auschwitz im Bild: Zur kritischen Analyse der Auschwitz-Alben', *Zeitschrift für Geschichtswissenschaft*, 63:7–8 (2015), 609–32.

29. See also Stone, *Histories of the Holocaust*, 154.

30. Yoysef Vaynberg, 'Kol Nidre in Auschwitz', in Jack Kugelmass and Jonathan Boyarin (eds.), *From a Ruined Garden: The Memorial Books of Polish Jewry*, 2nd edn (Bloomington: Indiana University Press, 1998), 234, from the Stryzow (Strizhuv) memorial book. The shofar was probably found in 'Canada', the barrack where inmates worked at sorting the clothing and other possessions of the deportees.

31. David Boder interview with Helen Tichauer in Jürgen Matthäus (ed.), *Approaching an Auschwitz Survivor: Holocaust Testimony and Its Transformations* (New York: Oxford University Press, 2009), 130. The original interview with David Boder was in German and an English transcript is online at: https://iit.aviaryplatform.com/collections/231/collection_resources/17690/transcript?u=t&keywords[]=helena&keywords[]=t&.

32. David Boder interview with Helen Tichauer in Matthäus (ed.), *Approaching an Auschwitz Survivor*, 131, 132.

33. Ibid., 132.

34. Ibid., 165.

35. Gertrud Deak, *A Woman Survives Auschwitz and the Death March*, Wiener Holocaust Library, P.III.h. (Auschwitz), no. 864 (1958), 7. Deak worked for a period in the 1960s for the Wiener Library; some of the incidents mentioned in her postwar account are also recounted in her book *A Cat Called Adolf* (London: Vallentine Mitchell, 1995).

36. Deak, *A Woman Survives Auschwitz and the Death March*, 8.

37. Gideon Greif, *We Wept Without Tears: Testimonies of the Jewish Sonderkommando from Auschwitz* (New Haven: Yale University Press, 2005), 180.

38. 'Report of Rudolf Vrba and Alfred Wetzler', in Henryk Świebocki (ed.), *London Has Been Informed . . . Reports by Auschwitz Escapees* (Oświęcim: Auschwitz-Birkenau State Museum, 2002), 214.

39. See Isabel Wollaston, 'Emerging from the Shadows? The Auschwitz Sonderkommando and the "Four Women" in History and Memory', *Holocaust Studies*, 20:3 (2014), 137–70.

40. Nicholas Chare and Dominic Williams, *Matters of Testimony: Interpreting the Scrolls of Auschwitz* (New York: Berghahn Books, 2016), 1–5.

41. Zalman Gradowski, 'Writings', in Ber Mark (ed.), *The Scrolls of Auschwitz* (Tel Aviv: Am Oved, 1985), 173.

42. Ibid., 175. See also Nicholas Chare and Dominic Williams (eds.), *Testimonies of Resistance: Representations of the Auschwitz-Birkenau Sonderkommando* (New York: Berghahn Books, 2019). Adorno and Horkheimer's classic work, *Dialectic of Enlightenment* (London: Verso, 1989 [1944]), begins (3): 'the fully enlightened earth radiates disaster triumphant'. This claim is itself heavily indebted to Walter Benjamin's famous statement that 'There is no document of civilization which is not at the same time a document of barbarism.' See Benjamin, 'Theses on the Philosophy of History', in *Illuminations*, ed. Hannah Arendt, trans. Harry Zohn (London: Fontana, 1992), 248.

43. Piper, *Auschwitz: How Many Perished*, 52, Table III.

44. Nikolaus Wachsmann, 'Being in Auschwitz: Lived Experience and the Holocaust', *TLS*, 24 January 2020.

45. Christian Gerlach, *The Extermination of the European Jews* (Cambridge: Cambridge University Press, 2016), 214.

46. Boaz Neumann, 'National Socialism, Holocaust, and Ecology', in Stone (ed.), *The Holocaust and Historical Methodology*, 112.

47. Naomi Sampson, *Hide: A Child's View of the Holocaust* (Lincoln: University of Nebraska Press, 2000), 74–5.

48. *The Diary of Dawid Sierakowiak: Five Notebooks from the Łódź Ghetto*, ed. Alan Adelson (London: Bloomsbury, 1997), 170 (entry for 20 May 1942). See my discussion in 'The Holocaust and "the Human"', in Richard H. King and Dan Stone (eds.), *Hannah Arendt and the Uses of History: Imperialism, Nation, Race, and Genocide* (New York: Berghahn Books, 2007), 232–49, and Tomasz Łysak, 'Holocaust Studies in the Era of Climate Change', in Ben Fletcher-Watson and Jana Phillips (eds.), *Humanities of the Future: Perspectives from the Past and Present* (Edinburgh: IASH Occasional Papers, 2020), 147–64.

49. Bartov, *Anatomy of a Genocide*, 244.

50. Buzha W., cited in Rebecca Clifford, *Survivors: Children's Lives after the Holocaust* (New Haven: Yale University Press, 2020), 252.

51. Neumann, 'National Socialism, Holocaust, and Ecology', 120.

52. Bloxham, *The Final Solution*, 252.

53. '"A Total Cleanup": Himmler's Order, July 19, 1942', in Dawidowicz (ed.), *A Holocaust Reader*, 97. The 'assembly camps' (*Sammellager*, i.e. forced labour installations) were at Warsaw, Cracow, Częstochowa, Radom and Lublin. See also Dwork, *Auschwitz and the Holocaust*, 21.

54. On Mühldorf, see Edith Raim, 'Mühldorf', in Megargee (ed.), *USHMM Encyclopedia*, vol. 1, part A, 500–3.

55. Jürgen Bassfreund, in Donald L. Niewyk (ed.), *Fresh Wounds: Early Narratives of Holocaust Survival* (Chapel Hill: University of North Carolina Press, 1998), 266–7. Boder's original interview with Jürgen Bassfreund is at: https://iit.aviaryplatform.com/collections/231/collection_resources/17583? u=t&keywords[]=Jurgen&keywords[]=Bassfreund.

56. Yittel Nechumah Bineth (Kornelia Paskusz), 'The Miracle of Our Survival', in Ferenc Laczó (ed.), *Confronting Devastation: Memoirs of Holocaust Survivors from Hungary* (Toronto: Azrieli Foundation, 2019), 149–57.

57. Sara Michalowicz, ITS Ermittlungsblatt betr. des Lagers Mittelsteine, 26 February 1950, ITS DAWL, 1.1.0.7/87764788. Mittelsteine was one of the Gross-Rosen sub-camps. For further discussion, see Stone, *Fate Unknown*, ch. 3.

58. Cited in Daniel Uziel, 'Jewish Slave Workers in the German Aviation Industry', in Claire Zalc and Tal Bruttmann (eds.), *Microhistories of the Holocaust* (New York: Berghahn Books, 2017), 160. On Markkleeberg, see Christine Schmidt van der Zanden, 'Women behind Barbed Wire: The Fate of Hungarian Jewish Women Reflected in ITS', *Freilegungen: Jahrbuch des International Tracing Service*, 4 (2015), 61–77.

59. Cited in Uziel, 'Jewish Slave Workers', 161.

60. Miriam Jung, University of Southern California Visual History Archive, interview 12042; Věra Hájková-Duxová, 'Such Was Life', in Anita Franková (ed.), *World without Human Dimensions: Four Women's Memories* (Prague: State Jewish Museum, 1991), 101. For more on Christianstadt, see Dan Stone, 'Christianstadt: Slave Labour and the Holocaust', in Stone, *Fascism, Nazism and the Holocaust: Challenging Histories* (London: Routledge, 2021), ch. 7.

61. Deak, *A Woman Survives Auschwitz and the Death March*, 10.

62. Ibid., 11–12.

63. Ibid., 13–14.

64. Ellie Mari Joelson, Testimony, Berlin, 26 November 1969, ITS DAWL, 5.1/82314060.

65. Rosa Rubin, Haifa, Testimony for Zentralstelle, Ludwigsburg, 18 February 1971, ITS DAWL, 5.1/82314068.

66. Michael J. Neufeld, 'Mittelbau Dora', in Megargee (ed.), *Encyclopedia of Camps and Ghettos 1933–1945*, vol. I, part B, 967.

67. See also Stone, *Fate Unknown*, ch. 3 on the sub-camps of Gross-Rosen and Auschwitz, and ch. 5 on the 'death marches'.

68. 'The German Concentration Camps', ITS DAWL, 6.1.1/82328575–8585. For fuller discussion, see Stone, *Fate Unknown*, ch. 3.

69. 'The German Concentration Camps', ITS DAWL, 6.1.1/82328575.

70. 'The German Concentration Camps', ITS DAWL, 6.1.1/82328578.

71. Gerlach, *The Extermination of the European Jews*, 199; Nikolaus Wachsmann, *KL: A History of the Nazi Concentration Camps* (London: Little, Brown, 2015), 466.

72. Jan Sehn, 'Protokół', 11 November 1950, ITS DAWL, 1.1.0.6/82338946 _1–8992_1.

73. Wachsmann, *KL*, 5.

74. Jens-Christian Wagner, 'War and Extermination in the Concentration Camps', in Jane Caplan and Nikolaus Wachsmann (eds.), *Concentration Camps in Nazi Germany: The New Histories* (London: Routledge, 2010), 135–6.

75. Marc Buggeln, 'Were Concentration Camp Prisoners Slaves? The Possibilities and Limits of Comparative History and Global Historical Perspectives', *International Review of Social History*, 53 (2008), 125.

76. Jens-Christian Wagner, 'Work and Extermination in the Concentration Camps', in Caplan and Wachsmann (eds.), *Concentration Camps in Nazi Germany*, 135–6. See also Karin Orth, *Das System der nationalsozialistischen Konzentrationslager: Eine politische Organisationsgeschichte* (Zurich: Pendo Verlag, 2002), 162–98; and Wachsmann, *KL*, 464–79 on the history of the sub-camps.

77. Mark Spoerer, 'The Nazi War Economy, the Forced Labor System, and the Murder of Jewish and Non-Jewish Workers', in Gigliotti and Earl (eds.), *A Companion to the Holocaust*, 142.

78. Geoffrey P. Megargee, 'Editor's Introduction to the Series and Volume I', in Megargee (ed.), *Encyclopedia of Camps and Ghettos 1933–1945* (Bloomington: Indiana University Press in association with the United States Holocaust Memorial Museum, 2009), vol. 1, part A, xxiii–xxiv.

79. For further discussion see Dan Stone, 'Ideologies of Race: The Construction and Suppression of Otherness in Nazi Germany', in Gigliotti and Earl (eds.), *A Companion to the Holocaust*, 59–74, and

Concentration Camps: A Very Short Introduction (Oxford: Oxford University Press, 2019), ch. 3.

80. Primo Levi, 'Arbeit macht frei' (1959), in *The Black Hole of Auschwitz*, trans. Sharon Wood (Cambridge: Polity Press, 2005), 9.

81. Milan Slavický, cited in Rudolf Mrázek, *The Complete Lives of Camp People: Colonialism, Fascism, Concentrated Modernity* (Durham, NC: Duke University Press, 2020), 108.

CHAPTER 7: GREAT IS THE WRATH:
'LIBERATION' AND ITS AFTERMATH

1. Tuvia Borzykowski, *Between Tumbling Walls*, trans. Mendel Kohansky (Tel Aviv: Hakkibutz Hameuchad Publishing House, 1976), 224. Borzykowski was a member of the Jewish Fighting Organization in the Warsaw ghetto; his memoir was first published in Yiddish in Poland in 1949, the year that he emigrated for Israel.

2. Niewyk, *Fresh Wounds*, 264–5; for the original transcript, see: https://iit. aviaryplatform.com/collections/231/collection_resources/17583?u=t&keyw ords[]=Jurgen&keywords[]=Bassfreund.

3. See my discussion in *Fate Unknown*, ch. 3.

4. Ludwig Hamburger, interview with David Boder, 26 August 1946, transcript online at: https://iit.aviaryplatform.com/collections/231/collection_resourc es/17619?u=t&keywords[]=Hamburger.

5. Helena Kubica, 'Die jüngsten Opfer der Todesmärsche von Auschwitz', *Freilegungen: Jahrbuch des International Tracing Service*, 2 (2013), 112–21.

6. Stefan Hördler, 'The Disintegration of the Racial Basis of the Concentration Camp System', in Pendas, Roseman and Wetzell (eds.), *Beyond the Racial State*, 498–9; Simone Gigliotti, Marc J. Masurovsky and Erik B. Steiner, 'From the Camp to the Road: Representing the Evacuations from Auschwitz, January 1945', in Anne Kelly Knowles, Tim Cole and Alberto Giordano (eds.), *Geographies of the Holocaust* (Bloomington: Indiana University Press, 2014), 195–7; Shmuel Krakowski, 'The Death Marches in the Period of the Evacuation of the Camps', in Yisrael Gutman and Avital Saf (eds.), *The Nazi Concentration Camps* (Jerusalem: Yad Vashem, 1984), 475–89; Bella Gutterman, *A Narrow Bridge to Life: Jewish Forced Labor and Survival in the Gross-Rosen Camp System, 1940–1945* (New York: Berghahn Books, 2008), 215; Stone, *Liberation of the Camps*, 57–61.

7. Krakowski, 'The Death Marches in the Period of the Evacuation of the Camps', 489.

8. Daniel Blatman, 'The Death Marches and the Final Phase of Nazi Genocide', in Caplan and Wachsmann (eds.), *Concentration Camps in Nazi Germany*, 167–85; Blatman, 'On the Traces of the Death Marches: The Historiographical Challenge', *Freilegungen: Jahrbuch des International Tracing Service*, 1 (2012), 85–107.

9. Tim Cole, *Holocaust Landscapes* (London: Bloomsbury, 2016), 182; Martin Clemens Winter, 'Evacuating the Camps: The Last Collective Crime of Nazi Germany', *Dapim: Studies on the Holocaust*, 29:3 (2015), 138–53. See also Daniel Blatman, '"Why Didn't They Mow Us Down Right Away?" The Death-March Experience in Survivors' Testimonies and Memoirs', in Norman J. W. Goda (ed.), *Jewish Histories of the Holocaust: New Transnational Approaches* (New York: Berghahn Books, 2014), 152–69; Leni Yahil, *The Holocaust: The Fate of European Jewry* (New York: Oxford University Press, 1991), 526–42; Christine Schmidt and Dan Stone, *Death Marches: Evidence and Memory* (London: Stephen Morris, 2021).

10. Gigliotti, Masurovsky and Steiner, 'From the Camp to the Road', 217.

11. Raymond Phillips (ed.), *Trial of Josef Kramer and Forty-Four Others (The Belsen Trial)* (London: William Hodge and Company, 1949), 285.

12. Herzberg, *Amor Fati*, 76.

13. Ibid., 77.

14. Cited in Joachim Neander, 'Auschwitz – Grosswerther – Gunskirchen: A Nine Months' Odyssey Through Eight Nazi Concentration Camps', *Yad Vashem Studies*, 28 (2000), 307.

15. Cited in Yahil, *The Holocaust*, 540.

16. Deak, *A Woman Survives Auschwitz and the Death March*, 15.

17. Thomas Buergenthal, *A Lucky Child: A Memoir of Surviving Auschwitz as a Young Boy* (London: Profile Books, 2015), 89–90.

18. Ibid., 98.

19. Herzberg, *Amor Fati*, 85.

20. See Christopher E. Mauriello, *Forced Confrontation: The Politics of Dead Bodies in Germany at the End of World War II* (Lanham, MD: Lexington Books, 2017).

21. Creasman in Sam Dann (ed.), *Dachau 29 April 1945: The Rainbow Liberation Memoirs* (Lubbock: Texas Tech University Press, 1998), 42.

22. Lt George Moise, 'Concentration Camp at Nordhausen', in Kevin Mahoney (ed.), *1945: The Year of Liberation* (Washington, DC: United States Holocaust Memorial Museum, 1995), 136–7.

23. Isaac Levy, *Witness to Evil: Bergen-Belsen 1945* (London: Peter Halban, 1995), 10.

24. Constantine Simonov, *The Lublin Extermination Camp* (Moscow: Foreign Languages Publishing House, 1944).

25. See especially Vasily Grossman, 'The Hell of Treblinka', in his *The Road: Short Fiction and Articles* (London: MacLehose Press, 2011), 126–79. Jan Tomasz Gross with Irena Grudzińska Gross, *Golden Harvest: Events at the Periphery of the Holocaust* (New York: Oxford University Press, 2012).

26. Derrick Sington, *Belsen Uncovered* (London: Duckworth, 1946), 16.

27. Ibid., 47.

28. Paul Kemp, 'The Liberation of Bergen-Belsen Concentration Camp in April 1945: The Testimony of Those Involved', *Imperial War Museum Review*, 5 (1990), 33. See also Hagit Lavsky, 'The Day After: Bergen-Belsen from Concentration Camp to the Centre of the Jewish Survivors in Germany', *German History*, 11:1 (1993), 36–59; Johannes-Dieter Steinert, *Nach Holocaust und Zwangsarbeit: Britische humanitäre Hilfe in Deutschland. Die Helfer, die Befreiten und die Deutschen* (Osnabrück: Secolo, 2007).

29. Gonin cited in Kemp, 'The Liberation of Bergen-Belsen Concentration Camp in April 1945', 32.

30. Major Charles Philip Sharp, *Notes. From 1 Jan 45*, 57, Philip Sharp Collection, USHMM, Washington, DC, 2004.664.3; Anita Lasker-Wallfisch, 'A Survivor's Memories of Belsen', in Suzanne Bardgett and David Cesarani (eds.), *Belsen 1945: New Historical Perspectives* (London: Vallentine Mitchell, 2006), 25; Glyn Hughes, evidence for the prosecution, 18 September 1945, in Phillips (ed.), *Trial of Josef Kramer and Forty-Four Others*, 33.

31. W. R. F. Collis, 'Belsen Camp: A Preliminary Report', *British Medical Journal* (9 June 1945), 815.

32. Garcia cited in Florian Freund, *Concentration Camp Ebensee: Subcamp of Mauthausen* (Vienna: Austrian Resistance Archives, 1998), 57–9.

33. Norbert Wollheim, 'Belsen's Place in the Process of "Death-and-Rebirth" of the Jewish People', in Irgun Sheerit Hapleitah (ed.), *Belsen* (Tel Aviv: Irgun Sheerit Hapleita Me'Haezor Habriti, 1957), 52.

34. Michał Głowiński, *The Black Seasons*, trans. Marci Shore (Evanston: Northwestern University Press, 2005), 126–7. On the local context, see Eliyana Adler, 'Hrubieszów at the Crossroads: Polish Jews Navigate the German and Soviet Occupations', *Holocaust and Genocide Studies*, 28:1 (2014), 1–30.

35. Isaac Goodfriend in Brewster Chamberlin and Marcia Feldman (eds.), *The Liberation of the Nazi Concentration Camps 1945: Eyewitness Accounts of the*

Liberators (Washington, DC: United States Holocaust Memorial Council, 1987), 145–6.

36. Bernard Warsager, interview with David Boder, 1 September 1946, transcript online at: https://iit.aviaryplatform.com/collections/231/collection_resources/17692/transcript?u=t&keywords[]=bernard&keywords[]=warsage&.

37. Cited in Eva Kolinsky, 'Experiences of Survival', *Leo Baeck Institute Yearbook*, 44 (1999), 260.

38. Evelyn Le Chêne, *Mauthausen: The History of a Death Camp* (London: Methuen & Co., 1971), 169.

39. Miriam Warburg, 'Conditions of Jewish Children in a Bavarian Rehabilitation Camp', in *Jews in Europe To-day: Two Reports by Jewish Relief Workers in Germany* (London: Jewish Central Information Office, November 1945); Wiener Holocaust Library, Henriques Papers, HA6A-3/3/78/v.

40. The Harrison Report is reproduced in Leonard Dinnerstein, *America and the Survivors of the Holocaust* (New York: Columbia University Press, 1982), 291–305, quotations here from 291–2 and 300–1. It is also online at: https://germanhistorydocs.ghi-dc.org/pdf/eng/Harrison_Report_ENG.pdf.

41. See, for example, Eliana Hadjisavvas, '"From Dachau to Cyprus": Jewish Refugees and the Cyprus Internment Camps – Relief and Rehabilitation, 1946–1949', in Bardgett, Schmidt and Stone (eds.), *Beyond Camps and Forced Labour*, 145–64.

42. Wall, letter of 31 October 1945, in Michael Feldberg, '"The Day is Short and the Task is Great": Reports from Jewish Military Chaplains in Europe, 1945–1947', *American Jewish History*, 91:3–4 (2003), 621.

43. Y. Marguliets et al., *A zikorn far Rivne* (1947), cited in Gabriel Finder, 'Yizkor! Commemoration of the Dead by Jewish Displaced Persons in Postwar Germany', in Alon Confino, Paul Betts and Dirk Schumann (eds.), *Between Mass Death and Individual Loss: The Place of the Dead in Twentieth-Century Germany* (New York: Berghahn Books, 2008), 241.

44. See, for example, Claudette Bloch, 'Avant-Propos', in Amicale des Déportés d'Auschwitz (ed.), *Témoignages sur Auschwitz* (Paris: Édition de l'Amicale des Déportés d'Auschwitz, 1946), 1 ('De nombreux récits ont déjà été publiés relatant les atrocités commises par les nazis dans les camps se trouvant autour d'Auschwitz').

45. *Unzer Sztime*, 20 (15 May 1947): 'Ein Nazi-Urteil im Nachkriegsdeutschland', in Hildegard Harck (ed.), *Unzer Sztyme: Jiddische Quellen zur Geschichte der*

jüdischen Gemeinden in der Britischen Zone 1945–1947 (Kiel: Landeszentrale für politische Bildung Schleswig-Holstein, 2004), 77.

46. See, for example, Anna Holian, 'The Architecture of Jewish Trade in Postwar Germany: Jewish Shops and Shopkeepers between Provisionality and Permanence', *Jewish Social Studies*, 23:1 (2017), 101–33; *Unzer Sztime*, 17 (25 January 1947): 'Hooligan-Überfall auf Juden in Hannover', in Harck (ed.), *Unzer Sztyme*, 72.

47. Cited in Laura Jockusch, *Collect and Record! Jewish Holocaust Documentation in Early Postwar Europe* (New York: Oxford University Press, 2012), 130–1, 142.

48. Norbert Horowitz, 'Yiddish Theatre of She'erit Hapleta', in *From the Recent Past* (New York: Congress for Jewish Culture, 1955), vol. 1, 160 (Yiddish), cited in Ella Florsheim, 'Yiddish Theater in the DP Camps', *Yad Vashem Studies*, 40:2 (2012), 107–8. 'Katzet' = KZ, 'concentration camp'.

49. Marian Zyd in *Di Jidisze Cajtung* (Buenos Aires), 2 November 1945, cited in Florsheim, 'Yiddish Theater', 127. See also Sophie Fetthauer, *Musik und Theater im DP-Camp Bergen-Belsen: Zum Kulturleben der jüdischen Displaced Persons 1945–1950* (Neumünster: von Bockel Verlag, 2012).

50. Richard Crossman, *Palestine Mission: A Personal Record* (London: Hamish Hamilton, 1946), 85

51. Hanna Yablonka, 'Holocaust Survivors in Israel: Time for an Initial Taking of Stock', in Dalia Ofer, Françoise S. Ouzan and Judith Tydor Baumel-Schwartz (eds.), *Holocaust Survivors: Resettlement, Memories, Identities* (New York: Berghahn Books, 2012), 187. On *'She'erit hapletah'*, see in the same volume, Zeev Mankowitz, 'She'erit Hapletah: The Surviving Remnant. An Overview', 10–15.

52. Abramovicz to Jewish Committee for Relief Abroad (London), 20 December 1945; Wiener Holocaust Library (WHL), Henriques Papers, HA6A-1/3/21.

53. Abramovicz to JCRA, 6 June 1946; WHL, Henriques Papers, HA6B-2-15/6/C.

54. Gringauz cited in Zeev W. Mankowitz, *Life between Memory and Hope: The Survivors of the Holocaust in Occupied Germany* (Cambridge: Cambridge University Press, 2002), 283.

55. Jacqueline Mesnil-Amar, *Maman, What Are We Called Now?*, trans. Francine Yorke (London: Persephone Books, 2015), 161–2.

56. Pieter Lagrou, *The Legacy of Nazi Occupation: Patriotic Memory and National Recovery in Western Europe, 1945–1965* (Cambridge: Cambridge University Press, 2000).

57. On the elderly, see Dan Stone, '"Somehow the Pathetic Dumb Suffering of These Elderly People Moves Me More than Anything": Caring for Elderly Holocaust Survivors in the Immediate Postwar Years', *Holocaust and Genocide Studies*, 32:3 (2018), 384–403. On children, Debórah Dwork, *Children with a Star: Jewish Youth in Nazi Europe* (New Haven: Yale University Press, 1991); Simone Gigliotti and Monica Tempian (eds.), *The Young Victims of the Nazi Regime: Migration, the Holocaust and Postwar Displacement* (London: Bloomsbury Academic, 2016); Stone, *Fate Unknown*, ch. 8.

58. Dawn Skorczewski and Bettine Siertsema, '"The Kind of Spirit that People Still Kept": VHA Testimonies of Amsterdam's Diamond Jews', *Holocaust Studies*, 26:1 (2020), 62–84; Bettine Siertsema, *The Rescue of Belsen's Diamond Children* (Houndmills: Palgrave Macmillan, 2022); Christine Schmidt, '"Privilege and Trauma": Sieg Maandag's Climb Upwards', *American Imago*, 80 (2023); Gunnar S. Paulsson, *Secret City: The Hidden Jews of Warsaw, 1940–1945* (New Haven: Yale University Press, 2002); Barbara Engelking and Jan Grabowski (eds.), *Night without End: The Fate of Jews in German-Occupied Poland* (Jerusalem: Yad Vashem, 2022).

59. Głowiński, *The Black Seasons*, 82.

CHAPTER 8: HOLOCAUST MEMORY

1. Herzberg, *Amor Fati*, 59

2. Comment at YIVO online event, *Holocaust Scholarship on Trial*, 16 February 2021: https://www.youtube.com/watch?v=jqYs8S2w_kY&feature=youtu.be. Engelking and Grabowski are the book's editors (the two volumes contain over 1,700 pages written by nine authors). Gross was earlier threatened with prosecution for 'defaming the Polish nation', but the case was dropped after an international outcry. It seems that the ruling party is looking for other ways to continue their campaign. For the broader political context in Poland, see Jörg Hackmann, 'Defending the "Good Name" of the Polish Nation: Politics of History as a Battlefield in Poland, 2015–2018', *Journal of Genocide Research*, 20:4 (2018), 587–606.

3. Jan Grabowski, 'Holocaust History under Siege', lecture at the Museum of London, 17 November 2021.

4. Report of the Academic Board Working Group on Racism and Prejudice, UCL, 16 December 2020, 63–4.

5. Compare Timothy Snyder: https://www.nytimes.com/2021/01/09/magazine/trump-coup.html, with Richard Evans: https://www.newstatesman.com/world/2021/01/new-statesman-trump-era.

6. Barry Langford, 'British Cinema and the Holocaust'; Sue Vice, 'British Holocaust Literature', both in Tom Lawson and Andy Pearce (eds.), *The Palgrave Handbook of Britain and the Holocaust* (Houndmills: Palgrave Macmillan, 2020), 261–80 and 281–300; Victoria Stewart, 'Glimpsing the Holocaust in Post-war Detective Fiction', *Patterns of Prejudice*, 53:1 (2019), 74–85.

7. Daniel Levy and Natan Sznaider, 'Memory Unbound: The Holocaust and the Formation of Cosmopolitan Memory', *European Journal of Social Theory*, 5:1 (2002), 87–106; Levy and Sznaider, 'The Institutionalization of Cosmopolitan Morality: The Holocaust and Human Rights', *Journal of Human Rights*, 3:2 (2004), 143–57.

8. Robert Deneri and François Perrot, `Reconnaissance de la Route de Cham, 22 et 23 juillet 1991', 14 August 1991: https://asso-flossenburg.com/wp-content/uploads/2020/02/1991-07-Reconnaissance-de-la-route-de-CHAM-R-Deneri-et-F-Perrot.pdf. See also Christine Schmidt and Dan Stone, *Death Marches: Evidence and Memory* (London: Stephen Morris, 2021), catalogue of an exhibition shown at the Wiener Holocaust Library and the Holocaust Exhibition and Learning Centre, University of Huddersfield, June–August 2021.

9. Andrei S. Markovits and Rebecca S. Hayden, '"Holocaust" Before and After the Event: Reactions in West Germany and Austria', in Rabinbach and Zipes (eds.), *Germans and Jews since the Holocaust*, 234.

10. Tony Kushner, *The Holocaust and the Liberal Imagination: A Social and Cultural History* (Oxford: Blackwell, 1994), 6.

11. Kushner, *The Holocaust and the Liberal Imagination*, 244: 'early attempts to historicise the subject by Reitlinger and Poliakov, while laying the foundations for future research, made little popular impact at the time'.

12. Mary Fulbrook, *Reckonings: Legacies of Nazi Persecution and the Quest for Justice* (Oxford: Oxford University Press, 2018), 281–2. See also Annette Weinke, *Eine Gesellschaft ermittelt gegen sich selbst: Die Geschichte der Zentralen Stelle Ludwigsburg 1958–2008*, 2nd edn (Darmstadt: Wissenschaftliche Buchgesellschaft, 2009).

13. Melanie A. Sully, 'The Waldheim Connection', in F. Parkinson (ed.), *Conquering the Past: Austrian Nazism Yesterday and Today* (Detroit: Wayne State University Press, 1989), 294–312.

14. Richard von Weizsäcker, Address to the Bundestag, 8 May 1985, in Geoffrey Hartman (ed.), *Bitburg in Moral and Political Perspective* (Bloomington: Indiana University Press, 1986), 264–5.

15. Ernst Nolte, 'Between Historical Legend and Revisionism? The Third Reich in the Perspective of 1980', in James Knowlton and Truett Cates (eds.), *Forever in the Shadow of Hitler? Original Documents of the* Historikerstreit, *the Controversy Concerning the Singularity of the Holocaust* (Atlantic Highlands, NJ: Humanities Press, 1993), 14. The original appeared in the *Frankfurter Allgemeine Zeitung*, 24 July 1980. See also Nolte, *Three Faces of Fascism* (London: Weidenfeld & Nicolson, 1965 [orig. 1963]).

16. Michael Stürmer, 'History in a Land without History', in Knowlton and Cates (eds.), *Forever in the Shadow of Hitler?*, 16.

17. Jürgen Habermas, 'A Kind of Settlement of Damages: The Apologetic Tendencies in German History Writing' (11 July 1986); 'On the Public Use of History: The Official Self-Understanding of the Federal Republic is Breaking Up' (7 November 1986), both in Knowlton and Cates (eds.), *Forever in the Shadow of Hitler?*, 43, 165.

18. Lagrou, *Legacy of Nazi Occupation*.

19. Henry Rousso, *The Vichy Syndrome: History and Memory in France since 1944* (Cambridge, Mass.: Harvard University Press, 1991); Éric Conan and Henry Rousso, *Vichy: An Ever-Present Past* (Hanover, NH: University Press of New England, 1998).

20. Norman G. Finkelstein, *The Holocaust Industry: Reflections on the Exploitation of Jewish Suffering* (London: Verso, 2000).

21. For a more measured, though still somewhat conspiratorial analysis, see Peter Novick, *The Holocaust and Collective Memory: The American Experience* (London: Bloomsbury, 2000).

22. Andy Pearce, *Holocaust Consciousness in Contemporary Britain* (London: Routledge, 2014). See also the chapters in Lawson and Pearce (eds.), *The Palgrave Handbook of Britain and the Holocaust*.

23. On the connection between the Holocaust and human rights legislation, compare Johannes Morsink, *The Universal Declaration of Human Rights and the Holocaust: An Endangered Connection* (Washington, DC: Georgetown University Press, 2019) with Marco Duranti, 'The Holocaust, the Legacy of 1789 and the Birth of International Human Rights Law: Revisiting the Foundation Myth', *Journal of Genocide Research*, 14:2 (2012), 159–71. See also Nathan Kurz, '"Hide a Fact Rather than State It": The Holocaust, the 1940s Human Rights Surge, and the Cosmopolitan Imperative of International Law', *Journal of Genocide Research*, 23:1 (2021), 37–57;

Kurz, *Jewish Internationalism and Human Rights after the Holocaust* (Cambridge: Cambridge University Press, 2020); James Loeffler, *Rooted Cosmopolitans: Jews and Human Rights in the Twentieth Century* (New Haven: Yale University Press, 2018); Loeffler, 'Becoming Cleopatra: The Forgotten Zionism of Raphael Lemkin', *Journal of Genocide Research*, 19:3 (2017), 340–60. Samuel Moyn, *The Last Utopia: Human Rights in History* (Cambridge, Mass.: The Belknap Press of Harvard University Press, 2010) argues that human rights is largely a construct of the 1970s. On *yizker-bikher*, see Jack Kugelmass and Jonathan Boyarin, *From a Ruined Garden: The Memorial Books of Polish Jewry*, 2nd edn (Bloomington: Indiana University Press, 1998).

24. See, for example, Mark L. Smith, *The Yiddish Historians and the Struggle for a Jewish History of the Holocaust* (Detroit: Wayne State University Press, 2019).

25. Jie-Hyun Lim, 'Triple Victimhood: On the Mnemonic Confluence of the Holocaust, Stalinist Crime, and Colonial Genocide', *Journal of Genocide Research*, 23:1 (2021), 105–26.

26. Jacob S. Eder, *Holocaust Angst: The Federal Republic of Germany and American Holocaust Memory since the 1970s* (New York: Oxford University Press, 2016); Carole Fink, *West Germany and Israel: Foreign Relations, Domestic Politics, and the Cold War, 1965–1974* (Cambridge: Cambridge University Press, 2019).

27. Maria Mälksöo, 'The Memory Politics of Becoming European: The East European Subalterns and the Collective Memory of Europe', *European Journal of International Relations*, 15:4 (2009), 653–80; Lidia Zessin-Jurek, 'The Rise of an East European Community of Memory? On Lobbying for the Gulag Memory via Brussels', in Małgorzata Pakier and Joanna Wawrzyniak (eds.), *Memory and Change in Europe: Eastern Perspectives* (New York: Berghahn Books, 2016), 131–49; Jelena Subotić, *Yellow Star, Red Star: Holocaust Remembrance after Communism* (Ithaca: Cornell University Press, 2019); Ljiljana Radonić (ed.), *The Holocaust/Genocide Template in Eastern Europe*, special issue of *Journal of Genocide Research*, 20:4 (2018).

28. These unexpected connections are the subject of Michael Rothberg, *Multidirectional Memory: Remembering the Holocaust in the Age of Decolonization* (Stanford: Stanford University Press, 2009).

29. Carolyn J. Dean, *The Moral Witness: Trials and Testimony after Genocide* (Ithaca: Cornell University Press, 2019). See also Emma Kuby, *Political Survivors: The Resistance, the Cold War, and the Fight against Concentration Camps after 1945* (Ithaca: Cornell University Press, 2019).

30. The phrase is Dirk Moses'; see 'Genocide and the Terror of History', *Parallax*, 17:4 (2011), 91. See also Dan Stone, 'Genocide and Memory', in Bloxham and Moses (eds.), *The Oxford Handbook of Genocide Studies*, 102–19.

31. Herzberg, *Amor Fati*, 89.

32. See Marko Živković, 'The Wish to be a Jew: The Power of the Jewish Trope in the Yugoslav Conflict', *Cahiers de l'URMIS*, 6 (2000), 69–84; David B. MacDonald, *Balkan Holocausts? Serbian and Croatian Victim-Centred Propaganda and the War in Yugoslavia* (Manchester: Manchester University Press, 2002). See also Filip David, *The House of Remembering and Forgetting*, trans. Christina Pribichevich Zorić (London: Peter Owen, 2017).

33. A. Dirk Moses, '"White Genocide" and the Ethics of Public Analysis', *Journal of Genocide Research*, 21:2 (2019), 201–13; Patrik Hermansson, David Lawrence, Joe Mulhall and Simon Murdoch, *The International Alt-Right: Fascism for the 21st Century?* (London: Routledge, 2020).

34. The phrase is Tony Judt's; see *Postwar: A History of Europe since 1945* (London: William Heinemann, 2005), 803: 'Holocaust recognition is our contemporary European entry ticket.'

35. Dovid Katz, 'The Baltic Movement to Obfuscate the Holocaust', in Alex J. Kay and David Stahel (eds.), *Mass Violence in Nazi-Occupied Europe* (Bloomington: Indiana University Press, 2018), 236. See also John-Paul Himka and Joanna Beata Michlic, 'Introduction', in Himka and Michlic (eds.), *Bringing the Dark Past to Light: The Reception of the Holocaust in Postcommunist Eastern Europe* (Lincoln: University of Nebraska Press, 2013), 1–24, e.g. 7: 'The theme of Judeocommunism . . . serves to justify and minimize any wrongdoing against the Jews during the Holocaust and force the narrative of one's own victimhood during World War II and the post-1945 communist period.'

36. Compare, for example, Mälksoo, 'The Memory Politics of Becoming European' with Michael Shafir, 'Four Pitfalls West and East: Universalization, Double Genocide, Obfuscation and Competitive Martyrdom as New Forms of Holocaust Negation', *Revista de Istorie a Evreilor din România*, 4–5 (2019–20), esp. 443–75, 446–7.

37. Judt, *Postwar*, 804.

38. Cited in István Rév, 'Liberty Square, Budapest: How Hungary Won the Second World War', *Journal of Genocide Research*, 20:4 (2018), 623. See also Dan Stone, 'On Neighbours and Those Knocking at the Door: Holocaust Memory and Europe's Refugee Crisis', *Patterns of Prejudice*, 52:2–3 (2018), 231–43.

39. For further detail, see Dan Stone, 'Integrated Approaches and Boundaries in Holocaust Scholarship', in Roseman and Stone (eds.), *The Cambridge History of the Holocaust*, vol. 1.

40. See, for example, Jan Burzlaff, 'The Holocaust and Slavery? Working Towards a Comparative History of Genocide and Mass Violence', *Journal of Genocide Research*, 22:3 (2020), 354–66, esp. 358–9.

41. Aimé Césaire, *Discourse on Colonialism* (New York: Monthly Review Press, 1972 [orig. 1955]), 14. For a more recent restatement of the argument, see Vinay Lal, 'Genocide, Barbaric Others, and the Violence of Categories: A Response to Omer Bartov', *American Historical Review*, 103:4 (1998), 1187–90.

42. See Anonymous, 'Palestine between German Memory Politics and (De-)Colonial Thought', *Journal of Genocide Research,* 23:3 (2020), online at: https://doi.org/10.1080/14623528.2020.1847852.

43. Ralf Michaels, cited in Anonymous, 'Palestine between German Memory Politics', 6.

44. Grabowski, 'Germany Is Fueling a False History of the Holocaust across Europe'. For critical admiration of the Germans' approach to the past, see Susan Neiman, *Learning from the Germans: Confronting Race and the Memory of Evil* (London: Penguin, 2020).

45. Michael Rothberg, 'Comparing Comparisons: From the "Historikerstreit" to the Mbembe Affair', *Geschichte der Gegenwart* (23 September 2020), online at: https://geschichtedergegenwart.ch/comparing-comparisons-from-the-historikerstreit-to-the-mbembe-affair/.

46. On 'mnemonic connections', see Lim, 'Triple Victimhood'; Benoît Challand, '1989, Contested Memories and the Shifting Cognitive Maps of Europe', *European Journal of Social Theory*, 12:3 (2009), 397–408. And on 'security paranoia', see A. Dirk Moses, *The Problems of Genocide: Permanent Security and the Language of Transgression* (New York: Cambridge University Press, 2021).

47. Zygmunt Bauman, *Modernity and the Holocaust* (Cambridge: Polity Press, 1989). See my discussion in *Histories of the Holocaust*, ch. 3.

48. For further discussion, see Dan Stone, *Constructing the Holocaust: A Study in Historiography* (London: Vallentine Mitchell, 2003), esp. ch. 7: 'Modernity and the Origins of the Holocaust'.

49. Morris Edward Opler, 'The Bio-social Basis of Thought in the Third Reich', *American Sociological Review*, 10:6 (1945), 776–83 (783).

50. Michael D. Weinman, 'Arendt and the Legitimate Expectation of Hospitality and Membership Today', *Moral Philosophy and Politics*, 5:1 (2018), 127–49.

51. Jean-François Lyotard, *The Differend: Phrases in Dispute* (Manchester: Manchester University Press, 1988), 106.

52. Norman Manea, *The Hooligan's Return: A Memoir*, trans. Angela Jianu (New York: Farrar, Straus and Giroux, 2003), 224.

53. Manea, *Hooligan's Return*, 244.

54. Yannis Boutaris, Speech for Holocaust Memorial Day, 30 January 2018, online at: https://www.facebook.com/alex.moissis/posts/10212981136936138.

CONCLUSION

1. Hanna Krall, 'To Outwit God', in *The Subtenant and to Outwit God* (Evanston: Northwestern University Press, 1992), 222.

2. Hannah Arendt, 'Truth and Politics', in *Between Past and Future: Eight Exercises in Political Thought* (New York: Penguin, 1993 [1961]), 239.

3. Katharine Burdekin, *Swastika Night* (New York: Feminist Press, 1985), 72. The book was originally published by Gollancz in 1937 under the pseudonym Murray Constantine.

4. Burdekin, *Swastika Night*, 148–9.

5. Jacqueline Mesnil-Amar, *Maman, What Are We Called Now?*, trans. Francine Yorke (London: Persephone Books, 2015), 152–3. Originally published in the article, 'Those Who Sleep at Night', *Bulletin du service central des déportés israélites*, 20 September 1945. I am aware that Mesnil-Amar's statement is unfair to the medieval world!

6. See Patrik Hermansson, David Lawrence, Joe Mulhall and Simon Murdoch, *The International Alt-Right: Fascism for the 21st Century?* (London: Routledge, 2020), esp. part III.

7. Lawrence L. Langer, *Admitting the Holocaust* (New York: Oxford University Press, 1995), 183.

8. E. M. Cioran, *A Short History of Decay* (London: Quartet, 1990), 179.

Select Bibliography

Abel, Theodore, *Why Hitler Came to Power* (Cambridge, Mass.: Harvard University Press, 1986)

Alexievich, Svetlana, *Second-Hand Time*, trans. Bela Shayevich (London: Fitzcarraldo Editions, 2016)

Allwork, Larissa, and Rachel Pistol (eds.), *The Jews, the Holocaust and the Public: The Legacies of David Cesarani* (Houndmills: Palgrave Macmillan, 2020)

Antoniou, Giorgos, and A. Dirk Moses (eds.), *The Holocaust in Greece* (Cambridge: Cambridge University Press, 2018)

Arad, Yitzhak, *The Operation Reinhard Death Camps: Belzec, Sobibor, Treblinka*, rev. edn (Bloomington: Indiana University Press, 2018)

Arad, Yitzhak, Yisrael Gutman and Abraham Margaliot (eds.), *Documents on the Holocaust: Selected Sources on the Destruction of the Jews of Germany and Austria, Poland, and the Soviet Union*, 4th edn (Jerusalem: Yad Vashem, 1990)

Arendt, Hannah, *Essays in Understanding, 1930–1954: Uncollected and Unpublished Works by Hannah Arendt*, ed. Jerome Kohn (New York: Harcourt Brace & Company, 1994)

Bajohr, Frank, and Andrea Löw (eds.), *Der Holocaust: Ergebnisse und neue Fragen der Forschung* (Frankfurt am Main: Fischer Taschenbuch Verlag, 2015)

Bankier, David (ed.), *Probing the Depths of German Antisemitism: German Society and the Persecution of the Jews, 1933–1941* (New York: Berghahn Books, 2000)

Bankier, David, and Dan Michman (eds.), *Holocaust Historiography in Context: Emergence, Challenges, Polemics and Achievements* (Jerusalem: Yad Vashem, 2008)

Bardgett, Suzanne, and David Cesarani (eds.), *Belsen 1945: New Historical Perspectives* (London: Vallentine Mitchell, 2006)

Bartov, Omer, *Anatomy of a Genocide: The Life and Death of a Town Called Buczacz* (New York: Simon & Schuster, 2018)

Bashford, Alison, and Philippa Levine (eds.), *The Oxford Handbook of the History of Eugenics* (Oxford: Oxford University Press, 2010)

Bauman, Zygmunt, *Modernity and the Holocaust* (Cambridge: Polity Press, 1989)

Bloch, Ernst, *Heritage of Our Times*, trans. Neville and Stephen Plaice (Cambridge: Polity Press, 1991)

Bloxham, Donald, *The Final Solution: A Genocide* (Oxford: Oxford University Press, 2009)

Borggräfe, Henning, Christian Höschler and Isabel Panek (eds.), *Tracing and Documenting Nazi Victims Past and Present* (Berlin: De Gruyter, 2020)

Boum, Aomar, and Sarah Abrevaya Stein (eds.), *The Holocaust and North Africa* (Stanford: Stanford University Press, 2019)

Brandon, Ray, and Wendy Lower (eds.), *The Shoah in Ukraine: History, Testimony, Memorialization* (Bloomington: Indiana University Press, 2008)

Browning, Christopher R., *The Path to Genocide: Essays on Launching the Final Solution* (Cambridge: Cambridge University Press, 1992)

Browning, Christopher R., *Ordinary Men: Reserve Police Battalion 101 and the Final Solution in Poland* (New York: HarperPerennial, 1993)

Browning, Christopher R., with a contribution by Jürgen Matthäus, *The Origins of the Final Solution: The Evolution of Nazi Jewish Policy, September 1939–March 1942* (London: William Heinemann, 2004)

Browning, Christopher R., Peter Hayes and Raul Hilberg, *German Railroads, Jewish Souls: The Reichsbahn, Bureaucracy, and the Final Solution* (New York: Berghahn Books, 2020)

Buergenthal, Thomas, *A Lucky Child: A Memoir of Surviving Auschwitz as a Young Boy* (London: Profile Books, 2015)

Buller, E. Amy, *Darkness over Germany: A Warning from History* (London: Arcadia Books, 2017 [1943])

Burdekin, Katharine, *Swastika Night* (New York: Feminist Press, 1985)

Caplan, Jane, and Nikolaus Wachsmann (eds.), *Concentration Camps in Nazi Germany: The New Histories* (London: Routledge, 2010)

Cesarani, David, *Final Solution: The Fate of the Jews 1933–49* (London: Macmillan, 2016)

Chamberlin, Brewster, and Marcia Feldman (eds.), *The Liberation of the Nazi Concentration Camps 1945: Eyewitness Accounts of the Liberators* (Washington, DC: United States Holocaust Memorial Council, 1987)

Chapoutot, Johann, *The Law of Blood: Thinking and Acting as a Nazi* (Cambridge, Mass.: Harvard University Press, 2018)

Chare, Nicholas, and Dominic Williams, *Matters of Testimony: Interpreting the Scrolls of Auschwitz* (New York: Berghahn Books, 2016)

Clifford, Rebecca, *Survivors: Children's Lives after the Holocaust* (New Haven: Yale University Press, 2020)

Collingwood, R. G., *Essays in Political Philosophy*, ed. David Boucher (Oxford: Clarendon Press, 1989)

Confino, Alon, *Foundational Pasts: The Holocaust as Historical Understanding* (New York: Cambridge University Press, 2012)

Confino, Alon, *A World without Jews: The Nazi Imagination from Persecution to Genocide* (New Haven: Yale University Press, 2014)

Crossman, Richard, *Palestine Mission: A Personal Record* (London: Hamish Hamilton, 1946)

Dafinger, Johannes, and Dieter Pohl (eds.), *A New Nationalist Europe under Hitler: Concepts of Europe and Transnational Networks in the National Socialist Sphere of Influence, 1933–1945* (London: Routledge, 2019)

Dawidowicz, Lucy S. (ed.), *A Holocaust Reader* (West Orange, NJ: Behrman House, 1976)

Dillon, Christopher, *Dachau and the SS: A Schooling in Violence* (Oxford: Oxford University Press, 2015)

Diner, Dan, *Beyond the Conceivable: Studies on Germany, Nazism, and the Holocaust* (Berkeley: University of California Press, 2000)

Dinnerstein, Leonard, *America and the Survivors of the Holocaust* (New York: Columbia University Press, 1982)

Dodd, Martha, *My Years in Germany* (London: Victor Gollancz, 1939)

Donat, Alexander (ed.), *The Death Camp Treblinka: A Documentary* (New York: Holocaust Library, 1979)

Dumitru, Diana, *The State, Antisemitism and Collaboration in the Holocaust: The Borderlands of Romania and the Soviet Union* (Cambridge: Cambridge University Press, 2016)

Dwork, Debórah, and Robert Jan Van Pelt, *Holocaust: A History* (London: John Murray, 2002)

Edele, Mark, Sheila Fitzpatrick and Atina Grossmann (eds.), *Shelter from the Holocaust: Rethinking Jewish Survival in the Soviet Union* (Detroit: Wayne State University Press, 2017)

Ehrenreich, Eric, *The Nazi Ancestral Proof: Genealogy, Racial Science, and the Final Solution* (Bloomington: Indiana University Press, 2007)

Elias, Norbert, *Studien über die Deutschen: Machtkämpfe und Habitusentwicklung im 19. Und 20. Jahrhundert* (Frankfurt am Main: Suhrkamp Taschenbuch Verlag, 1994)

Erckner, S., *Hitler's Conspiracy against Peace* (London: Victor Gollancz, 1937)

Evans, Richard, *The Coming of the Third Reich* (New York: Penguin Books, 2003)

Fogu, Claudio, Wulf Kansteiner, and Todd Presner (eds.), *Probing the Ethics of Holocaust Culture* (Cambridge, Mass.: Harvard University Press, 2016)

Frenkel, Françoise, *No Place to Lay One's Head*, trans. Stephanie Smee (London: Pushkin Press, 2018)

Friedlander, Henry, *The Origins of Nazi Genocide: From Euthanasia to the Final Solution* (Chapel Hill: University of North Carolina Press, 1995)

Friedländer, Saul, *Memory, History, and the Extermination of the Jews of Europe* (Bloomington: Indiana University Press, 1993)

Friedländer, Saul, *Nazi Germany and the Jews*, vol. 1: *The Years of Persecution, 1933–1939* (London: Weidenfeld & Nicolson, 1997)

Friedländer, Saul, *The Years of Extermination: Nazi Germany and the Jews 1939–1945* (New York: HarperCollins, 2007)

Friedländer, Saul, *Where Memory Leads: My Life* (New York: Other Press, 2016)

Friedländer, Saul (ed.), *Probing the Limits of Representation: Nazism and the 'Final Solution'* (Cambridge, Mass.: Harvard University Press, 1992)

Fritzsche, Peter, *Germans into Nazis* (Cambridge, Mass.: Harvard University Press, 1998)

Fritzsche, Peter, *Life and Death in the Third Reich* (Cambridge, Mass.: The Belknap Press of Harvard University Press, 2008)

Garbarini, Alexandra, *Numbered Days: Diaries and the Holocaust* (New Haven: Yale University Press, 2006)

Garbarini, Alexandra (ed.), *Jewish Responses to Persecution*, vol. 2: *1938–1940* (Lanham, MD: AltaMira Press in association with the United States Holocaust Memorial Museum, 2011)

Gerlach, Christian, *The Extermination of the European Jews* (Cambridge: Cambridge University Press, 2016)

Gerwarth, Robert, *Hitler's Hangman: The Life of Heydrich* (New Haven: Yale University Press, 2011)

Głowiński, Michał, *The Black Seasons*, trans. Marci Shore (Evanston: Northwestern University Press, 2005)

Goldberg, Amos, *Trauma in First Person: Diary Writing during the Holocaust* (Bloomington: Indiana University Press, 2017)

Goldberg, Amos, and Haim Hazan (eds.), *Marking Evil: Holocaust Memory in the Global Age* (New York: Berghahn Books, 2015)

Greif, Gideon, *We Wept Without Tears: Testimonies of the Jewish Sonderkommando from Auschwitz* (New Haven: Yale University Press, 2005)

Gruner, Wolf, and Jörg Osterloh (eds.), *The Greater German Reich and the Jews: Nazi Persecution Policies in the Annexed Territories 1935–1945* (New York: Berghahn Books, 2015)

Gruner, Wolf, and Steven J. Ross (eds.), *New Perspectives on Kristallnacht: After 80 Years, the Nazi Pogrom in Global Comparison* (West Lafayette, IND: Purdue University Press, 2019)

Gutman, Yisrael, and Livia Rothkirchen (eds.), *The Catastrophe of European Jewry: Antecedents – History – Reflections* (Jerusalem: Yad Vashem, n.d. [1976])

Hagen, Paul, *Will Germany Crack? A Factual Report on Germany from Within*, trans. Anna Caples (London: Victor Gollancz, 1943)

Haffner, Sebastian, *Defying Hitler: A Memoir* (London: Phoenix, 2003)

Haffner, Sebastian, *Germany: Jekyll and Hyde. An Eyewitness Analysis of Nazi Germany* (London: Libris, 2005 [1940])

Hájková, Anna, *The Last Ghetto: An Everyday History of Theresienstadt, 1941–1945* (Oxford: Oxford University Press, 2020)

Harck, Hildegard (ed.), *Unzer Sztyme: Jiddische Quellen zur Geschichte der jüdischen Gemeinden in der Britischen Zone 1945–1947* (Kiel: Landeszentrale für politische Bildung Schleswig-Holstein, 2004)

Harten, Hans-Christian, *Himmlers Lehrer: Die weltanschauliche Schulung in der SS 1933–1945* (Paderborn: Ferdinand Schöningh, 2014)

Hartman, Geoffrey (ed.), *Bitburg in Moral and Political Perspective* (Bloomington: Indiana University Press, 1986)

Hayes, Peter, *Why? Explaining the Holocaust* (New York: W. W. Norton, 2017)

Hensel, Jürgen, and Stephan Lehnstaedt (eds.), *Arbeit in den nationalsozialistischen Ghettos* (Osnabrück: fibre Verlag, 2013)

Herbert, Ulrich (ed.), *National Socialist Extermination Policies: Contemporary German Perspectives and Controversies* (New York: Berghahn Books, 2000)

Herf, Jeffrey, *The Jewish Enemy: Nazi Propaganda during World War II and the Holocaust* (Cambridge, Mass.: The Belknap Press of Harvard University Press, 2006)

Herzberg, Abel Jacob, *Amor Fati: Seven Essays on Bergen-Belsen* (Göttingen: Wallstein Verlag, 2016)

Hilberg, Raul, *The Destruction of the European Jews*, rev. edn (New York: Holmes & Meier, 1985)

Himka, John-Paul, and Joanna Beata Michlic (eds.), *Bringing the Dark Past to Light: The Reception of the Holocaust in Postcommunist Europe* (Lincoln: University of Nebraska Press, 2013)

Horwitz, Gordon J., *In the Shadow of Death: Living Outside the Gates of Mauthausen* (New York: The Free Press, 1990)

Horwitz, Gordon J., *Ghettostadt: Łódź and the Making of a Nazi City* (Cambridge, Mass.: The Belknap Press of Harvard University Press, 2008)

Hutton, Christopher M., *Race and the Third Reich: Linguistics, Racial Anthropology and Genetics in the Dialectic of* Volk (Cambridge: Polity, 2005)

Ingrao, Christian, *Believe and Destroy: Intellectuals in the SS War Machine* (Cambridge: Polity Press, 2013)

Jasch, Hans-Christian, and Christoph Kreutzmüller (eds.), *The Participants: The Men of the Wannsee Conference* (New York: Berghahn Books, 2017)

Jinks, Rebecca, *Representing Genocide: The Holocaust as Paradigm?* (London: Bloomsbury, 2016)

Jockusch, Laura, *Collect and Record! Jewish Holocaust Documentation in Early Postwar Europe* (New York: Oxford University Press, 2012)

Kay, Alex J., *Empire of Destruction: A History of Nazi Mass Killing* (New Haven: Yale University Press, 2021)

Kerenji, Emil (ed.), *Jewish Responses to Persecution*, vol. 4: *1942–1943* (Lanham, MD: Rowman & Littlefield in association with the United States Holocaust Memorial Museum, 2015)

Kershaw, Ian, *Hitler, the Germans and the Final Solution* (New Haven: Yale University Press, 2008)

Klee, Ernst, *'Euthanasie' im NS-Staat: Die 'Vernichtung lebensunwerten Lebens'* (Frankfurt am Main: Suhrkamp Taschenbuch Verlag, 1985)

Klee, Ernst, Willi Dressen and Volker Riess (eds.), *'Those Were the Days': The Holocaust as Seen by the Perpetrators and Bystanders* (London: Hamish Hamilton, 1991)

Knowlton, James, and Truett Cates (eds.), *Forever in the Shadow of Hitler? Original Documents of the* Historikerstreit, *the Controversy Concerning the Singularity of the Holocaust* (Atlantic Highlands, NJ: Humanities Press, 1993)

Koker, David, *At the Edge of the Abyss: A Concentration Camp Diary, 1943–1944*, trans. Robert Jan van Pelt (Evanston: Northwestern University Press, 2012)

Kolnai, Aurel, *The War Against the West* (London: Victor Gollancz, 1938)

Koonz, Claudia, *The Nazi Conscience* (Cambridge, Mass.: The Belknap Press of Harvard University Press, 2003)

Korb, Alexander, *Im Schatten des Weltkriegs: Massengewalt der Ustaša gegen Serben, Juden und Roma in Kroatien 1941–1945* (Hamburg: Hamburger Edition, 2013)

Kreutzmüller, Christoph, and Jonathan R. Zatlin (eds.), *Dispossession: Plundering German Jewry, 1933–1953* (Ann Arbor: University of Michigan Press, 2021)

Kuby, Emma, *Political Survivors: The Resistance, the Cold War, and the Fight against Concentration Camps after 1945* (Ithaca: Cornell University Press, 2019)

Kugelmass, Jack, and Jonathan Boyarin (eds.), *From a Ruined Garden: The Memorial Books of Polish Jewry*, 2nd edn (Bloomington: Indiana University Press, 1998)

Kühne, Thomas, *Belonging and Genocide: Hitler's Community, 1918–1945* (New Haven: Yale University Press, 2010)

Kundnani, Hans, *Utopia or Auschwitz: Germany's 1968 Generation and the Holocaust* (London: C. Hurst & Co., 2009)

Kushner, Tony, *The Holocaust and the Liberal Imagination: A Social and Cultural History* (Oxford: Blackwell, 1994)

Laczó, Ferenc (ed.), *Confronting Devastation: Memoirs of Holocaust Survivors from Hungary* (Toronto: Azrieli Foundation, 2019)

Langer, Lawrence L., *Holocaust Testimonies: The Ruins of Memory* (New Haven: Yale University Press, 1991)

Langer, Lawrence L., *Admitting the Holocaust* (New York: Oxford University Press, 1995)

Láníček, Jan, and Jan Lambertz (eds.), *More than Parcels: Wartime Aid for Jews in Nazi-Era Camps and Ghettos* (Detroit: Wayne State University Press, 2022)

Le Chêne, Evelyn, *Mauthausen: The History of a Death Camp* (London: Methuen & Co., 1971)

Levi, Primo, *The Black Hole of Auschwitz*, trans. Sharon Wood (Cambridge: Polity Press, 2005)

Levis Sullam, Simon, *The Italian Executioners: The Genocide of the Jews of Italy* (Princeton: Princeton University Press, 2018)

Levitt, Ruth (ed.), *Pogrom November 1938: Testimonies from 'Kristallnacht'* (London: Souvenir Press, 2015)

Levy, Isaac, *Witness to Evil: Bergen-Belsen 1945* (London: Peter Halban, 1995)

Lévy-Hass, Hanna, *Diary of Bergen-Belsen, 1944–1945* (Chicago: Haymarket, 2009)

Lingens-Reiner, Ella, *Prisoners of Fear* (London: Victor Gollancz, 1948)

Longerich, Peter, *Hitler: A Life* (Oxford: Oxford University Press, 2019)

Lower, Wendy, and Lauren Faulkner Rossi (eds.), *Lessons and Legacies*, vol. 12: *New Directions in Holocaust Research and Education* (Evanston: Northwestern University Press, 2017)

Mahoney, Kevin (ed.), *1945: The Year of Liberation* (Washington, DC: United States Holocaust Memorial Museum, 1995)

Maier, Charles S., *The Unmasterable Past: History, Holocaust, and German National Identity* (Cambridge, Mass.: Harvard University Press, 1988)

Malinowski, Bronislaw, *Freedom and Civilization* (Bloomington: Indiana University Press, 1960 [1944])

Manea, Norman, *The Hooligan's Return: A Memoir*, trans. Angela Jianu (New York: Farrar, Straus and Giroux, 2003)

Mankowitz, Zeev W., *Life between Memory and Hope: The Survivors of the Holocaust in Occupied Germany* (Cambridge: Cambridge University Press, 2002)

Mark, Ber (ed.), *The Scrolls of Auschwitz* (Tel Aviv: Am Oved, 1985)

Marrus, Michael R., and Robert O. Paxton, *Vichy France and the Jews*, 2nd edn (Stanford: Stanford University Press, 2019)

Matthäus, Jürgen (ed.), *Approaching an Auschwitz Survivor: Holocaust Testimony and Its Transformations* (New York: Oxford University Press, 2009)

Matthäus, Jürgen (ed.), *Jewish Responses to Persecution*, vol. 3: *1941–1942* (Lanham, MD: AltaMira Press in association with the United States Holocaust Memorial Museum, 2013)

Matthäus, Jürgen, and Frank Bajohr (eds.), *The Political Diary of Alfred Rosenberg and the Onset of the Holocaust* (Lanham, MD: Rowman & Littlefield in association with the United States Holocaust Memorial Museum, 2015)

Matthäus, Jürgen, and Mark Roseman (eds.), *Jewish Responses to Persecution*, vol. 1: *1933–1938* (Lanham, MD: AltaMira Press in association with the United States Holocaust Memorial Museum, 2010)

Megargee, Geoffrey P. (ed.), *United States Holocaust Memorial Museum Encyclopedia of Camps and Ghettos 1933–1945*, vol. 1: *Early Camps, Youth Camps, and Concentration Camps and Subcamps under the SS-Business Administration Main Office (WVHA)* (Bloomington: Indiana University Press in association with the United States Holocaust Memorial Museum, 2009)

Mesnil-Amar, Jacqueline, *Maman, What Are We Called Now?*, trans. Francine Yorke (London: Persephone Books, 2015)

Meyer, Beate, Hermann Simon and Chana Schütz (eds.), *Jews in Nazi Berlin: From Kristallnacht to Liberation* (Chicago: University of Chicago Press, 2009)

Michman, Dan, 'Why Did Heydrich Write the *Schnellbrief*? A Remark on the Reason and on Its Significance', *Yad Vashem Studies*, 32 (2004), 433–47

Michman, Dan, *The Emergence of Jewish Ghettos during the Holocaust* (Cambridge: Cambridge University Press, 2011)

Milch, Baruch, *Can Heaven Be Void?*, ed. Shosh Milch-Avigal, trans. Helen Kaye (Jerusalem: Yad Vashem, 2003)

Miller Lane, Barbara, and Leila J. Rupp (eds.), *Nazi Ideology before 1933: A Documentation* (Manchester: Manchester University Press, 1978)

Moses, A. Dirk (ed.), *Empire, Colony, Genocide: Conquest, Occupation and Subaltern Resistance in World History* (New York: Berghahn Books, 2008)

Mulisch, Harry, *Criminal Case 40/61, the Trial of Adolf Eichmann: An Eyewitness Account* (Philadelphia: University of Pennsylvania Press, 2005)

Munk, Frank, *The Legacy of Nazism: The Economic and Social Consequences of Totalitarianism* (New York: The Macmillan Company, 1943)

Neumann, Boaz, *Die Weltanschauung des Nazismus: Raum, Körper, Sprache* (Göttingen: Wallstein, 2010)

Newton, Verne W. (ed.), *FDR and the Holocaust* (New York: Palgrave Macmillan, 1996)

Niewyk, Donald L. (ed.), *Fresh Wounds: Early Narratives of Holocaust Survival* (Chapel Hill: University of North Carolina Press, 1998)

Pegelow Kaplan, Thomas, and Wolf Gruner (eds.), *Resisting Persecution: Jews and Their Petitions during the Holocaust* (New York: Berghahn Books, 2020)

Pendas, Devin O., Mark Roseman and Richard F. Wetzell (eds.), *Beyond the Racial State: Rethinking Nazi Germany* (New York: Cambridge University Press, 2017)

Phillips, Raymond (ed.), *Trial of Josef Kramer and Forty-Four Others (The Belsen Trial)* (London: William Hodge and Company, 1949)

Postone, Moishe, and Eric Santner (eds.), *Catastrophe and Meaning: The Holocaust and the Twentieth Century* (Chicago: University of Chicago Press, 2003)

Poznanski, Renée, *Jews in France during World War II*, trans. Nathan Bracher (Hanover: Brandeis University Press, 2001)

Rabinbach, Anson, and Sander L. Gilman (eds.), *The Third Reich Sourcebook* (Berkeley: University of California Press, 2013)

Rabinbach, Anson, and Jack Zipes (eds.), *Germans and Jews since the Holocaust: The Changing Situation in West Germany* (New York: Holmes & Meier, 1986)

Rabinovici, Doron, *Eichmann's Jews: The Jewish Administration of Holocaust Vienna, 1938–1945* (Cambridge: Polity Press, 2011)

Rich, Ian, *Holocaust Perpetrators of the German Police Battalions: The Mass Murder of Jewish Civilians, 1940–1942* (London: Bloomsbury, 2018)

Roseman, Mark, *The Villa, the Lake, the Meeting: Wannsee and the Final Solution* (London: Penguin, 2003)

Roseman, Mark, and Dan Stone (eds.), *The Cambridge History of the Holocaust*, vol. 1 (Cambridge: Cambridge University Press, 2023)

Roskies, David G. (ed.), *Voices from the Warsaw Ghetto: Writing Our History* (New Haven: Yale University Press, 2019)

Rupnow, Dirk, *Judenforschung im Dritten Reich: Wissenschaft zwischen Politik, Propaganda und Ideologie* (Baden-Baden: Nomos Verlagsgesellschaft, 2011)

Rutherford, Phillip T., *Prelude to the Final Solution: The Nazi Program for Deporting Ethnic Poles, 1939–1941* (Lawrence: University Press of Kansas, 2007)

Sait, Bryce, *The Indoctrination of the Wehrmacht: Nazi Ideology and the War Crimes of the German Military* (New York: Berghahn Books, 2019)

Sakowicz, Kazimierz, *Ponary Diary, 1941–1943: A Bystander's Account of a Mass Murder*, ed. Yitzhak Arad (New Haven: Yale University Press, 2005)

Seghers, Anna, *The Seventh Cross*, trans. Margot Battauer Dembo (London: Virago, 2019)

Seibel, Wolfgang, *Persecution and Rescue: The Politics of the 'Final Solution' in France, 1940–1944*, trans. Ciaran Cronin (Ann Arbor: University of Michigan Press, 2016)

Selinger, Menachem Mendel, *Wir sind so weit . . . The Story of a Jewish Family in Nazi Europe. Memories and Thoughts 1939–1945*, trans. Robert Burns (Milan: Il Faggio, 2020)

Sierakowiak, Dawid, *The Diary of Dawid Sierakowiak: Five Notebooks from the Łódź Ghetto*, ed. Alan Adelson (London: Bloomsbury, 1997)

Simonov, Constantine, *The Lublin Extermination Camp* (Moscow: Foreign Languages Publishing House, 1944)

Sington, Derrick, *Belsen Uncovered* (London: Duckworth, 1946)

Sloan, Jacob (ed.), *Notes from the Warsaw Ghetto: The Journal of Emmanuel Ringelblum* (New York: Schocken Books, 1974)

Smith, Mark L., *The Yiddish Historians and the Struggle for a Jewish History of the Holocaust* (Detroit: Wayne State University Press, 2019)

Spiegel, Isaiah, *Ghetto Kingdom: Tales of the Łódź Ghetto* (Evanston: Northwestern University Press, 1998)

Steber, Martina, and Bernhard Gotto (eds.), *Visions of Community in Nazi Germany: Social Engineering and Private Lives* (Oxford: Oxford University Press, 2014)

Steinweis, Alan E., *Kristallnacht 1938* (Cambridge, Mass.: The Belknap Press of Harvard University Press, 2009)

Stone, Dan, *Histories of the Holocaust* (Oxford: Oxford University Press, 2010)

Stone, Dan, *Responses to Nazism in Britain, 1933–1939: Before War and Holocaust*, 2nd edn (Houndmills: Palgrave Macmillan, 2012)

Stone, Dan, *Goodbye to All That? The Story of Europe since 1945* (Oxford: Oxford University Press, 2014)

Stone, Dan, *The Liberation of the Camps: The End of the Holocaust and Its Aftermath* (New Haven: Yale University Press, 2015)

Stone, Dan, *Concentration Camps: A Very Short Introduction* (Oxford: Oxford University Press, 2019)

Stone, Dan, *Fascism, Nazism and the Holocaust: Challenging Histories* (London: Routledge, 2021)

Stone, Dan, *Fate Unknown: The Search for the Missing after World War II and the Holocaust* (Oxford: Oxford University Press, 2023)

Stone, Dan (ed.), *The Historiography of the Holocaust* (Houndmills: Palgrave Macmillan, 2004)

Stone, Dan (ed.), *The Holocaust and Historical Methodology* (New York: Berghahn Books, 2012)

Stone, Lewi, 'Quantifying the Holocaust: Hyperintense Kill Rates during the Nazi Genocide', *Science Advances*, 5:1 (2019)

Świebocki, Henryk (ed.), *London Has Been Informed . . . Reports by Auschwitz Escapees* (Oświęcim: Auschwitz-Birkenau State Museum, 2002)

Tal, Uriel, *Religion, Politics and Ideology in the Third Reich: Selected Essays* (London: Routledge, 2004)

Teicher, Amir, *Social Mendelism: Genetics and the Politics of Race in Germany, 1900–1948* (Cambridge: Cambridge University Press, 2020)

Traşcă, Ottmar (ed.), *'Chestiunea evreiască' în documente militare române, 1941–1944* (Bucharest: Institutul European, 2010)

Traşcă, Ottmar, and Dennis Deletant (eds.), *Al III-lea Reich şi Holocaustul din România 1940–1944: Documente din arhivele germane* (Bucharest: Editura Institutului Naţional pentru Studierea Holocaustului din România 'Elie Wiesel', 2007)

Vági, Zoltán, and Gábor Kádár with László Csősz, *The Holocaust in Hungary: Evolution of a Genocide* (Lanham, MD: AltaMira Press in association with the United States Holocaust Memorial Museum, 2013)

Varshizky, Amit, 'The Metaphysics of Race: Revisiting Nazism and Religion', *Central European History*, 52:2 (2019), 252–88

Vastenhout, Laurien, *Between Community and Collaboration: 'Jewish Councils' in Western Europe under Nazi Occupation* (Cambridge: Cambridge University Press, 2022)

Viereck, Peter, *Meta-Politics: The Roots of the Nazi Mind*, rev. edn (New York: Capricorn Books, 1965 [1941])

Voegelin, Eric, *Collected Works of Eric Voegelin*, vol. 2: *Race and State* (Baton Rouge: Louisiana State University Press, 1997 [1933])

Wachsmann, Nikolaus, *KL: A History of the Nazi Concentration Camps* (London: Little, Brown, 2015)

Walke, Anika, *Pioneers and Partisans: An Oral History of Nazi Genocide in Belarussia* (New York: Oxford University Press, 2015)

Warburg, G., *Six Years of Hitler: The Jews under the Nazi Regime* (London: George Allen & Unwin, 1939)

Weiss-Wendt, Anton, and Rory Yeomans (eds.), *Racial Science in Hitler's New Europe, 1938–1945* (Lincoln: University of Nebraska Press, 2013)

White, Joseph R. (ed.), *United States Holocaust Memorial Museum Encyclopedia of Camps and Ghettos*, vol. 3: *Camps and Ghettos under European Regimes Aligned with Nazi Germany* (Bloomington: Indiana University Press, 2018)

Wildt, Michael, *Hitler's* Volksgemeinschaft *and the Dynamics of Radical Exclusion: Violence against Jews in Provincial Germany, 1919–1939* (New York: Berghahn Books, 2012)

Wolfson, Leah (ed.), *Jewish Responses to Persecution*, vol. 5: *1944–1946* (Lanham, MD: Rowman & Littlefield in association with the United States Holocaust Memorial Museum, 2015)

Wünschmann, Kim, *Before Auschwitz: Jewish Prisoners in the Prewar Concentration Camps* (Cambridge, Mass.: Harvard University Press, 2015)

Wyman, David (ed.), *The World Reacts to the Holocaust* (Baltimore: Johns Hopkins University Press, 1996)

Yeomans, Rory, *Visions of Annihilation: The Ustasha Regime and the Cultural Politics of Fascism 1941–1945* (Pittsburgh: University of Pittsburgh Press, 2013)

Zalc, Claire, and Tal Bruttmann (eds.), *Microhistories of the Holocaust* (New York: Berghahn Books, 2017)

Zełkowicz, Josef, *In Those Terrible Days: Writings from the Łódź Ghetto*, ed. Michal Unger, trans. Naftali Greenwood (Jerusalem: Yad Vashem, 2002)

Zeltser, Arkadi (ed.), *To Pour Out My Bitter Soul: Letters of Jews from the USSR, 1941–1945* (Jerusalem: Yad Vashem, 2016)

Index

Funkkaserne DP camp, near Munich, 212
futurism, 2

G

Galen, Clemens August Graf von, Bishop of
    Münster, 86, 87
Galton, Francis, 83
Garcia, Max, 241
Gebhardsdorf (Gross-Rosen sub-camp), 216
gender: female attacks on Jews, 54, 123;
    female Jews left behind in Germany,
    66, 111–12; female survivors at Belsen,
    238–9; gendered studies, xliv, xlvii; incel
    culture of the manosphere, 300; murder
    of women in Lithuania, 127; trauma of
    rape of, xii; violent masculinity across
    wartime Europe, 187; women in slave-
    labour sub-camps, 213–17; women seen
    as breeding machines, 84–5; women's
    experience in Auschwitz, 203–5; women's
    experience of 'death marches,' 230–4
genocide studies, xlvi
Georgia, 292
Gercke, Achim, 43
German Democratic Republic
    (GDR), 269-70
Germany: Alternative für Deutschland,
    xxviii; American zone in post-war period,
    244, 246, 247, 248; British zone in post-
    war era, 246, 247, 248; crimes of the
    Wehrmacht exhibition (1995), xxvi; DP
    (displaced persons) camps, xxiii, xli–xlii,
    212; failings of post-war justice system,
    251; Great War military dictatorship,
    7; history of anti-Black racism in, 289;
    Holocaust distortion in, 282–3, 287–9;
    and Holocaust's singularity/'uniqueness,'
    271–2, 282, 287–90; impact of First World
    War, 7; Jewish survivors living in, 256;
    post-war antisemitism in, 251; post-war
    democracy, xliii, 291; 'process of coming
    to terms with the past' in, 270–4, 282,
    287–8; returnees from Soviet Union
    labelled 'infiltrees,' 246; reunification at
    end of Cold War, xxvi; Russian POWs
    in after Great War, 10–11; sensitivity
    towards Israel in, 287–8; Wilhelmine
    Empire, 7, 25 *see also* Nazism/Nazi
    Germany; Weimar Republic; West
    Germany
Gestapo, 37, 76, 82
ghettos: Białystok ghetto, Poland, 97;
    Brzeziny ghetto, Poland, 92; conditions
    in, 91, 93–7, 105, 128, 133, 172–5, 192,
    210; Cracow-Podgorze ghetto, Poland,
    92; creation/emergence of in Poland,
    81, 82, 90–3; deaths from starvation in,
    xv, xix, 192; as dehumanising places
    of humiliation, 95–7, 133–4, 172–4, 175,
    210; deportation to death camps from,
    93, 96, 97, 133, 189–90, 193–4; Djurin
    ghetto, Transnistria, 133–4; as genocidal,
    93–4, 98, 164, 192, 199–200, 209, 210;
    in Hungary, 161; intra-Nazi debate
    about Polish Jews in, xxxv, 92–3; Jewish
    Councils tasked with administering, 91,
    95, 96–7, 135; Kovno (Kaunas) ghetto,
    Poland, 96; liquidation of in Poland
    (1942 onwards), 195, 219, 266; Łódź
    ghetto, x–xii, 79, 81, 92, 93, 95–6, 97, 113,
    133, 210; Minsk ghetto, 122; Pabianice
    ghetto, Poland, 92; resistance fighters
    of Warsaw ghetto, xxiv, 190, 192, 193,
    195, 225; in Soviet Union, 122, 128;
    Theresienstadt, 113–14, 115, 167, 200, 222,
    227, 237; in Transnistria, 133–4, 172–7;
    Tulisków ghetto, Poland, 92; Warsaw
    ghetto, xxiv, 62, 92, 94–5, 134, 189, 190,
    192, 193, 195, 225, 301
Givon, Miriam, 214
Globke, Hans, 269-70
Globocnik, Odilo, 191, 192, 211
Głowinski, Michał, 35, 242, 259–60
Gobineau, Arthur de, 2
Goebbels, Joseph, 1, 22, 45, 48, 75, 81, 140;
    'The Jews Are Guilty' speech (November
    1941), 110; and *Kristallnacht*, 50, 51–2
Goering, Hermann, 54, 55, 97, 136, 197
Goga, Octavian, 98
Gollancz, Victor, 41, 44, 45–7
Gonchar, Tumer, 128
Gonin, M.W., 239
Goodfriend, Isaac, 243

German project, xiii, xiv–xvi, xxxvii–xxxviii, 145–51, 153–4, 159–79, 289, 294; Operation Harvest Festival (November 1943), 175, 195–6; perpetrators' enjoyment, 170, 187; process of arriving at genocidal programme, xx–xxii, xxxiii–xxxvi, 52–3, 57, 81–3, 85–8, 89–101, 104–10, 117–18, 196–200; ratlines for escape to South America, xxv; response of the 'free world,' xxxviii, 180–1; roots of in genocidal fantasy, xx–xxii, xxvii, 36, 53, 87–8, 99–101, 291–2; as series of interlocking local genocides, 148–50; sexualized aspect of violence, xii, 39, 170, 205; systematic mass deportations commence (1942), 139–40; 'territorial solution' as itself genocidal, 88, 98, 100–1; transition from 'euthanasia' to, 87–8, 136, 191–2, 200; and unexpected longevity of war in east, 92, 100, 115, 207–8; unrelenting ferocity in Eastern Europe, xxxv–xxxvi, 79–82, 103–7, 108–11, 119–29, 130–6, 190–1; use of gas vans, xxxvi, 86, 108, 136, 190; use of term, xxvi, 149, 152, 278; Wehrmacht direct involvement, xxvi, 79, 82, 103–4, 107, 108–9, 117–18, 123, 125, 186; Western Europe as always part of Final Solution, 90, 141–2 see also Wannsee Conference (20 January 1942) and other Holocaust entries
Holocaust (1978 NBC TV series), xxvi, 269
Holocaust denial, 280–1
Holocaust education, xiv, xxvii, xxviii, xxx–xxxi, xliii, 291–2, 293
Holocaust Educational Trust, xxviii
Holocaust Memorial Day, 275–6
Holocaust memory/consciousness: absence of slave-labour sub-camps, 221; *Auschwitz Album*, 163, 202; 'beautifying' of Holocaust, xlii, 281; collecting of survivors' accounts, xlvi, 251–2, 260, 261, 276–7, 278; consequences leading to good, xliii, 291; as contested by radical/far right, xlii, 268, 280, 281, 282–3, 294; dark psychological legacy of fascism, xliii, 291–2, 293, 294; dialogue with colonial brutality and slavery, xxiv, 274, 277, 286–7,

289; discourse of 'double genocide,' xxvi, xxix, 272, 283, 289; and end of Cold War, 268, 273, 277; as fixed part of culture today, 267–8, 276–7; GDR's publication of '*Brown Book*,' 269; in geopolitics, 277, 278, 280; Holocaust as banalized and exploited, xlii, 268; 'Holocaust industry' notion, xliv, 275; Holocaust museums, xiv–xv, xix, xxviii–xxix, 149, 267, 275, 281, 284; Holocaust-related cultural production, xiv, xxvi–xxvii, 267, 268, 269; iconography/images, xxvii, xl, xli, 163, 201–2; 'industrial murder' notion, xii, xv, xix, 199, 201–2, 205; instrumentalized to justify pre-emptive strikes, 280; Manea on public commemorations, 293–4; material written in Yiddish, xlvii, 206–7, 276; modern Holocaust distortion, 281–5, 287–9; move from 'war crime to trauma drama,' xlii, 268; need to face radical conclusions led to, xliii, 291, 302–3; oral history projects, 278; overestimation of impact of, xxx; place of Holocaust in world history, 286–8, 288–9; in the post-truth age, 279–90; 'progressive' narrative of, 268, 268–79; right wing use of in culture wars, 265–6; and rise of xenophobic nationalism, xxvii–xxx, 279–7, 291–5; selective memory criminalizing scholarship, 263–5; stages in development of, 268–74; stages of 'collective memory' passed through, xlii, 268; in UK, 275; and United Nations (2005), xxvii–xxviii, 277; in USA, 275; vast, interdisciplinary literature on, xlvi; writing of *Yizker Bikher* (memorial books), xlv, 251, 276; Yad Vashem, Israel, xxiv, 149, 278
Holocaust survivors: age and class as factors in survival, 259; Allied medical relief at 'liberated' camps, 239–2; Central Historical Commission (Munich), 251–2; collecting of testimony/evidence, xlvi, 251–2, 260, 261, 276–7, 278; and continued antisemitism, xii, xxiii, xxiv–xxv, 243, 244, 246, 248; of the 'death marches,' 223–5, 230–5, 238, 268; deaths just before/

Japan, 116; attack on Pearl Harbor, 136–7
Jewish Brigade, 178–9
Jewish Historical Institute (ZIH,
    Warsaw), 276
Jewish Relief Unit, 239
Jews: bundist tradition in Eastern Europe,
    254; émigrés from Nazi Germany, xxxiv,
    13, 28, 31, 36, 44, 47, 53, 57, 58–60, 65; focus
    on in this book, xlviii–xlix; instinctive
    post-war Zionism, xxiii, xxiv, xli, 249, 254,
    255–6; Jewish reservation (Judenreservat)
    plans (Nisko Project), 88, 92, 97; Nazi
    academic study of (Judenforschung),
    21; Nazi Madagascar plan, xxxv, 88,
    97–8, 100–1; Nazi 'territorial solution,'
    xxxv, 88, 91, 92, 97–8, 100–1; as not a
    homogeneous community, 61–2, 254, 255;
    overlooked in Gaullist narrative, 273-4;
    population in Poland at beginning of
    war, 79; religious faith of, x–xi, xxxvi,
    l, 111, 202–3; Romaniots in Greece, 147,
    148; and Roosevelt administration,
    181–2; Sephardic, 147, 148, 294; as small
    percentage of German population, 14;
    as traditional Other of the Christian
    West, xlix–l, 25–6; transnational
    economic dispossession of, 47–8, 52–3,
    58, 65, 70, 76–7, 267, 269; Yiddish-
    speaking communities in Romania,
    171–7 see also antisemitism; Holocaust
    victims, Jewish
Judt, Tony, 284
Jung, Miriam, 215

K

Kaiserwald Riga concentration camp,
    109, 225
Kállay, Miklós, 160
Kammler, Hans, 199
Kann, Gerhard, 59
Karski, Jan, 94–5
Katz, Sally, 253
Kaunas, 'death dealer of,' 126
Kershaw, Ian, xxii, 106
Kindertransport, xxv
Klages, Ludwig, 55

Klein, Gideon, 221
Klonicki, Aryeh, 133
Kohl, Helmut, 271
Kolnai, Aurel, The War Against the West
    (1938), 15–16
Koonz, Claudia, 21–2
Korber, Mirjam, 133–4
Kovner, Abba, 178–9, 186
Krall, Hanna, 297
Kreutzer, Paul, 228
Krieck, Ernst, 15–16, 22, 23, 27
Królikowski, Jerzy, 190
Krupka (Krupki, Belarus), 103–4
Krzepicki, Abraham, 189–90, 193
Kurfürstendamm riot, 45–6
Kvaternik, Slavko, 109–10

L

Landmesser, August, 42–3
Langer, Lawrence, xiii, xlii, 96, 302
Lasker-Wallfisch, Anita, 240
Laski, Harold, 13, 29
Laski, Neville, 5
Latvia, xxxvi, 108–9, 135–6, 137, 141
Le Chêne, Evelyn, 247
Le Pen, Jean-Marie, xxx
League of Nations, 67
Lebensphilosophie, 2
Lebensraum (living space) concept, xxi–xxii,
    4–5, 12, 78, 99, 100, 116–17, 119–20, 198
Leese, Arnold, 98
Leipzig-Thekla (sub-camp of
    Buchenwald), 234
Lenz, Fritz, 22
Leszczynska, Filomena, 263–4
Levi, Primo, 205, 220, 244, 258
Levy, Isaac, 237
Lévy-Hass, Hanna, x
'liberation' of camps: of Auschwitz, xxviii,
    225, 237; of Belsen, xl, 235, 237, 238,
    239–41; callousness of guards and local
    populations, 241; deaths just before/
    soon after, xli, 235–6, 240; encounter
    between inmates and the Allied soldiers,
    241; images from, xl, xli; by Red Army,
    195, 225, 237; shock of Allied soldiers,

V

W

About the Author

DAN STONE is a professor of modern history and director of the Holocaust Research Institute at Royal Holloway, University of London. He is the author or editor of numerous articles and books, including: *Histories of the Holocaust*; *The Liberation of the Camps: The End of the Holocaust and Its Aftermath*; and *Concentration Camps: A Very Short Introduction*.

About Mariner Books

Mariner Books traces its beginnings to 1832 when William Ticknor cofounded the Old Corner Bookstore in Boston, from which he would run the legendary firm Ticknor and Fields, publisher of Ralph Waldo Emerson, Harriet Beecher Stowe, Nathaniel Hawthorne, and Henry David Thoreau. Following Ticknor's death, Henry Oscar Houghton acquired Ticknor and Fields and, in 1880, formed Houghton Mifflin, which later merged with venerable Harcourt Publishing to form Houghton Mifflin Harcourt. HarperCollins purchased HMH's trade publishing business in 2021 and reestablished their storied lists and editorial team under the name Mariner Books.

Uniting the legacies of Houghton Mifflin, Harcourt Brace, and Ticknor and Fields, Mariner Books continues one of the great traditions in American bookselling. Our imprints have introduced an incomparable roster of enduring classics, including Hawthorne's *The Scarlet Letter*, Thoreau's *Walden*, Willa Cather's *O Pioneers!*, Virginia Woolf's *To the Lighthouse*, W.E.B. Du Bois's *Black Reconstruction*, J.R.R. Tolkien's *The Lord of the Rings*, Carson McCullers's *The Heart Is a Lonely Hunter*, Ann Petry's *The Narrows*, George Orwell's *Animal Farm* and *Nineteen Eighty-Four*, Rachel Carson's *Silent Spring*, Margaret Walker's *Jubilee*, Italo Calvino's *Invisible Cities*, Alice Walker's *The Color Purple*, Margaret Atwood's *The Handmaid's Tale*, Tim O'Brien's *The Things They Carried*, Philip Roth's *The Plot Against America*, Jhumpa Lahiri's *Interpreter of Maladies*, and many others. Today Mariner Books remains proudly committed to the craft of fine publishing established nearly two centuries ago at the Old Corner Bookstore.